R/C PILOT'S HANDBOOK

BASIC TO ADVANCED FLYING TECHNIQUES FROM THE PROS

From the Publishers of
MODEL
AIRPLANE
NEWS

TABLE OF CONTENTS

Group Editor-in-Chief: **Tom Atwood** • Technical Editor: **Roger Post Jr.** • Editor: **Gerry Yarrish**
Copy Director: **Lynne Sewell** • Managing Art Director: **Alan J. Palermo**
Publication Coordinators: **Kathleen J. Doherty, Debra D. Sharp** • Book Design: **Angela A. Carpenter**
Staff Photographer: **Walter Sidas** • Image Technician: **Christopher Hoffmaster**
Production Manager: **Mary Reid McElwee**

Copyright© 1995 by Air Age Inc.   ISBN: 0-911295-38-0

Published by Air Age Inc., 251 Danbury Rd., Wilton, CT 06897. Dr. L.V. DeFrancesco, Chairman of the Board; M. F. Doyle, Chief Executive Officer; Louis V. DeFrancesco Jr., Group Publisher; Y. DeFrancesco, Publisher; Gary Dolzall, Associate Publisher.
PRINTED IN THE USA

INTRODUCTION

For most of us, flying is the most enjoyable part of R/C aeromodeling. Many top fliers advise that to speed the development of your flying skills, you should fly as many different types of R/C aircraft as you can, because the lessons you learn from each in some fashion apply to all. We would probably all agree that truly proficient R/C pilots have mastered a set of skills that, in some sense, is as diverse as the R/C aircraft they're likely to fly.

Fair enough, but once you have your hands on that new airplane—and are counting the days until you can take it to the flying field—wouldn't it be helpful to have ready access to the insights and techniques of a top flier who is a master at flying that type of aircraft? Suppose you are interested in competing; wouldn't it be helpful to be advised by a pro who has taken home the gold? That was the inspiration for this book.

In this unique volume, we have assembled flying-technique articles by nearly three dozen of the leading R/C pilots of our time, and we include brief author biographies that include details of their most notable R/C accomplishments. We have tried to cover every major arena of R/C flying and to answer any questions you might have. Whether you are a beginner or a seasoned sport-flying pro, this book should be a gold mine that will accelerate your progress whenever you take the next step in R/C aeromodeling.

Newcomers will benefit greatly from the "Basic Techniques" section because it covers the fundamentals of flying. Instructional "how to's" in these chapters will help keep those precious aircraft in one piece! Novice to intermediate sport fliers will appreciate the information in the "Intermediate Flying Skills" chapters; read these, and you will quickly advance to the next flying level. If you really want to tear up the sky, the "Aerobatics" section has what you're looking for. Performing precision aerobatics gives you a sense of accomplishment like no other flying skill. It also impresses the others at the flying field!

For up-and-coming competitors as well as serious competition fliers, we have three jam-packed sections that will help you take home that first-place trophy. Check out "Scale," "Racing" and "Soaring," and your flying in these categories will greatly improve.

The last section was designed for those who have a special flying interest. Electric competitions, combat, competition fun flying, flying the planes of yesterday and blasting away with ducted fans are the subjects covered here.

It's our hope that your R/C flying skills progress as quickly as possible. Assimilate the information in this book, and you'll become a safer and more proficient pilot, and you'll no doubt have more fun in this enjoyable sport. Good luck and happy landings.

Roger Post Jr.

Roger Post Jr.—Technical Editor

Tom Atwood

Tom Atwood—Group Editor-in-Chief

SECTION 1

BASIC TECHNIQUES

There are so many things to learn when you first start to fly R/C airplanes that you may feel a little overwhelmed. The chapters in this section will help you sort out what is important and make sense of it all. If you're still earning your wings, "Getting into R/C Planes" by *Model Airplane News* columnist and test pilot David Baron is a must-read. The nuances of flight technique explained by Roger Post Jr. (technical editor of this book and a full-scale pilot) in "How to Use the Rudder" will help you further improve your basic flying skills.

Once you become comfortable in the air, the next step is to refine your landings. In "Approach to Landing," full-scale pilot Bob Gilbert provides an excellent basic approach to getting your model on the ground in one piece. "How to Avoid the Stall/Crash Quandary" by seasoned R/C flying pro Dan Parsons (also a full-scale pilot) will ring true for many pilots, and "The Merry

Modelers' Mindset" by Roy L. Clough Jr.—an inventive modeler who has been a pioneer in the hobby and a contributor to *Model Airplane News* since the early '50s—recounts his approach to training yourself to make instinctive (and correct) control inputs.

Finally, "How to Avoid Crashing" by Roger Post Jr. gives you valuable tips that will prevent your plane from falling out of the sky. Most basic questions asked by novice fliers (and some that should be asked more often by intermediate fliers) are answered in these six chapters, so read on!

CHAPTER 1

Getting into R/C Planes

by David C. Baron

Welcome to the wonderful sport of model aviation. Model flying machines have been around for a long time. Some of the oldest known flying models have been found buried with pharaohs in Egyptian pyramids. Building an airworthy machine with one's own hands is a very rewarding experi-

When learning to fly, a .40-size trainer is a good plane to start with. It will have good handling characteristics and will be very stable in the landing configuration.

ence. To do so is to conquer a medium that, for thousands of years, has been a barrier that mankind could only dream about. Although flight is commonplace today, the allure and magic of soaring above the earth is alive and well.

Model aviation is unique because it challenges all, from the youngest dreamers to highly educated engineers. You can explore any facet of flight; there are high-technology models of prehistoric birds that fly by flapping their wings, and there are models of jets with real turbine engines. But complexity and high cost do not make the model; the rewards of flight can be garnered from a folded sheet of paper. Planes can be controlled by radio or tether, or simply by rising air currents without any more assistance from the pilot than their release into the air.

The many incredible models that you see in this book are the creations and experiences of some of the most talented builders and fliers from around the country. Though the insight demonstrated in this collection is meant for modelers looking to further their skills, it will also benefit newcomers to the hobby. Much of this knowledge is the result of the best education known to humankind—that gained by

trial and error. By appreciating the lessons shared by these masters, you will be able to expand your own goals as you explore what this hobby holds for you.

STARTING OUT

Most beginners dream of having a P-51 Mustang or a B-17 bomber. This is wonderful, as long as some slick salesman does not reward this ambition with such an unsuitable first model. These scale planes require building and flying skills that must be developed through experience. Don't jump the gun. The most successful first models are plain and simple because first, you must learn to fly, and your first plane is merely a tool to achieve that end.

FIRST STEPS

The best way to start learning about R/C airplanes is to go to your local hobby shop, look in some modeling magazines and check out the local flying field. You'll also want to join the Academy of Model Aeronautics (AMA). For $42, AMA membership offers a monthly magazine and $2.5 million in liability insurance. Most flying clubs require AMA membership (or comparable insurance) in their bylaws, so you'll need to join to fly.

I can't overemphasize the value of joining the local flying club. In nearly every club, you will find several individuals willing to help you learn what you need to know to get started. They will be able to tell you which type of trainer plane to buy, which type of engine, radio and accessories you will need and how you should build and set up your plane. Most clubs have one or more people designated to recruit and train new members, but modelers tend to be sociable, friendly types anyway, so many more will be of great assistance on an informal basis. Don't be afraid to ask questions, or to let your interest in joining in be known!

To find out where the local club is, drop by your hobby shop. The proprietor is usually in the hobby and can tell you where the field is. He will also be a great resource about products that you'll need for the hobby. If there is no local hobby

If you can, find a qualified instructor to help you learn to fly. Judge anyone who wants to help you by how well he flies his own model.

Tools of the Trade

To get started in radio control model planes, you'll need some basic tools and equipment. Most people already own most, if not all, of the tools needed to build and set up a radio-controlled model. You don't need a professionally equipped workshop to build R/C models. The most basic item is a good, straight and level workbench or table. This building surface is used to build straight and true wings, fuselages and the like (assuming you are interested in building kits; some planes come built).

A piece of plywood on top of a couple of sawhorses won't really serve the modeler well because it will be flimsy, and the plywood won't stay straight for long. The sawhorses should be cross-braced so they won't wobble. A better solution is an inexpensive hollow-core, lauan door from a home-improvement center or a lumberyard. Most centers have damaged-goods sales, and you'd be surprised how inexpensive a damaged door can be. If one side has a bad gash, the other side will usually be perfect for model building. The wood surface is smooth and easy to push pins into (you can also cover the surface with cork), and these doors are made so they won't warp. Even if you don't have a shop or a work room, one of these doors can easily be slid under a bed when not in use (sorta like a "roll-away" workshop!).

Tool Tips

Nothing is more frustrating than not having the right tools for the job and not being able to find tools when you need them. The following hints will help you in your workshop.

- Stay organized, and store tools in a box or a drawer. Keep loose tools, pins and building scraps away from the work surface. This minimizes dings in your model and speeds construction.
- Work on one thing at a time. If you're building a wing, fuselage bulkheads and landing-gear wires will get in the way if they're placed on the bench.
- Use a pegboard or shelves to store tools and supplies, which should be in plain view and easy to reach.
- If you build over the plans (a common practice), cover them with clear plastic, wax paper or MonoKote backing material to protect them from glue (MonoKote is a type of Mylar plastic covering material for models). Also, cut the plans into sections so that you can work on the wing, tail, or fuselage easily without folding the plans or having them hang off the edge of the table.
- Always use sharp tools—especially hobby knives. Buy packages of blades, and keep the package handy. You won't save much money by using dull blades, but you will produce a less precise cut.
- Have a good source of light. Illuminate your work area so no glare or shadows are cast. Less eyestrain makes building more enjoyable.

shop, you can contact the AMA for information on flying fields near you. Their number is (317) 287-1256. Because most R/C clubs are AMA-chartered, the AMA will probably be able to tell you where your nearest field is. You might also check out the local high school athletic fields. Sometimes, these are sanctioned as glider or electric-glider flying fields (and, occasionally, for glow-powered planes as well).

TIME, SPACE AND BUDGET
How much time do you have for building? This is often the deciding factor in choosing a model. I know of many modelers

who have plenty of time on their hands, but would rather spend their time flying than building. It suits them just fine to buy a plane that's ready to fly, so they can head right for the field. Other modelers love the planning, construction, finishing and detailing. For them, their most recently built plane is their current masterpiece. Many of these planes fly only occasionally under perfect conditions, and still others never fly; the builder feels satisfied that the plane has been completed. Don't overlook the importance of building space; the size of your workbench can dictate your next plane just as much as your wallet

can! Other considerations are the size of your workshop's door and the car you drive. I know many modelers who consider fitting their creations into their cars one of the most pleasant challenges during planning and construction.

WHAT YOU WILL NEED
Most people ask me, "How much does it cost to get into the hobby?" My answer is between $300 and $500. These figures can vary slightly, depending on the deals you find. If you look in the newspaper, you might find a good deal on a used R/C plane that has an engine and a radio, but make sure you know what you're getting. If possible, ask an experienced modeler to go with you and look the plane over. Sometimes, hobby shops have planes that are ready to fly, and they often have decent price tags. Shopping around, knowing what you want and knowing what is a high-quality product will enable you to determine the cost.

All kits require some assembly, and most require more than an hour or two of building effort. Many modelers enjoy the building process. If you wish to spend less time on building, you can purchase an "almost ready to fly" (ARF) kit. Some kits are prebuilt but not covered with plastic film. These are called "almost ready to cover" (ARC) kits. The idea here is to create any color scheme you like, instead of accepting an out-of-the-box scheme.

Basic items that will be part of your first purchase (see "Tools of the Trade" for more details) include:
- trainer kit;
- engine;
- glow driver (to light the glow plug);
- torque starter and power supply if not combined (to turn the engine over when starting);
- fuel and fuel pump;
- 4-channel radio (includes transmitter, receiver and servos).

DO YOU KNOW WHERE YOU WILL FLY?
You are lucky if there is an organized flying site in your area. Is it suitable for the type of model that you have in mind? It's time to establish which direction your interest will take—essentially, a choice between gliders and powered trainers. Both have unique requirements. If you do not have any type of flying activity in your area, consider the following.

Gliders require one of two phenomena for sustained flight: either a substantial slope that faces the wind, or open space next to a source of thermals (rising hot air currents). Large asphalt parking lots next to open fields create this scenario very well. The sun on the asphalt is the catalyst for the rising thermal. Getting your unpowered model into the air for thermals is accomplished with a winch-launching system or a high-start. (A high-start is a giant slingshot!) Slope soaring is possible when you have a hill that faces the wind. The wind must blow up the slope and be of suitable force to support the glider. On

Beginners may find it more challenging, but flying a tail-dragger will make you more of an accomplished pilot than flying any other type of plane.

very steep cliffs, this wind can be as few as 10 knots. On more shallow slopes, you may need a stronger wind.

Powered trainers are still gliders in a sense, but the space needed for flight is different. Unless you're willing to always hand-launch your plane, you will need a suitable place to take off from and land again. For beginners, landings often require a substantial open area because landing your plane precisely will be one of your first major challenges.

GLIDERS AND POWERED GLIDERS
I suggest that you choose a simple glider that has only rudder and elevator control. The use of ailerons and/or flaps requires much more complex construction and should be reserved for a later model. Mastering just the rudder will be excellent training for your fingers. All of what you learn with the rudder will be instantly applicable to ailerons when you get to that experience level.

It's best to learn to fly winch-launched models with the assistance and guidance of experienced modelers, because the skills needed to get the plane to a safe, high altitude and to fly it down are learned. Without experienced help, this would be a major undertaking.

Powered gliders are gaining popularity. Whether gas or electric, this option for getting a plane into the air is very sound. Most gliders have slow flying speeds, which are critical to early success. You need time to think about the proper con-

trols to give your plane; if your plane is traveling too quickly, it may reach the ground before the proper control input can be made. There are quite a few excellent electric gliders on the market. These have the added benefit of being non-offensive (no noise), so you don't have to leave civilization to fly them.

YOUR FIRST PLANE
The .40-size trainers with flat-bottom airfoils are the most popular trainers. A flat-bottom airfoil amkes wing construction simpler. A good trainer will possess very stable handling characteristics, especially at slow speeds, and it will be of rugged construction. (By "rugged" I don't mean heavy, but it should be able to take the abuse of hard landings.) The .40 size refers to the engine size and equates to .4 cubic inch. This engine size seems to be the most popular.

Note that you can save money by investing in a 4-channel radio, but a more capable radio will fly more advanced models as you develop your modeling and flying skills. If you buy a 4-channel radio, your second model can only be a 4-channel model. If you buy a 6- to 10-channel radio, your next plane could have flaps or retractable gear as well as the standard four channels.

In case you're wondering, the standard four channels are aileron, elevator, throttle and rudder. It might be worth spending a little extra money on a better radio now, rather than spending more money later. Also, if you buy what is referred to as a "programmable" radio, you can put two to eight models on one transmitter (it depends on which radio you buy). Programmable radios offer myriad combinations of control inputs.

LEARNING ON YOUR OWN
If there is no instructor available, then you may have no choice but to go it alone. If so, I strongly urge that you choose a glider as your first plane for two reasons.
• First: mastering engine installation and setup without guidance may really be complicated and therefore slow your learning experience. This does not even address the knowledge required to start the engine and keep it running. Before you can concentrate on the intricacies of learning to fly, there is much to know about engines and making them run reliably.
• Second: with a glider, any open space is a flying field. If the grass is long, so much the better. I guarantee that your first landings won't be pretty, and tall grass is the most forgiving thing that you can crash into! Without engines, gliders are generally lighter and crash better, and that means

fewer broken pieces. Less weight means less inertia, and that results in less impact energy. Spend more time flying, less time repairing!

YOUR FIRST PLANE IS A TOOL
Though you may have grand expectations of your first plane, its function is simply to teach you (or more correctly, your hands) to fly. Many who decide to build and fly model planes already have a great deal of knowledge about aeronautics and aviation. This is good, and it is an asset, but when it comes to your first flight, don't expect it to be easy. On many occasions, I have seen full-scale pilots with thousands of hours be humbled by mere balsa wood. The reason is that, though they have excellent practical knowledge

At the Field
When you have your beautiful model built and ready to go, you will need some field-support equipment that wasn't included in your kit. Here's a list of useful and required equipment:
• a tote box to carry all your supplies;
• a fuel can and a pump (either mechanical or electric);
• a battery (if you have an electric pump);
• a supply of glow plugs specified by the engine manufacturer (these serve the same purpose as spark plugs in gas engines);
• a glow-plug wrench;
• spare props and a prop wrench (you'll want to balance your props at home);
• a glow driver—usually a single Ni-Cd, battery-powered unit used to "light" the glow plug when you start the engine, which runs on its own thereafter;
• about 24 inches of fuel line and a short piece of ⅛-inch brass tube to fuel and de-fuel your model;
• a chicken stick for turning the prop while you start the engine;
• a small mat to place under the engine while you work on it at the field so that small screws and other items don't become lost in the grass;
• an adjustable wrench;
• paper towels and spray cleaner to clean the model after flying (the exhaust tends to spray oil residue on portions of the model);
• small and long screwdrivers (common and Phillips);
• a complete set of Allen wrenches.

Other Niceties

Other things make the day at the flying field more enjoyable. If your interest in flying model airplanes blossoms, these items will become more important:

- electric starter and starter battery;
- DC/DC field battery charger for transmitter and receiver;
- folding table or small stand for model;
- folding chair;
- bug spray;
- sunblock;
- sunglasses;
- small first-aid kit;
- wide-brim hat (baseball caps let your ears become sunburned);
- cooler for soft drinks and snacks;
- small trash bag (keep your field clean!).

Perhaps the most important thing to take is a friend. At least make arrangements to meet someone at the field. It's more fun to fly with someone, and it's much safer. This is especially true for beginners who have yet to solo. An accomplished instructor will save your model from destruction as you learn to master its controls; he can save you money and make the hobby a lot more enjoyable. Crashes sometimes happen, even with an instructor, but they're far less likely. Above all else, have fun and be safe!

about flight, they are used to using their brains, eyes, hands, feet and the seat of their pants to fly. They may be used to the luxury of an altimeter, an air-speed indicator and a compass to help them decide their next command. But with a radio-control model, all the "feel" is moved to a displaced perspective. Your position is not the model's position, and your eyes and fingers are all that link you to the plane as it makes its way through the sky.

Let's think about this for a minute. You are flying your plane from a fixed position on the side of the runway, and your plane is traveling through the air. While you and the runway are in fixed positions, you do not have the luxury of looking away from your aircraft. Your concentration on it must be absolute. Use your peripheral vision to look at the ground. The plane's life expectancy depends on how well you fly around those obstacles and objects around you. The Air Force calls this "situational awareness." It will become a most valuable skill.

WHAT TO EXPECT

How much is enough? Because we live in the Nintendo™ generation, we are not used to having proportional control over our video games. Proportional control is the ability to move the controls very slightly and have the corresponding control surface of the plane be deflected a similar amount. It's like the steering wheel in a car. The speed at which your plane reacts to your commands will surprise you, and the faster your plane goes, the quicker it will respond. New pilots tend to over-control their models. This is quite natural and is caused by a natural desire to see the plane respond to commands. Because you may not think the plane is responding yet, you induce a little bit more rate of change. Yet, like a car on the highway, changing lanes is best done smoothly. If you are too abrupt with your controls, you will not "feel" the tell-tale feedback of the plane. It tells a lot about how it responds if it takes a fraction of a second to initiate a turn or a change of altitude. You need to remember this for the next turn you make and to time the completion of a turn so that the plane finishes with its wings level going in the direction you want it to. This becomes very critical when you are aligning your plane with the runway for landing.

WHEN LEFT IS RIGHT AND RIGHT IS LEFT...

When your plane is pointed away from you, the controls are accurately represented, you move the "stick" to the left and the

plane goes left. At other times, the plane is pointed at you (coming toward you), and when you want to direct the plane to go to "your" right, it requires that you move the stick to the left! You can only relate to the plane insofar as its position is relative to you. There are many ways to visualize yourself "in the cockpit," instead of on the ground. One way is to turn your body so that you are always facing in the same direction as the plane is going. This is helpful, but be prepared to do a lot of flying the plane toward you by looking over your shoulder. Many instructors teach students that, if the plane is coming at you and you get confused, move the stick in the direction of the wing that appears to be down. This will return the plane to level flight. This simple rule may save your plane when you are in a pinch!

FINAL THOUGHTS

There is still a tremendous amount to learn. Study the information that comes with the radio, kit, engine and accessories. Take strongly into consideration all of the suggestions that "experts" provide (some suggestions are smarter than others), and never be bashful about getting a second opinion. Planes in flight may not get a second chance!

Always judge the "experts" by the skills they demonstrate with their own models. If you haven't witnessed their skills, don't let them show you how good they are with your model because they "don't have their plane with them today."

What makes this hobby rewarding is that once you know how to fly, you wear all the hats. You are the builder, the pit crew, the pilot, the engineer and the planner for the next challenge. Nothing compares with the joy that success brings. Happy landings! ◆

ABOUT THE AUTHOR

David Baron

David has been a modeler for more than 28 years. His interests include giant-scale, helicopters, sailplanes, floatplanes, trainers, aerobatic planes, electrics and fun-fly competition. He also

designs and scratch-builds many types of planes, and he is the consummate test pilot. David co-owned a hobby shop for two years and is a multi-engine, commercial/instrument-rated pilot. He won fifth place in the '91 Fun Fly Nats and is a valued contributor to Model Airplane News.

CHAPTER 2

How to Use the Rudder

by Roger Post Jr.

Did you start out on a 4-channel trainer and learn to fly with just your right thumb? Or did you learn on a 3-channel airplane (rudder included) only to upgrade to four channels and forget about the benefits of the rudder? Maybe you're an old single-stick flier who has finally bought a two-stick transmitter. If you fit any of these descriptions, you'll find this chapter useful.

HOW THE RUDDER WORKS

The rudder controls the plane along its vertical axis. To visualize the vertical axis, just picture a horse on a carousel; then change the horse into a plane, and the pole runs vertically through its center of gravity (CG). The plane will pivot around this pole, which is the vertical axis. The movement around the vertical axis is known as yaw.

◆ **Move the rudder to the right.** The decreased camber on the left side of the vertical tail creates a lower pressure while the increased camber on the right side creates a higher pressure. As a result of these opposing pressures, the tail swings to the left and the nose moves to the right.

◆ **Move the rudder to the left.** The opposite happens: the tail swings right and the nose moves left.

The rudder can also induce roll around the longitudinal axis (but more about that later). When you set up your plane's rudder deflection, make sure that you have a lot of throw and that it's equal in both directions. With the rudder, a little input can do a lot, and a lot of input—at the right moment—could save your plane.

USING RUDDER ON THE GROUND

◆ **Taxiing.** Do you have problems taxiing into the takeoff position? If you do, you'll find it beneficial to practice taxiing with the throttle set just above idle. The throttle will control your forward speed, so use it sparingly. If your plane happens to get stuck while it's taxiing, wiggle the rudder stick back and forth while you give some bursts of throttle. This will usually get the model to advance. On airplanes with nose gear, a little up-elevator helps, too.

◆ **On takeoff.** Do you get frustrated with the aircraft straying to the left on takeoff runs? I'll tell you why this happens and how you can correct it. Three things will cause an airplane to veer to the left during the takeoff run:
• engine torque;
• spiraling slipstream;
• gyroscopic precession.
Four things will cause it to veer to the left during climb-out:
• the aforementioned factors;
• asymmetrical thrust.
In the following, numbers 2, 3 and 4 are quotes from "Sanderson's Private Pilot Manual," by Sanderson (published by Jeppensen & Co., 1972).

1. Engine torque. Just imagine a vertical torque roll—prop spins right, plane rolls left.

2. Spiraling slipstream. "The propeller also induces a slipstream rotation which causes a change in flow direction across the vertical stabilizer. Due to the direction of propeller rotation, the slipstream strikes the left surface of the vertical fin causing the airplane to yaw left."

3. Gyroscopic precession. "Can be explained as the resultant action or deflection of the spinning object when a force is applied to this object. The reaction to a force applied to a gyro acts approximately 90 degrees in the direction of rotation from the point where the force is applied. Therefore, if an airplane is rapidly moved from a nose-high pitch attitude to a nose-low pitch attitude, gyroscopic precession will create a tendency for the nose to yaw to the left. The left-turning force is quite apparent in tail-wheel type airplanes as the tail is raised on the takeoff roll."

4. Asymmetrical thrust. "In a propeller-driven airplane at a high angle of attack, asymmetrical thrust is created because the

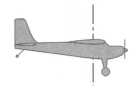

VERTICAL AXIS

FIGURE 1A
Location of the vertical axis. The plane pivots around this axis, and that's known as "yaw."

LONGITUDINAL AXIS

FIGURE 1B
The longitudinal axis extends from the nose to the tail.

descending propeller blade on the right side of the engine has a greater angle of attack than the ascending blade on the left. This produces greater thrust from the right

4-CHANNEL COORDINATED RIGHT TURN

FIGURE 2
These are the control inputs for a right-hand coordinated turn. Rudder and aileron are the first inputs. Once the plane banks, add in up-elevator to hold altitude and neutralize the bank input. (Note that the control-surface deflections have been exaggerated for clarity.)

side of the propeller, resulting in a left yaw known as "P-factor" (propeller factor). It should be remembered that P-factor creates a left-turning tendency only when the airplane is flying with a positive angle of attack. P-factor is not prevalent in level cruise flight since both propeller blades are at the same angle of attack, producing equal thrust."

As you can see, all these factors lead to a left-turning tendency that can be corrected only by using right rudder to keep the plane straight on takeoffs and climb-outs. If you have built a scale model of a plane that uses a counterclockwise prop rotation (as viewed from the cockpit), all the above principles would be reversed, and you would use left rudder to correct the right-hand yawing tendencies.

Many articles have been written on the subject of sub-fins and sub-rudders and how they help to counteract the one-sided effects of spiraling slipstream. One that comes to mind is Carl Risteen's article about flight performance in the August 1995 issue of *Model Airplane News*. A section of the article—on sub-fins and sub-rudders—helps to explain the benefits of having equal vertical areas above and below the thrust line.

◆ **Rudder use in the air (coordinated turns).** Did you ever notice your plane's tail slip in the direction of the turn while its nose swings in the opposite direction? This is adverse yaw at work. Rudder input that precedes aileron input will correct this and give you a smooth, coordinated turn. If you find it too difficult to move the left stick before the right stick, you can move

both sticks at the same time to achieve the desired effect.

At first, you might input too much rudder while you try to coordinate your turns. You'll recognize this when you see the tail of your plane go to the outside of the turn and not track neatly behind the nose. This is called "skidding." Coordinated turns can really make your flying look smooth and precise, but they do take practice.

◆ **Coupling.** Some fliers like to couple their rudder to their aileron stick and use only one thumb. In my opinion, this does not help you to develop any left-thumb agility, and it can fail you at the most inopportune time. For example: most coupled rudder inputs do not have adequate deflection; to correct an unusual attitude at a slow air speed during landing, the plane may need more rudder input than is available through coupling. The pilot uses the

FIGURE 3
The top drawing is a front view of a dihedralled wing. The bottom drawing shows the wing turning right on the vertical axis. You can see the bottom of the left panel and the top of the right.

aileron stick to correct the attitude, but the drag of the down aileron creates some adverse yaw and stalls the wing at the slow air speed, and the plane crashes. Ailerons will only correct a yaw misalignment when the plane has adequate air speed, but it takes some time to react; the correction looks awkward, and if you were in a full-size plane, it would feel

awkward. Precise, smooth, coordinated turns require both thumbs.

3-CHANNEL FLIGHT

If you start with a 3-channel airplane, it will probably have some dihedral for lateral control stability. The more dihedral the plane has, the more it will try to right itself when placed in a banked attitude. This dihedral creates some interesting control responses when you fly inverted.

Now, before I cover inverted, rudder-only flight, let's talk about how the rudder makes the wing react. When you give a rudder command, the wing half that's on the outside of the turn generates more lift because of its new angle of attack in relation to the relative wind. The best way to visualize this is to have a friend hold a dihedralled wing in front of you (leading edge faces you). Imagine that your line of vision is the relative wind. Now have your friend rotate the wing slightly on its vertical axis. You will start to see more of the bottom of the wing panel that's on the outside of the turn and more of the top that's on the inside. The relative wind is now blowing diagonally across the wing and pushing up on the bottom of the leading edge of the outside panel and pushing down on the top of the trailing edge of the inside panel. So the wing panels act as a large set of ailerons. If you give a significant amount of rudder input, the outside wing will eventually rise and go over the top of the fuselage and create a roll on the longitudinal axis. It won't be an axial roll by any means, but it will be a smooth, slow roll with some added down-elevator in the appropriate spot; and you can do barrel rolls of various roll rates and sizes.

I have rolled many Florio Flyer Nifty 50s with great results. I've even rolled rudder-only, polyhedral gliders and trainers (with some funny-looking results).

It seems that the shape of the wingtip also helps a plane's rolling ability. With the flat-bottom wing, a tip that slants upward from the bottom to the top will help the plane to roll.

◆ **Inverted.** Frustrated with 3-channel, dihedral-wing aircraft in inverted flight? Maybe these tips will help you.

First, enter inverted flight by doing a half loop or half roll. Once you are inverted, to maintain altitude, you must maintain an adequate power input. Also, to achieve a slight, positive angle of attack, add some down-elevator; but don't add so much that you stall the wing.

3-CHANNEL INVERTED LEFT TURN

FIGURE 4
When you fly a 3-channel plane inverted, right rudder input makes the plane go to the right, and left rudder makes it go to the left. Here we see an inverted plane with left-turn control inputs. The arrow on the left indicates that the wing will drop and allow the plane to turn in that direction.

Now the fun begins! Believe it or not, if you move the rudder stick to the right, the plane will actually turn right (this right-hand turn is relative to how you see the plane from the ground while it's flying *away* from you). From the plane's perspective, the nose initially swings to the *plane's* right (your left), and then the left wing (on your right side) drops, and the plane turns to its left (your right). You may find that, to get the plane to bank in the desired direction, the rudder input has to be increased. Once the plane has started to bank, add enough down-elevator to maintain altitude and turn the plane. The amount of elevator input determines the tightness of the turn. To prevent the plane from rolling right-side up, you'll probably have to add some opposite rudder. This combination is a bit tricky to master at first because you'll probably input more control than is necessary. But once you've learned how not to over-control, you'll achieve a smooth, inverted turn.

From here, the best thing to do is to practice horizontal figure-8s. This exercise will help you to balance your right- and left-hand inverted turning abilities. Any confusion about right or left (whether the plane is coming toward you or flying away from you) can be alleviated just by always thinking that you're flying right-side up. If the plane is coming toward you (inverted), the rule still applies: *move the*

stick toward the low wing. Of course, the elevator is opposite.

4-CHANNEL FLIGHT

When you fly a 4-channel aircraft, inverted coordinated flight will require input from both thumbs. An airplane with no dihedral and a symmetrical airfoil uses opposite thumb inputs to coordinate its inverted turns. This is because the rudder reacts as you would expect it to: left rudder makes the plane go right and right rudder makes the plane go left (viewed from the ground with the plane moving away from you). So when you initiate an inverted turn, right rudder will make the plane's nose turn left. Add left aileron (ailerons are the

4-CHANNEL INVERTED COORDINATED RIGHT TURN

FIGURE 5
The rudder input yaws the nose in the direction of the turn. The aileron input will bank the wing, and the down-elevator input will maintain altitude and help tighten up the turn. (Again, the bank controls are used first, and then the added elevator holds the altitude. Control inputs are exaggerated for clarity.)

same right-side up or inverted) and some down-elevator, and you have an inverted coordinated turn. Of course, the reverse rudder and aileron inputs are used for a right-hand turn. If the plane is flying toward you, to level it, move the aileron stick toward the low wing. Because the leveling should be a coordinated input, the

rudder stick will move in the opposite direction to the aileron stick.

If your 4-channel plane has dihedral and a flat-bottom wing, you'll need a greater angle of attack to maintain level inverted flight. This is where achieving smooth, coordinated turns becomes tricky. Once you're inverted, to eliminate the need for a lot of down-elevator, it helps to add some down-trim. For a left turn, push the sticks toward each other; for a right turn, pull them apart. To tighten up the turn, add some down-elevator. If the wing starts to drop too much, add the opposite turn control to prevent the plane from rolling right-side up. I've found that only very small inputs on the sticks are needed to achieve a smooth, coordinated turn.

If you're flying in windy conditions, your thumbs will constantly be making minute lateral movements. Some extra down-elevator and added power inputs might be needed while turning. This gives you a busy set of thumbs. All the motion, however, is very close to the center of the neutral stick position. Practice this one with enough recovery altitude to allow you to *roll* out if you get into trouble. All you have to do is move both sticks in the same direction, and the plane will roll right-side up.

◆ **Left-hand practice.** When you fly, is your left hand off the rudder (throttle) stick? Does your plane go in because your left thumb reacts too slowly? The follow-ing exercise will wake up that sleeping left thumb and help to bring that plane home in one piece.

Once your plane has reached a safe altitude, you can try to fly it with just your left hand. Yes, it's true; an airplane will fly with just left-hand inputs. You need to reduce your throttle and to input some up-elevator trim so that the model will maintain altitude hands-off. Also, trim it so that it's laterally stable (aileron and rudder trim). Now all you need to do is turn the plane with the rudder and add some power if you start to lose altitude (power is altitude). If your right bank becomes too steep, input some opposite rudder. To prevent the plane from overbanking, you may find that you have to hold some left rudder and added power. This will give you a nice, smooth turn. When you've finished the turn, level the wings with a little more left rudder, reduce the power setting to where it was for level flight, and neutralize the rudder stick. The opposite applies if you turn to the left.

Some things to keep in mind when you use just your left hand are:
• Put your right hand in your pocket or behind your back, and use it only if it's absolutely necessary.
• Smooth, minute control inputs are necessary (over-controlling will make the plane go all over the sky and cause great frustration).
• If you lose altitude, add power.
• Always practice with recovery altitude.

FINAL THOUGHTS

I hope this answers some of your questions about the rudder and why you need to use it. Waking up your left-hand inputs (in the Mode II transmitter configuration) will save your model and allow you to spend more time flying and less time rebuilding. Try to set up your 3-channel plane with rudder and power on the left stick and elevator on the right. If you have a computer radio, you can "slave" the aileron stick to the rudder channel; that way, if you forget to use your left stick in time, you can save your plane instinctively with the right hand.

Good luck, and keep those planes in one piece. ◆

ABOUT THE AUTHOR

Roger Post Jr.

Roger was introduced to R/C flying by his father more than 30 years ago. Since then, he has built and flown many types of aircraft and instructed beginning and intermediate pilots. He holds a private pilot's license and is currently towing gliders and working on an instrument rating. Roger already holds an instrument rating in the musical field because he has been a professional drummer/percussionist for 27 years. Sometime during these 27 years, he lived and worked as a full-time musician in NYC, but he has since taken a real job as associate editor of Model Airplane News. He is currently the president of the FLYRC club in Connecticut and is having a great time.

CHAPTER 3

Approach to Landing

by Bob Gilbert

MANY R/C pilots fly all the time; they make a lot of landings and wreck a lot of planes. They typically make only one landing in each flight, and it's performed only as a necessity. Although they may be accomplished, high-time pilots, they haven't mastered landings. These pilots usually get the plane back to the field in one piece and, in doing so, often run off the side or the end of the runway.

Taking off is infinitely easier than landing, especially with the overpowered aircraft seen at the field, and many people feel that if they know how to take off, then they automatically know how to land. If any of this describes you, please read on.

These steps are designed to help you become proficient in the execution of landings. To master landings, there are two things you must do:
• find a technique that works for you and your airplane;
• practice and then practice some more.

The technique that I describe is borrowed from Roger Maves, who taught me

then take this article to the field and read the important parts again before you fly. Happy landings!

EIGHT STEPS

◆ **Aircraft selection.** I strongly suggest that you use a 3-channel trainer. If you're using a 4-channel aircraft, and you really know how to control the rudder, then go ahead and use it. Be honest with yourself. If you don't know how to keep the aircraft straight ahead on takeoffs and landings, go back to that good old 3-channel rig.

◆ **The pattern.** Refer to the pictorial provided, and learn the basic parts of the pattern. Memorize the position of the *key point*. This point is the most important ingredient for successful landings.

Go to your local airport, and watch the full-size aircraft fly the pattern. Notice that it's rectangular and that it's normally flown with four distinct turns. (The turn from downwind to final is often flown as one sweeping 180-degree turn, but I don't recommend this. See the diagram.)

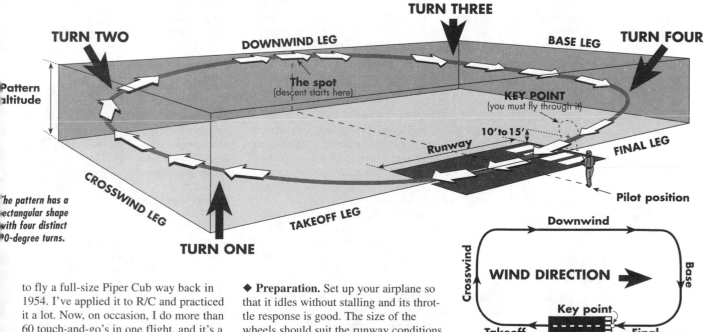

TURN THREE

TURN TWO DOWNWIND LEG BASE LEG **TURN FOUR**

Pattern altitude

The spot (descent starts here)

KEY POINT (you must fly through it)

10' to 15'

Runway

FINAL LEG

Pilot position

The pattern has a rectangular shape with four distinct 90-degree turns.

CROSSWIND LEG

TAKEOFF LEG

TURN ONE

Downwind

Crosswind · WIND DIRECTION → · Base

Key point

Takeoff · Final

The pattern viewed from above.

to fly a full-size Piper Cub way back in 1954. I've applied it to R/C and practiced it a lot. Now, on occasion, I do more than 60 touch-and-go's in one flight, and it's a lot of fun. So here goes. Read it a few times, set up your aircraft properly, and

◆ **Preparation.** Set up your airplane so that it idles without stalling and its throttle response is good. The size of the wheels should suit the runway conditions. I don't care how small the plane is or what the kit calls for. On grass, the

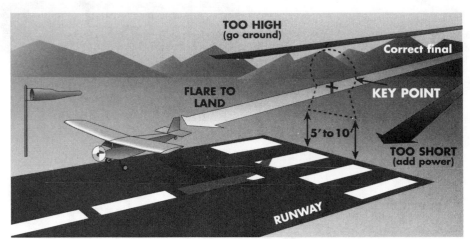

To land successfully, the model flies through the key position with the power pulled back. If it's too low, add power; if it's too high, go around.

wheels should be no less than 2¾ inches in diameter, and you should also remove the wheel pants.

Now it's time to fly. Be sure to operate in accordance with the rules of the field. Try to pick a time when there aren't many others there so that your operations won't interfere with theirs.

◆ **Throttle and stalls.** Take off and climb to altitude out of the pattern. At this point, you must learn and practice how to use the throttle correctly and how to perform straight-ahead stalls. To start, slowly reduce the throttle while you hold the aircraft straight ahead and at a constant altitude. Reduce the throttle until the plane reaches idle, and feed in up-elevator until the aircraft stalls. A trainer-type plane (low wing loading) may stall straight ahead. A plane with a higher wing loading may drop one of its wings and then its nose. To recover, add some power and up-elevator. Full throttle isn't necessary.

Practice this stall and recovery until you recognize the speed at which the aircraft stalls. This will also enable you to practice with the throttle—something that you must learn to operate to make good landings.

◆ **Fly the pattern.** Return the plane to the pattern area. Keep it at a constant altitude, and fly the rectangular pattern until you're comfortable with it (especially the four 90-degree turns). Fly at a moderate speed—certainly at less than full throttle. When you feel that you know how to fly the pattern, move on to the next step.

◆ **Go-arounds.** Look at the runway, and find the key point. It's about 10 or 15 feet above the approach end of the runway. To make a good landing, you must fly through the key point. To learn this, make a series of go-arounds. Every landing

approach need not be followed by a landing. If the approach is poor, the landing will be poor. A good approach will generally produce a good landing. You should make a go-around whenever it's apparent that the approach isn't good.

The assumption at this time is that the wind is light to nonexistent. Don't attempt these exercises in high wind until you've gained some experience. The landing approach starts when the aircraft is on the downwind leg opposite you. When it's in that position, reduce the throttle. Most trainers glide well enough to allow you to close the throttle completely. Start the descent. Control the speed by changing the pitch attitude—nose-up or down. Make a nice, gradual turn to base and continue to descend. Keep the aircraft speed slow, but stay well above the stall speed. If you descend below the desired glide path with insufficient speed to pull the plane's nose up without stalling, add a little power. Keep the key point in mind and turn to final, with the nose heading right through the key point. When the plane is just above the end of the runway, going through the key point, apply some (not full) throttle to go around. (Using less than full throttle reduces the engine's torque output, so less rudder correction is required to keep the aircraft straight.) Climb to the normal pattern altitude, and repeat the procedure.

Determine the altitude at which you want to fly and precisely where you should cut the throttle. Find the spot in the sky that allows you to close the throttle completely and come through the key point at close to stall speed, without ever opening the throttle. The plane should glide from the midpoint of the downwind leg all the way to the runway. You're trying to achieve a full stall just inches above the runway. If the plane passes through

the key point too rapidly, it will overshoot the runway, in which case, you should perform a go-around. If the plane is below the key point, it will crash; as soon as you see that you have insufficient altitude, throttle up and go around.

When you've mastered going through the key point with the throttle closed and at just above stall speed, you're ready to move on to the next step.

◆ **Landing...at last.** If you've really practiced the approaches and go-arounds, you'll have no trouble with landings. Just continue through the key point with throttle off, and feed in a little more "up" to cause the aircraft to stall when it touches the runway, i.e., flare. That's all there is to it! If the aircraft starts to veer off to either side and there's sufficient runway, apply some throttle and correct with rudder. Again, applying less than full throttle will help to keep the plane on the ground.

Touch-and-go's are easier to manage if you feed in some throttle a few inches before touchdown. This keeps the prop turning through the grass—and possibly the dirt—and gives you much better rudder control when the plane leaves the runway.

◆ **Handling the wind.** When landing in a substantial headwind, the base leg will be in a little closer, and the final approach leg will be steeper. Don't be afraid to point the nose downward to keep the speed up. It may also help to maintain a little power until the plane is about a foot above the runway.

I hope these steps are helpful. Remember: no crashes allowed; keep 'em flying. ◆

ABOUT THE AUTHOR

Bob Gilbert

In 1947, Bob looked to the sky and saw a large, free-flight airplane powered by a model engine. From that day forward, he was hooked on flight. First, he learned U-control. He spent four years in the U.S. Air Force in B-29s (logging 1,000 hours) and then signed on with Grumman Aircraft's engineering department. In time, he obtained his private pilot's license and assembled and flew a Taylorcraft BC12-D, which sparked his interest in R/C. This wasn't without its challenges; though Bob learned to solo a full-size Cub in 6 hours, he crashed 12 R/C planes before one landed in one piece. Bob now enjoys sport flying and fun flys. The slower they fly, the better he likes them.

CHAPTER 4

How to Avoid the Stall/Crash Quandary

by Dan Parsons

The stall—a pilot-induced error—has probably caused more R/C plane crashes than any other mistake (possibly more than all other mistakes combined). Why do the pilots do this? Because they don't really understand what keeps a plane in the air and, more specifically, why the wing stalls.

To minimize the number of crashes caused by wing stalling, it's essential that an R/C pilot understand the hows and wherefores of this classic plane wrecker. The fundamentals aren't difficult to grasp, but putting this knowledge to practical use will require that the pilot study, practice, be disciplined and, most important of all, train his reflexes so that he does the correct things at critical times.

WING AERODYNAMICS

First, I'll review how a wing supports a plane in flight—aerodynamics. As the wing is propelled through the air, it develops lift. The amount of lift developed by a particular wing airfoil under a given set of atmospheric conditions is determined by the angle at which the wing meets the oncoming "relative" wind and by the wing's speed through the air.

This angle is known as the angle of attack (AOA), and it's measured from the wing's chord line to the line of the relative wind (see Figure 1). Here, "relative wind" means the air moving past the wing, and it has nothing to do with the wind that blows at us as we stand on the ground. This relative wind is produced solely by the wing's being moved through the air. Thus, the relative wind always comes at the plane from the direction in which the plane is traveling. For example: if the plane is going straight up, the relative wind is coming straight "down" at the plane; if the plane is going straight down, the relative wind is coming straight "up" at the plane, and so on. This is an important concept that all R/C pilots should clearly understand.

Dave Smith has the RWR Racing Stiletto in its landing configuration (slow flight) at the 1994 Galveston Unlimited Races. Note the high angle of attack, which is always required for low-speed flight.

◆ **Wing lift.** The lift developed by a particular wing is determined by many factors, including:
  —its airfoil;
  —its angle of attack (AOA);
  —its speed through the air.

Thus, the lift that supports an airborne plane is generated by the combination of a higher AOA and a lower speed, or a lower AOA and a higher speed. Low-speed flight is always at a high AOA, and high-speed flight is always at a low AOA.

As mentioned previously, the larger a wing's AOA, the greater the lift—up to a critical angle. Increase the AOA beyond this critical angle, and total wing lift suddenly decreases very rapidly. And you know what happens next: the plane starts to fall out of the sky.

This sudden loss of lift caused by the wing's having too large an AOA is called the wing's "stalling point." I want to emphasize that with most of the airfoils that we R/C'ers use, this sudden loss of lift is just that—sudden and complete. In other words, one moment, your plane is flying through the air with maximum lift from its wing and, suddenly, with too large an AOA, the wing stalls and lift disappears. The plane immediately heads for the ground—usually with its nose pointing almost straight down and often in a

spin. In its stalled condition, the wing has all the lift of a round rock!

◆ *Remember: a wing always stalls because its AOA has been increased past the critical or stalling AOA (typically 16 to 18 degrees).*

It's even more important to understand and remember that the pilot *always* controls the AOA. How so? Because he operates the AOA controller, otherwise known as the elevator. When he puts in up-elevator, the tail drops, thus raising the nose, increasing the wing's AOA and decreasing the plane's air speed.

◆ *So what should a pilot do to avoid stalling his plane?*

It's very simple: if he does not increase the wing's AOA with the elevator beyond the critical stalling angle, his plane will never stall. Caution: too much engine power with incorrect trims or incidence

could stall the plane.

I said the answer was simple, but always following this "law" under all flying conditions is neither simple nor easy. It's difficult, and it can only be accomplished by knowing thoroughly what a stall is, what causes it and how it can be prevented—combined with plenty of flight experience.

Other than knowing safe flying practices, understanding what causes the stall and how it can be prevented are probably the most important lessons about flying that the R/C pilot has to learn. Combined with knowing how to handle the unintentional stall, this knowledge will eliminate many crashes. This is particularly pertinent for modelers who fly scale models, which generally have heavier wing loadings. Over the years, I've seen many beautiful planes crash and often be destroyed because the pilot did not understand the stall.

◆ *Why do so many R/C pilots unintentionally stall their planes and crash?*

Because they believe the elevator is what makes a plane go up! It's easy to understand why: first, the name itself—elevator; second, up-elevator does cause the typical model to go up for a while until the critical AOA is reached and the wing stalls; and third, many of the "flying movies" we've all seen always show the pilot pulling up to go up.

Thus, when combined with the "feeling" that the elevator is always the "go-up" and "hold-up" control, there's enough misleading information out there to get many pilots into deep trouble.

Here I want to clarify a very important point. I've been using the term, "unintentional stall." These stalls don't usually occur during normal, full-powered flight, but during bad takeoffs, tight aerobatic maneuvers, the low-altitude terror of sagging engine power or no power, and—finally— during landing approaches. And it's during just such flight situations that many planes fall victim to the stall/crash quandary because the pilot tries to "hold" the plane in the air with full up-elevator and holds it all the way to the crash point.

The pilot must have it ingrained in his mind—and, eventually, in his reflexes—that the elevator is not the "always-go-up" control; it's the AOA controller. I can't overemphasize this: the elevator is the AOA controller. And that's all it is!

◆ *If the elevator doesn't make a plane go up (except temporarily, as the plane bleeds off speed), what does?*

The engine's power does! This brings up another very important point. At full throttle, most R/C models have much more power than is required to maintain minimum-speed level flight. During level flight, this "excess" power is converted into higher speed (low AOA). Thus, when the pilot wants his plane to go up, all he has to do is hold some up-elevator to increase the AOA and thus lift, and the plane goes up and its speed goes down. If the angle of climb isn't too steep, the plane could continue to climb out of sight. The "excess" power has been used to lift the plane to a higher altitude. It's easy to understand why many pilots fall into the trap of thinking the elevator is what always makes their planes go up.

Now, let's assume a pilot flies his plane at reduced power that will just maintain level flight by greatly increasing the AOA to just below the stalling AOA. The pilot tries to go up by putting in some up-elevator, but there's no available excess power to climb, so the plane doesn't go up. If the

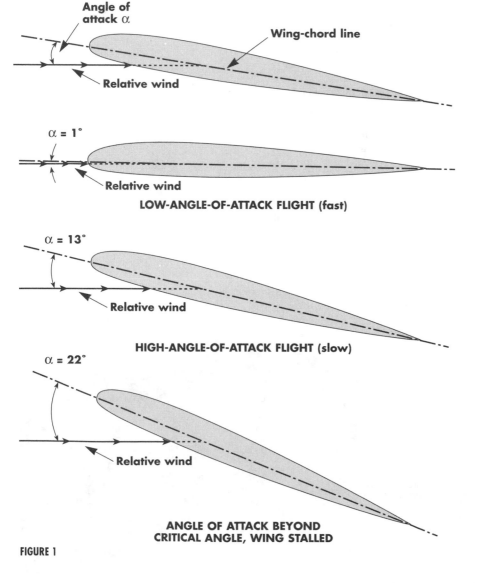

ANGLE OF ATTACK BEYOND CRITICAL ANGLE, WING STALLED

FIGURE 1

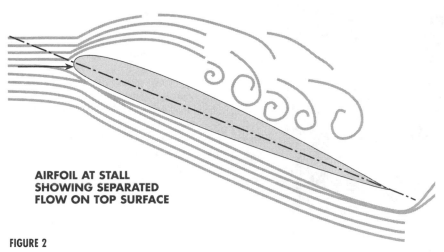

**AIRFOIL AT STALL
SHOWING SEPARATED
FLOW ON TOP SURFACE**

FIGURE 2

pilot continues to hold this up-elevator, he will increase the AOA beyond the critical AOA, the wing will stall, and the plane, instead of going up, will go down very rapidly. And if he doesn't get off that elevator, his plane will crash—the stall-crash quandary

◆ *To repeat, for emphasis, why did the wing stall?*
Because the pilot, using the AOA controller—the elevator—increased the AOA beyond the stalling AOA, and his plane fell out of the air.

This shows that it isn't up-elevator that makes a plane climb; it is the *power of the engine.* Take away that power and all the up-elevator in the world won't make that plane go up or even stay airborne; in fact, it will do the opposite: if the pilot insists on holding up-elevator, the plane will go down rapidly and crash.

And the sad truth is that many pilots of R/C models (and of full-scale planes, too) have never gotten these all-important fundamentals clear in their minds. The many models that are stalled and crashed attest to this. Every crash caused by a stall is caused by improper control of the AOA, i.e., by the pilot's grossly misusing the elevator.

Earlier, I mentioned the spin; it's time for an explanation. The spin is an important factor in the stall-crash quandary because after a plane is stalled and held in that condition, it will often spin. Therefore, the R/C pilot must understand the fundamentals of the spin and what he must do to get out of one.

THE SPIN
The spin is but an extension of the stall. When a wing is completely stalled and kept stalled, the plane will often fall off into a spin, its nose pointing almost

straight down and the plane rotating either to the right or to the left. This rotation is called "autorotation" and is caused by a rather complicated series of events.

It is important to realize that when in a spin, either the right wing or the left wing is always in a stalled condition, and that

means a high AOA beyond the critical angle. As long as that half of the wing remains stalled (by the pilot holding full up-elevator), the plane will remain in a spin all the way to the ground.

◆ **Recovering from a spin.** This is usually very simple: just release all the controls, thus lowering the AOA; this un-stalls the wing, and the spinning stops. Then *ease* the plane out of its dive after it has regained sufficient flying speed. Be careful not to add up-elevator too soon or too hard, or you might stall the wing again and pop right back into a spin.

Some planes will not recover from a spin just by having their controls neutralized; then things get more complicated. Usually, neutralizing the controls and then giving opposite rudder to the rotation of the spin will bring the plane out of the spin. If this doesn't do it, adding some down-elevator and changing the engine power might work. Once in a while, nothing works, and the plane will spin all the way to the ground.

I've been talking about spins that develop out of an unintentional stall. Most reasonably proficient R/C fliers will do spins on purpose because they're fun and rather spectacular. To expedite spin entry, full rudder is always applied at the same time

Dan Parsons, with his scratch-designed deHavilland Hornet twin-engine fighter—12 years old and still flying strong.

as full up-elevator, and full aileron is also often used in the same direction as the rudder.

Caution: opposite direction aileron may

Our author's deHavilland Hornet twin-engine fighter on a high-speed low pass. Note the low angle of attack, which is associated with high-speed flight.

FINAL THOUGHTS

In conclusion, it is *always* the pilot who stalls the plane—unintentionally or otherwise. The elevator is not the "go-up" or "hold-up" device; it's the AOA controller. Holding up-elevator too long or applying it too rapidly increases the wing's AOA past the critical point and the wing stalls. The only way to un-stall the wing is to release the up-elevator to lower the AOA. The pilot must give that poor wing a chance to fly!

For approximately a third of the time that it takes to build even a modest R/C model, the builder/pilot could study, learn and practice these important fundamentals and save himself much disappointment, frustration and money. ◆

ABOUT THE AUTHOR

Dan Parsons

Dan has been involved in R/C since 1952. His primary interest is designing, building and flying "different" WW II fighter-type scale models. His first twin was an 84-inch-span ME 210 fighter/bomber. He started flying it in 1961 and flew it for three years on reeds. His latest is an 80-inch deHavilland Hornet fighter that he has been flying for 13 years. Since 1951, Dan has been living in Albuquerque, NM. He retired from Sandia National Labs in 1977 where he worked for 25 years as a photo-optical engineer. When he isn't going to meets all over the country, he's writing articles on R/C, consulting on mini-RPVs and running Dan Parsons Products.

produce the possibly dangerous flat spin.

I want to stress these very important facts:

When a plane is heading toward the ground, almost straight down in a sudden, unintentional spin, it is psychologically and reflex-wise very difficult for the unskilled pilot to get off what he thinks is the "up" control—the elevator. Yet this is the first action that he has to take if his plane is to be saved. This is a perfect example of why a pilot has to understand the elevator/AOA/stall connection if he's to fly without falling victim to the stall/crash quandary. He must not only

understand this, but he must also develop his reflexes by practicing until he does the right things to recover during the emergency of an unintentional stall-spin.

Flying an R/C plane is more difficult than flying a full-scale plane for several reasons, two of them major:

—the absence of an air-speed indicator;

—because you aren't sitting in it, you don't have the "feel" for the plane that can warn you that you are close to stalling the wing.

Having talked to many R/C/full-scale pilots and being a full-scale pilot myself, I can attest that R/C planes are more difficult to fly.

CHAPTER 5

The Merry Modelers' Mindset

OR

Training one's brain to minimize stupid mistakes is easier than building a new plane

by Roy L. Clough Jr.

Years ago, when R/C models were few and far between, an accident steered me toward an attitude adjustment. It has worked for me through more than four decades of every sort of model flying. Today, with the proliferation of R/C, it seems more applicable than ever.

I had picked up a control-line handle upside-down. Thirty-five seconds later, staring down at the wreckage, I wondered, was I really all that stupid? Accidents don't just happen. Something causes them. Why had I done that? Was it just natural-born rattle-headedness or something deeply psychological?

Salvaging the remains, I mulled over some silly gaffes that I had seen committed by other modelers. Many had real savvy, but savvy hadn't prevented them from ruining the onboard ignition batteries then in use by accidentally connecting boosters backward or discovering an empty tank halfway up a wingover. Picking up handles upside-down has happened to the best of us. Worse yet, I've watched people who knew better succumb to momentary confusion and, when their plane was in an awkward position, they made the wrong move and pow!—into the ground.

I decided it was time to *really* think things through—but carefully. Too often, thinking things through degenerates into a review and confirmation of one's systematized prejudices—not a good way to arrive at new insights.

Example: most of us share the prejudice that a set of rules, memorized for recall when the action starts, can guide anybody through any complex operation. But when I started to formulate rules to remember when flying a model plane, I soon realized that things happen too fast. My recall of rote learning couldn't keep up with a model wheeling around the sky. What was needed was not a set of rules to cover every situation but a don't-think-about-it-do-it kind of automatic reaction.

Well, of course! Isn't that what training is all about? After months, maybe years, of practice, one automatically responds with the right moves. But just jumping in and practicing might not be the best idea.

Much of practicing consists of finding out what won't work. You start learning to do things right as a result of doing them wrong. Meantime, while you're learning the things that *do* work, you have to examine each one to make sure it doesn't contain the seeds of a bad habit that will cause problems later. Long before you've practiced enough to do things automatically, you wind up with a head full of caveats about things you shouldn't do *that* way but must do *this* way.

Take control line. The first thing you learn is that pulling up lifts the plane's nose. It makes it climb. But not always. Only when the engine is running. But not always even then: only when there is enough air speed. But sometimes, you can get enough air speed by "whipping." Then "up" will make it climb *without* the engine running, etc., etc. Long before your reactions get to be automatic, everything you've learned gets tied up in a confusing bunch of qualifiers. Your plane heads for

Here's an example of what can happen when the Merry Modelers' Mindset is not set. Think things through, and know what control inputs to use before you make a sudden move.

the ground upside-down, but before you can sift through the qualifiers and come up with the right response—blam! Of course, you *know* that when a plane is upside-down, the elevator "works backward." You should have given it "down" to raise the nose out of trouble. Right?

Down at the other end of the field, your friend, looking at the remains of his R/C plane, did something similar. Hacking around near the ground, he got momentarily confused. Pow! He should have remembered that controls are *reversed* when a plane is inverted. Right? Wrong. Dead wrong in both cases.

Bear with me. Many years ago, when I started thinking about these things, I looked for the lowest common denominator. I found it in my head. Don't laugh. You've got one, too. It's called a mind. It resides in that gray lump between your ears where everything you relate to gets sorted out. The mind has a peculiar characteristic that is simultaneously its most valuable asset and its most dangerous feature: it's always trying to rig itself for full automatic. After a stimulus has been repeated a few times, its subsequent inputs aren't evaluated but *recognized;* the mind reacts "without thinking." Over a period, a headful of recognition-reactions accumulate. There's a name for it: mindset.

A *mindset* is a fixed attitude or disposition that automatically determines an

AMA 3254

RUDDER

The rudder stick swings the nose of the plane toward the wingtip on the side to which it is moved.

When the rudder points up, its response is "right." When it points down, its response is "wrong."

individual's response to a thing or a situation. It has very little to do with *thinking;* it exists as a labor-saving alternative to conscious evaluation: recognize bug. Stomp bug!

ACQUIRE A USEFUL MINDSET

Suppose you could easily acquire a *useful* mindset about model airplanes. Suppose you could approach building and flying with a pre-loaded "natural disposition" to make correct responses. You could short-circuit much of the make-a-mistake-and-correct-it aspect of learning. Interested?

Meet the Merry Modelers' Mindset. But be forewarned: it's contagious—an infectious mind-virus that's almost impossible to get rid of once you've been exposed. The reason it works is rooted in something called "semantics"—a fancy word that means, basically, that the things we are *able* to think about are creatures of the reality defined (and limited) for us by our language. The fact is, language is the biggest mindset of all. It is what makes the Merry Modelers' Mindset possible. It's not a set of rules. It's a "revelation" of obvious relationships. Once it sits firmly under your piloting cap, you'll have the happy assurance that future crashes will not be the result of momentary confusion or stupid mistakes. They'll be mechanical failures or the result of your own bad judgment.

Here's the revelation: from molecular levels on up, reality presents itself to our senses as a combination of two comple-

Nick Ziroli—who definitely has a merry mindset—concentrates on flying his P-38 at a fun-scale meet. His spotter seems to have the same concentration as well.

mentary polarities—positive and negative. For model plane purposes, we accept, as positives: yes, true, forward, pushed, extended, on, ahead, up, clockwise, top, front, center, inside, right, red, beginning, same, more, always, clear (and their synonyms). Negatives: no, false, backward, pulled, retracted, off, to the rear, down, counterclockwise, bottom, rear, rim, outside, left, black, ending, opposite, less, never, obstructed (and their synonyms).

How it works: control line—*front* wing lead-in is connected to *up*-elevator, the *rear* to *down.* Control lines are *always* laid out with the control handle's *"up"* facing *ahead* in the direction in which the plane will take off.

For any powered plane, switches are *"on"* if their tabs, toggles, and/or slides are pointed *upward* or *forward* with respect to their location on the plane. Battery connectors have the *positive* pole to the *front* or *uppermost* and, with round connectors, the *center (inside)* pole is *positive* and the *outer* rim is *negative.*

Fuel filler is *positive*; vent air is *negative.* Arrange tank connections so that the filler line is either in the *front,* on *top,* or at the *right.* The vent line is at the *rear,* on the *bottom,* or to the *left.* The filler line feeds *into* the carburetor; the vent line goes *out* to the exhaust. Even with the tank totally enclosed and out of sight, you

instantly know which line is which.

Any plane that's ready to fly is prepped *positive.* Switches are *positive, "on."*

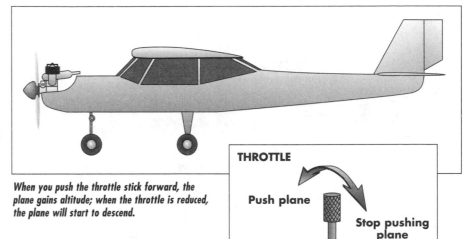

When you push the throttle stick forward, the plane gains altitude; when the throttle is reduced, the plane will start to descend.

THROTTLE

Push plane

Stop pushing plane

Controls are *positive;* the handle is laid out with the *up* wire facing *ahead.* The free-flight timer is set to *"on."* The R/C transmitter switch when *on* is *"up"* (is pushed *"in"* for some), the antenna is *extended,* and the receiver switch is *"on."* Servo-*reverse* switches are *no* if *not* checked; they become *yes* when they are *verified.* Controls function, *yes.* Range check *verified* is *yes.* Engine running is *on.* Positive across the board and if the field is *clear,* flight is *"on."*

toward its corresponding left or right wingtip. The rudder also points a finger to remind you its control response will be *right* or apparently *wrong.* When the rudder points *up* at the sky, the rudder stick is *"right."* It swings the nose of the plane in the direction it is moved. When the plane is inverted and the rudder points *down* at the ground, the rudder stick is *"wrong"* and swings the nose of the plane's apparent image *opposite* to the direction in which it is moved. Get comfortable with the concept of the plane's apparent image. It pops up again in aileron control.

The elevator stick *pushes* the nose *toward* the wheels or *pulls* the nose *away* from the wheels. In either control-line or R/C flying, never think of the elevator as *up* or *down.* The elevator changes the attitude of the plane. Whether it gains or loses altitude depends on other factors, such as thrust and the direction in which it is moving. You decide what attitude change is appropriate for a particular maneuver or to avoid a crunch. The wheels will tell you which way to move the stick. (Don't worry about what will happen when you move up to using retracting landing gear.

Aileron stick motions always rotate the plane in the same direction, regardless of whether it's upright or inverted. Therefore, a wiggle of the stick easily tells you whether a distant plane is coming or going.

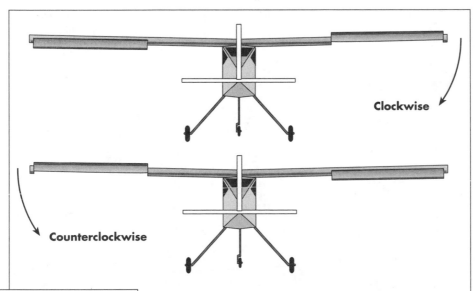

Clockwise

Counterclockwise

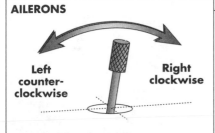

AILERONS

Left counter-clockwise

Right clockwise

When the model is airborne, all the following statements become *true,* regardless of the position of the plane, whether right side up, inverted, nose down or nose up or on its side. Mindset stuff here: you *push* the plane with the throttle stick. You *pull* back to stop *pushing* it. The rudder stick always *swings* the nose of the plane

By then, you'll *know* which side is up.)

The aileron stick moved *right* rotates the plane (from its point of view) *clockwise*. Moved *left,* the plane rotates *counter-*

Never think of the elevator stick as "the up-and-down control." Throttle makes the plane go up. Gravity brings it down. The elevator stick controls attitude.

clockwise. You can think of the aileron stick as *pushing* its corresponding wingtip *toward* the wheels. When you have *pushed* the wingtip to the angle of bank you need, let go of the stick.

The great thing about the aileron stick is that the apparent visual image of the plane responds in the same way whether the plane is right-side up or inverted. Thus, a quick waggle of the stick tells you instantly whether a distant plane is coming or going regardless of which side is up.

This apparent image thing that makes the ailerons seem to work the same either side up is also a great comfort when making inverted low-level passes. Just note,

ELEVATOR

Toward wheels

Away from wheels

before you move it, what the pointing finger of the rudder is telling you about *its* response.

There you go. Don't even think about moving the sticks in a *different* way when the plane gets into an unusual attitude. The plane always reacts in the same way to control inputs, regardless of its position against the sky. Your job is to decide where

you want it to go and *aim* it with the sticks.

Modifications to your planes may be mechanically minor even though psychologically important. Might as well get to it. Just rearrange switch positions, fuel lines and charging jacks to conform to your new mindset. You probably won't be able to get it out of your head once you've been exposed. ◆

ABOUT THE AUTHOR

Roy L. Clough Jr.

It was Gordon Light's 1935 Wakefield winner that inspired Roy to start designing and building rubber-powered planes. From the outset, he built innovative creations such as helicopters, ornithopters and autogyros. Many flopped, but the successes kept him at it. His writing career began with an appreciative nod from Popular Science Workshop editor Harry Walton, then it was on to publications such as Popular Mechanics and Air Trails. Always a loner, Roy recently joined the Winnipesaukee R/C'ers in his home state of New Hampshire and now enjoys the camaraderie of fellow modelers. His affiliation with Model Airplane News began in the '50s with editor Howard G. McEntee, who urged him to design several unorthodox models, and it continues to this day.

CHAPTER 6

How to Avoid Crashing

by Roger Post Jr.

I n 30 years of flying R/C, I have become well versed in the art of getting out of crash situations. My training as a full-scale pilot has sharpened my understanding of some of these techniques.

Recently, while watching videotapes of model crashes—"Oops" and "Son of Oops," produced by Propwash Video Productions, 2973 Berman St., Las Vegas, NV; (702) 731-5217—I realized that a number of crashes could have been avoided had the pilots better understood how and when to use throttle and rudder. At low altitudes, left-hand inputs (throttle and rudder—assuming you fly in Mode II) are critical to surviving stalls or near-stall situations, yet many modelers instinctively input aileron and elevator commands and lose their models in the process. Had other guidelines been followed, many models in the videos could have been saved. So I would like to share some of these alternative procedures with you.

Using preflight checklists also helps to minimize crashes. I've included sample checklists here. When I was training for my pilot's license, everyone commented on how long I took to preflight an aircraft. Well, I just let them talk, because I knew that a thorough preflight could save my life. The same approach can be applied to your model.

PREPARE FOR TAKEOFF

Once all checks have been completed, you're ready for flight. Takeoffs present the first chance of crashing. When you start your ground run, simultaneously increase power and add a little right rudder. As the plane gathers speed and tends to veer left, increase the right rudder input. Don't try to correct the left-hand veering tendencies with aileron. Ailerons are ineffective at slow air speeds, and they will only cause

adverse yaw, i.e., the downward-deflected aileron generates drag that pulls that wing back. The left-hand turning is a yaw problem, and rudder corrects yaw.

Once the plane has reached an adequate air speed, pull the elevator stick back a degree or two. The airplane should climb out at a nice 20- to 30-degree angle to the horizon. On your climb-out, keep your wings level with the ailerons, and keep your ground track straight with the rudder.

◆ **Crosswind takeoffs.** Crosswinds can cause crashes if the correct transmitter controls are not used. The guiding principle: to prevent the plane from flipping over, bank the upwind wingtip down. Following full-scale practice, aileron input starts during the ground roll and decreases slightly as speed increases. Once the plane has taken off, rolling slightly into the wind directs the lift, generated by the wings, into the wind and

counteracts the model's sideways drift.

Wind velocity and direction and ground speed determine how much you lower the upwind wingtip. If your ground speed is slow, you need more aileron into the wind. As ground speed increases, decrease the aileron input. If the crosswind speed is high, you need more

FIGURE 1
Right-hand crosswind landing with the incorrect control inputs to recover from a high right-wingtip attitude. The added right aileron creates adverse yaw, and the up-elevator slows the air speed. The plane stalls and crashes. (Note that the deflections have been exaggerated for clarity.)

ILLUSTRATIONS BY DALE TREECE ©1995

aileron input, and if there's just a gentle breeze, you need only a little.

Rudder is used to keep your model tracking straight and to counteract torque and the other factors that tend to swing a model's nose to the left during takeoff. If needed, after takeoff, you can "crab" into the wind to ensure a straight track.

If, right after takeoff, the wind starts to flip your model over (the upwind wing starts rolling upward), follow the rules that apply in a near-stall or stall condition. Use your rudder to correct the bank angle: to roll level, input right rudder and relieve a little back-pressure on the elevator stick, i.e., reduce up-elevator to pitch the nose down and regain air speed. Don't use the ailerons for bank correction when you're in this precarious situation.

CLIMB-OUT

◆ **Stalling on climb-out.** After your plane has taken off, don't pull the nose up

Preflight Checklist

Always check—
- Engine and its mounting bolts.
- Firewall mount.
- Prop nut and muffler bolts.
- Firewall attachment to the fuselage. Grab the plane by the prop, and hang the model in a vertical position. Sometimes, I gently shake the plane as an added check. It can ruin your day if the engine comes off the plane.

Examine the airframe.
Look for—
- Stress cracks.
- Proper landing-gear and wheel attachment. (I've seen many good aircraft lose wheels in flight and cartwheel on landing because of a wheel-less landing-gear strut.)
- Broken or loose hinges and linkages.
- Properly attached tail surfaces.
- Correctly attached wings that are strong enough. To check your wing's strength, pick up the model by the wingtips. If the wing feels weak, it will never support the weight of an aircraft in a multi-G turn.
- Fuel-tank clunk and your fuel line and filter. These can adversely affect your fuel intake. Pinholes or a loose fuel-filter housing can allow air to enter the fuel mixture and cause the engine to run lean.
- CG placement—last, but by no means least.

too high, or you will lose air speed and stall the wing. The only way to save a model that has stalled is to push the elevator stick forward to decrease the angle of attack and increase air speed. If you are not already at full throttle, add throttle.

Remember that power is altitude, and pitch is air speed. The only way to gain altitude is with the engine running at max rpm. The only way to gain air speed is by pitching the nose down.

When you're near a stall, or fighting your way out of a stalled condition, correct any wing-dropping tendencies with the rudder—not the ailerons! To level the wings, add rudder in the direction of the high wingtip. This will yaw the model toward the high wing. This yawing momentarily increases the air speed of the low wing and increases lift on the low wingtip, causing it to rise.

If, instead, you were to apply full aileron to roll the plane level at this critical moment, you would probably throw the lower wing into a deep stall. The downward-deflected aileron would add drag and further slow the lower wing, and there would be no recovery at a low altitude.

◆ **Engine-out on climb-out.** If your engine quits on takeoff, try to glide straight ahead. Turning 180 degrees depletes your air speed and usually results in a stall and a crash. If you can't go straight ahead, then turn gently with your rudder, and push the nose down to gain air speed. Do not use the ailerons unless you need to slip the plane into a particular spot to avoid striking an object. If your engine

starts to lean out on takeoff, reduce your power to about 75 percent, and keep your climb-out angle shallow by easing up on the elevator-stick pressure.

WHEN AIRBORNE

◆ **In-flight emergencies.** In-flight emergencies are another major cause of aircraft crashes. If you feel something is wrong, pull back the power immediately. Don't wait until the wing has flexed to the point

1. Corrections for a stall on takeoff: full power and a little down-elevator.

2. Corrections for a high, right wingtip on a right-crosswind takeoff and climb-out.

3. Control inputs for a right-crosswind landing. Inputs have been slightly exaggerated to show clarity of movement.

Author's note: the thumbs are placed off the tops of the sticks to allow a better visualization of the stick movements.

at which it's two separate pieces. A reduction of power can save your airframe from an in-flight breakup.

◆ **Unusual attitudes.** Aerobatic maneuvers, such as spins and inverted flight, frequently result in crashes. To get out of a spin or a flat spin, use opposite rudder to stop the model's autorotation, then add down-elevator to get the wing "un-stalled" and flying again. Next, gently ease in the power. After you've done all of this, make sure the wings are level, and pull back on the elevator stick to resume straight-and-level flight.

With inverted-flight recovery, you should remember two things: to get out of a tense situation, either push the elevator stick forward, or roll the plane right-side up with aileron.

When a plane is flying directly toward you, move the transmitter sticks in the direction of the low wing. This will correct any unwanted bank angle and prevent your plane from flipping over.

Altitude can give you and your plane another chance. I can't stress enough the importance of practicing any kind of

FIGURE 2
Right-hand cross-wind landing with the correct control inputs to recover from a high right-wingtip attitude. Power is added, rudder is used to correct the high right-wing attitude, and the elevator is deflected down to gain some air speed. (Note that the deflections have been exaggerated for clarity.)

maneuver, recovery technique, etc., at a *higher than normal* altitude.

◆ **Air density.** Let's touch briefly on air density and aircraft performance. On cold days, your airplane will seem as if it can do anything. On hot days, it will seem as if it can't get out of its own way. More crashes happen on hot days because there are fewer air molecules per cubic foot for the plane and propeller to bite into. Therefore, you must think ahead before attempting anything on a hot day. It takes your airplane much longer to recover from an unusual attitude on a hot day than it will on a cold day.

LANDINGS

Too many R/C pilots land their airplanes improperly. The most common error is landing too fast. Try to touch down with absolutely no bounce. To do this, slow the aircraft down during your landing-pattern setup. On the downwind leg, pull back the throttle, and add some up-trim to achieve a slightly nose-down, slow descent. The more throttle you take out, the more up-trim you must add. Sometimes, I pull back my throttle trim first and then use my main throttle stick to control my descent. This saves me from having to try to find the throttle trim at that critical approach moment.

At this point, with your plane slowing down, it's best to turn it with the rudder and control the descent with the throttle. I always teach students to keep their left-hand thumb on the left stick and to move both sticks in the same direction for better coordinated flight. Small input corrections are necessary at this time to keep the model on track. Too many planes have been dumped because pilots over-controlled

on final approach. Try to keep your plane flying straight from final to touchdown. In full-scale flying, pilots track the final approach in line with the runway's center line. Just because you have a large landing area at your disposal, it doesn't mean that you don't have to practice precision approaches and landings.

Whether the wind is blowing straight down the runway or across it, for a smooth landing, you should anticipate

this question in mind: "If my engine quits now, can I make it to the field?" A strong wind will push you away; in that event, keep the airplane closer to the field.

Once the plane is over the runway, let it come into ground effect and settle itself. Bleed off any excess air speed with minute up-elevator inputs. After touchdown, hold full up-elevator, and let the plane roll to a stop. Correct any directional problems with the rudder. If you touch down at the

Engine Check

Nothing spoils a flight more than an engine failure on takeoff. Always set your high end first, and check it by holding the model with its nose pointing straight up. It should hold max rpm with the nose high and change to a slightly richer mixture with the nose low.

It's easy to adjust idle. Put your throttle setting on low, and see how the engine sounds. If it gurgles, sputters and quits, it's too rich. High rpm probably mean it's too lean. Check it by advancing the throttle rapidly. You should have a smooth transition with no burps or gurgles. On landing, if you need to do a go-around, you'll want a reliable transition from idle to max power. Also, remember that an engine will lean out a little in the air, so don't set it for max rpm on the ground.

AIR DENSITY

A good engine run-up is essential for good performance. Make sure that you take into consideration the air temperature and the air density when you adjust your needle valve. On a cold day, the air molecules are very dense (thick), so there's more air per cubic foot, and your engine will need a richer setting (less air). On a warm day, the air is less dense (much thinner) with fewer air molecules per cubic foot, and your engine will need a leaner setting (more air) to run well.

having to make corrective actions. If the plane approaches the runway straight into a headwind, maintain a higher throttle setting to ensure that it reaches the field. You can also shorten your downwind leg, base leg and final-approach pattern. Try to keep

proper landing speed, you should have little or no bounce. If you do bounce with a hard impact, add a little power to keep up your air speed. Any kind of contact with the ground will diminish air speed. This will usually put the plane in a nose-high, low-air-speed configuration—a primary setup for a low-speed stall.

◆ **Stall recovery during landings.** If you do stall in this landing configuration—either on final or after a bounced touchdown—you must add power! Then

Radio Check

- Secure the battery leads and servo connections so that they won't come apart in the air.
- Check your receiver batteries.
- Range-check the radio.
- Check the movement of the control surfaces for the correct response.
- Check your landing gear, if you have retracts.
- Listen for any servo noise and for binding linkage movements. If the servos are not quiet with the transmitter sticks in neutral, you can be sure that you are drawing power from your battery.
- Make sure you have your frequency pin before you turn on your transmitter!
- Check trims, and don't forget to fully extend the transmitter antenna!

add some down-elevator, and correct any wing-dropping tendencies with rudder. A stall after a bounced touchdown can lead to a cartwheel and all sorts of other gymnastics. How fast you are with these inputs determines whether your plane will live to fly again.

◆ **Dead-stick landings.** Suppose your

engine quits on the approach. Keep up your air speed by lowering your aircraft's nose a little. Once you're sure that you can make the field, start to ease in some up-elevator to help you slow down. Then use the technique described earler to complete your touchdown.

◆ **Crosswind landings.** Always keep some aileron into the wind. As in crosswind takeoffs, air speed and wind velocity determine how much aileron you need to input. To keep your ground track straight, counteract the rolling effect of the aileron input with some opposite rudder. This is called "cross controlling," and it puts you into a forward slip (the upwind, banked-down wingtip is yawed slightly forward), but it allows you to land without the plane flipping into a knife-edge attitude because of a wind gust underneath the upwind wing.

If your plane does begin to flip (roll downwind) on the approach, add power to increase airflow over the tail surfaces, use your rudder to correct the banking of the wings, and add down-elevator to keep your air speed up. On the other hand, if you're set for a touchdown and the upwind wing starts to drop faster than you'd like, add more opposite rudder and a little power. You can groove a beautiful crosswind landing with these inputs, but you must be quick and be able to anticipate what the plane will do.

PAY ATTENTION AND STAY FOCUSED!

Aside from using left-gimbal control inputs during problematic, low-speed, low-altitude

situations, always use your eyes and ears to maintain a *total awareness* of your situation. Don't fly with tunnel vision. Be aware of the other planes in the air. I've seen many crashes and near misses caused by someone not paying attention to what was going on around him. Call out your intentions to the others, and if you need help in the air, ask for it. Pride has ruined many a good airplane.

Inaccurate depth perception is another problem that can result in a crash. When your plane gets too far away for you to tell its attitude, give it a command that your eyes will easily pick out, e.g., full up-elevator. Usually, a very abrupt attitude change will help you to determine whether you're coming or going or whether you're right-side up or right-side down.

If you're close to the ground, tree shadows can fog up your attitude perception. If you can, stay above the trees on your approach until your eyes are able to perceive the plane's attitude. Try not to make approaches with the setting sun as a backdrop. If you have no other choice, make sure you have a good pair of sunglasses that enable you to look near the sun and still see the plane coming toward you. If necessary, block the sun with your transmitter.

I hope these tips will help you keep your pride and joy in one piece. I believe in promoting safety and pilot proficiency; the more we discuss and practice them, the better off we will all be. Good luck and happy landings. ◆

To learn about the author of this chapter, see page 18.

INTERMEDIATE FLYING SKILLS

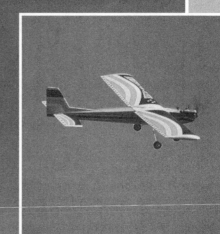

This section takes R/C flying a step further. Dan Parsons explains a flying technique we should all know in "Tail-Dragger vs. Trike Gear"; and master R/C aerobatic flier and aircraft designer Dave Patrick provides more essentials in "Crosswind Takeoff and Landing."

Adding another engine always makes things interesting. Our good friend Nick Ziroli, a master scale designer, builder and flier of worldwide renown, gives some helpful advice in "The Multi-Engine Experience." Dan Parsons follows up with some more helpful hints on multi-engine flying. *Model Airplane News* "RPM" columnist Dave Gierke, who pioneered the testing of model engines, props and airframes using downlink telemetry, offers key insights into matching these components in "Maximizing Engine Performance."

Optimized performance assumes proper balancing: Larry Renger, an accomplished model aerodynamicist and designer, explains what you need to know in "Fine-Tune Your CG by Flight Testing." When your thumbs have mastered cross-controlling, slipping your plane will give you hours of landing pleasure. Look at Roger Post Jr.'s "How to Slip an Airplane" for all the answers.

CHAPTER 7

Tail-Dragger vs. Trike Gear

by Dan Parsons

Back in the really early days of radio control—the late '30s—the only R/C models were tail-draggers. Most models were tail-draggers until somewhere around 1960, when the pattern fliers started to switch to trike gear. I can't remember just when the switch occurred, but I believe it was after the tail-dragger Astro Hog was flown to fame by Bob Dunham. Bob won the pattern class at the Nats three years in a row, and then he retired. Now, there was a flier— certainly the best of his day; no doubt about it.

Anyway, back to the coming of the trike gear. Once the switch to trike gear had started in pattern (probably because of the taxiing requirement), it soon became a stampede. The influence of pattern was such that the hearts and minds of modelers (and the kit manufacturers) switched to trike gear for almost everything that flew, except of course, scale models of tail-draggers (also known as "conventional geared" planes). The tail-dragger's traditionally poor reputation also played a significant role in this switch.

ADVANTAGES OF A TAIL-DRAGGER

I steadfastly maintain that this poor reputation is not deserved, and what follows will, I hope, convince you that the tail-dragger should be held in high esteem by all R/C modelers. I must stress that the success of a tail-dragger depends on the proper setup of the two main wheels, and that this is assumed all through my discussion. Later on, I'll describe this setup.

I've been flying R/C planes for 42 years and, in that time, I've built a grand total of two planes with trike gear. But I've flown many planes with trike gear because I instructed new R/C'ers, and I know the trike gear well.

Looking at the list I've made of the advantages and disadvantages of the tail-dragger, I find that the advantages outnumber the disadvantages. I'll discuss all of its good features first, and by the time I get to the "poor" features, you may agree that a tail-dragger really doesn't have any that merit mention.

You may shake your head in disbelief at some of the good features I discuss because of the deeply entrenched bad reputation of the tail-dragger. But please, just keep reading.

◆ From a construction standpoint, a tail-dragger's landing gear is easier to install than that on a trike gear. In a trike gear, the nose wheel and its linkage compete for space with the engine and the fuel tank, especially if you retract the nose wheel. Conversely, the steerable tail wheel of a tail-dragger is much simpler to install and seldom gets in the way of anything.

◆ Once in operation, you'll find the tail wheel virtually trouble-free for many months of flying. If the support bracket wears out or the wire strut breaks, they can be quickly and easily replaced. Conversely, the nose wheel in a trike gear requires considerable maintenance and frequent adjustments. After all, it's in a vulnerable position and takes quite a pounding, as does its driving servo.

◆ Because a tail wheel and its strut are much smaller than a nose-wheel assembly, they create less drag, and that allows your plane to fly better at a given power setting. Less drag also helps your plane get back to the runway when the engine unexpectedly dies. The couple of ounces that you save don't hurt, either.

A classic wheel landing of the RWR Racing Team's Unlimited Stiletto by Chuck Collier at the Galveston Races in 1994. Note the slight nose-down attitude. Chuck was probably holding just a bit of down-elevator. No bounce and a long, straight rollout followed this perfect touchdown.

◆ Here's an advantage that many of you may scoff at. I happen to think it's one of the most important and would have listed it first, but you might have thought me nuts and read no further. You ready? A properly rigged tail-dragger will break far fewer props than a trike gear. (Just a reminder, I'm always talking about a properly rigged tail-dragger; this is of utmost importance.) An improperly rigged tail-dragger will eat not only props, but also your lunch and your patience; and, in the worst case, it will prevent you from flying and will probably cause considerable damage to your plane.

I'm sure that you've often landed a trike gear a little hard in a slight nose-down attitude and heard that familiar "tick" of the prop blade hitting the runway. With a wooden prop, you've just made another expensive landing. Or perhaps, after a landing, you've turned a little too fast and your plane has tipped "into the corner"; there goes another prop. The same thing is easy to do if you taxi too fast, particularly as you turn crosswind. But it's amazing how hard you can drive a tail-dragger into a slight nose-down landing and not damage the prop—even after a bounce. A fast turn that causes tip-dragging doesn't usually damage it either. About the only time you'll bust a prop is by nosing over because you stubbed the

A T-6 at the Galveston 1994 Races assumes the proper three-point attitude just prior to a perfect, no-bounce stall landing. The T-6 is a notorious "bouncer," but not this time.

ing. Ideally, in a stall landing, the wing stalls just an instant before the wheels (two mains and a tail wheel) touch the runway, thereby ensuring that the plane remains on the runway because so little lift remains. In a wheel landing, you actually fly the plane onto the runway well above its stall speed, in a level or slightly nose-down attitude. The photos show these two types of landings.

◆ The previous advantage leads naturally into this one—the challenge of a tail-dragger. I imagine you've heard the phrase, "Real pilots fly tail-draggers." It is definitely more challenging to make a good landing with a tail-dragger than with a trike gear. I guarantee that with a tail-dragger, a well-executed stall landing is a

for sharpening up your approach and landing techniques, particularly if you throw in many different approach patterns. (I'm surprised that so few R/C'ers know about and participate in touch-and-go contests.)

◆ Many scale models are tail-draggers, so anyone who plans to go into scale should be familiar with the takeoff and landing techniques of tail-draggers. I like to start new students in tail-draggers so that they learn the handling techniques from the start. Once you've mastered tail-dragger technique, a trike gear is a walk in the park. Learning in the reverse order is not nearly as quick and easy. (By the way, I feel the same about full-size planes, having learned to fly in a tail-dragger.)

◆ Looks. This advantage is strictly an opinion of mine. Here, I'm referring to non-scale planes; I think many of the so-called "trainers" and the everyday sport planes look better as tail-draggers. By the way, the Ugly Stik—one of the most popular designs ever kitted—is easily converted into an excellent tail-dragger that is as good, or better than any I've ever flown. As for improving its appearance, I'm not making any rash claims about that!

DISADVANTAGES OF A TAIL-DRAGGER

Well, I've finally run out of the advantages of tail-draggers and, to be fair, I have to list the disadvantages. Try as I might, I can come up with only two.

◆ First, most tail-draggers will not handle a crosswind takeoff as well as most trike gears. This is only important in contest flying though, because in everyday sport flying, we just take off into the wind or don't worry about drifting during our takeoff run.

◆ The other disadvantage, and I won't concede that it really is a disadvantage, is ground handling. With little or no wind, a tail-dragger is just as good (or better) than a trike gear in the ground-handling depart-

A big Spitfire in the correct three-point attitude just before a solid, no-bounce stall landing (note the up-elevator).

wheels on a sharp ridge or caught them in a crack. Caution: if you mount the main gear too close to the CG, the nosing-over tendency will be aggravated and you'll start to break props.

When you become familiar with your properly rigged tail-dragger, you'll probably make many flights without breaking the prop.

◆ A tail-dragger allows you to choose between a stall landing and a wheel land-

delight to accomplish (and to watch) and will leave you feeling good. A wheel landing with no bounce is another thing of beauty.

I've spent many an hour with friends having touch-and-go contests in which we take turns shooting touch-and-go's (with the same plane) to see who can make the best landings. Though enjoyable with a trike gear, this is really fun with a tail-dragger, especially with a plane like the Pitts. Touch-and-go contests are also great

ment. Even in winds of up to 10mph, I've seen tail-draggers do a creditable job of ground handling. Besides, haven't you seen many a trike gear tipped "into the corner" by a quartering tailwind that busts the prop?

RIGGING AND SETUP

Now, on to the most important thing to know about non-scale tail-draggers: how to set up and rig them. Though these principles apply to scale models as well, with a scale model, you often have little or no choice as to how you correctly position the main gear—the secret to having a well-behaved tail-dragger. For example, many—if not most—biplanes have their main gear too far forward of the CG and are therefore tough to handle on takeoff and landing. The poor reputation of the tail-dragger has been largely earned by its built-in tendency to ground loop during the takeoff run and the landing rollout, and by its (sometimes wild) bouncing on landing. It has also been earned by its poor ground handling and taxiing capabilities. An improperly rigged tail-dragger will do all of the above and more.

The secrets to reducing (or eliminating) these problems and to producing a pussy-cat are:

• Position the main gear in the proper place in relation to the plane's CG.
• Have lots of tail-wheel movement.
• Toe-in the main wheels about 1 or 2 degrees. It's as simple as that. So, to obtain a well-behaved tail-dragger, place the wheel axles approximately 1¾ inch forward of the CG and swing that tail wheel! (See Figures 1 and 2.)

To repeat, the bad ground looping and bouncing tendencies of an improperly rigged tail-dragger are caused (almost completely) by having the wheel too far forward of the CG. The closer the wheel axles are to the CG, the more stable and tame the tail-dragger becomes. But there is a limit to how close the axles can be because of the increasing nosing-over tendency. Like most engineering problems, it's a compromise. By experimenting, I've found that the 1¾-inch distance works well for me on a typical .60-size plane. This distance certainly isn't ironclad and may vary with different types of models, so I suggest that you experiment with your own plane. The larger the plane, the larger this distance should be.

LANDING

◆ **Stall landing.** In a perfect stall landing, the model is held off (with its wheels just above the runway) by the continuous and smooth application of increasing up-elevator; this bleeds off the excess speed above the stall, and the plane neither rises nor falls. Then, just as the elevator stick nears its maximum up-travel, the model stalls, and all three wheels (two mains and a tail wheel) softly and simultaneously touch the runway. To softly touch the run-

Rob "The Kid" Pastor makes another classic wheel landing with his Unlimited Stiletto racer at the 1994 Galveston Races. No bounce and a long, straight roll-out followed this well-executed touchdown.

way after stalling, the wheels should not be more than 1 inch above the runway because the bottom falls out of most models when they stall (the type and thickness of the airfoil affects this; some are much gentler than others).

A complication that could arise is if, at any time before the stall, the wheels touch while you're holding up-elevator, your plane will bounce. The amount of bounce will depend on your speed above the stall, how much up you're holding and the type of plane. Biplanes are particularly notorious for this type of bounce because most have their main gear too far forward (which also makes them want to ground-loop). Remember, for a no-bounce stall landing, the plane must be completely stalled before the wheels touch, and the elevator stick should be all the way back. Full up-elevator should ensure that the plane is stalled and remains so.

So, as you can see, several things have to be just right to get a perfect stall landing. That's where the challenge comes in, and that's why it makes you feel so good when you get that perfect stall landing.

◆ **Wheel landing.** In some respects, the wheel-landing technique is simpler than

the stall-landing technique. Instead of holding the plane off with increasing up-elevator until the stall, put it into a level attitude with its wheels just above the runway. *[Editor's note: this level attitude can be set using a little power and some up-elevator trim.]* Then release any up-elevator and allow the plane to land. The secret here is to make absolutely sure you're off up-elevator at the moment of wheel contact. In fact, proper wheel-landing technique requires that you apply and hold some down-elevator just before wheel contact. This flies the plane onto the runway and holds it there. Psychologically, I've always found flying a plane (full-size or model) onto the runway rather difficult; but the technique can be learned, and it really works.

The wheel landing is particularly useful during strong, gusty winds because the higher air speed and lower angle of attack of the model just before touchdown provide better response and therefore better control.

TAKEOFF

I have gone on at length about landing a tail-dragger, so some words on takeoff technique are certainly in order. With some exceptions, takeoff is easier than landing for a tail-dragger. One exception is a scale plane with long landing-gear legs and a powerful engine. This combination will often produce a tendency to nose-over during the first part of the take-off roll. To prevent the plane from nosing over, hold full up-elevator at the start of the takeoff, and ease the power in smoothly over 4 or 5 seconds. As the plane picks up speed, start to ease off the up-elevator to allow the tail to rise. When the tail is up, the fuselage is parallel to the ground and the plane is close to takeoff speed, all the up-elevator input should be out, and the plane should be running along nicely on its wheels. Allow the speed to increase further, then gently ease the plane off the runway. I use this technique on all tail-draggers just to keep in practice, because the coordination and timing required between throttle and elevator application is considerable.

You're probably wondering about feed-

coordinated and timed with your other control applications, and only practice will make perfect. Believe me, a well-executed takeoff with a tail-dragger (particularly scale) is a thing of beauty and great satis-

degrees, maybe more; again, experiment.

Installing a steerable tail wheel on most non-scale planes is a simple job. Just attach one of the available tail-wheel brackets to the underside of the fuselage with the wheel-strut pivot axis lined up with the rudder hinge line. But before you attach the bracket to the fuselage, install the strut and axle wire in the bracket, and then form the driving arm or tiller so that it extends along the underside of the rudder (see Figure 2). Slip a U-shaped piece of sheet metal over the driving arm of the strut and onto either side of the rudder, and then fasten it to the rudder. To prevent metal-to-metal contact, slip a piece of fuel tubing over the driving arm. The rudder is now directly driving the tail wheel.

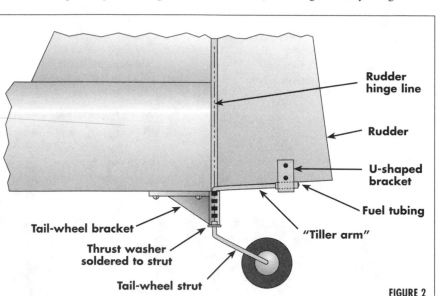

Rudder hinge line

Rudder

U-shaped bracket

Fuel tubing

Tail-wheel bracket

"Tiller arm"

Thrust washer soldered to strut

Tail-wheel strut

FIGURE 2

ing in some right rudder to stop the plane from swinging left during the takeoff roll, especially in the early part. Some right rudder is usually required, but more is required when the tail comes up. The amount depends on the plane and how it's trimmed. This right rudder also has to be

faction—that old challenge again.

I have to back up a little here to discuss ground handling. Though it's true that main-gear placement is important for ground handling, tail-wheel movement is even more important. Put lots of angular movement in the tail wheel—30 to 40

A tail wheel can be driven independently of the rudder by running a separate pushrod from the other side of your rudder servo to the driving arm (or tiller) of the tail-wheel strut. This technique allows the tail wheel to turn more or less than the rudder; usually, you want it to turn more. But the simpler rudder-drive system does work well in most cases, and I recommend it for a first try.

Well, there it is: the case for tail-draggers. Give one a try; I know you'll love it. Many pattern fliers have, and they like 'em! ◆

To learn about the author of this chapter, see page 24.

CHAPTER 8

Crosswind Takeoff and Landing

by Dave Patrick

One of the questions I'm most often asked is how to fly in a crosswind. Many pilots get intimidated when the wind isn't blowing straight down the runway, and that's understandable. Although it's a bit difficult to fly in a crosswind, anyone can learn to do it well. It just takes a little understanding, some practice and forethought. Though having this skill is imperative in competition, it's also very helpful to the beginner/sport flier, so I strongly recommend that all pilots try to understand crosswind effects and how to compensate.

CROSSWIND TAKEOFFS

I'm sure there are many ways to accomplish crosswind takeoffs successfully, but one thing is sure: when you learn how to handle a crosswind successfully during takeoff, you'll not only be a safer pilot, but you'll also have a lot more fun—especially on windy days when other fliers are grounded.

◆ **In the beginning**. In crosswind-takeoff conditions, some modelers cheat by taking off into the wind instead of straight down the center of the runway. There's nothing wrong with this in itself, but if you always do it, you'll never learn proper crosswind technique (see Figure 1).

If the wind is coming from the pit or the spectator area (and it often does), this "cheating" can be dangerous. The real answer is to learn how to maintain full

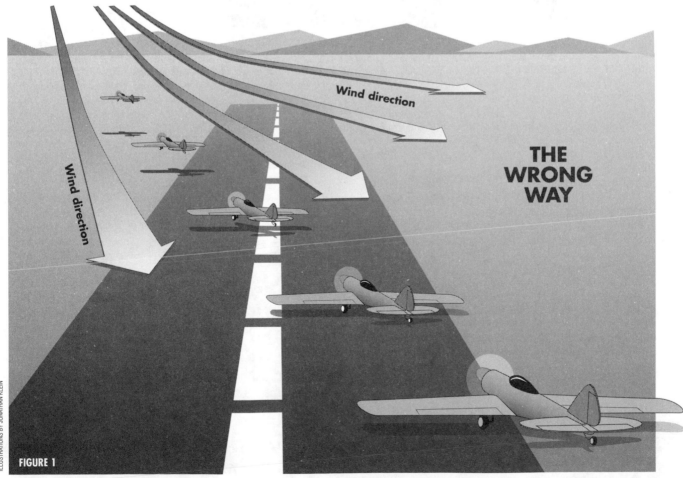

Wind direction

Wind direction

THE WRONG WAY

FIGURE 1

ILLUSTRATIONS BY JONATHAN KLEIN

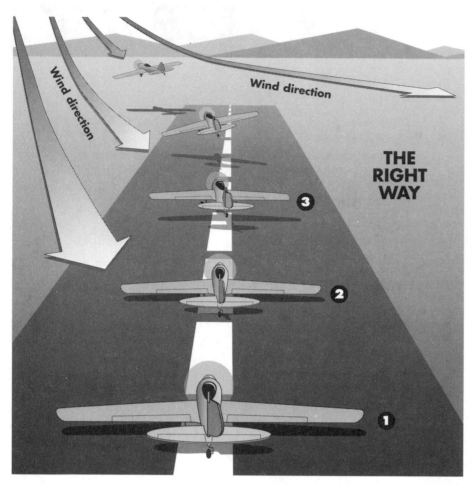

Wind direction

Wind direction

Wind direction

THE RIGHT WAY

FIGURE 2

1. At this point, you might need lots of right rudder to prevent the plane from "weathervaning" into the wind.

2. As the plane picks up speed, you'll need less rudder to keep it tracking down the center line.

3. After rotation, the aircraft must be allowed to point into the wind or "crab" slightly to compensate for the crosswind. When the plane is airborne and on its way, you may have to maintain a little right rudder during climb-out to compensate for torque.

climb out gradually, e.g., at a 5- to 10-degree angle. As you rotate, also remove any right-aileron input; from here, use ailerons to maintain level wings.

During most climb-outs, I keep some right rudder in to counteract torque and to maintain a straight track. In a crosswind takeoff, it's important to use the rudder to correct the heading as well.

◆ **Practice!** If the wind is from the left during takeoff, you'll have to apply left aileron and right rudder during the take-off. Then, as speed builds, you'll need less rudder until you reach the point (during climb-out) at which you'll need just enough right rudder to counteract torque (see Figure 2). Practice makes perfect, and every plane is different. It isn't unusual to find me at the airfield just practicing take-offs and landings instead of the usual aer-obatics. Knowing what to do ahead of time will really help you with those cross-wind takeoffs. Don't be intimidated. With the proper skills, it's amazing how strong a crosswind you'll be able to handle.

FLYING IN A CROSSWIND

◆ **Heading and track.** There are two ways to fly an aircraft in a crosswind. One, which is really a constant process, involves compensating for the wind by adjusting the heading to get the desired

control while going down the center of the runway. If you're reluctant to go straight down the center, on your first attempts, go easy on yourself by compromising the angle of your takeoff run. As you build proficiency, you can work your way to taking off right down the center line. With practice, there's no reason why you shouldn't be able to take off in a 90-degree crosswind.

In a competition last summer, this prac-tice really paid off for me. I flew in a 15-knot wind that was blowing at a 90-degree angle to the runway center line. It was a long day for the competitors who couldn't handle a crosswind!

Before you even start to roll down the runway, try to get a "feel" for what's going to happen by paying close attention to the wind's direction and strength. Before take-off, pilots of full-scale aircraft are repeatedly given this information, because it has a dra-matic effect on a plane's handling.

◆ **Let's go!** Let's look at a takeoff that has a fairly strong crosswind coming from your right. First, you should input a little right aileron, or at least be prepared to input right aileron to prevent the wind from getting under the upwind wing and

possibly flipping the aircraft over. Then, because the tail will try to "weathervane" the aircraft into the wind, apply left rudder during the initial takeoff roll (this is the opposite of what you'd usually require on a calm day). The amount of right-aileron you input will depend on the strength and direc-tion of the cross-wind, the size of the fin and rudder and how much power you apply.

As speed builds, you'll use less left rudder. When the air-craft is about to lift off, you may need to apply right rudder to keep the aircraft cen-tered on the runway.

When your air-craft is ready to lift off, don't horse it off. Gently rotate it, allowing plenty of air speed to build, then

FIGURE 3

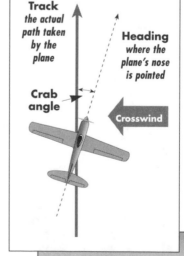

Track the actual path taken by the plane

Heading where the plane's nose is pointed

Crab angle

Crosswind

Typical landing-approach angle of approximately 6 degrees

track. Remember, "heading" is the direction in which the plane is pointed; "track" is the actual path in which the airplane flies (see Figure 3). The other method is to fly the maneuvers straight and to intermittently compensate for crosswind-induced drift by flying a separate maneuver altogether. Different types of competitions require different techniques, and using the wrong one can cost you big points!

◆ **How much angle?** In most situations, I recommend that you use the technique in which you adjust the heading to establish proper track. Let's say you simply want to make a pass down the runway center line. The wind is blowing into your face at 10mph, your model air speed is at an even 100mph, and you're flying from right to left. To have your plane fly down the runway over the center line, you must point its nose to the right at some angle. A scale drawing can show you the appropriate compensation angle.

For this example, let's use a unit of

length, e.g., 1 inch, to equal 10mph in a sketch as shown in Figures 5A-C. This also shows graphically what the compensation angle should look like. Take note of this angle, because it will be a key measure of proper heading when your plane is in the air. While we're at it, why don't you try a few more sketches using 20 and 25mph as your crosswinds; interesting, eh? Don't put the sketchpad away yet; try the same drawing but with faster air speeds such as 75 and 50mph.

These sketches will work even if the crosswind is at an angle other than 90 degrees (see Figure 5B, which illustrates a 15mph crosswind at 45 degrees). I'm not suggesting that you take a sketchpad to the contest site, but this exercise will give you some idea of the relationship between air speed, the strength and angle of the crosswind and how much compensation you may need.

◆ **Varying the angle.** Now that we've learned to compensate for a crosswind by pointing the nose into the wind at a partic-

CRAB-ANGLE COMPARISONS
These drawings show angles with a 50mph approach. Notice how much less of a "crab" is required as the crosswind angle decreases.

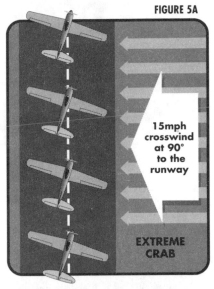

FIGURE 5A

15mph crosswind at 90° to the runway

EXTREME CRAB

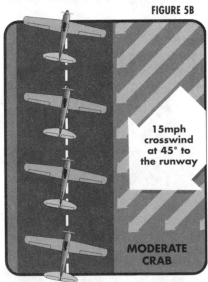

FIGURE 5B

15mph crosswind at 45° to the runway

MODERATE CRAB

FIGURE 5C

15mph crosswind at 10° to the runway

SLIGHT CRAB

FIGURE 4

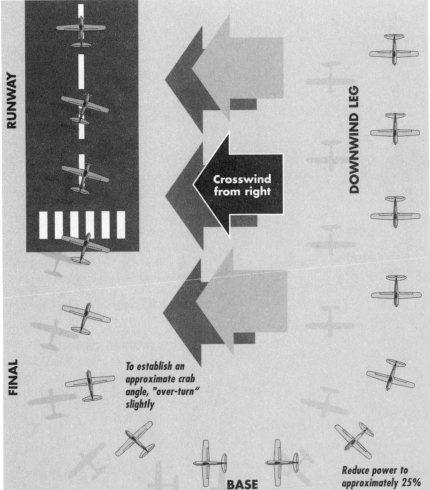

RUNWAY

Crosswind from right

DOWNWIND LEG

FINAL

To establish an approximate crab angle, "over-turn" slightly

BASE

Reduce power to approximately 25%

ular angle, let's really put this technique to practical use. If you were to fly totally by the book, as your plane changed speed during its flight (as in a loop), you'd have to change the compensation angle (throughout the maneuver). This doesn't look good, and if you're being judged, it usually doesn't score well. I've developed a few tricks that help to hide the corrections. I've even been told it seems as though the crosswind has died down.

It's really quite simple. During a pass, such as a slow roll, use more angle than is needed per the calculation noted above. Then, immediately after, when you perform a stall turn or some vertical maneuver, use a smaller angle. During horizontal passes, the compensation angle is hard to see, so you can use more, but in vertical maneuvers, the compensation really shows, so you use less. Overall, the average compensation is about right, so you can maintain the proper position, and it will look as if your plane handles a crosswind really well (but you and I know how it's really done).

◆ **Flying the angle.** Let's think about what it means to fly at the proper angle or heading. I've heard modelers comment, "Gee, sure is a strong crosswind today; your plane must have a very powerful rudder." Some people seem to think that to compensate for a crosswind, you must constantly fight it with rudder inputs. The truth is that once you have established the compensation angle, that's it; your control surfaces are at neutral, and your plane is in an aerodynamically stable position. There isn't a problem with weathervaning. It's impossible; the airplane is only "aware" of the relative wind. It doesn't know it's tracking right down the runway!

If you want to roll your plane perfectly down the runway center line, approach the line with the correct heading for the wind, then roll. When performing the roll as you would in calmer conditions, the nose of the plane will continue to point at the pre-established heading. You'll finish the maneuver with the heading you started with—and will still be on the center line. Easy, eh? This is also true of a loop. Approach at the correct

angle, perform the loop and voilà!

◆ **Changing angles in flight.** As you gain altitude in a loop, your air speed will diminish, and if you keep the same angle, the plane will be "blown in" to some degree. I advise you to add a little more angle as you gain altitude and lose air speed. Or you can just try to avoid doing huge loops, because the slower speeds

they entail offer greater exposure to crosswind. Anyway, on the down portion of the loop, you'll have an opportunity to make up most of what you lost.

When you're in competition, observe others to determine the compensation angles that might work best for you. And if you're up first? Oh, well! Your experience and one allowable dead pass will have to give you an idea of where to start. After that, if you find yourself drifting in, add more angle, and feel your way through.

CROSSWIND LANDINGS

Now comes the fun part: landing your aircraft in one piece in a crosswind! It isn't that difficult, but you'll have to follow a fairly basic formula. Then you'll have to practice and build up your confidence on the sticks to make it happen. Try to work on your proficiency a little at a time; trust me, you can't cram all this in at once, and there's no Evelyn Wood Speed Flight-Training course available yet!

FIGURE 6

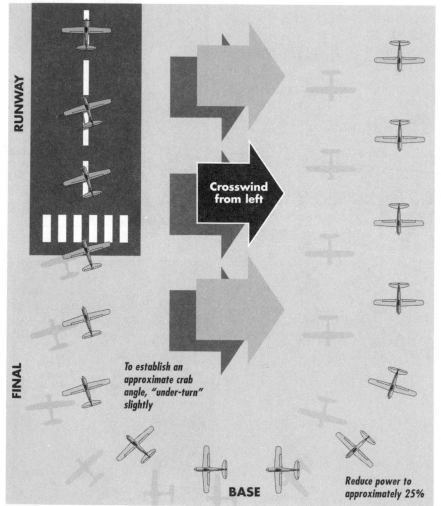

RUNWAY

FINAL

Crosswind from left

To establish an approximate crab angle, "under-turn" slightly

BASE

Reduce power to approximately 25%

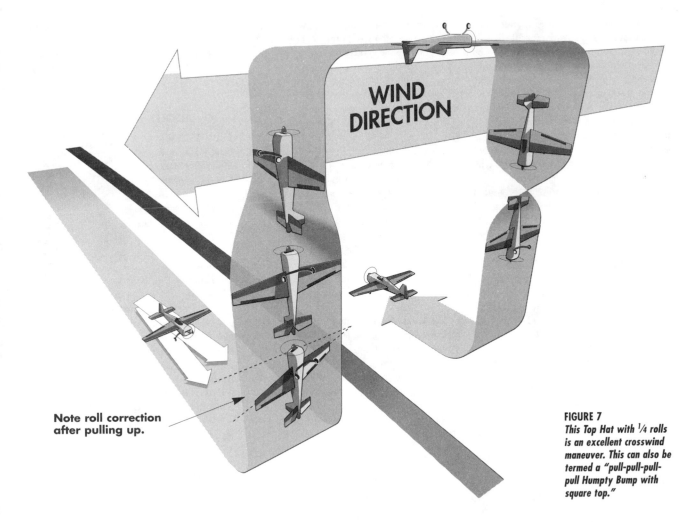

WIND DIRECTION

Note roll correction after pulling up.

FIGURE 7
This Top Hat with ¼ rolls is an excellent crosswind maneuver. This can also be termed a "pull-pull-pull-pull Humpty Bump with square top."

◆ **Before we start.** Regardless of conditions, the key to any landing is a good approach. When a crosswind is blowing, a longer approach is strongly recommended, as this allows you more time to get set up properly and time to settle into the right approach angle. Also, if you end up on an approach that you're not happy with, don't hesitate to go around and try again. Finally, be consistent and fly a rectangular landing pattern every time you land.

◆ **How strong is this crosswind?** The strength of a crosswind is determined by its speed and direction. For a given wind speed, the effect of a crosswind on your plane will greatly depend on the crosswind's angle. For example, a 15mph crosswind at 90 degrees to the runway can be quite difficult to contend with; at 45 degrees, it's not too bad, and at 10 degrees, you'll hardly notice it. Be sure to have a clear picture of how the wind will affect your aircraft before you take off.

◆ **The approach.** During a landing approach, two basic techniques can help compensate for a crosswind. The easier technique is to establish a natural "crab" angle so that the plane's track is parallel to the runway and the fuselage is angled slightly into the wind (see Figures 4 and 6). The hard way is to side-slip the aircraft with respect to the relative wind by maintaining a heading and a track that are parallel to the runway. (At this point, the fuselage is parallel to the runway.) This is difficult to do from the ground. We'll focus on the easy way because it's just as effective.

Turning from base into final establishes the crab angle, which is determined by the crosswind. Take a guess, and observe what happens. If, for example, your plane has too much of a crab angle, gently turn it to reduce the angle slightly. Don't go overboard trying to yaw or rudder-turn to correct, because at low air speeds, you may find your plane in a spin–literally. Also, try to keep your approach speed constant from the turn going onto base. A good final approach speed is about halfway between stall and cruise speeds, or at about a 25-percent power setting. But planes differ, and while you practice, experiment to determine the best approach speed for your particular plane. The stronger the cross-

wind, the faster I like to fly the approach.

◆ **Flare.** Now that you've flown a nice approach to the runway, it's time to prepare for touchdown. Although the flare will be conventional, it does have a very important twist. You have to add some rudder to get rid of the crab angle that you established during your approach. The best technique is to wait until the last moment before touchdown and apply rudder very gently to reduce the chance of a spin. Applying the rudder reduces the side load on the landing gear and establishes a straight roll-out. Keep in mind that wind velocity is sometimes dramatically less closer to the ground so, as you begin your flare, be prepared for a loss of lift during the last couple of feet.

◆ **The hard way—side-slip.** Assume that the wind is coming from the right. To make the plane track correctly, it must yaw slightly to the right, but to side-slip it properly, you must add enough left rudder to straighten the fuselage's relative alignment so that it's parallel to the runway.

To compensate for the rudder-induced turn, add opposite aileron (here, right aileron). Now you have significant additional drag, and the airplane will slow down to the point of stalling. To prevent this, apply down-elevator to maintain the airplane's approach speed. This will generate a steeper approach angle. Add power to return to the original approach angle (about 6 percent). It's a complicated maneuver that requires a lot of mixing of the right amount of control inputs. Side-slipping on approach in a crosswind can make for a very busy approach!

There's really no need to be grounded when there's a crosswind. Once you've mastered the proper techniques, you'll be surprised at how well your plane handles.

THE FULL-SCALE APPROACH

In full-scale aerobatics, it's nearly impossible for the pilot to compensate for wind. This is because he sits inside the cockpit. He does not have the great advantage that R/C fliers have: the ability to observe the aircraft from the ground. Full-scale aerobatics pilots don't even try to compensate for wind-drift during maneuvers. They simply make sure that heading and track are always the same. Instead of attempting to point the nose of the aircraft into the wind, they perform a crosswind maneuver that repositions the aircraft upwind. There are two problems with this technique. If it's really windy, full-scale pilots can be blown right out of the box in which they're flying. If they try to perform too many maneuvers between their crosswind maneuvers, this problem is compounded. The second problem is that, viewed from the ground, the maneuvers look more like they should look if the pilot is compensating for the wind conditions to ensure perfect roundness and symmetry.

If it's calm, the pilot has a lot of freedom with the size of the crosswind maneuver. When the crosswind is strong, he has to take full advantage of the maneuver to place the aircraft as far upwind as possible. The crosswind maneuver can vary, but it's usually something like a Top Hat with $\frac{1}{4}$ rolls (see Figure 7).

Regular pattern flying allows compensation during the maneuvers, but in International Miniature Aerobatic Club (IMAC) contests, pilots fly by heading as they do in full-scale aerobatics. It's interesting that at the TOC, which in many ways is an IMAC contest, changes in heading are allowed as they are in pattern contests.

As usual, practice makes perfect. Don't be intimidated by that crosswind; fly in it and learn! I hope this has shed some light on the subject of the crosswind. ◆

ABOUT THE AUTHOR

Dave Patrick

Dave was born in Montreal, Canada, and by the age of nine had built many control-line models and started designing and building free-flight versions. He remained active in the hobby and, at age 25, was introduced to pattern aerobatics with the gift of a .60-size pattern ship. He went on to become Canadian National Champion three times and made the Canadian international team four times. He has won gold and bronze world championship medals and, at last count, has won or placed in more than 60 aerobatics competitions. He has starred in several instructional videos and is a columnist for Model Airplane News. As vice president of Carl Goldberg Models, he is responsible for designing and marketing some of the most popular R/C kits sold.

CHAPTER 9

The Multi-Engine Experience

by Nick Ziroli Sr.

For those who have not tried it, building and flying multi-engine R/C models can be an exciting new experience. In the past, only more adventurous modelers would attempt a twin-engine plane; a plane with more than two engines was a real rarity. These models generally did not last long, and when they went, the thrill went with them. Seldom do I recall someone building a follow-up twin; they were just too unreliable—both in their radio systems and engines. These problems are a thing of the past.

BE PREPARED!

◆ **Radio systems.** When properly installed and maintained, radio systems are now unbelievably reliable. There are many potential failure points at both the transmitter and airplane, but they seldom fail. Even the low-cost basic system is extremely reliable—a tribute to the manufacturer. I have found the electronics of the system to be the most trouble-free.

◆ **Batteries.** These are the most frequent source of failure, for the most part, mechanically. Internal structural breakdown or external cell connectors and leads are sources of trouble. In spite of this, our current battery packs are very reliable, and by using one of the many cycling and test systems available, we can significantly reduce the chance of failure. Battery prices are reasonable, so it doesn't make sense to fly with a questionable one; replace it.

◆ **Servos.** I believe that servos are the second most frequent cause of failure in a system. Some of this is because of the nature of the device; it contains a motor, gears, potentiometers and bearings—all items that wear out. Again, the newer servos are far more reliable than earlier ones ever were. Proper installation is something the manufacturer has no control over, however, and it's probably the cause of most servo failures. Improper mounting—too tight or in direct contact with the airframe—can allow engine vibration to affect the servo and cause an early failure. Overloading the servo with tight pushrods

should also be avoided. With proper installation, servos should give good service for many flying hours.

◆ **Engines.** These have been the biggest source of problems in multi-engine model flying. Modern glow-plug engine design and excellent carburetors in both 2-stroke and especially 4-stroke engines have increased their reliability and ease of operation. This increases the chances of success and aircraft longevity.

About 20 years ago, I designed and built two, twin-engine, scale R/C models—a .21-powered B-25 and a .30 Wankel-powered F5F Skyrocket. I found it difficult to get a good, reliable engine run on both engines through a full flight. This took away most of the enjoyment of flying these models, so they didn't get flown much.

My modeling activities are now devoted pretty much to giant-scale warbirds; many multi-engine warbirds are great candidates for modeling in a large scale (I prefer the 100- to 120-inch-wingspan range). Power for my models has exclusively been gasoline engines—for single-engine aircraft as well as twins. My experience over the last 15-plus years with this type of engine has shown it to be exceptionally reliable. When the carburetor and linkages

Here's an example of an in-line twin—the Cessna 336 Skymaster. If one engine quits, there aren't any engine-out-related torque problems.

have been adjusted, they seldom require attention from one year to the next. Your chain saw doesn't have to be adjusted every time you use it; generally, these are the same type of engines, using a diaphragm-pump carburetor. With these carburetors, fuel-tank location and fuel draw aren't a problem. I hate to think of how many glow-engine-powered twins I've seen meet their end mainly because of poor needle-valve adjustments. On the other hand, there are those piloted by experts such as Dan Parsons and Art Johnson that fly on year after year.

◆ **Fuels.** I'm particular about the fuel I use; it's always fresh, and what goes into the fuel tanks is clean. In the fill line that runs from my fuel container to the model's fuel tank, there's a filter, and there's also one in the engine feed line. These are not just filter screens but, rather, paper, motorcycle-type fuel filters—small versions of those found on automobiles. Inside the carburetor, there's a small filter screen that requires attention periodically (once a season is often enough for the amount of flying I do, and I find very little accumulated dirt).

CONSTRUCTION METHODS

Building a multi-engine model is not much different from building a single-engine one. But certain areas, i.e., nacelles and firewalls, benefit from extra strengthening. Engine resonation can be a very destructive force; obviously, the more slowly the props turn, the lower will be the vibration and resonance. Of course, the props must be turning fast enough to produce enough thrust to fly the model. A

little prop testing and modifying can yield a worthwhile increase in performance.

◆ **Engine mounts and props.** Powered by a pair of Zenoah G-38s, my 114-inch-span P-61 Black Widow was self-destructing because of engine resonance and vibration. A servo failed, and hinges

Nick runs up the engines on his P-61 Black Widow. Good engine performance is critical for twin flying, so make sure everything works consistently well on the ground.

were becoming very sloppy. Because the full-scale P-61 was fast (370mph), I wanted a good rate of speed for the model. I tried 18x6-10 Zinger props, and they worked just as I wanted them to. It was, however, soon apparent that the high speed of the engines was taking its toll on the model. The engines are hard-mounted, which doesn't help.

I swapped the props for 20x6-10s that had been cut down to a diameter of 19 inches. These turned a little more slowly—below the destructive point—yet still gave plenty of speed. During more than a season of flying the P-61, I had no more problems with the airframe.

I had no problems with my previous twin Beechcraft D-18, which had hard-mounted engines, so I hadn't used soft mounts on my P-61. The D-18's short, large-diameter nacelles mounted on a very thick, rigid, center section may have isolated the engines from each other enough to reduce damaging resonation. Also, I used 20x8 (scale diameter) props, which turn more slowly. These props flew the D-18 to perfection and the P-61 (a similar size) rather poorly. Props must be matched to the model and engines to obtain the desired performance.

My new, 114-inch-span P-38 has its two Zenoah G-45 engines soft-mounted—or rather, not really soft-mounted, but more isolated by rubber from the airframe. If engine mounts are too soft, the engine will not operate properly; it might be difficult to start and will not idle as it should. To spread the mounting points out as far as is practical, I mount the engine on a larger mounting plate. In the case of the P-38, this plate is ⅛-inch-thick, 4x6-inch aluminum. The firewall overhangs the sides of the engine box so that the locknuts are accessible from the outside and can be

At the '95 Delaware Warbird Fly-In, there were many multi-engine aircraft. During a break in the action, the spectators went out onto the field for a closer look at these spectacular planes.

The author's P-38 on a flyby at the Delaware Warbird meet. This is one of Nick's newest designs; it flies very well and it looks great in the air.

held with a wrench while the bolts are tightened.

Available from Cirrus Ventures and Nick Ziroli Plans, I like the quality of Scale Aviation's engine-vibration isolators. They are available in three hardnesses (durometer figures of 50, 60 and 70) and with 5mm or 1/4-inch bolts. With the G-45, I used the 60s with 5mm hardware, and they seem good. To make them harder, these can be tightened down, or for a softer mount, they can be left a little looser. By adjusting each corner, small spinner-to-cowl alignment corrections can be made. Be careful here because you're also changing the thrust line. J'Tec's Snuf Vibe is a similar system, and I'm sure there are others. (I haven't researched the market.)

◆ **Throttle linkages.** I always pay close attention to these; I make every effort to obtain the same linkage positions and travel on both throttle plates. Servo-output arms and bellcranks are set up to travel through the same arcs and angles. When this is done correctly, the engines will operate in sync over their entire speed range. I've found that it really isn't so important to ensure that they're in perfect sync as long as they're both running. Off-speed engines are more noticeable during takeoff than during any other part of the flight. Here, a turn toward the slower engine will usually be obvious. Once in the air, the unevenness of the thrust is less apparent. It's worth the extra effort to make the engines run in sync, even if only for the even sound.

At the field, one of the most asked questions is, "How is it with one engine out?" In the case of the P-61 and P-38, I must reply that I don't know because I've never had one go out. The D-18 is another story; I put an engine out a number of times and always managed to get it back on the ground in one piece—except for the last time it happened! If the engines were idled back too far, the electric-pump-operated smoke system would flood

the engines with smoke fluid and make one or the other engine quit.

This problem could have easily been remedied: a switch added to the throttle servo could have cut off the pumps whenever the throttle was reduced to below 3/4 power. But rather than go to the trouble of doing that (no more than a one-hour job), I always decided that the *next* time, I would remember *not* to cut the power with the smoke on. That's all fine until things get a little busy at the transmitter—like the fateful day at Rhinebeck. While doing my freestyle performance, I attempted a wingover with the smoke and power on throughout the maneuver. Well, I got a little too vertical and too slow to cut a nice smoking arc through the sky, so I decided to turn the maneuver into a stall turn, for which I had to cut the power. As the D-18 rotated 180 degrees, it looked great with all that smoke, so I let it fall a long way to make a spectacular low-level pull-out. At the bottom, I put the power to the model and it spun one way; I over-controlled it, and it spun the other way; and into the woods it went! Smoke fluid had put one engine out. My memory didn't serve me well that day. If I had spent an hour on making it foolproof, I would probably still

have my all-time favorite model.

The one-engine-out capability depends a great deal on when and where it occurs. No twin, except a push/pull, is in good shape when it loses an engine during takeoff. The steeper the takeoff angle, the worse the consequence if an engine is lost. I never take off and do a steep climb-out; instead, I fly a climbing racetrack pattern,

gaining about 100 feet in the circuit. If the engines sound good after the first pass, I proceed with the flight. Whenever they don't sound right—and sound is the only thing you have to go by—I land the plane. Engine rpm have to be quite far off before you realize you need to make a trim change. At any sign of engine trouble, land and investigate.

When an engine is lost at altitude, cutting back to idle may not be the best thing to do. If you're flying a warbird or a heavy model, the chances are it will come down pretty fast, and you may be lower than you think and faster than you anticipated. At this point, you'll have to power back up again and maintain control of the airplane—not always easy to do. It's better to maintain a fair amount of power and get the control of the model sorted out while you still have enough altitude. Get the plane to the approach end of the runway, then reduce power for landing. Try to avoid reducing power and then increasing it quickly. This is sure to lead to disaster.

Also, don't be so short on your approach that you have to power up to stretch out the landing. If the field is such that you can land short without damaging the model, land short, if you have to. But

This Me-110 would be a good plane to check out if you want to get into twins. It flies well, is quite stable and has good engine-out characteristics.

you're really looking for an approach that's a little higher and faster. Don't try to impress anyone by trying to put your model at your feet. Like you, spectators will be just as happy to see it on the ground undamaged.

◆ **Thrust-line offsets.** Having the correct engine thrust-line offsets can help takeoffs and an engine-out situation. I have tried a variety of setups and have settled on zero offset for the left engine and between 2 and 3 degrees of right thrust in the right engine. (Engines are left or right from the point of view of sitting in the airplane.) I arrived at this as my prefer-

Bill Steffes' incredible Beech D-18 on final approach. This beautiful model was loaded with amazing details and its performance was as stupendous as its looks. It scored well at Top Gun and other scale competitions.

ence after building and flying the D-18 with the scale 2 degrees out-thrust on each engine. The left-hand torque of two large propellers was difficult to overcome during takeoffs. Full right rudder was not always enough to overcome the torque, and if the wind wasn't coming from exactly the right direction, a good takeoff was a rarity. I thought that if I removed the left thrust from the left engine, the offset thrust line pulling the airplane to the right would be mostly canceled out by the torque to the left. Adding a little more than 2 degrees of right thrust to the right

engine would make it pull to the right about the same amount as torque would take it to the left.

This setup worked well on the D-18 and required very little right rudder during take-off. I've used the same offsets on all my twins since—tail-draggers and those with tricycle landing gear. The single-engine performance will also be much improved by using these thrust offsets. Before the D-18 crashed, I had the chance to prove it a number of times; no amount of thrust-line offset would have saved it. Only a better memory could have saved *that* one.

If you have dreamed of a giant-scale two-, three- or four-engine model, now may be the time to give it a try. I don't believe that gasoline engines will get any more reliable than they are now; and they're the key to a successful project.

For scratch-builders, there are a number

of plans available for scale, multi-engine planes; contact Nick Ziroli Plans and Don Smith Plans. If you don't like cutting out your own parts from plans, there's a solution: certain companies specialize in cutting kits from plans drawn up by other companies; contact The Aeroplane Works, All-American Kit Cutters and Madden Model Products. I'm familiar with their work and find it of excellent quality.

Now may be the time to satisfy that multi-engine desire. Everything is available to make it happen. Good luck! ◆

ABOUT THE AUTHOR

Nick Ziroli

Nick was born in Bridgeport, CT, in 1935. His model-building endeavors have spanned more than 50 years. In 1951, he flew his first R/C model—a Live Wire trainer. Nick worked in the precision electrical/mechanical industry where his expertise included high-reliability potentiometers, gyros and relays. In 1969, he founded his model airplane company—Major Model and Mfg. This business developed into an engineering company dealing with all types of aerospace models and drones. Early on (1979), Nick saw the potential of the giant-scale movement and started a plans business to support this area of the hobby. His plans have since become very popular. The business has recently been turned over to Nick Jr., who is planning even bigger and better things.

CHAPTER 10

Multi-Engine Techniques

by Dan Parsons

T hough multi-engine R/C models have been around for many years (I flew my first twin, an ME 210, in 1960), few are seen at even the largest meets. A few years ago, I attended a big fly-in at Greenville, SC; 267 pilots took along more than 400 planes, but only four were multis. Why is this? Two main reasons: few kits or even plans are available for multis; and multis—especially scale—

A down-and-dirty B-25—a popular subject for twin-engine aircraft, and it flies very well.

have a well-founded reputation for being short-lived. I think many modelers are interested in multis, particularly twins, but they've often seen twins have engine problems with disastrous results. They then conclude, "That isn't for me."

Here, I'll discuss the differences between and problems of multi-engine R/C models and the solutions to those problems. I hope to encourage more modelers to try them. I'll be talking about twin-engine models, but the same principles apply to models with more than two engines.

I want to stress that there are a few big differences between building and flying a single-engine model and a twin-engine model. It's extremely important—and I can't over-stress this point—that any modeler who plans to build and fly a twin should know about and understand these differences.

Now, a quick run-through on design and construction basics.

DESIGN BASICS

The engines are in the wings, so the fuselage structure can be kept light because it only attaches the tail feathers to the wing. And speaking of lightness, it's imperative

to keep the tail feathers light because many twins have short nose arms and long tail arms, so they tend to become tail-heavy. Don't let those two engines that stick out from the wing fool you into thinking you have plenty of weight forward and therefore don't have to worry about being tail-heavy.

The engines should be set straight ahead (no right or left thrust) with 1 to 2 degrees of downthrust. For most twins, I think it's best to operate the throttles with one servo and to have a separate fuel tank for each engine (each tank should be set up just as it would be in a single-engine plane). Also, if at all possible, have a hatch to allow easy access to each tank. In twins, engine reliability is an absolute must, so the engines and fuel system must be easy to get at—both to solve problems and to perform routine maintenance.

With many twins, you can simplify construction by building the engine nacelles as separate units—just like a fuselage—and then gluing them onto the completed and covered wing. I've done this with all my twins, and it works very well.

Most twins are fast, so to help prevent flutter, it's imperative to keep the control

Here's a close-up of a beautifully detailed C-47—a very stable platform for the multi-engine design.

surfaces light and the linkages tight and stiff. If in doubt, statically balance the control surfaces.

With the rather simple construction dif-

This F-82 in an overhead pass is a great photo-op. The F-82 is two mated P-51Fs, and it was designed to be a long-range fighter escort. It's a very popular model for twin-engine flying.

ferences out of the way, let's get on to the preparations for flying.

PREPARE FOR TAKEOFF

By far the most important factor in flying twin-engine models is to keep both engines running properly, especially at the full-power setting. Sounds plausible, doesn't it? But in practice, most new twin fliers concern themselves much more with engine synchronization than with having each engine set for proper running. Wrong! Wrong! Wrong! Engine synchronization isn't really a problem, whereas setting each engine properly is critical and must be the primary concern. Sadly, the lives of a high percentage of scale twins are very short, and the primary reason for their loss is the unexpected loss of one engine. Fortunately, it's easy to set the engines properly.

Here's the "secret" to setting the engines so that they run reliably flight after flight.

Treat and set each engine just as if it were on a single-engine model. Simple? You bet! With the plane horizontal and the throttle wide open, have the engine running rich so that it's 4-cycling, then

lean it until you obtain a solid 2-cycle. Then hold the model vertical for at least 10 seconds to make sure that the engine is not running too lean. Ideally, when the model goes to the vertical, engine rpm should increase slightly. If the engine sags at all, it's too lean.

When you're satisfied that the first engine has been set correctly, shut it down, start the other one and go through the same procedure. It's a good idea to "richen" each engine very slightly from these settings, just to be on the super-safe side. Check each engine's idle setting, and adjust it to obtain a reliable idle; but give priority to absolutely reliable running at the full-power setting.

Now here's the crucial part of this whole engine-setting procedure. When you fire up both engines to fly and do your full-power check with the plane held both horizontal and vertical, do not—I repeat, do not—touch the needle valve of either engine. Most of the time (and this still surprises me), the engines will pull closely into sync, especially when the model is held vertical. If they're a bit out of sync, don't worry about it! Go fly! If they're way out of sync, shut both engines down and go through the previous engine-setting procedures, one engine at a time. You'll probably get it right the second time around.

I can't overemphasize the importance of *not* tweaking one or both of the needle

valves while both engines are running. If you do, you run the real risk of getting at least one engine too lean and losing it shortly after takeoff (worst case) or on the climb-out.

Once the engines have been set so that they operate properly in the air, they will

usually remain so all day or even during an entire weekend of flying, unless there's a drastic change in the temperature or humidity. To be on the super-safe side, however, I always check the engines before each flight by holding the plane vertical for approximately 10 seconds with the engines at full power.

Over 12 years, using these engine-setting procedures before more than 400 flights with my deHavilland Hornet, I've had nearly perfect engine sync on an estimated 85 percent of flights and have had only two engine failures because one was set too lean.

In both cases, I was flying with several other planes and couldn't hear my engines most of the time. Thus, when one went lean, I couldn't hear it so kept flying until it overheated and quit. This is one of the best reasons to set your engines properly and then just slightly richer than if you were flying a single-engine plane—not too rich, mind you, or you'll lose significant power and waste fuel. Ah, the challenges of twin-engine flying.

Any twin, especially a tail-dragger, has the occasional problem of swinging out of control at the start of the takeoff roll because one engine comes up ahead of the other one. If this happens (and it will), immediately abort the takeoff by chopping the power. By the way, proper "abort" action requires that you think about it just before you advance the throttle; chances

The British team at a recent Top Gun Invitational readies their Mosquito for flight. This fighter/bomber was made of plywood and served the British quite well during WW II. As you can see, for safety reasons, it's always a good idea to have some helpers when preparing a multi-engine plane for flight.

are, you'll get lots of practice with your first twin.

Generally speaking, I've found it helps to come up on the power slowly while holding full up-elevator to keep the tail wheel on the ground to provide steering during the early part of the takeoff roll.

Remember, a multi has very little prop blast over the rudder. As the air speed increases, the rudder begins to bite the air, and I can ease off the elevator while smoothly advancing the throttle. It's a closely coordinated procedure that works beautifully when done correctly. It takes practice and concentration, but that's part of the constant challenge of twin flying, and it's what keeps it so interesting.

Nick Ziroli's P-38 flies by the reviewing stand. Nick did an outstanding job on this great-looking model, and it flies well, too.

WHEN AN ENGINE QUITS

Even though you always set the engines on your twin properly, once in a great while, you'll lose an engine owing to plug failure or something as inexcusable as forgetting to refill one tank (I've done that). So, what's the best procedure to follow when you lose an engine?—depends on your speed and the power setting.

First, if you're flying fast at full power—straight and level—and lose an engine, you probably won't even know it at first, especially if other planes are flying and you can't hear your engines well. Your plane will gradually slow down and perhaps assume a slight yawing attitude into the dead engine. You'll think (or somebody may tell you), "I believe I've [you've] lost an engine." Once you even suspect this, prepare to land ASAP.

If you have plenty of altitude, no problem; just throttle back to a couple of clicks above idle, and come in to land. Keep the nose down slightly to keep your speed up and make gentle, rudder-coordinated turns. Make a fairly high approach and ease in any power on the good engine if you need to lengthen the glide. A little power on that good engine helps you lengthen the glide quite a lot. Don't use any more power than you have to; don't get low on the approach; and don't get slow!

If you lose an engine while climbing out or doing a maneuver at slow speed and full power, the plane will probably flip up and over in a snap-like action. When you see this, immediately throttle back to idle and concentrate on getting the plane stabilized by keeping the nose

down to pick up safe flying speed. Then gently level off. If you still have plenty of altitude at this point, follow the procedures previously discussed.

If you lose an engine while flying low at high speed, you'll have to keep full or nearly full power on the good engine to keep up your speed and maintain what precious altitude you have. Don't let your plane's nose come up and thus bleed off speed; make coordinated, gentle turns, and you'll have an excellent chance to make it back to the field.

If you have the misfortune of losing an engine while low and slow at full power, the plane will probably do a "whoop-dee-do," and you'll probably have bought the farm.

DON'T KICK IN RUDDER

When you lose an engine, don't worry which engine quit. Believe me, you probably won't know which engine you've lost for quite a while, so don't even think about kicking in opposite rudder or rudder trim.

In the surprise, excitement, fear and tension following the loss of an engine—especially if the plane does an immediate

Coupling Engines and Rudder

Multi-engine models have a distinct advantage when taxiing on water. A few years ago, during a water fly-in on a beautiful lake in British Columbia, Canada, I watched several large flying boats being taxied with ease in windy conditions. The fliers accomplished this by having a switching system that tied the engine on each side of the wing into the rudder action. If the pilot wanted to turn right, he'd give right rudder, and the left engine, on advancing the throttle, would come up on power while the right engine remained at idle. The result was an immediate right turn, regardless of the wind.

Once in takeoff position and headed into the wind, this coupling of the engines and rudder is disengaged, and a normal takeoff is made. Come to think of it, this would work fine on land-based multi-engine models also, though I've never seen it.

whoop-dee-do—I guarantee that you won't know which engine went out, much less which rudder and/or rudder trim you ought to put in. And if you kick in the wrong rudder, you may well do your plane in right then and there. (Pilots of full-scale craft have shut down and feathered the good engine, and they're sitting in the plane!)

In other words, just continue to control

Dennis Richardson stands guard over a group of multi-engine warbirds. They seem to be more popular than ever because of engine reliability and improved control systems.

One of the fun things to do with warbirds is to replicate their military functions as accurately as possible. This C-47 has a parachute cargo drop rigged for an in-flight action sequence.

ENGINE SIZE

Engine size is very important. One engine must be powerful enough to maintain the plane's altitude and sufficient speed to allow good controllability. Err on the side of engines that are too large; you can always throttle back.

So, there you have it: easy and enjoyable twin flying is simply a matter of having reliable engines that run just as they always do on your old, trusty, single-engine, weekend sport flier. Just think of the engines on your twin as two singles that just happen to be joined by a wing, and set them accordingly. Do this, and I

your plane with the sticks so that it's flying properly. This is much easier said than done, but it's exactly what top fliers such as Ted White, Frank Noll, Stinger Wallace, Al Casey, Tom Street and Bob Frey do when confronted with an engine-out. They automatically move the sticks to maintain the proper attitude and speed, and it always works.

Speaking of turns with one engine, I'm sure you've heard the old saying, "Never turn into the dead engine." In fact, there's nothing wrong with turning into the dead engine, as long as you keep the turn gentle. In fact, turning into the dead engine is the natural inclination for your twin. It may well be easier than turning into the running engine; this will probably require forceful use of the rudder that will create more drag and slow you down.

To summarize: turning into the dead engine is OK; just keep the control actions gentle.

Never ever make a go-around on one engine because your approach is too high—unless you're an exceptional pilot, which also says that you're especially good on the rudder. Go straight ahead no

matter what—better that than a sure up-and-over snap into the ground and total destruction.

This WW II B-25 is waiting for action. The ground crew must be close by, and the flight crew is probably in a briefing. This plane was used as a fighter and a bomber and was well-liked by multi-engine pilots during the war.

Ninety-nine percent of your twin-engine flying can be completely free of all these problems if you just set the engines properly so that you don't lose one. This is why I stress the importance of knowing how to set the engines and of religiously sticking to this procedure.

guarantee you'll have invigorating, wonderful and always challenging times with your twin. Besides, where else can you get that magical sound? ◆

To learn about the author of this chapter, see page 24.

CHAPTER 11

Maximizing Engine Performance

by Dave Gierke

Before most of us learned how to fly R/C successfully, the performance of the model wasn't a great concern. Of course it had to have forgiving flight characteristics, be large enough to be seen at 300 to 400 feet of altitude and land easily. With time, most modelers graduate to more sophisticated aircraft intended for aerobatics, racing, scale or high performance sport planes. Performance in terms of vertical climb, horizontal speed, takeoff distance, scale speed, etc., become more important to discriminating enthusiasts.

Kit manufacturers usually allow for a choice of engine types and a range of sizes for their products. Which is best? Which will provide the maximum performance? Competitors have found that making the correct component choice is absolutely necessary if winning is the goal. Many seasoned competitors design their own models; the selection of the correct engine for these designs is very important.

The simplest method of selection is to copy what the winner is using. This is the often utilized technique; if it's good enough for Chip, it's good enough for me! Unfortunately for the copycat, great performance isn't guaranteed. If the model isn't built straight or it's heavier, it probably won't fly properly. If you use a different propeller or perhaps it isn't balanced or doesn't track, it can't deliver all of the engine's power for propulsion. When performance robbing mistakes produce an inferior model that doesn't perform like the original, the standard cry amounts to: "He must be doing something to that engine," or "He must be using more nitro than me," or "The kit isn't the same as the original; he's using a special airfoil." Similar excuses can be heard in all specialized events, but the conclusion is hard to avoid: experts have some "secret" products or techniques that allow them an edge.

SECRETS

Although there may be a secret or two out there, the overwhelming majority of experts gain performance advantages through hard work and knowing what to do. Choosing the correct components

comes first; tailoring them into a smooth, efficient combination is next. Strange as it may seem, recognizing when the combination is working correctly is probably the most difficult part of the formula.

Over the years I've heard many experts say: "I've told him everything there is to know about building and setting-up the model, and he still can't get it to perform!" Similar stories have been told about engine modifications. An expert can spend hours explaining and detailing procedures designed to improve engine performance to a beginner, only to have the resultant powerplant turn out to be a disaster. These experiences tend to make novices wary of what experts tell them. Experts tend to become frustrated when the recipient of their advice fails to improve. Eventually, the expert decides to keep his advice to himself rather than be accused of delivering false information. An expert's reluctance to divulge information is now construed to mean: secrets really do exist out there—catch 22!

LEARNING ABOUT PERFORMANCE

If secrets are a myth, then how does a serious enthusiast gain practical informa-

Getting ready for a test session with a new engine, a variety of props, telemetry and the "Airtrax" test model...; the author and his toys!

tion? Would you be surprised to learn that there are no shortcuts? It's OK to ask the resident expert specific questions concerning some phase of his model or its system, such as, "Why are you directing most of the inlet cooling air directly at the cylinder head?" This type of question will probably impress the expert that you are observant,

Atmospheric conditions can be measured with a variety of instruments such as this sling psychrometer.

and he will probably be happy to explain the setup. Conversely, don't expect much of an answer (other than a grunt) if you ask, "How do you get so much power when the model climbs vertically?" If you had half a day, that question might not be fully answerable!

If you've decided to become more proficient at the hobby, remember this: it's not the length of time you've been in the hobby that counts the most; it's how quickly you progress on the learning curve. This reminds me of the story about an experienced employee who consistently has difficulty performing routine tasks; his disgusted boss explains the situation to a colleague: "Harold's been with us for five years; too bad he's repeated his first year's experience five times!" If you stay in the hobby for several years, you'll get to know someone like Harold!

Observe
The first law of learning performance enhancement is to *observe* everything that's going on, especially with advanced modelers. Make a point of walking up and down the flight line at your local field to see what the other guy is doing. If you really want to accelerate on the learning curve, attend as many contests as you can; watch how these mysterious people function; ask the pointed question when there's a break in the action, but beware: asking questions during the heat of competition can be hazardous to your health!

Read
The second law of learning performance enhancement is to *read* everything and

anything associated with your type of model and its systems. Specialization is what I'm talking about; the universal expert doesn't exist; there aren't enough hours in the day or days in a lifetime to learn everything you need to know about all model types! Besides the current literature, ask your friends if you can read their old magazines. Ten years is a long time in the genesis of a specific competition event, especially when following technical refinements, but history provides valuable insight. If you're perceptive, you might be able to extrapolate trends into the future. Don't laugh, it has been done before.

Unfortunately, rule changes interrupt an otherwise wonderful progression in technology. An example of this interruption (and there are many) raised its ubiquitous head when the R/C aerobatics rules committee allowed 4-stroke engines to have twice the cylinder displacement of 2-stroke designs (1.20ci. to 0.60ci). As you might expect, there was a great rush by manufacturers to develop the 4-stroke engine, and normal technological evaluation was skewed.

Building
The third law of learning performance enhancement, and one of the most important: *build*, build and build some more! There isn't a substitute for *just doing it*. Almost-ready-to-fly models (ARFs) have improved in their design and quality over the years, and they're certainly great for getting you into the air quickly, but you learn precious little about *building* a model. When you construct your own model, either from a kit or from scratch (from plans), you quickly develop an appreciation for certain techniques, like building a straight wing. Many R/C'ers think that modern programmable computer radios offer a solution for twisted wings— without penalty. This is wrong. I know several experts who would readily (if not gleefully) step on a twisted wing before tweaking-in corrective aileron trim; the additional drag simply can't be tolerated. This might seem extreme to the uninitiated, but many models built by experts never see the light

of day after their initial testing.

Besides the revered, "It feels great to build it myself" syndrome, you'll be constantly thinking about flying performance during those long winter months occupied with construction, finishing and equipment installation.

Flying
The fourth law of learning performance enhancement techniques is to *fly*, fly and fly some more. There is no substitute for boring holes in the sky! We used to keep track of how much flying we did by the gallons of fuel burned; it was easier than keeping a log of actual flights. However, keeping a log of a model's setup and performance is important in understanding how it can be improved. It might seem too simple to be effective, but keeping track of the variables provides a base line for adjustments that may be used later. These variables include: fuel (manufacturer, nitromethane and lubricating oil content); propeller (manufacturer, diameter and pitch); glow plug (manufacturer, reach, heat range); tachometer readings for high speed and idle; trim settings for the control surfaces; atmospheric conditions and notes, e.g., the 11x9 APC prop was not tracking and was replaced with a similar unit; rpm increased 200.

Atmospherics
Appreciating the importance of atmospheric conditions can't be overstated. The Wright brothers historically significant flights of December 1903 were achieved when the temperature was near 35 degrees and the air was *dense*. They were confused when their improved version of

The aneroid barometer will tell you the barometric pressure at the field. Measuring the pressure will help you determine how the engine will run.

the Kitty Hawk Flyer wouldn't take off at the Huffman Prairie site near Dayton in the spring and summer of 1904. They were stymied primarily because the air temperature was 30 to 50 degrees higher than Kitty Hawk, along with higher humidity. The density of the air controls the amount of lift generated by the wing as well as the power produced by the engine. Today, the phenomena is known as *density altitude*; and it's closely monitored in full-size aviation due to its tremendous effect on aircraft performance.

Strangely, density altitude receives little attention from modelers. Perhaps it's because our power-to-weight ratios (engine power to model weight) are so favorable compared to full-scale aircraft, that it's not considered important. Maybe it's because no one is sitting in the cockpit when the stall-spin occurs!

To the performance enhancement person, atmospheric conditions should be near the top of the priority list. There are several ways to gather important weather data; the simplest method is to listen to the weather forecast in your vehicle on the way to the flying field. Note the temperature, pressure and relative humidity; write these into your log at the field. If you stay at the field for several hours, note and record the air temperature hourly. Atmospheric pressure usually stabilizes, unless there's a weather system moving in. In that case, you might consider packing up and going home before you get wet!

For the serious enthusiast: take your own weather instruments! Actually, you only need a sling psychrometer and a barometer of the aneroid variety (a round analog dial face with a spiral, bi-metallic sensor). The psychrometer consists of a wet and dry bulb thermometer. The dry bulb provides the air temperature directly, while using it with the wet bulb a special graph allows you to determine the water vapor pressure of the air. By knowing these three factors, the density altitude is quickly computed from a graph or formula. Example: if the temperature is 60 degrees F, the pressure 29.92 inches of mercury, and the water-vapor pressure is 0, the density altitude (commonly called Relative Air Density [RAD]) is 100 percent; this is the standard, or base line, against which all other weather combinations are compared. Example: if the RAD computes to 94 percent, you can expect a

reduction of 6 percent in aircraft and engine performance compared to standard conditions (100 percent). By keeping careful records of changes required to restore or partially restore the model's performance, you will know what to adjust if similar weather conditions occur in the future. For low performance conditions described above, increasing the nitromethane content of the fuel along with reducing the propeller's diameter and/or pitch, may restore some of the engine's performance. By increasing the model's flying speed, lost lift may be restored, since it's proportional to the square of the velocity increase factor $(L=V^2)$. Example: a model flying straight and level at 100mph has its velocity increased to 120mph by opening the throttle. The velocity increase factor is 120/100 = 1.2. Lift is increased 1.2^2 = 1.44.

Some may think it strange that an individual might spend time keeping close track of the weather. These are the same people who ask the expert why his airplane has unlimited vertical performance! There's a nice instrument available at speed shops (automotive); it's known as a *temperature compensated barometer*. It has an analog scale, calibrated directly to percent density altitude (RAD). Although it's not quite as accurate as the previous method (it doesn't take humidity into consideration), it's very user friendly. Oh, by the way, why do you think it can be found in a speed shop?

MAXIMIZING PERFORMANCE
Where to start?
Forces

Airplanes constantly deal with four forces: gravity, air-drag, lift and thrust. There's no doubt about it, if you fly within the atmosphere of this or any other planet you'll have to deal with gravity and air-drag. These are the villans of aerodynamics.

They must be offset by the lift of the wing and thrust of the propeller or reaction engine (jet or rocket).

Early flying machine thinkers such as Leonardo envisioned lift and propulsion being provided by the flapping wing—like a bird. Unfortunately, this method has proven extremely difficult for human tech-

VAPOR PRESSURE CHART

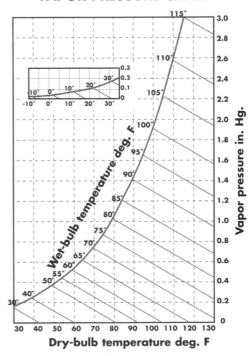

nology to achieve! Nineteenth-century experimenters, including Britain's insightful Sir George Cayley, suggested decoupling the lift and thrust components of the flapping wing. The concept resulted in a fixed wing providing lift and a propeller providing thrust. This may seem obvious today, but it wasn't nearly as crystal-clear in 1896 when professor Langley of the Smithsonian Institution successfully flew his fixed-wing, steam-powered, propeller-driven free-flight model (4 meters wingspan) over the Potomac River near Washington D.C. Some diehard experimenters continued to pursue flappers even after this highly publicized success. With the fixed-wing concept firmly entrenched, most experimenters concentrated on developing technology to handle thrust and lift independently.

Heavy models

Gravity acts upon the model's mass (for our purposes, weight) and must be overcome by the lift of the wing. The wing develops lift because of its airfoil shape and angle of attack (angle between the relative wind and the chord line of the air-

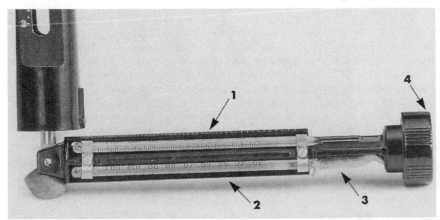

Components of the sling psychrometer: 1—dry-bulb thermometer; 2—wet-bulb thermometer; 3—cotton sock; 4—water reservoir.

foil) and velocity through the air. Heavy airplanes can overcome gravity by flying faster, increasing the wing's angle of attack, or a combination of the two. In either case, unwanted air-drag is increased.

With few exceptions, experts are concerned with constructing the lightest possible models. To the uninitiated, their seemingly obsessive pursuit of this goal may seem compulsive or silly. After all, who in their right mind would hollow balsa wingtips to a thickness of a credit card to save 10 grams? Look at the situation from their point of view: theoretically, a super lightweight aerobatics aircraft could fly with a lighter, smaller displacement engine because the thrust required to overcome air-drag is less with the wing flying at a relatively low angle of attack. A more likely scenario would have the model using the

one needs an in-flight failure attributed to a poorly stressed model. Conversely, all serious racers build to minimum weight requirements.

Propellers

Many modelers fail to appreciate the importance of propellers. Experts pay great attention to this frequently overlooked segment of powered modeling; if there are secrets to high performance, they're probably hiding out with this unobtrusive component!

In the late 1960s, I was getting started in R/C pylon racing. Back then, many of the system components had to be developed by the individual, including the racing engines. I spent hundreds of hours modifying and testing the SuperTigre G-40 ABC engine to attain the maximum possible performance. Fellow East Coast

spending my time developing engines, Pete was learning about propellers! He was delivering his engine's horsepower more efficiently into thrust; in other words, his prop was doing a much better job of changing rotary power into linear force. At the time, I couldn't believe the propeller made that much difference! From that point forward, I paid much greater attention to propellers.

Here's what I observed at a recent national pylon-racing championship: the event was FAI (international class). Three West Coast competitors who worked together as a team were sharing the same propeller! Now, these guys weren't cheap; they each took dozens of props to the competition. However, they found that this one propeller performed better than anything else they had. Why? That's the big question. No one really knows why one prop will perform better than an exact duplicate, but it does. The scene was humorous: after his flight, one guy would remove the prop from his engine and hand it to the next person, who, in turn, handed it to the third guy after his flight. What a tragedy if someone had broken it on landing!

How do you evaluate propellers? In pylon racing, it's relatively simple: the fastest race time generally tells you that you have a pretty good prop. For pattern aircraft, the evaluation of propellers is much more subjective in nature—unless you have an onboard telemetry system for providing rpm and air-speed data.

Torque and horsepower

Pattern aircraft fly closer to the engine's torque peak rpm than the horsepower peak rpm. The reason is directly associated with the 2-stroke cycle engine. It has to run at high rpm to develop its maximum horsepower; it's the nature of the beast. Unfortunately, operating the 2-stroker at these high rpm requires running with an unreasonably small propeller. Since .60-size pattern ships don't perform too well with 11x4 or 9x10 propellers, the only alternative, short of changing to a 4-stroke cycle engine, is to load it with a sensible prop, which slows the machinery.

Unluckily, a quick glance at any torque and horsepower graph will show that when torque is at its peak, horsepower isn't. Manufacturers have partially alleviated this problem by developing tuned exhaust systems that give the 2-stroker a kick in the backplate at lower rpm. Since horsepower is the product of torque and rpm, an increase in torque effectively boosts the horsepower within a narrow rpm band; this helps the model perform

Here's the airborne unit mounted on the plane. 1—telemetry transmitter (under canopy); 2—Pitot tube, which takes in the ram air for the measurements.

most powerful engine allowed by the rules and exhibiting unlimited vertical performance! So, in response to the earlier question about vertical performance: it's the weight, and that's the truth!

For pylon racers, a lightweight model means greater speed over the racecourse because there's less induced drag (drag generated by the wing) at low angles of attack. For safety, pylon-racing events have minimum weight requirements; this eliminates many questionable materials and construction techniques associated with lightweight models. Other than the "Let's see a crash" spectator appeal, no

competitor Pete Reed was also using the Tigre for his racers. Pete used to tease that his engines were more powerful than my own. Of course this challenge led to an rpm contest at one of the races which we both attended.

By using the same test propeller (9x6 Top Flite Super M), the engine that turned the highest was producing the greatest horsepower. My engine out-turned his by almost 600rpm! The smile on my face abruptly disappeared when Pete blew by me in a heat race. What did he know that I didn't? After thinking about it for a while, the answer became obvious: while I was

difficult maneuvers such as vertical climbs while using a practical propeller.

Torque and horsepower graphs

Between Mike Billinton and me, many 2-stroke engines have been dynamometer tested. The "dyno" is an apparatus that measures an engine's torque (crankshaft twisting force) at regular intervals throughout its operational speed range. From this data, horsepower characteristics can be calculated. Representative torque and horsepower graphs display these characteristics in relation to rpm. Helpful information can be extracted from these performance graphs, including how to determine the best rpm to load your engine for a given application.

Racers

Getting a model from point A to point B in the shortest period of time requires power. Ideally, we want a racing engine to operate at its peak horsepower speed (rpm) at all times during a race. Regrettably, current engine and propeller control technology doesn't allow us to accomplish this—yet—but it might happen in the near future.

The typical racing engine is affected by in-flight forces that cause it to slow down and speed up. These rpm changes cause the horsepower to increase or decrease accordingly. If the propeller load isn't allowing the engine to attain its ideal rpm during straight flight, its horsepower will be further reduced when negotiating tight pylon turns due to slowing of the model.

There are several solutions to this dilemma. First, prop the engine to operate slightly beyond the peak horsepower rpm.

When loaded down in a turn, the rpm will drop, but horsepower will remain closer to its peak, providing faster acceleration to maximum velocity. Second; if the pilot flies a smooth course around the pylons, air-drag fluctuations will be kept to a minimum, allowing the engine to perform closer to its peak horsepower rpm. The next time you watch a pylon race, notice how smoothly the experts fly compared with the also-rans.

Horsepower vs. rpm graphs indicate

Telemetry system: left, R/C talker (receiver); center, airborne transmitter; right, airspeed sensor.

what the in-air rpm should be. The next step is to determine the peaked ground rpm. As you know, the engine-propeller combination unloads (speeds up) as the model makes the transition from static ground conditions to dynamic flight. The question becomes, "How much does it speed up?" With onboard telemetry equipment the answer is simple: read the ground-based tachometer while the model is flying! I've found that the degree of engine unload isn't predictable. Variables such as the internal design of the engine, drag characteristics of the model and style

of the propeller influence the results. If you don't have telemetry, the next best thing is a systematic evaluation of props by comparing actual race times. However, horsepower performance graphs give you a reasonable starting point for developing competitive propellers.

Aerobatic and high-performance sport models

Aerobatic models are also dependent upon horsepower to perform high load maneuvers, especially unlimited vertical climbs which act directly against the force of gravity. As discussed previously, tiny propellers are required to operate near the engine's horsepower peak. This has proven to be inefficient and impractical for this type of model.

As a compromise, aerobatic engines are forced to operate at a lower rpm, which allows them to turn a much larger prop because they're operating nearer the torque peak. As with racing planes, the question is, "How do I determine the best in-air rpm?" The answer is telemetry. However, by empirical methods a variety of props can be evaluated simply by flying them. By watching the air speed and listening to the engine rpm while performing maneuvers such as loops and climbs, the application of available horsepower can be monitored. If rpm drop too much, air speed will rapidly degrade and sluggish control will result. By substituting a propeller with slightly lower pitch and/or diameter, rpm will increase to a more favorable horsepower and performance level.

The observant modeler can subjectively analyze a model's performance without telemetry. If the model climbs 300 feet before losing air speed, compared to 400 feet with another propeller, the choice is obvious—almost. Large-diameter/low-pitch propellers will give excellent vertical performance while sacrificing air speed everywhere else; it attains its vertical performance because the engine is operating closer to the peak horsepower rpm. This

The hand-held telemetry receiver (ground unit) and the ever important clipboard for note taking.

may be acceptable to some fliers; however, the sound of an engine screaming its guts out (especially in dives) while flying slowly isn't the direction most of us choose to pursue.

FUTURE PERFORMANCE

Crystal ball gazing is always fun, especially when it pertains to R/C aircraft.

duced their prop-drive unit, which was designed for 60-size engines. By gearing down the output shaft speed (a double-belt drive was utilized), an effective boost in thrust was realized by propellers in the 20- to 24-inch-diameter range, operating at about 6,000rpm. Du-Bro claimed that models weighing up to 30 pounds could be flown with their system.

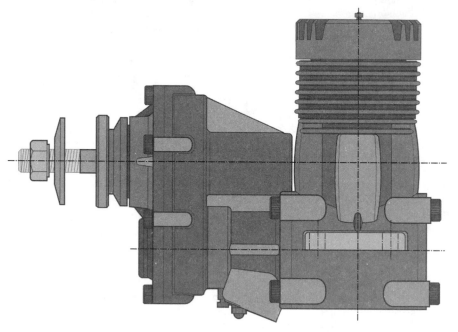

O.S. Max .61 FSR GS-A2 geared engine

Because technology is capable of producing stunning new developments, here's a few that would secure enhanced aircraft performance:

Geared 2-stroke engines

By gearing the output shaft of a 2-stroke engine to operate at about $\frac{1}{2}$ speed, large and efficient propellers have the ability to propel large, heavy aerobatic and scale models with authority. This system has the advantage of operating the engine near its peak horsepower rpm while doubling the torque at the propeller shaft.

Another benefit of the relatively slow turning propeller shaft is the dramatic reduction in propeller *noise*. This may come as a shock, but high rpm propeller noise is more difficult to contend with than exhaust noise. Once the exhaust has been quieted below that of the propeller, continued improvement depends on propeller efficiency—converting more of the prop's input energy into usable thrust and less into noise—a very difficult problem. Presently, the best technical fix is to reduce propeller rpm.

Back in 1977, Du-Bro Products intro-

In 1982, O.S. Engines produced a 10cc engine that featured an integral crankshaft/propeller shaft front housing with helical gear reduction. Originally, O.S. planned to offer many combinations of gear ratios and propeller shaft locations but apparently settled on two: the C-1 and C-2 models; these located the propeller shaft below the crankshaft with a ratio of 1.4 to 1, or 1.9 to 1. About the same time, Webra Engines offered their version of the encased gearbox for the popular Speed .61; with a gear reduction of 1.66 to 1, the unit offered an alternative to the O.S. design while providing the flexibility of four attachment locations on the engine. Unfortunately, these units were expensive (between $100 and $130) and weren't widely accepted. Perhaps the concept was ahead of its time, but in my opinion, Du-Bro, O.S. and Webra had the right idea. Look for renewed interest in this old idea from progressive manufacturers.

Improved 2-stroke engines

The FAI (international rules-making body) has finally removed the cylinder displacement advantage from 4-stroke engines. By

equalizing the maximum allowable cylinder displacement at 1.2ci for competition events such as aerobatics, 2-stroke and 4-stroke designs now compete on a level playing field. Most knowledgeable observers believe the performance pendulum will now swing toward 2-stroke designs.

Unfortunately, the 2-stroke design has its faults. The major knock against it has always been its low level of brake mean effective pressure (bmep) throughout its practical rpm range. Low mean cylinder pressures produce low torque at the crankshaft. As expected, they can't turn large propellers at relatively low rpm. Over the years, engineers have improved the situation significantly by incorporating better cylinder porting, scavenging and exhaust systems; however, the weakness persists because they continue to promote high rpm applications with flashy but out-of-reach horsepower numbers, as we touched upon earlier.

Designers need to abandon the obsolete notion that 2-strokers always need to run *fast* to realize high performance. A recent paradigm shift strongly suggests that the engine should be redesigned, concentrating on improved low rpm bmep and torque—even if some horsepower is sacrificed! Let's face it: other than in specialized racing events, high rpm horsepower is wasted on the majority of R/C fliers!

Keep in mind that horsepower is the product of the engine's torque and rpm; it controls the *rate* at which maneuvers are performed and the speed in straight and level flight. When engine speed is reduced as proposed, chunks of horsepower are also sliced off. The only practical way to replace some of this performance potential is to increase the bmep - this is much harder to do than designing the engine to run faster! Here's a list of things that will help:
1. Increase the strength of the crankcase and reciprocating components to withstand the increased bmep.
2. Adjust the induction and cylinder port timing to match lower shaft speeds:
3. Apply innovative new porting configurations, such as the cylinder packing *colliding stream* system as used in modern motorcycle designs.
4. Use higher compression ratios.
5. Utilize tuned exhaust systems to provide a boost at the peak torque rpm, rather than the peak horsepower speed.

The 2-stroke engine can be persuaded to change its ways. It's not going to be easy, but it's possible. Irvine Engines has pointed the way with their revolutionary Quiet .40 engine, which emphasizes low rpm torque. The goal must be to develop an engine that will function at 10,000rpm with practical propellers. Imagine this "torquer" 2-stroke coupled to a gear reduction propeller shaft; how large would you like the propeller to be?

A NEW ENGINE DESIGN

What's really needed is a totally new engine design—one that embodies the best characteristics of both the 2-stroke and 4-stroke concepts. The 2-stroke engine is good because it produces a power event each revolution of the crankshaft, while the 4-stroke engine demonstrates excellent cylinder scavenging characteristics.

How about an engine that transfers its air-fuel mixture through a ring of circumferential ports (drilled holes) in the lower end of its cylinder sleeve (piston controlled, as with a 2-stroke design) and exhausts through a pair of 4-stroke-type poppet valves in the cylinder head? The valves can be actuated by a standard pushrod valve train that utilizes a camshaft modified to open the valves with each revolution of the crankshaft.

The advantage of this type of engine centers on its ability to scavenge the cylinder of exhaust gases while minimizing mixing with the fresh air-fuel charge. This will undoubtedly generate much higher cylinder pressures, torque and horsepower—at *lower rpm!*

Many readers will recognize this engine as the diesel 2-stroke uniflow design, which is widely used to power trucks. Our miniature engine will differ from its truck counterpart in several important ways:
1. The diesel transfers only air into the cylinder from a positive displacement supercharger; ours transfers the air-fuel *mixture* from the crankcase to the cylinder via crankcase compression—just like current 2-stroke designs.
2. The diesel ignition occurs by injecting fuel directly into the highly compressed and heated air charge within the cylinder; ours ignites the compressed air-fuel charge by a standard glow plug or spark plug.
3. Lubricating oil will be mixed in the fuel—as with standard 2-stroke practice; since the air-fuel mixture passes through the crankcase, it's easy to service with after-run oil, unlike miniature 4-strokers.
4. A reed valve will admit the air-fuel mixture from the carburetor to the crankcase. The reed valve possesses variable timing because it's acted upon by the strength and duration of pressure changes within the crankcase throughout the engine's speed range. It provides excellent starting characteristics, positive idle and throttle response along with adequate mixture delivery at the moderate speeds expected from this design.

Does this sound too good to be true? Maybe, but initial testing utilizing a modified 4-stroke cycle engine has been encouraging. Further development will be necessary; strength of materials is a concern since the design produces significantly more cylinder pressure than traditional designs. Optimizing port and valve timing configurations in order to provide the desired low speed operation is time consuming but straightforward.

at any throttle setting, is desirable.

Fixed-pitch propellers operate best within a narrow air-speed range. Above that range, an over-speeding engine risks mechanical failure, while under-speeding (overloading) inevitably causes overheating problems. An example of the fixed-pitch predicament is the takeoff mode of operation, where low pitch is desired for high thrust and short ground runs. Unfortunately, low-pitch props provide

TORQUE AND HORSEPOWER GRAPH AND CHART

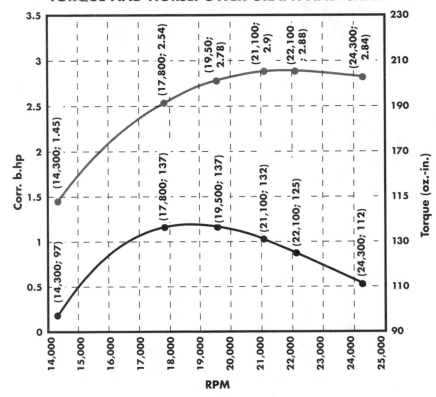

RPM	Torque	Corr. b.hp	b.hp	Corr. factor	Distance
14,000					
14,300	97	1.45	1.38	1.05	1.632
17,800	137	2.54	2.42	1.05	2.305
19,500	137	2.78	2.65	1.05	2.317
21,100	132	2.90	2.76	1.05	2.226
22,100	125	2.88	2.74	1.05	2.1
24,300	112	2.84	2.70	1.05	1.889
25,000					

Wet bulb (F)	65
Dry bulb (F)	75
Bar. pres (Hg)	29.34
Vap. pres (Hg)	0.5

CONSTANT-SPEED PROPELLERS

For years, full-scale aircraft have benefited from constant-speed propeller technology. The concept is simple: use a variable-pitch propeller to control engine speed in all modes of flight. From earlier discussions concerning engine rpm and horsepower production, it should be apparent that operating at (or near) peak horsepower,

unsatisfactory high-speed (cruise) performance in most applications. High-pitch props offer superior high-speed performance at the expense of prolonged and dangerous takeoff runs; 1930s pylon racers were glaring examples of this potentially disastrous situation. Pilots of these highly loaded speedsters had to hold them on the ground until sufficient speed had been attained; impatiently lifting off too soon risked encountering the deadly stall-spin phenomenon, which often proved fatal.

Prior to the advent of the *controllable-variable pitch* propeller (c.v.p.), most full-scale aircraft manufacturers provided pro-

The rpm sensor for telemetry system (photo-cell). It takes the measurements off the revolving propeller.

pellers that sacrificed top speed to improve takeoff—a necessary compromise. The c.v.p. propeller eliminates the need to compromise—at the expense of simplicity. Model aviation pattern fliers had the opportunity to experience using these propellers in the late 1970s. The servo-operated propeller of German manufacture was a hot item on the national and international scene for a while until eventually falling into disfavor. Most fliers couldn't handle the additional task of manually adjusting the pitch for individual maneuvers. Many didn't like the performance of the propeller in terms of producing efficient thrust.

Off-the-shelf technology offers the ability to make the c.v.p. propeller an automatic system, requiring no in-flight commands by the pilot to obtain optimum engine-aircraft performance. A photocell or Hall Effect sensor detects engine rpm and sends this information to a microprocessor that maintains a constant shaft speed. This is achieved by interfacing a standard servo between the controller and the variable-pitch propeller; subsequent pitch adjustments control the load on the engine—a classic example of automatic feedback!

Several companies have offered controllers for other applications, which would function satisfactorily for the constant-speed system. Joe Utasi of Jomar (now EMS) manufactured a unit for synchronizing the rpm of multiple engine applications. Another controller—the Tachtron—synchronized the speed of a helicopter's tail rotor to that of its main rotor. The Utasi unit controls the slave engine's throttle to attain synchronization.

Although the constant-speed propeller is an improvement, it isn't a panacea. When the aircraft noses down into a dive, the load is reduced and the controller signals for an increase of the propeller's pitch. This produces an acceleration, something that most pattern fliers try to avoid by manually throttling back. What we really need is a system that maintains *constant aircraft speed!*

It has been suggested that an engine torque sensor would be useful in signaling for a throttle and/or pitch change. Another interesting approach involves the application of a Pitot tube or similar air-speed sensor to signal appropriate microprocessor interventions.

This discussion prompted fellow modeler and engineer extraordinaire, Franklin Vassallo, to recall the following anecdote:

"I am reminded of a story told to me by one of my colleagues at the former Cornell Aeronautical Laboratory in Buffalo, NY. While attending a church service, Galileo observed the altar candle oscillating on its chain in a period (time) which appeared to be independent of its swing arc length. Finding this to be remarkable, he set out to establish the theory of the pendulum which, indeed, showed the period to be a function of the square root of the pendulum arm length (assuming no friction). He then fashioned a rudimentary clock mechanism (without escapement) to test its ability to indicate time. He revealed the mechanism at a demonstration for his peers. Following the demonstration, where the clock eventually stopped for lack of sustaining impetus, the observers questioned its utility for keeping time continuously. Galileo remarked that he had established the pendulum as a *means* of keeping time, it was now up to others to determine the specific *method* by which its motion could be sustained. Of course, the escapement was later invented, allowing clocks based upon pendulum action to be used—even to the present day."

We have a similar situation here; the *means* for control of speed is pitch and throttle. The specific method has yet to be developed.

CONCLUSIONS

Not everyone is willing to pay the price to attain high performance. It requires hard work, persistence, perseverance and dedication to achieving a goal. If you follow the general outline presented here, success will guarantee that someone will eventually approach you at the flying field and ask, "How do you get so much power when the model climbs vertically?" ◆

ABOUT THE AUTHOR

Dave Gierke

Dave has been involved with model aviation since the age of seven. For 47 years, he has been designing, constructing and competing with his models on a national level. He has published more than 20 articles since 1967 and is a columnist for Model Airplane News. His award-winning work treats subjects such as model design, engine testing, atmospheric effects on performance, analysis of 2-stroke oils and finishing techniques. Dave holds his masters from the State University College at Buffalo and, in 1978, was named Teacher of the Year for New York State. He resides in Lancaster, NY, with his wife Carolyn.

CHAPTER 12

Fine-Tune Your CG by Flight Testing

by Larry Renger

The plans told you exactly where to balance the airplane—right? What's that about messing with ballast and incidence? The plane flies, so who needs it? Well, that depends on whether you want to be a good pilot or not. The best pilots have planes that respond to their every input; they don't require constant control just to maintain heading. The ideal is a model that will do what *you* want it to, not what it happens to be set up to do.

Let's compare it with driving a car. Let's say you have an old clunker that has encountered its share of potholes and curbs. The front-end alignment is shot, the wheels aren't balanced, and the tires are bald. Add a rainstorm. OK, if you're a really good driver, you'll probably still be able to go pretty fast and actually live to tell about it, but if you aren't…. Who needs it! I'd prefer a modern suspension with the best all-weather tires and the best maintenance I can afford to keep my tail out of the weeds. You want a machine that does *not* have a mind of its own. It should go exactly where and when you want and how you want it to. Unexpected responses can be fatal when driving a car, and they can total your model. My purpose here is to detail the techniques you need to use to tune your model to respond smoothly and appropriately to the type of flying *you* do.

The designer told you where to balance the model, and you did it, so what's the big deal? Well, models differ—even the same design built by the same modeler from the same materials. We just can't build airplanes so perfectly that they don't require adjustments. In addition, a model's designer will tell you a "safe" CG location that will work every time. But it will almost never be the "best" CG location for your particular model.

STATE OF TUNE

First, consider your level of expertise and the type of model you fly. Every type has a particular character and will respond to pilot input according to the level of his skills. Let's discuss a few of these types:

◆ **Trainers** are basically stable. If you

get into trouble, it's best to let go of the sticks and wait for the model to resume flying by itself. Lots of altitude helps, of course, but the model is completely stable flying itself. The classic old-timer free-flight with minimal power comes to mind as a comparison—no pilot input required. In flying of this type, the term "radio influenced" seems more apt than "radio controlled."

On the next level are the so-called "aileron trainers." Here, you want a plane that rights itself, responds in a moderate manner to control inputs and doesn't require lightning-fast reflexes.

◆ **High-performance or competition aerobatic models**—the third basic level of stability. Here, the ideal is a model that's precisely neutral in all stability axes, i.e., it goes exactly where it was last pointed, until told to do something else. The pilot has to be totally in command, but the reward is a level of response and flying precision that can be achieved in no other way. Mind you, this level of neutrality is usually combined with extremely sensitive control inputs, so the average Sunday pilot wouldn't find the models flyable. For the sport pilot, neutral stability with mild control sensitivity can make for pleasant flying.

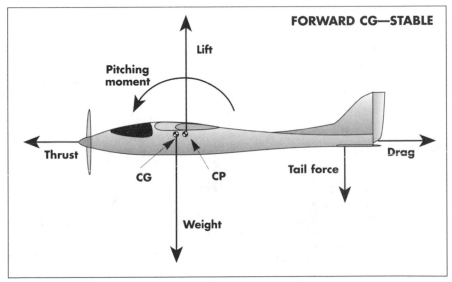

FORWARD CG—STABLE

FIGURE 1
Stable margin (slightly nose-heavy). This drawing shows a case in which the CG is ahead of the center of pressure (CP). The weight adds to the wing's nose-down pitching moment, and they both must be countered by a downforce at the tail. This is the most classic stable configuration. As speed picks up, the wing and tail forces increase, but the weight moment does not. As a result, forces are unbalanced and the nose comes up; this reduces speed.

TAKING A DIVE!

The dive test measures how sensitive a model is to changes of speed while holding constant as many other variables as possible. The validity of the test has long been controversial, because it doesn't seem to work with all models.

In a very practical sense, the test also measures a model's margin of stability. It compares its flight in a horizontal, stable mode to one in which it's flying faster—in effect, two points on the net pitching moment curve.

The model is trimmed to be stable (no accelerations) in level flight, then pitched down and returned to the same trimmed flight. The model is no longer in equilibrium because lift is reduced and the model is accelerating. As a result, the model will respond to the pitch trim more than the weight balance.

If you were flying tail-heavy with a lifting stab, the model would pitch downward. If you were flying nose-heavy with a downward-lifting stab, the model would pitch up. If trim is neutral, the model will fly straight.

Note that the results are the reverse of the obvious. Tail-heavy causes the nose to go down; nose-heavy makes the nose come up. See Figures 1 through 5 to understand why this is so.

Note that forces are assumed to work on a horizontal line through the CG. In fact, the problem is at least two-dimensional in that the thrust, drag and lift all work in different vertical planes. My aim here is just to get the pitching moment concept across.

CG VS. CONTROL SENSITIVITY— and other related factors

In model aircraft setup, one of the most difficult things is to distinguish between such factors as basic design, trim, center of gravity location, control sensitivity and engine thrust line. The key is to evolve a technique to isolate each factor in turn.

It would be the work of a lifetime to start with a clean sheet of paper and come up with a totally new design that worked well; 99.9 percent of "new" model designs are adaptations of previous designs. The most successful models are the result of refinements made by a modeler who, over a period of time, builds several versions of

the same model and makes small modifications every time. (As they say, "The name changed, but the moments are the same.")

Dealing with the entire range of adjustments, design changes and settings required to develop a new airplane design is certainly beyond the scope of this chapter. For the purposes of this chapter, you should be working with a well-established design that generally works for anyone.

The author with a short-coupled polyhedral slope soarer in the hills of California.

So let's just try to set up the CG for a model that has been built and set up correctly. The plan is to make *your* model perform as well as possible.

First, the model must be built and aligned correctly. You really do have to make all those funny measurements to ensure that the wings are at right angles to

the fuselage, the tail is parallel to the wing in both the vertical and the horizontal directions, and that the vertical tail is straight along the fuselage and at 90 degrees to the horizontal stabilizer.

INITIAL SETUP

Set the controls as recommended in the instructions or on the plans. If settings aren't given, about 20 degrees of throw in each direction on all surfaces is a good starting point. For most designs, this should give you a pretty docile model. If the design uses full "flying" surfaces, for starters, throw should be limited to about 10 degrees. The key here is to have a model that's rather *unresponsive* so you can distinguish the model's stability from

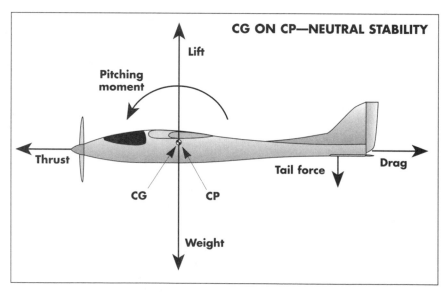

FIGURE 2
Zero margin of stability (neutral CG). Here, the condition is neutrally stable. The weight is on the CP, and the model's forces are the balance of the tail force versus the pitching moment. If speed picks up, the forces stay in balance and no pitching happens.

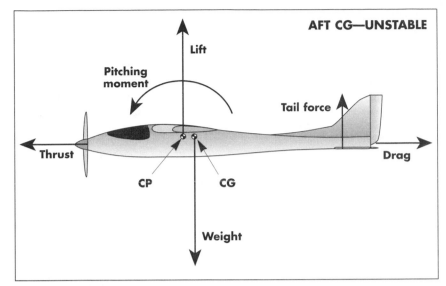

FIGURE 3
Negative margin (slightly tail-heavy, unstable)—uh-oh! This one means instant death. Here, the CG is behind the CP and is countering the pitching moment. Tail force may be zero or even a force lifting upward (sounds very efficient, and it is). The bad news is that it's "speed unstable." As speed picks up, the tail force and wing pitching moment overpower the weight force, pitch the nose down and increase speed more. The result is a divergent instability.

the control input response. It's very easy to think that a model is tail-heavy, when the real problem is too much elevator control input.

Set the CG as suggested by the model's designer. Generally, I expect the designer to define a "safe" position with a little extra margin of stability to keep us out of trouble. In other words, the CG is farther forward than it really needs to be, so all the models built from the design will fly OK. From here, we'll proceed through a process to achieve the ideal balance point for your model and style of flying.

POWER OFF!

As mentioned before, for a model, one of the most difficult elements in setting any aspect of trim is to isolate it from the other factors that affect a model's aerodynamics. By setting the control sensitivities low, we eliminate one distraction. The next item to isolate is the power or thrust effect. Not surprisingly, to do this, you must turn your model into a glider (or close to one). Initially, find a power setting that lets the model fly comfortably in level flight, but at a power setting that's as low as possible.

On a glider or an airplane with power off, trim for a glide at minimum sink angle (maximum lift-to-drag ratio). The blade speed will be noticeably faster than the stall, or even minimum sink-rate speeds, but not so fast that you have to point the nose down noticeably. Typically, it's the point at which people say the glider is "on the step."

Here we get to the famous (or infamous) "dive test." The idea is to compare the model flight in level trim to the same model in a faster, nose-down attitude. (See the "Taking a Dive" sidebar and the figures for details on what's happening aerodynamically.)

The dive test is very simple, but if the model to be tested is a trainer, it's probably better to have an experienced pilot do the dive testing.

Set up your plane to fly level or, in the case of a glider, in a smooth glide at the best glide angle. If the model is truly unstable, you won't be able to get that smooth glide in the first place. Add nose weight until you can get a steady glide or smooth level flight. Mechanical problems—slop in the control linkages or servo-centering problems—can give you trouble here, too.

The control surfaces must be free enough to return to the same place every time.

Having achieved level flight, just put the model into a steep dive, release the controls, and observe the resulting flight path. The results and the actions to take are as follows:
• If the model turns in either direction, you have a misalignment or warp, and you must fix that before you try to tune the model. If all is well in that department, here's how to set the model.

◆ **Trainers.** The airplane should pull out of the dive in 20 fuselage lengths or so, and it should return by itself to steady level flight after a stall or two. If the model pulls out very quickly but never settles down to steady flight (it may even accelerate in the stalls until it loops), it's very nose-heavy. Move the CG back no more than 1 percent of the chord at a time. When the CG is within 2 percent of optimum, the model will probably fly OK.
• If, however, the model takes a long time to pull out, or the dive steepens, you should move the CG forward. Again, keep the changes small, and repeat the tests until the model flies perfectly.

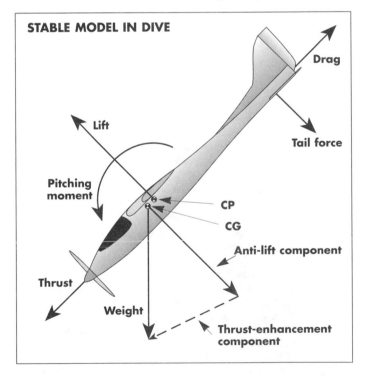

FIGURE 4
A stable model in a dive. Here we take the case shown in Figure 1 and put it in a dive. As you can see, one component of the weight vector now augments thrust, and the other component of weight (counter to the wing lift) is reduced. As a result, speed picks up because the forward force exceeds the rearward. The tail force, wing pitching moment and the wing lift all increase together. Because the weight pitching moment is decreased and the aerodynamic pitching moment is increased, the model has a rotational acceleration (nose up). It is also lifted upward by the net force unbalance toward the top of the airplane. This is a stabilizing action.

• If the model shows odd characteristics such as a nice pull-out in a mild dive, but it tucks under in a steep dive, you need to really dig in and do some research and re-designing, but that's way beyond the scope of this chapter, so *good luck!*

◆ **Intermediate models.** Here you are, trying for a model that's just slightly stable, i.e., it will tend to find its own level flight

tank nearly empty. During this part of the flight, the CG is in its farthest aft position, and you don't want to have to deal with a model becoming unstable just when you're trying to land!

• For this type of model, repeat the dive test until the model goes absolutely straight until you actively use the controls to pull it out, i.e., it has no speed sensitivity at all. To confirm that you have a truly

ing in for a kit, and its response to the dive test was odd. It had an under-cambered wing with a sloped, pitching moment curve. Initially, when trimmed to fly smoothly and be stable in very slight dives, it would tuck under in a steep dive. We found a CG and incidence that pulled the model out reliably in the dive test, as required for a trainer glider design. In normal flight, however, the model would gallop and end up in a series of uncontrolled stalls. Because the glider had only rudder control—no elevator—this was a disaster!

The problem was not with the test, but with the model. Ultimately, a change to the stabilizer airfoil was required to solve the problem. A new series of dive tests showed that with the modified stab, the model flew well when balanced as shown on the plans.

I assume that you're working with a properly designed model.

FINAL THOUGHTS

That is really all there is to it, but realize that we're dealing with only one of a number of interacting controls here. We assumed a well-designed model. This means that if you get the pitch CG correct, it will be in the right place for spiral stability, rolling, knife-edge flight and everything else. When you have the correct CG, you can move on to adjusting the thrust-line angles and control sensitivity to fine-tune the model. ◆

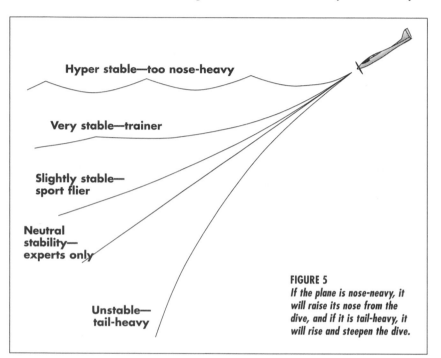

Hyper stable—too nose-heavy

Very stable—trainer

Slightly stable—sport flier

Neutral stability—experts only

Unstable—tail-heavy

FIGURE 5
If the plane is nose-neavy, it will raise its nose from the dive, and if it is tail-heavy, it will rise and steepen the dive.

at all times, but it isn't a fanatic about it. You should look for a gently curved, nose-up flight path when the model is released in the dive. This will result in a model that shouldn't stall at all at the end of the dive, but will end up transitioning to smooth level flight. The statement about steepening dives applies here, of course. You'll probably find that, to get the model just right, you'll have to get the CG within about 1 percent of perfect.

◆ **Expert models.** The goal for an expert-class model is to have the plane achieve exact neutral stability. It goes where you point it until it is told to do something else. This type of stability is only achievable on airplanes that were designed to have it. You can't trim a trainer to be truly neutral at all speeds. The airfoils and moments have to work together to give you this capability.

• It's important to perform this test on a high-performance powered model with the

neutral model, do the same test inverted! If that's a bit beyond your skills, compare the elevator stick position needed for inverted level flight with that needed for upright flight. There should be no difference.

STRIKING A BALANCE

When a plane has too much stability, its up-and-down oscillation never settles back to smooth flight. This is generally more difficult to deal with than a tuck-under. In full-scale aviation, an excess of stability coupled with oversensitive controls results in pilot-induced oscillation, which is occasionally fatal.

I contend that the dive test always works, but it may not tell you what you want to know. An unstable model can be flown, and one that has unusual pitch characteristics to the airfoil may fly stably in many conditions, but will be unstable in the dive test. Sometimes, the test may tell you that you should modify your design.

For example, I had a model I was tun-

ABOUT THE AUTHOR

Larry Renger

Larry's first "own design" was a glider that he cut out of ⅟₆-inch balsa by bearing down repeatedly with a pencil. He says that, "being too cheap to buy kits," he designed his own models throughout high school. During college at MIT, with the patient tutelage of Ray Harlan, he captured many indoor national records. As an avid sci-fi fan, he was also interested in rockets, so he invented the first forward engine boost glider for an Estes Industries design competition. After a stint in aerospace engineering, Larry broke into the model industry at Estes, Fox Engines and finally, Cox Hobbies. Money talks, however, and he spent 11 years at Mattel working on He-Man™, Hot Wheels™, etc. Larry is now back at Cox as director of engineering, and he's loving it!

CHAPTER 13

How to Slip an Airplane

by Roger Post Jr.

Have you ever, on final approach, found yourself flying too high or too fast? Have you had to cope with a strong crosswind or make a landing approach over an obstruction? Or have you been forced to land in a tight spot? Slipping can help us to overcome all of these and let us land our planes safely.

In the old days, full-scale pilots would slip their planes to make the approach angle steeper without gaining air speed. This was particularly helpful in emergency situations, short-field landings and landings over obstacles. With the invention of flaps, the art of slipping seems to have taken a back seat. If you visit a small airport, you might be lucky enough to see somebody flying a tail-dragger (without flaps) and doing slips on the approach. Seeing it done with a full-size aircraft will greatly enhance your ability to create a slip with your model.

TYPES OF SLIP

◆ **Forward slip.** This allows the pilot to lose altitude without increasing air speed because the plane's fuselage ends up in a position that's 10 to 30 degrees off the center line of the approach. This offset fuselage, which is now acting as a large speed brake against the relative wind, helps to slow the aircraft down. The offset fuselage is created by lowering one of the wingtips (with aileron input) into the crosswind or relative wind and adding a large amount of opposite rudder, e.g., right aileron plus left rudder. The plane is actually slipping in a forward direction of flight.

At this point, your rate of descent (feet per minute loss) can be controlled by the amount of aileron and rudder you use. If you need to lose a large amount of altitude in a short forward distance, you increase the aileron input and counteract the rolling tendency with more opposite

rudder. A shallower descent (which can be used over a longer forward distance) requires less aileron and opposite rudder input.

Besides using the fuselage as an air brake to control air speed, you can also use the pitch attitude of the nose. If you raise the nose, it will slow the plane down; if you lower the nose, your air speed increases. Slips are usually done with the throttle at idle, but it's sometimes necessary to add throttle to gain back a little of the lost altitude.

THE FORWARD SLIP

Here is the forward slip from the rear view. Note that in the third airplane down, the rudder shows a deflection to the left. This starts to realign the fuselage with the runway.

Remember: power is altitude; pitch is air speed.

The flight path of a forward slip is straight down the center line of the runway, but the nose of the aircraft is off the center line. The wind, landing setup, pilot preference, etc., will determine whether the nose is to the right or left of the center line.

◆ **Side slip.** This allows the aircraft's nose to remain on the heading while the plane slips sideways through a moving air mass. This is particularly useful in controlling the drift of an airplane. The drift is caused by strong crosswinds, and it will blow the plane off the center line of the runway. To keep on course, we must slip the plane with the ailerons and rudder, but our rudder input must be controlled so that the nose of the airplane stays parallel to the runway center line.

◆ **Knife-edge slip.** This is a variation on the side slip and can be used if you need to lose a lot of altitude and place the plane at the beginning of a runway that's bordered on both sides by tall trees. I had the opportunity to experience this in the back seat of an Aeronca Champion. What a ride that was! The side of the plane's fuselage was facing the ground, and we were falling in a knife-edge attitude. The nose was a little high, and the tail was a little low. The direction of the slip was a straight line to the ground. This attitude requires quite a bit of aileron input to get the wing perpendicular to the ground and a large amount of opposite rudder input to help counteract the rolling tendencies. The descent is controlled by the throttle and, once you're close to the touchdown point, you add some power (to get air flowing over the tail surfaces), kick in opposite rudder (to level the fuselage), level your wings with rudder and then aileron input and land the plane. Nothing to it!

HOW TO SLIP YOUR PLANE

• First, consider the type of plane you have and how much throw you have on your control surfaces. Most planes will slip well if they have more than the recommended throw on their rudder and ailerons.
• Second, it helps to have a large vertical fin and rudder. Some planes will slip with a small rudder, but to really nail a forward slip, you'll need a large rudder with lots of deflection.
• Third, you must practice the slips with plenty of altitude to recover in case your thumbs get mixed up.

THE SIDE SLIP

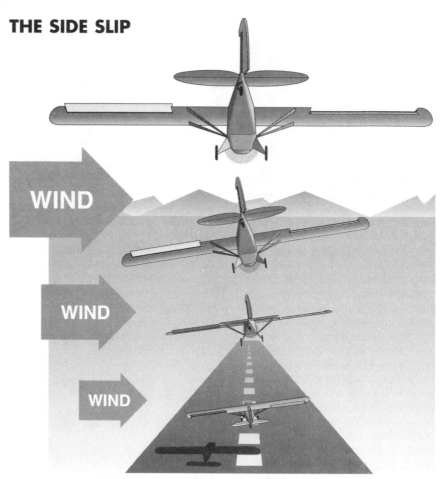

During a side slip, the plane is actually slipping through the moving air mass sideways. Its ground track remains on the runway heading.

FORWARD SLIP

Line up with the runway, and bank one of your wings down.

Here's the $64,000 question: which wing should I bank?

Assuming that you fly facing your runway and your runway is parallel to the flight line, you must first consider the wind direction. (I'll use compass headings to try to eliminate any confusion.) Your body faces north, and your runway runs east to west.
• *Wind is blowing from the northwest:* your plane approaches from the east with the right wing down.
• *Wind is from the northeast:* you approach from the west with the left wing down.
• *Wind is from the southeast:* you'll also approach from the west, but the right wing will be down.
• *Wind is from the southwest:* you'll approach from the east with the left wing down.

Rule of thumb: approach into the wind, and keep the plane's upwind wing lowered into the crosswind.

When there's little wind or it's blowing straight down the runway, the approach to landing direction can be the second consideration in determining which wing to bank. If your plane is right of the center line, you should bank the right wing down. If you approach from the left, the opposite applies. The position of obstructions in the flight path should also be considered when banking a wing for a slip. Finally, consider pilot preference; some of us are more comfortable banking a particular wing.

Having determined which wing to bank, we apply opposite rudder to counteract the rolling tendencies. The real trick to this cross-controlling is how much pressure you use on the sticks. You'll find that you're either spreading your thumbs or pushing them together. One of the sticks might have more input than the other, but this will change as the procedure moves further along. What changes it?: wind speed and direction; how much altitude you'd like to lose; having a short distance over the ground to lose a lot of altitude; the height of the obstructions; the speed of the approach; the size of the control surfaces and how much throw they have.

When the wind speed is high and its direction is angled far off the center line, you must lower the upwind wing more to prevent the plane from drifting off course. Your aileron stick will have a little more input than usual, and your rudder stick input will balance out the aileron deflection so that the plane performs a side slip. (The nose of the plane is still lined up with the runway.) If you need to lose a lot of altitude over a short forward distance, you can add in more aileron and counteract with enough opposite rudder to make the plane go into a forward slip.

KNIFE-EDGE SLIP

The knife-edge slip is a steeper version of the side slip. The wing is almost perpendicular to the ground, and the flight path is more of a straight line to the ground rather than forward or sideways. For this one, your sticks could be pushed in or spread out almost all of the way. You'll lose altitude very quickly with this one, so be ready to add throttle to control your rate of descent. Watching real airplanes do slips and practicing on your part to re-create what you see will help your thumbs to respond automatically.

Caution: don't put the plane into a cross-controlled slip and freeze your thumbs. As the slip progresses, you'll have to adjust the plane's attitude with small stick inputs. You may need more rudder or less aileron or vice versa, and you'll have to make these minute adjustments to keep the plane slipping over the intended ground track. This hand/eye coordination takes some time to perfect, so be patient, and practice it with plenty of recovery altitude.

In a forward slip, the plane's air speed will be greatly reduced by the exposed side of the fuselage. This is a handy feature to know in case you come in for a low pass and your engine quits. Just throw the plane into a forward slip, and you have an instant speed brake. If this is done properly, you can land on the runway and not overshoot it. If you lose too much altitude and look as though you will be landing short of the runway (engine still running), add power to gain the altitude back.

You may find yourself feeding in a little up-elevator through the entire slipping process. This is all right if you have sufficient air speed to prevent the plane from stalling. Remember that a forward slip will

The knife-edge slip is a more severe side slip that allows the plane to lose altitude at a faster rate than the other slips. It can also be used to land in between obstructions.

reduce your air speed and any up-elevator will further reduce the air speed because of the increased angle of attack. This could send you into a stall, maybe even a knife-edge stall, if your wing happens to be banked at a drastic angle. Don't be afraid of a lower-than-usual nose attitude when you practice your slips. If things get too complicated all at once, add power, straighten the fuselage with opposite rudder, level the wings with the ailerons and then go around and try again. A bad approach makes for an even worse landing.

LANDING AFTER A SLIP

Now that you've worked out how to lose altitude and control air speed and are able to keep the ground track straight, you must straighten the plane out to land. To straighten out the fuselage (if you're in a forward slip), simply reverse the rudder input. Level the wings with the ailerons, and flare into a three-point landing. If there's a crosswind, keep the upwind wing lower with some aileron input, steer with the rudder and perform a wheel landing. Remember to gradually increase your

THE KNIFE-EDGE SLIP

aileron input into the crosswind as your rollout speed decreases. This will prevent your plane from flipping over after the landing has been completed. At the end of a side slip, you will not need to straighten anything out, but you will have to keep the upwind wing lower in the ground-effect phase of the landing and remember to increase your aileron into the wind during the rollout.

You will find that, with practice, your thumbs will get the feel of how to control the slip. You'll see that a forward slip will use more rudder than a side slip.

Two things to keep in mind:
• The side slip's ground track will stay straight, but the plane will actually be slipping sideways through the moving air mass.
• In a forward slip, the plane is actually slipping in a forward direction relative to the runway.

I hope this helps you understand the slip a little more and, if you can, I highly recommend that you find a good tail-dragger pilot who'll take you up and show you how the real thing is done. Slipping a Piper Cub on an approach with the side doors and the window open is a great way to spend a summer day. Good luck, and practice with recovery altitude.   ◆

To learn about the author of this chapter, see page 18.

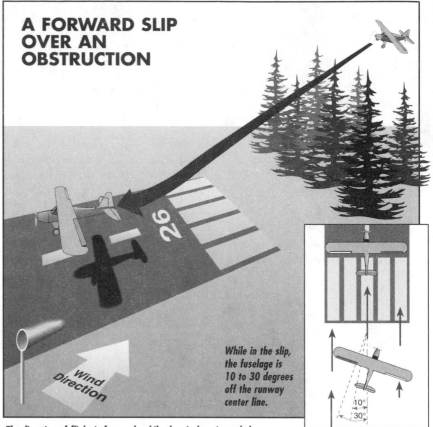

A FORWARD SLIP OVER AN OBSTRUCTION

Wind Direction

While in the slip, the fuselage is 10 to 30 degrees off the runway center line.

10°
30°

The direction of flight is forward, while the airplane is angled off of the center line. As the plane approaches the runway, the fuselage is realigned with the runway center line.

AEROBATICS

SECTION THREE
AEROBATICS

The pursuit of aerobatic proficiency is probably one of the main reasons we all get into this hobby. There are many approaches to aerobatics, and this section reflects that diversity. If hot-dogging is your goal, experienced R/C show pilot and aerobatic model designer Frank Noll Jr. provides the basics in "Hot-Dogging it with Frank Noll Jr."

In "The Art of Low-Power Aerobatics," world-famous electric scale modeler and R/C show pilot Keith Shaw offers useful lessons that also apply to glow aircraft that are not over-powered. If you wish to put on an air show for the local crowd, be sure to read Shaw's chapter.

Another who has amazed crowds at R/C gatherings with antics such as dragging a fin in the grass during inverted flight is Stinger Wallace. Pick up some of his tips in "Hotshot Flying—*Stinger* Style."

Interested in the fast-paced action of competition fun flying? In "Fun-Fly Competition," fun-fly airplane designer and champion Jerry L. Smith offers basic advice that will equip you to enter the highly competitive fun-fly circuit. This chapter will really keep that plane and those thumbs "dancing." So, read thoroughly, and don't be afraid to try the moves!

Looking to trim your airplane for better aerobatic flight? Accomplished model designer and aerobatic slope pilot Jef Raskin tells you how to trim your sailplane to best achieve those graceful gyrations in the sky in "How to Trim Sailplanes for Aerobatics." These lessons also apply to sport planes.

CHAPTER 14

Hot-Dogging it with Frank Noll Jr.

by Frank Noll Jr. and Dwight Doench

I f you think you're bold and have lots of grit, let's explore a place in the world of model aviation that many R/C fliers dream of, but very few reach: the gyrating, upside-down, inside-out world of the hot-dogger. This freestyle aerobatics haven can be found lurking around the outer fringes of precision aerobatics and pattern flying. The only difference is that a good hot-dog pilot is tough to find. In the sport of R/C flying, it isn't easy to make an airplane do more moves in less space than the "best of all the rest."

I like to think of hot-dog flying as a form of self-expression in which "Style is everything," as they say. On one hand, I might sound as though I'm flying on thin air here, but when I snap and roll my giant-scale Christen Eagle or IMAC through a show routine, my adrenaline really gets pumping (even after more than 30 years in this great hobby).

Even if your own flying experience is limited somewhat in the aerobatics department, don't worry; you'll set the sky ablaze at the show center in due course. But first, let's go over some technical aspects of setting up your airplane so it will become a mean hot-dog flying machine.

TYPES OF PLANE

When talking about the right "type" of airplane for this high-jeopardy style of flying, it's important to know what we are discussing. All my show flying is done with giant-scale aircraft that meet current IMAA standards.

I recommend two types of aircraft:
◆ **Scale designs**—such as the Lazer and the Extra Series, and for bipe enthusiasts, the Pitts and the Ultimate designs.

◆ **Non-scale sport**—for the more price-conscious model aviators. These include the Stinger and the Impulse Plus.

Whichever of these you go with—scale or non-scale—it makes no difference; they all have the handling characteristics needed for the extreme stuff I'll talk about later. But for now, let's say you've already selected your hot-dog flying

machine and have built it and covered it. If you're wondering how to set up an airplane to "strut the stuff," read on.

SETTING UP

Your airplane can be set up to fly as smoothly or as erratically as your heart desires. Let's go over a few tips for making your plane's personality shine in the handling department.

Servo throws are critical for making your plane do the maneuvers included in the hot-dogger's repertoire. They put the heat into your airplane's handling characteristics, and they give its flight envelope another dimension. Therefore, you need to increase the throw in all your control surfaces.

Move your pushrod extensions all the way out to the end of your servo arms. This will increase the pivoting radius of the arm and cause your control surface to be deflected more. Even though your plane will be more erratic with this setup, there are ways to desensitize this overkill on the throws and smooth out the bumpy spots in your hot-dog routine.

SERVOS

Enough can't be said about the importance of using high-torque servos or large servos for your high-performance needs. Trust me; you need the torque power to hold the control surfaces in place against

The author with his One Design. Frank manufactures this kit and uses it during his air show performances.

the air pressure that's created by the plane's air speed. The high loads generated during this style of flying can rip an airplane apart when control surfaces flutter, and that can strip out the gears in your "standard" servo setup.

Another option for making your control surfaces more durable is to rig each one up with a dual-servo setup on the surface. For example, you could put one on each side of the rudder as well as one on each bottom panel of the elevator and ailerons. Anything less is suicide in giant-scale circles.

RADIOS

When you set your radio for hot-dogging, I suggest that you use a transmitter that's at least equipped with dual rates. I prefer it because it gives me added extension on my control-surface throws. While flying on low rates, I can make my airplane as

docile as a newborn pup; but when I kick in the highs—watch out! My plane has suddenly turned into a pit bull with an attitude.

Because they're becoming more popular at flying sites, let's briefly touch on programmable radios. They offer an exciting option over standard radio systems because they enable you to fly maneuvers while mixing out the airplane's otherwise inherently bad tendencies, such as pitching to the belly (tucking under) or rolling out with the rudder. Manual transmitters aren't equipped with this nifty self-correcting feature.

BALANCING

Now for one last thing with regard to your airplane's ability to handle hot-dog maneuvers: where do you set up your plane's center of gravity (CG)? Finding

the ideal CG for hot-dogging will take some experimentation on your part. Obviously, most airplanes come with the CG problem somewhat resolved by their designers. This is usually adequate for knocking around the sky. For the hot-dog jockey, things will have to be changed to some degree.

If you position the CG forward of the recommended spot, your airplane will be more stable on the upside of its performance envelope, but sluggish on the downside.

If you move the CG aft of the recommended spot, your control surfaces will become sensitized, thereby enhancing the plane's handling characteristics. The only drawback to the aft CG location is that your plane will be less stable.

Keep pushing the CG around until you find an ideal spot that offers the most versatility in freestyle and hot-dog aerobatics.

ENGINES

We have covered just about everything you can do to make your airplane stand up on end. The last item on our hot-dogging preflight checklist is the engine. Depending on how you use it, your engine can be a killer or a lifesaver. Therefore, I suggest that you hang a good, reliable engine that has lots of power on your plane's firewall. Ideally, you should use one that has a 2:1 power-to-weight ratio. Otherwise, you'll be forced to make up for your plane's sluggish handling by coaxing it through maneuvers with increased air speed.

As for propping the engine, I usually go with a large-diameter propeller that has a little pitch. This provides optimum rpm with added thrust, but it does sacrifice speed. After all, nothing beats brute power for getting out of trouble.

The fuel that you use is important to your engine's performance. Glow fuel (or methanol) wins hands down for me because its chemical makeup is more stable than those of gasoline and alcohol. If reliability is your so-called copilot through this whole hot-dogging ordeal, why not stay with the best that money can buy?

PSYCHING UP

During your hot-dogging apprenticeship, you'll discover that it's necessary to push yourself past your own "comfort zone," so to speak. This takes lots of practice, along with a few hits and near misses. Make the best of this learning experience. Push yourself beyond this zone. A good way to begin is to continually slow your plane down until it reaches its stall zone. Then correct the stall, and remember which

BASIC STALL TURN

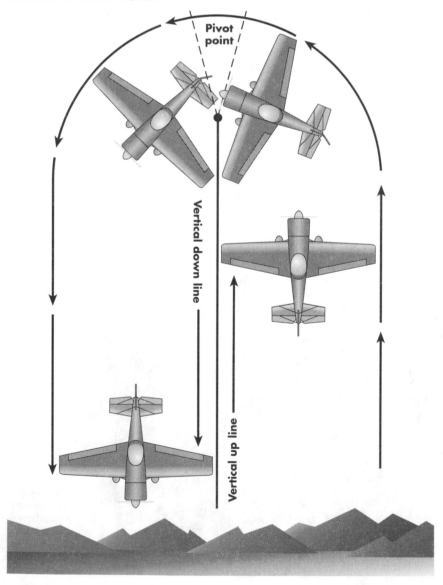

Pivot point

Vertical down line

Vertical up line

FOUR-POINT HAMMERHEAD TURN

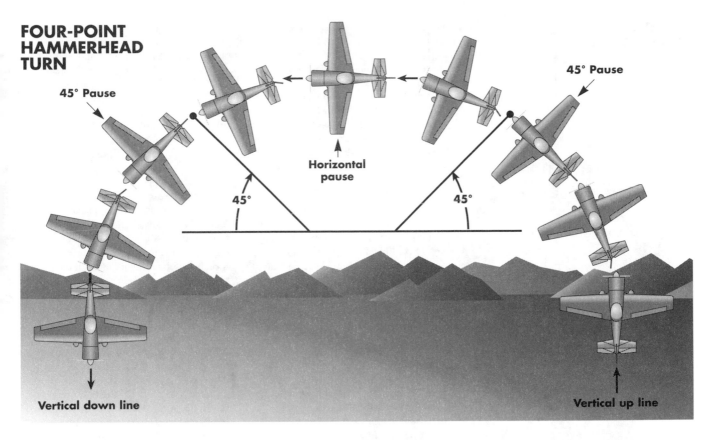

45° Pause

45° Pause

Horizontal pause

45°

45°

Vertical down line

Vertical up line

inputs you used. Stall it in the upright; stall it in the inverted; and stall it in the knife-edge, too. Know when and where it quits flying. You won't be sorry in the end.

Before you begin to practice the maneuvers I'll go over next, always remember to loosen up before doing hot-dog maneuvers. Do a few rolls, loops and whatever else you've learned along the way. Do variations of each. Change your approaches from left to right, and then reverse them. You'll be surprised at how quickly you'll pick up the basics of these maneuvers. Practice them until they are as automatic as driving your car.

MANEUVERS

Basically, hot-dog maneuvers are offshoots of precision aerobatics; the only difference is that you cluster several moves into one to give your routine a livelier quality. In reality, this is what hot-dogging is about: action and reaction. So, let's begin.

◆ **Stall turns.** The stall turn is the most basic move in freestyle aerobatics. In fact, it was probably the first risky aerobatic maneuver you learned. No matter how poorly you do it, you'll eventually master it, and you'll even cut out that nasty flopping over in the top of the maneuver. A well-executed stall turn consists of nothing more than pulling your airplane up the vertical axis with your elevator input,

allowing it to slow "just enough," then throwing some rudder into it. This rudder action pivots it back down the same vertical axis along which it climbed.

In short, the key is to stay on the vertical line going up, pivot around without flying over the top, and come back down the same vertical line. Flying over the top can be remedied by cutting back on the throttle until the plane slows down and then throwing in your rudder input. A short blast on the throttle is also helpful in pivoting the tail over the top.

Another approach to the stall turn is to realign yourself with the airplane and fly it "dead ahead" in front of you instead of down at either end of the flying field. With this new reference point established, you'll be able to rotate the airplane directly in front of you so that its top is facing ¼ turn to the right or left of you on the vertical line. Next, kick the rudder over until the airplane pivots onto its side and stops in a horizontal attitude (much like a knife-edge); then apply opposite rudder to stop the plane's momentum. After that, throw your initial rudder input back in. This will send the plane back down the same vertical line as you used for your climb. All this rudder action at the end should give you a squared-off stall turn.

A third way to do this maneuver is to fly it in the 4-point segments. With this approach, you kick the rudder in just before

the airplane comes to a stop in the climb and then kick it in a second time. This second pop makes the airplane track off the vertical at a 45-degree angle. Use the same rudder input a third time to put the plane horizontal. Hit the rudder input a fourth time, and the plane will pivot down out of the horizontal at a 45-degree angle. Kick the rudder input one last time, and you should head back down the vertical line.

With all this rudder action, you should have created a pattern in which your stall turn resembles half an octagon. Just remember, when you use this method, maintain identical rudder inputs in all four segments. A few words of caution: when you attempt any of these variations on the stall turn, be sure to start with plenty of altitude built into the maneuver, because the ground has a way of coming up fast.

◆ **Vertical rolls.** Another maneuver that air-show crowds love is the vertical roll. Like the stall turn, this move is done by flying up the vertical axis. The concept behind the vertical roll is deception; the airplane appears to be doing more than it actually is. This is done by using the best attributes of both the airplane and the radio. The airplane should have optimum power for going ballistic, while the radio should be outfitted with rate differentials. If your plane's power is less than adequate, you can compensate by clicking on

FOUR-POINT VERTICAL ROLL

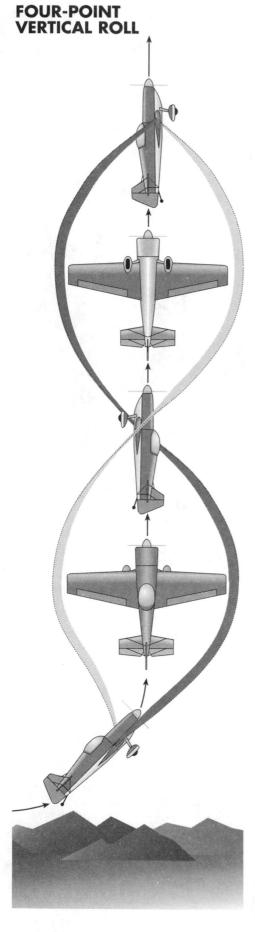

your high rate. You'll not only generate more rolls in the vertical, but you'll also make the airplane appear to be doing more than it actually is. This is where the deception comes in.

A simple exercise to practice this is alternately rolling one way and then the other going up the vertical line as well as coming down it. Once again, make sure you have enough clearance at the bottom to recover.

Vertical rolls can also be done in a variety of combinations, including 4- and 8-point segments. A good warm-up exercise is to roll your plane going up as well as coming down. Mix combinations until you're proficient at exiting the maneuver at your desired heading. After a while, you'll get the hang of it. In addition, it isn't necessary to keep the roll going up and out of sight into the clouds. A stall at the top provides a nice recovery when you fly out of the top of a 4-point vertical roll. Another escape route is to push or pull the airplane back over the top and end the maneuver straight and level.

In my opinion, vertical rolls are easier than all the other rolling maneuvers because fighting gravity is easier than flying the horizontal line that dominates the rest of aerobatic flying. Another advantage is that they don't use as much area in the hot-dog box as horizontal maneuvers. The payoff here is that everything happens right in front of you.

◆ **Knife-edges.** Now I'll discuss knife-edge circles and rolling circles. Basically, if you can do a knife-edge circle, a rolling circle will be no big deal. Because I touched on the knife-edge concept when I discussed the stall turn and the rudder throw that's used to hold it, there's only one more thing to cover: steering with your airplane's elevator. Otherwise, everything else stays the same. It sounds scary, especially when the plane is coming at you around that fourth quadrant. Nonetheless, this is about as complicated as the knife-edge circle gets. Because you have this maneuver under control, let's move on to the rolling circle.

◆ **Rolling circles.** These are the most difficult of all horizontal maneuvers because you are constantly changing inputs on the sticks. An easy way to break into a rolling circle is to start out by flying a knife-edge circle. There are only two approaches to setting up the knife-edge circle. These will evolve into a sequence of rolls. First, establish whether you will push the airplane around the circle from right to left or pull it around from the opposite direction.

Also, it isn't uncommon for beginners to play it safe and fly in one direction using only their elevator inputs. All they're really doing is randomly steering around the circle and adding rolls without any rudder input whatsoever. This tactic usually produces a rolling circle with about 30 or 40 rolls in rapid succession, and it looks out of sync with regard to timing. This is fine at first, but sooner or later, you have to push yourself to mix rudder into each roll.

I prefer to use the rudder, elevator and ailerons to finesse the airplane around the circle. This allows me to execute the same number of rolls in each quarter (or half circle) to give the maneuver a smoother look by effectively mixing all three control surfaces.

One of the most deceptive rolling circles is that in which the airplane makes just one roll within the circle. It looks difficult because it seems as though you're fighting the airplane all the way around the circle when, in fact, you aren't. You are really doing nothing more than flying a standard left turn for the first quarter of the circle. After your plane has completed the first quadrant of the circle, turn it up on the knife-edge by inputting full right rudder. It's worth noting that the full right rudder and the elevator are working together here by skidding the airplane around the rear of the circle when the plane is inverted. At this point, you neutralize the rudder back to zero, and begin the left-hand inverted turn in the third quadrant. Now, throw in the left rudder and down-elevator during the third quadrant of the circle, and then ease out the down-elevator while you add a little up-elevator to bring the airplane back around to its point of origin. As difficult as this may sound, this hot-dog maneuver's bark is worse than its bite. One last thing before moving on to the snap roll: if you do the slow rolling circle to the outside, just reverse all your inputs on the control surfaces.

◆ **Snap rolls.** Snap rolls are those jumpy moves that, on the one hand, suspend the action but, on the other, add to it. In a snap roll, your airplane is thrown into a set of violent twists, rolls and other nondescript gyrations.

The easiest snap roll is a single one that starts and ends in the upright position. Confused? Don't be. Here's an easy tip to remember for doing a snap roll. Always lead your snap roll with the elevator (before you throw your other sticks in with this maneuver). This goes for both the inside and the outside versions.

Leading with the elevator eliminates the downward pitching motion in the plane after it has recovered and exited the snap. Actually, the airplane's nose should be level or tilted up somewhat to enable you to resume level flight without losing altitude. The elevator trick also helps when you do a 1½ snap roll; it prolongs the airplane's level flight as it exits horizontally. You can do variations on the snap roll by stopping the roll in the knife-edge, but remember: plan your rudder inputs so you're ready when the airplane stops snapping.

◆ **Spins.** Spins are nothing more than vertical snap rolls in which the airplane has been stalled out completely before it spirals toward the ground. Whether it's an upright or an inverted spin makes little difference. Because you lose altitude rapidly, the most critical point is the exit point. In exiting a spin, you need to neutralize all your controls. Then add opposite rudder to stop the rotation and down-elevator to get your wing flying again. This will allow the plane's rotation to stop and its nose to drop, and it will give it enough air speed to fly out at the bottom.

Upright and inverted spins are basically the same, with the exception of a few minor inputs on the controls. One of the easiest ways to go into an inverted flat spin is to go into a regular inverted spin.

ROLLING CIRCLE

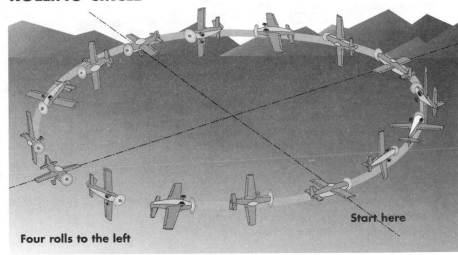

Four rolls to the left

Start here

Once the airplane has started spinning, cross-control it with the ailerons until the airplane flattens out on its back. In a sense, your ailerons pick up one wingtip, and that makes the airplane flatten out and slows its deceleration even more. Don't forget, you're still running full throttle, and you've still got full down-elevator and rudder in. If, by chance, you have too much aileron, the airplane will roll out in the other direction. Don't forget that the CG is farther back. This makes executing spins a lot easier, plus it beefs up your airplane's other handling characteristics.

◆ **Lomcevaks.** This is the most talked about maneuver in the world of R/C aerobatics. Everybody is in awe of this "sleight of hand" work on the sticks. I do not have the space here to go into all the ways in which this end-over-end, tumbling maneuver can be done; therefore, I'll simplify things.

When you enter a Lomcevak, start the maneuver with a left (or right) snap roll; rotate the plane 1½ times with ailerons, elevator and rudder inputs in the inside-snap-roll position, then throw in full down-elevator. This radical up/down-

KNIFE-EDGE CIRCLE

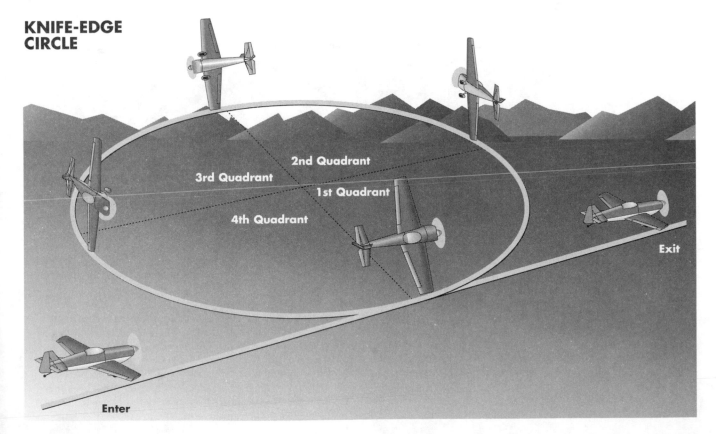

2nd Quadrant

3rd Quadrant

1st Quadrant

4th Quadrant

Exit

Enter

elevator input will literally cause the airplane's tail to swing over the top while the nose pitches into a downward tumble. If your airplane is slightly tail-heavy with lots of control-surface throw, your Lomcevak should resemble a tumbling, outside corkscrew, which is exactly what we are working toward here.

Also, you can up the ante on your airplane's ability to go into a Lomcevak by pushing its CG even farther back and increasing the control-surface throws even more. With this enhancement, your airplane will become extremely active during the "up" side of the Lomcevak move. One problem does exist with this enhancement: it inadvertently hinders the airplane's ability to perform other maneuvers. So make a plan before you go for such extreme setup measures.

◆ **Torque rolls.** The torque roll is the granddaddy of all hot-dog maneuvers. Everybody wants to know how to do it! Yet most pilots have a tough time maintaining their airplane dangling against the thrust generated by its own propeller in a vertical position.

A few additional matters must be covered before you attempt a torque roll:
• Make sure that, with the exception of the ailerons, your radio's high rates are on.
• On the firewall, mount enough power to swing a large-diameter prop that will

ONE INSIDE ROLLING CIRCLE TO THE LEFT

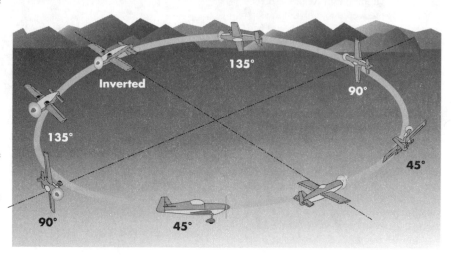

gives the most thrust. With these conditions met, the airplane should be nearly ready to torque roll on its own. All you need to do now is to bring your piloting skills up to speed.

When you enter a torque roll, the key is to be able to simultaneously pull the airplane up and slow it down so that the tail is directly beneath the nose. This attitude is critical because, if you don't do it, the airplane will wander aimlessly above with little hope of remaining in the vertical axis. Throws and inputs won't help at this stage of the maneuver, so fly out, and try

it. I call this the "zone" where everything comes together effortlessly.

Sometimes, when your plane hangs on the vertical axis, it may wander or have its tail blown out from under it. Then what do you do? I jump on the rudder and elevator inputs so that I can get the airplane back into that so-called zone quickly; otherwise, the maneuver dies a quick death. How can its pilot stay with an airplane when its top gets turned around to the other side?

For many, confusion seems to reign here. One remedy is to imagine yourself

SNAP ROLL

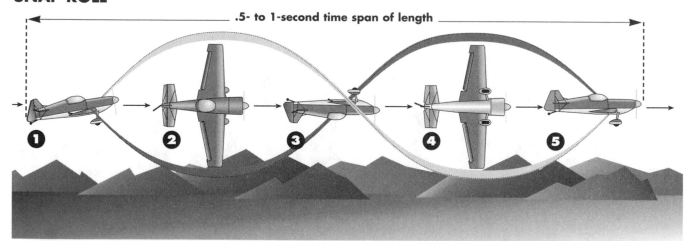

1. Pitch nose up with up-elevator to prevent loss of altitude. 2. Add aileron and rudder. 3-4. Right aileron and rudder while still holding up-elevator. 5. Exit straight and level (relax controls).

allow your plane to hover in the vertical (just as the rotor blades do for a helicopter). The big propeller also adds stability to the torque roll by acting like a gyro, which helps to keep the tail under the airplane.
• Learn where your engine's peak power ratio resides and which throttle setting

it again. Often, you'll know a particular torque roll will be successful because of certain cues from the sticks and the airplane's behavior. The airplane will actually begin to rotate in the stationary attitude on its own axis without climbing or falling in the vertical line. When it reaches this point, little stick input is needed to maintain

sitting in the cockpit and visualize the inputs that would be necessary if you were on the other side. You can practice this even while you watch television. Eventually, you'll master this maneuver to the point at which you won't even think about it; it will almost like being on automatic pilot.

Another problem that plagues fliers who are learning torque rolls is that they have trouble keeping up with the airplane's rotation. An easy fix is to isolate and correct the problem with one control surface at a time and to keep control inputs to a minimum. Pure and simple: make one correction at a time, and see what happens.

Assuming you already have your airplane hanging as stationary as can be, remember that inputting ailerons is a waste of time. At this point, they are virtually ineffective, unless they extend inward next to the fuselage—something that isn't seen too often in giant-scale airplanes.

OK, you have your aircraft hovering, pointing straight up. Its torquing or rotating action is not caused by your input on the control surfaces, but by the twisting force—or torque—generated by the engine. If the airplane comes back down through its own propwash a bit, it will pivot around the vertical axis at a faster rate. This effect can be slowed down by adding more power on the throttle so the airplane climbs again and its roll rate slows. This move comes in handy when the airplane is descending faster than you feel comfortable with. Don't forget: power is your best friend when you do torque rolls. My only other suggestion is to get out and practice until you've mastered this maneuver and all the others discussed here.

AIR SHOWS AND FLIGHT DEMONSTRATIONS

People just love air shows; they're real crowd pleasers, no matter where you go. Giant-scale flight demos really get the crowd rocking—just like their full-scale counterparts. Many groups (fliers and non-fliers) invite me to show off my ability in the daredevil world of hot-dogging—R/C style. These people don't come to R/C air shows to watch guys fly straight and level. They want the hot stuff with all the fixings, so give them what they came for—action!

When you're proficient at hot-dogging, you should still be aware of a few artistic matters before you go out on the road and put on your own version of a hot-dogger's "show of shows." By artistic, I mean the music. Music makes the soul soar, and it

can make your performance soar. The type of music you incorporate isn't as important as your own personalized program of self-expression set to music. It will certainly make your performance memorable.

When I fly a hot-dogging show, I go for a good selection of "music to fly by"—something people are familiar with, or at

least recognize. For example, in my hot-dog demos, I orchestrate several songs into one medley for a full flight segment. I begin with a slow song, move along to a more upbeat tempo and finish with a beat that gets the crowd jumping. I look at music as the sizzle that "sells" the performance. The music really makes me fly

THE SPIN

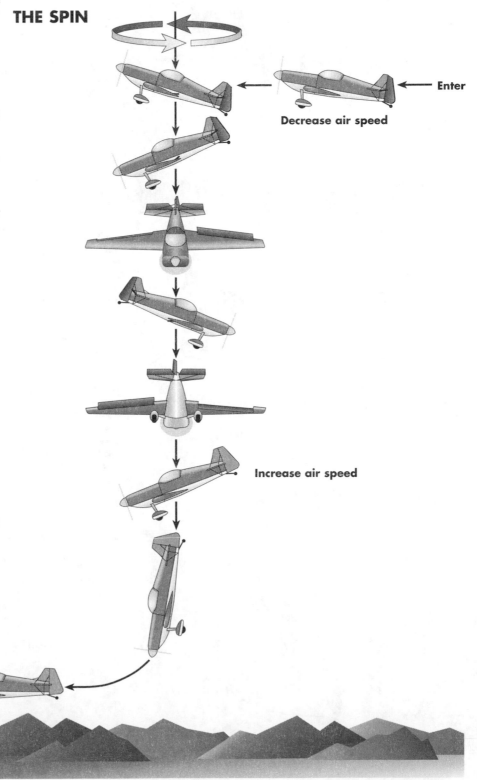

Enter

Decrease air speed

Increase air speed

Exit

LOMCEVAK
Traditional entry

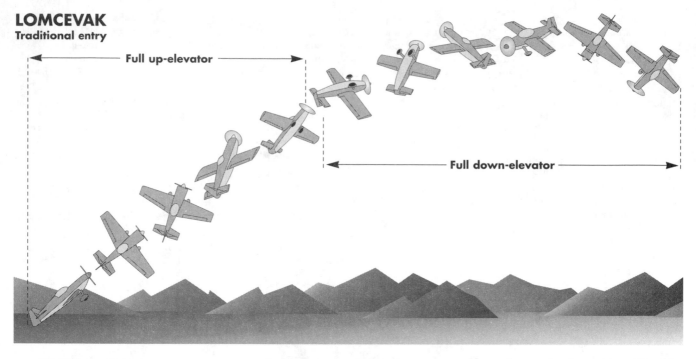

Full up-elevator

Full down-elevator

TORQUE ROLL

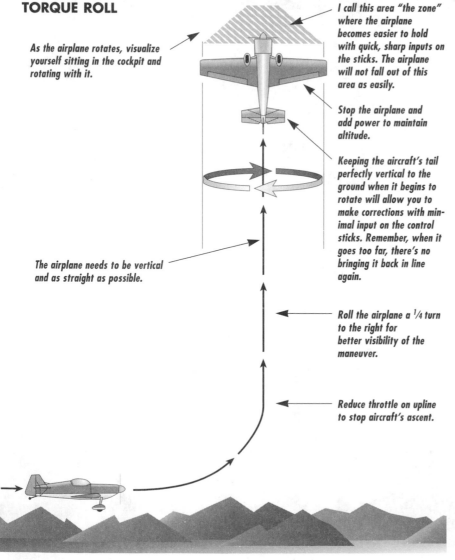

As the airplane rotates, visualize yourself sitting in the cockpit and rotating with it.

I call this area "the zone" where the airplane becomes easier to hold with quick, sharp inputs on the sticks. The airplane will not fall out of this area as easily.

Stop the airplane and add power to maintain altitude.

Keeping the aircraft's tail perfectly vertical to the ground when it begins to rotate will allow you to make corrections with minimal input on the control sticks. Remember, when it goes too far, there's no bringing it back in line again.

The airplane needs to be vertical and as straight as possible.

Roll the airplane a ¼ turn to the right for better visibility of the maneuver.

Reduce throttle on upline to stop aircraft's ascent.

better, because I'm interpreting and making my own variations on it.

Choreographed flying can be fun, especially when you keep your maneuvers in rhythm with the song—one smooth act that flows from takeoff to landing. I guess it's a lot like rubbing your head, patting your stomach and keeping beat with your feet all at the same time. This is a real challenge for the flier who has done everything and is looking for something beyond traditional precision work.

Looking to the future of hot-dogging—or freestyle flying, as it's sometimes called—I feel it will continue to grow. Competitions are popping up all across the land. The Tournament of Champions freestyle competition literally stole the show in 1994. It's here to stay; it's one of many avenues in model aviation that offer a thrill a second for the public as well as for the flier who ventures into this arena of high-risk flying. ◆

ABOUT THE AUTHOR
Frank Noll Jr.

Frank learned to fly 31 years ago at the age of seven. Since then, he has come to be known as one of the premier pilots in the United States. His talent has taken him to events in places such as Puerto Rico, Canada and Costa Rica. He is currently the president and owner of Eagle Aviation, which produces some of this country's finest R/C aerobatic aircraft. He has recently been named the associate vice president for AMA District III. He has done hundreds of demos at air shows across the country, thrilling audiences everywhere. Frank has been married for 15 years and has a 14-year-old son, Jason.

CHAPTER 15

The Art of Low-Power Aerobatics

by Keith Shaw

At any air show, you'll see many styles of flying. The public's favorites always seem to be the speed, thunder and close-quarter flying of the jet teams and the brutal precision of planes such as the Pitts, Laser, Extra and Sukhoi as they effortlessly perform intricate dances, without any apparent regard for gravity. My favorite acts, however, are those by stock or slightly modified "standard" aircraft flown on meager power, but still doing excellent aerobatics. I know that I am watching a real pilot who uses finely honed skills and senses to push the plane to the limit in pursuit of performance. My heroes include Bill Barber, Art Scholl, Duane Cole and Bob Hoover, so it should be no surprise that I try to emulate them when I fly replicas of their aircraft. This type of flying requires quite a different mind set from the usual one; you spend much more time "listening" to your plane than demanding that it follow your commands. Controls are squeezed rather than slammed, while everything possible is done to minimize drag; and, surprisingly, gravity becomes a very important *ally!*

While I find the pursuit of efficiency in aerobatics extremely gratifying in its own right, there are other reasons to learn these techniques. I've seen many a crash at a crowded, noisy airfield because the pilot didn't know his engine had quit. If the pilot had been paying attention to his aircraft's speed or handling characteristics instead of to the engine noise, a safe dead-stick landing could have saved the plane. For competition fliers, a crucial flight score might be salvaged even with a bad engine run. Electric fliers will gain great rewards,

because efficient flying can dramatically reduce power consumption and extend flight time.

The biggest benefit, however, will be in learning to be a better pilot. After a while, the continuing observation of the subtle visual cues and control interactions will become second nature as you develop a "feel" for the aircraft. At that point, the loop is complete, and you are now a real pilot, completely unaware of the transmitter in your hands.

A LITTLE BIT OF PHYSICS

Please, don't be frightened! I promise not to snow you under with any equations, but there are just a couple of concepts to be discussed.

◆ **The balance of forces.** I think everyone has seen the sketch of an airplane in level flight when lift equals weight and thrust matches drag (see Figure 1). Though this is pretty simplistic, it will serve for our purposes. Assuming the

BALANCE OF FORCES

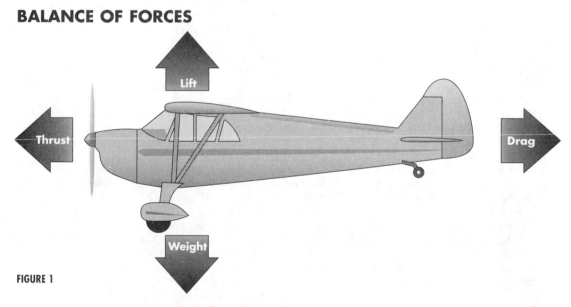

FIGURE 1

plane is in level flight, an increase in thrust will cause an acceleration, and the speed will increase until the drag rises to just equal the thrust. At this point, the forces are once again in balance, only the plane is flying somewhat faster. If the lift is increased, either by an increase in camber or an increase in the angle of attack, the plane will climb, or it could be made to carry more weight in level flight.

Unfortunately, things aren't this simple. The balance-of-forces concept implies that there is no interaction between the lift/weight and the thrust/drag components. The drag that most people think

especially near stall, induced drag can dramatically affect how a plane handles.

◆ **Conservation of energy**—the other physics lesson, and it's probably the most important tenet in flying aerobatics. A plane's potential energy is related to the height it is flying above the ground, while its kinetic energy is a function of speed.

surfaces are moved off neutral, they do not deflect the air as most people think, but they change the airfoil's camber, thereby changing the lift coefficient and unfortunately, the induced drag. If a plane has any warps, most modelers just offset the appropriate control surface. This causes induced trim drag, so it's much better to remove the warps. Similarly, if the plane

CENTER OF GRAVITY TEST

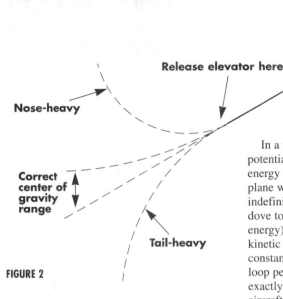

Release elevator here

30°

Nose-heavy

Correct center of gravity range

Tail-heavy

FIGURE 2

about is called *"form drag"*; it includes bulky fuselages, rigging, struts, exposed landing gear and engine cylinders. This type of drag gets worse as speed increases, and it's the major force that limits an airplane's top speed.

The "hidden" drag is called *induced* drag, and it's the penalty incurred in exchange for lift. The total lift of a wing (or any flying surface, for that matter) is dependent on its area, air speed and the airfoil's coefficient of lift (basically, a measure of how hard the airfoil must work to produce lift). The harder it has to work, the higher the lift coefficient and, unfortunately, the higher the induced drag. When a plane is flying fast, the necessary lift coefficient is quite low, so the induced drag is also low. That's why most pylon racers have very low-cambered airfoils—usually, just enough to produce the necessary extra lift for a turn. At low speeds, however, induced drag is the dominant type of drag, because the airfoil has to work very hard to create lift. To get the most efficient glide possible, sailplane designers go to excruciating lengths to choose and construct a wing that will produce the best lift-to-drag ratio. So we see that our lift force in the balance picture is coupled with the thrust/drag relationship. At slow speeds,

In a perfect world without drag, the potential energy added to the kinetic energy would be a constant. This perfect plane would fly at a constant altitude indefinitely, without needing a motor. If it dove to lose altitude (decrease in potential energy), it would gain speed (increased kinetic energy) to keep the total energy constant. It would roll effortlessly and loop perfectly, and entry speed would be exactly the exit speed. For an un-powered aircraft in the real world, however, drag acts as an energy siphon that gradually decreases the plane's total energy. To even maintain a constant air speed, it would have to slowly lose altitude, and the extra drag of aerobatics would lead to even more altitude loss. As an example, a loop could be performed in two ways: by exiting at the same altitude and a lower air speed, or at a slightly lower altitude with the same air speed. But by allowing this slight altitude loss, a properly trimmed and flown glider can do *any* aerobatic maneuver. If we install a small power system that can just replace the energy lost owing to drag, our plane can maintain altitude and perform aerobatics. With even more power, it could gain altitude and still hold a given air speed. Of course, we could get silly and become a Sukhoi, with enough horsepower to reach terminal speed while going straight up! But rather than solving the problem with excessive energy input, we can get much of the same effect by learning to control and minimize drag and, thus, reduce our energy requirements.

CONTROLLING DRAG

On a scale airplane, little can be done to reduce form drag, but there are several ways to reduce induced drag. As control

is not laterally balanced (one wing is heavy), it will require aileron and rudder trim to compensate, and, of course, this means unwanted drag. So that less control throw is needed, I also always seal the hinge line on all control surfaces to make them more aerodynamically efficient.

A very major source of drag comes from having an incorrect center of gravity—usually too nose-heavy. A nose-heavy plane has to carry up-elevator trim to maintain longitudinal stability. This means that the stabilizer is lifting downward, and that creates some induced trim drag. But what's worse is that the wing must now develop even more lift to maintain level flight—incurring even more drag! A little longitudinal stability is desirable for comfortable flying, but most kits and plans are highly over-stabilized.

Test your plane for correct CG using the following method (see Figure 2):
◆ Fly at half throttle and adjust the elevator trim until the plane can maintain hands-off level flight. Check this by making several passes without changing the throttle. You should be flying at an altitude of 100 to 150 feet.
◆ When the plane is nearing center stage, gently push it into a 30-degree dive, and hold it until the air speed has increased noticeably. At this point, take your hand off the stick and observe what happens.
◆ If the plane pulls up sharply, it's very nose-heavy. If it continues in the dive or pulls up slightly, its CG is just right. If it tries to tuck under, it's tail-heavy.

A bunch of extra advantages come with having a correct CG location. The amount of elevator throw necessary for any maneuver will decrease, and that will mean less control drag. There will be virtually no need for downthrust, which is an inept attempt to "fix" an over-stabilized aircraft's tendency to nose up as power is increased.

Another source of induced drag comes from trying to convince the wing to roll. Every method works by differentially changing the lift of the wing panels. Standard ailerons deflect to increase the camber (and lift) on one panel and decrease it on the other. Of course, the change in lift also causes a change in induced drag. The problem is that the drag force creates a yaw in the opposite direction to the roll; this is known as "adverse yaw." Imagine a right roll, in which the right wing aileron goes up (decreasing lift and drag) and the left wing aileron goes down (increasing lift and drag), producing a *right* roll but a *left* yaw. If the plane is flying fast and/or has a long fuselage or a large fin, the effect is minimal. But for a slow flying plane with large wings and a short-coupled fuselage, this adverse yaw can be strong enough to turn it in the wrong direction! Not only that, the yaw also swings the fuselage out of the flight path, causing a huge increase in drag. A vast amount of effort has gone into trying to tame this demon—using tricks such as differential aileron throw; aileron/rudder coupling; specially shaped ailerons that put out a drag-increasing "foot" on the up-going motion; and various spoilers and yaw flaps. The glitch is that all of these

envelope includes speeds just barely above stall, such as near the top of a loop or Immelmann. Before performing such maneuvers, it's best to practice slow flight to learn how the plane's handling characteristics change. Most modelers think that flying near stall speed is inviting certain disaster, but in truth, most planes are quite benign. Of course, extremely high wing loadings, warped wings and poorly crafted airfoils can degrade the stall handling characteristics.

To begin, fly at 150 to 200 feet while practicing a racetrack or lazy figure-8 pattern, and gradually decrease the power on each pass. Several things will become apparent at well above stall speed. Aileron authority will diminish and become sloppy, and adverse yaw will be much more noticeable, but fortunately, rudder control will usually stay solid all the way down to stall.

If the ailerons become too sloppy, try flying with rudder. Some planes, particularly those with barn-door ailerons, may experience "aileron reversal" at slow speed. What happens is that for a right-aileron turn, the down-going surface on the left wing panel effectively pushes the airfoil past stall. The loss of lift drops the left tip, making it seem to roll to the *left*.

elevator can be applied to return to level flight. With some practice, a plane can be flown continuously and carefully in a partial stall condition, usually with a little more power to compensate for the high induced drag.

As you become more confident, you'll appreciate the value of flying coordinated rudder to control adverse yaw, because you'll be able to turn and maneuver at much lower speeds. Flying lower will help to set these skills. It is also beneficial to do the same training inverted, particularly to help suppress the panic up-elevator response. Recovering from an inverted stall is almost the same as flying right side up, but you use slight *up*-elevator to get out of the stall.

Another anomaly occurs when trying to climb at slow speed: the plane tries to yaw to the left and needs right-rudder correction. This happens to any single-engine airplane with a right-handed-rotation propeller. This is *not* due to torque, gyroscopic precession, or circular airflow, but to an effect called the "P-factor." When a plane is in a slow-speed climb, the entire airplane—including the engine shaft—is at a high angle of attack. The descending propeller blade on the right side of the center line is at a higher angle of attack than the ascending blade, so it produces more thrust. This offsets the prop thrust to the right of the center line and yaws the plane to the left. When tail-draggers veer to the left on takeoff, it's because of the P-factor.

Kit designers try to help by building right thrust into the engine mount in an attempt to counteract the P-factor. But the yaw force is to the *right* when the plane is inverted, so the built-in right thrust just makes the problem worse, and it would require a lot of drag-producing left-rudder correction to overcome it. Understanding the source of these forces and learning to give the correct control inputs result in lower overall drag through maneuvers.

ENTRY AIR SPEED FOR LOOPS

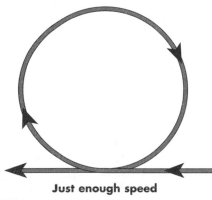

Just enough speed

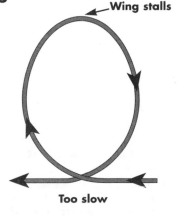

Wing stalls

Too slow

FIGURE 3

methods only help for upright flight, but they severely worsen the problem when a plane is inverted. The all-around best method is to learn to fly coordinated rudder, keeping the fuselage in line with the flight path and drag to a minimum.

PRACTICING SLOW FLIGHT

When a fast, highly powered aircraft performs aerobatics, it is usually well above stall speed. Snap rolls, Lomcevaks and other violent contortions are generated by forcing a high-speed wing stall. But for low-powered airplanes, the usable speed

My Gee Bee R-1 is notorious for this, so once it's turned onto final and begins to slow down, I never touch the ailerons, but fly it strictly on rudder.

Just above stall, elevator control fades, and the forward speed will rapidly drop owing to the very strong induced drag (high lift coefficient means high drag); the plane will mush forward and lose altitude. Stall recovery is best effected by applying slight down-elevator and increasing the power gradually. This decreases the induced drag and allows the wing to start lifting again, after which gradual up-

SIMPLE AEROBATICS

All basic maneuvers with the same entry and exit altitude—including loops, rolls, point rolls, figure-8s and stall turns—can be done with little horsepower. The only limitation is that the air speed must not drop below stall speed anywhere in the maneuver. A nice, round loop requires an entry speed of about twice stall speed. Higher entry speeds allow an increase in loop diameter. An entry speed that's too low will result in a stall, which makes a loop out of round at the top (the classic "Cub" loop is an example of this; see Figure 3). It's important to control the

AXIAL ROLL FOR GLIDERS

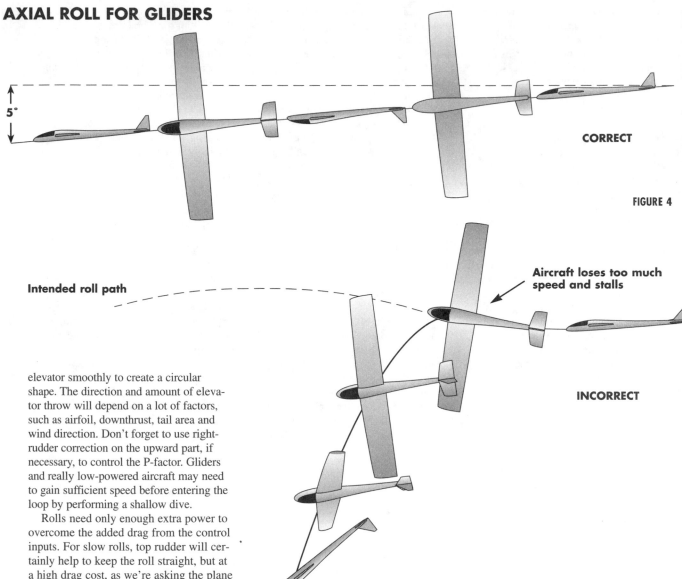

5°

CORRECT

FIGURE 4

Intended roll path

Aircraft loses too much speed and stalls

INCORRECT

FIGURE 5

elevator smoothly to create a circular shape. The direction and amount of elevator throw will depend on a lot of factors, such as airfoil, downthrust, tail area and wind direction. Don't forget to use right-rudder correction on the upward part, if necessary, to control the P-factor. Gliders and really low-powered aircraft may need to gain sufficient speed before entering the loop by performing a shallow dive.

Rolls need only enough extra power to overcome the added drag from the control inputs. For slow rolls, top rudder will certainly help to keep the roll straight, but at a high drag cost, as we're asking the plane to knife-edge in the first and third quadrants. Knife-edge flying is done with the wings vertical while using the fuselage as the wing—certainly a spectacular but very high-drag configuration!

Try to resist the urge to pull the nose of the plane above the horizon with rudder. Smaller corrections will still help, but they'll create much less drag. In point rolls, it's important to gently squeeze the aileron controls to prevent adverse yaw from starting a yaw oscillation. This not only looks bad, but it's also very difficult to damp out. The aileron input should be more like a sine wave than a set of staccato pulses. For gliders and very low-powered planes, the loss of energy caused by control drag may be offset by performing the roll on a shallow downward line (usually no more than 5 degrees; see Figure 4). Do not pull the nose of the plane above the horizon at any part of the roll, because the drag could increase so quickly that air

speed will drop below stall speed, and the plane will literally fall out of the sky (see Figure 5).

Cuban-8s can be done by allowing an altitude loss of about 5 feet on each half to compensate for the control losses. Even a pattern judge would have a difficult time spotting this loss. For stall turns, smoothly transition into the vertical and leave the engine at full power, not only to get the best possible height, but also to maintain rudder effectiveness. After the yaw has been initiated, the power can be reduced if you want to slow the descent.

◆ **Snap rolls** create very high drag and must be done carefully. The controls are easy: full up-elevator and aileron and rudder in the same direction for an inside snap; down-elevator and *crossed* aileron

and rudder for an outside snap. The tricky part is gauging the correct entry speed. If the entry speed is too high, the maneuver will look like a half barrel roll and a half snap. If it is too slow, the snap will quickly degrade into a spin. Even when this is done correctly, the plane will exit at a speed just above stall at which the controls are mushy. To stop the snap with the wings level, neutralize the controls, and then add opposite rudder and a little down-elevator.

For multiple snap rolls, the drag will keep increasing, so power will have to be added to prevent the plane from transitioning into a spin. If a snap roll is incorporated into another maneuver, such as the avalanche (loop with a snap at the top), a higher entry speed will be needed to prevent the snap roll from dropping the air speed too much and causing the loop to become asymmetric (see Figure 6).

◆ **Spins** are easy to do: at partial power, approach a stall, then add in up-elevator and rudder and ailerons in the same direction. If all you get is a spiral, try putting in rudder first, and when you see the yaw, add full up-elevator. When the wingtip stalls, dump in the ailerons. Some aircraft will spin without needing ailerons, but I find that the entry and exit are much more unpredictable and sloppy. Spin exit usually just requires that you release the controls, let the nose drop, gradually add power and return to level flight. If it's a little stubborn, keep the aileron and elevator neutralized, but feed in some rudder in the direction opposite the spin. When rotation ceases, add power and continue with the normal exit. Inverted spins are done similarly, but with down-elevator and the aileron and rudder controls crossed. Even gliders can spin, but air speed has to be a little higher because there's no prop blast on the tail. The rudder/elevator/aileron sequence seems to work best.

◆ **Altitude-gaining maneuvers** will always have a lower exit speed than they had at the start. Probably the hardest stunt to do well on low power is the Immelmann. Right when the speed is lowest and the P-factor is strongest, the plane will need to transition into inverted flight and then immediately try to do a half roll! Certainly, some extra entry speed would be very helpful, but the biggest problem is not in doing the half roll, but keeping the heading. Even though the adverse yaw tries to act like top rudder to help maintain altitude, the drag penalty is quite high and, if uncorrected, will pull the plane off heading as it approaches level flight. If we are doing a left half roll, adding some right rudder after the wings pass the vertical position will help keep the heading (see Figure 7). Another way to do the Immelmann involves a little cheating. It's done by doing a little less than a half loop and then starting the roll immediately. The wing will still be under positive G-force, so the adverse yaw will prevent the nose from hanging above the horizon; and it will be in the correct direction to help hold the heading. The nice thing about this method is that it does not require any rudder corrections.

◆ **Vertical roll**—one of the neatest maneuvers (usually considered a "macho-power" maneuver). With enough energy from a dive, even a glider can do one (my own record is *six* vertical rolls with a 2-meter slope glider). Once again, the roll part is relatively easy, but the transition back to level flight requires great care, due to very low air speed and massive P-factor effects from the prop. When pushing the nose down toward level flight, the plane is under substantial negative-G, so you'll need some left rudder to hold the heading. When the plane is level, the elevator must switch smoothly over to up, and because the plane will enter positive-G, the rudder correction has to switch to the right. Trying to hold level flight just above stall speed while trying to keep the heading and letting the plane gain speed is a fine balancing act. The "flub" that can occur is an unwanted spin caused by too low a speed and the up-elevator and right-rudder corrections. No problem! Just release the controls, do a normal spin exit, gain altitude and give it another try.

ENERGY MANAGEMENT

Now that you have practiced the individual maneuvers, it's time to link them into a pleasing air show. Probably the most time- and space-efficient format for aerobatics is

1,000 feet away may be the standard in pattern flying, but they are rarely suitable for scale air shows. The huge maneuvers not only require vast amount of power, but they also take longer to complete, so fewer can be done in a fixed time or energy allotment (such as with electric power). Flying closer with smaller maneuvers can look the same while saving a lot of energy; the only drawback is that errors will be more visible. A good box length is about six times the diameter of a comfortable loop. Some maneuvers can be altered to give the box some depth, but you should practice imagining a barrier on the near edge that *never* allows the plane any closer to the audience.

To make best use of the available energy, try to link maneuvers with matching entry and exit speeds, and practice them as a sequence. An example might be a loop at center stage, a stall turn at the turnaround, then a four-point roll, followed by a half Cuban-8. The result will be that you are in the same position on the same heading with about the same energy.

Another sequence can be created and

EFFECT OF ENTRY SPEED ON THE AVALANCHE

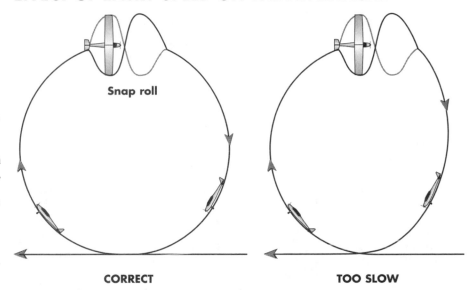

Snap roll

CORRECT

TOO SLOW

FIGURE 6

the "turnaround" layout in which maneuvers are performed at center stage and at both ends of a box. Some maneuvers are naturals for center stage; these include loops, rolls, point rolls, various figure-8s, and any maneuver that does not produce a change in direction. Direction-changing maneuvers, such as the stall turn, the Immelmann, split-S's, or half Cuban-8s, work best at the ends of the box.

The size of the box will depend on the energy available. Huge loops performed

practiced and added to the previous one, until a satisfying air-show routine emerges. If an altitude-gaining maneuver such as an Immelmann is used, the energy in the extra altitude can be invested in diving to get a higher entry speed for the maneuver that follows—a super-slow roll, avalanche, or vertical roll, or on an altitude-losing one—a spin or split-S. If the plane is getting too low, one of the turnaround maneuvers could be replaced with a climbing 180- or 540-degree turn.

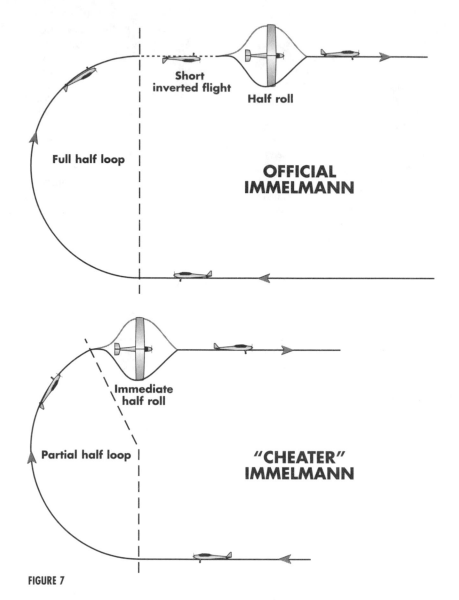

OFFICIAL IMMELMANN

Short inverted flight

Half roll

Full half loop

"CHEATER" IMMELMANN

Immediate half roll

Partial half loop

FIGURE 7

can be blended into the maneuvers themselves. For example, an uncorrected loop in a crosswind becomes a helix, but carefully adding rudder toward the wind will keep it straight. Keep practicing in all types of weather; it will make you a much better pilot.

FINAL THOUGHTS

Well, the path to success in flying low-powered aerobatics is before you. With much practice, careful analysis and diligent effort, you will become a real pilot. At that point, you will also know how to fly any plane in any conditions, as you'll need smaller corrections as power and speed go up.

I hope to see you at the air shows. If you have any comments or questions, you may write to me, but please include an SASE: Keith Shaw, 2756 Elmwood, Ann Arbor, MI 48104.   ◆

ABOUT THE AUTHOR

Keith Shaw

Keith is one of the foremost electric-flight modelers of our time, and his beautiful, scale, electric models have appeared frequently in the modeling press. Keith has been fascinated (some would say obsessed) with flying machines his entire life. After starting with free-flight and control-line models in the early '50s, Keith entered the world of R/C modeling around 1960 using homemade, vacuum-tube radio equipment. In 1975, while competing in pattern, scale and pylon, Keith became interested in electric flight. This interest has grown to dominate his time. He flies in several dozen air shows each summer to demonstrate the advantages of electric flight.

Keith is a senior research scientist at the University of Michigan, where he develops exotic instrumentation to study molecular structure. In his remaining "copious spare time," he enjoys rock 'n' roll and an occasional few hours of sleep.

The last major hurdle will be learning to fly your routine in real-life condtions—invariably crosswind or with heavy turbulence. With low power and speeds, their effects will be much more severe than normal. I suggest that you start with basic slow-flight practice and learn how the wind affects flight characteristics. Although I don't want to get into the "downwind turn" fiasco, I will tell you that making turns in a moving air mass using a plane with a finite acceleration can lead to some *very* exciting flying, so start with a little extra altitude. Under these conditions, I raise my base line for aerobatics by at least 30 feet. In crosswinds, the aerobatic flight line will drift, so corrections will constantly be needed. Initially, the corrections can be applied after each maneuver, but eventually, they

CHAPTER 16

Hotshot Flying— *Stinger* Style

by Stinger Wallace

We all know that model airplanes should be flown safely and, especially, that you should only experiment with one at a safe altitude and with a minimum number of spectators present. I strongly suggest that whenever you experiment and aren't comfortable with your airplane, you should be two, three, or four "mistakes" high so that you don't lose your airplane or cause any damage. Be familiar with your airplane and its flying characteristics. Each plane is different, and you should know what to expect if something goes wrong. My personal feeling is that it doesn't matter how far you have to walk to retrieve your model; it always beats having to rebuild it.

MANEUVERS

I'll cover some of my favorite maneuvers, step by step, in hopes that the information may help those of you who wish to improve your flying skills. I still keep a .40-size, high-performance airplane to help keep my reflexes tuned up. Such a plane is capable of any of the following:

◆ The low inverted pass down the runway. I started doing this stunt (my favorite!) with small sport planes many years ago. Believe me, it took several crashes to learn this maneuver. I've been able to fly most types of R/C aircraft (sport, scale, small and large) inverted. Some, of course, owing to their design and airfoils, are a lot easier to fly than others. But without a doubt, airplanes that were designed for aerobatics and pattern-style flight are much more suitable for inverted flight. A plane with a fully symmetrical airfoil design on the wing and the horizontal stabilizer in line with the airflow of the wing is best for this particular maneuver.

I like to set up for a low inverted pass by turning the airplane upside-down on the downwind leg of the pattern, then I make my turn slowly while keeping the plane inverted, and then I line up with the runway center line. As the plane approaches the runway, I maintain control but let it slowly descend to a comfortable altitude, and I complete the pass while holding a constant altitude.

Always consider where you're flying and the effects of different wind, humidity and temperature conditions. All these factors play an important part in keeping the airplane airborne and prevent it from meeting the ground unexpectedly.

In some cases, as you can see in the picture that was taken by Dan Parsons at the Joe Nall Memorial in 1993 (below), you can actually touch the ground with the vertical fin and still continue to fly with just the right amount of down-elevator. In this case, the field was soft grass, circumstances were just right, and the airplane continued to fly. This particular plane was scratch-built from an old set of plans that was designed by Andrews Quik Ray. It has a $\frac{1}{4}$x$\frac{3}{8}$-inch hardwood leading edge on the vertical fin that enables me to actually drag the fin on the ground. If this maneuver is performed off grass, there will be no damage. On asphalt, the most extensive repair will be a MonoKote patch

This is what I call a "rudder bump." The plane's fin and rudder are completely flat on the top; this allows me to drag the rudder along the grass for quite a distance.

on the fin tip or perhaps a broken prop.

You must realize that, if you take these risks, you are very likely to crash-land occasionally. Over the years, I have hit the ground when I wasn't trying to. It's a chance you take, but I've been very fortunate and have successfully completed the maneuver many times.

To keep elevator control and to be able to feel it through the transmitter stick, you must maintain sufficient speed. If you can't feel the elevator response through your thumb, you're in trouble; power up and go around. I've gone as far as putting landing gear on both the top and the bottom to serve as a training tool, but this does affect flight performance. Remember, reverse your control action when flying inverted.

◆ The rolling circle is always a crowd-pleaser. This is another maneuver that can only be completed with properly designed aircraft. You'll have far less trouble performing this maneuver with an airplane that grooves well and handles smoothly.

My favorite sequence is to roll the airplane with right aileron while using the elevator to turn the airplane in a left circle. Again, keep in mind that location, wind and temperature have a great deal to do with being able to successfully complete this maneuver. I not only try to concentrate on what the airplane is currently doing, but I also mentally prepare for the next move that I want the plane to do.

It works best for me to set up for this maneuver while the airplane is approaching me from the left and to start moving the aileron to the right. When the right wing goes down, apply down-elevator to turn the plane to the left. Hold slight down-elevator until the right wing has rotated to a horizontal position (airplane inverted). At this point, you should again be close to neutral on the elevator, while still holding slight right aileron tension. Now, switch to slight up-elevator as the right wing rotates to vertical. This continues the left turn of the circle.

When the right wing returns to horizontal (airplane upright), you should have elevator back to neutral and should have

completed about ¼ of the circle if you are doing a four-roll, rolling circle. Repeat this entire sequence for the next roll and ¼ circle, etc. You may also find that the slower you roll the airplane, the more rud-

My P-51 blazes past in a low flyby. This is one of the most thrilling maneuvers for spectators because they're anticipating a maneuver of some type, but I like to fool them by flying the straight line and blasting to vertical at the end of the run.

der you need to apply during the knife-edge point of the roll. If this is the case, when the right wing is in the down position, you may need left rudder; when the right wing is at the top, you may need right rudder. First, try the maneuver without rudder and see how your plane performs. When you have learned this much, you'll be able to vary the maneuver to include as many rolls as you wish (or are able) to complete.

For me, the most difficult maneuver is to do only one roll while completing a 360-degree circle. When you fly with the wings vertical (knife-edge), you will have to use some rudder to hold the fuselage straight during the maneuver. The faster

you perform the rolls, the less you will have to use the rudder. It takes practice to make that determination. Do whatever works best for you and your airplane. Remember that the method I've described

may not apply in a competitive situation. If you enter a contest, you must observe the rules that require a certain number of rolls, etc.

◆ The slow roll is another maneuver that appeals to the crowd and is fun to do. I like to start a long (1,000-foot) slow roll about 500 feet away from me in one direction and complete it about 500 feet in the other direction. This maneuver is similar to the rolling circle, although you concentrate on keeping the airplane flying in a straight line, as if on an imaginary string.

Start either up- or downwind, in whichever direction you feel more comfortable rolling your plane. While flying

This P-38 looks very majestic in the air. The maneuvers that I do with this plane are a little more scale-like. Quick, snappy maneuvers don't quite make it with this type of plane.

in a straight line, apply the aileron to roll in the direction you want. Let's use the right-hand roll as an example. Start by applying light right aileron (you may require light up-elevator). Then, as the right wing goes down to vertical, start applying the necessary left rudder to keep the fuselage straight, just as if you were flying knife-edge for a short time. Because the right wing is now slowly coming up to horizontal (inverted), you'll need the necessary down-elevator pressure to maintain level flight. As the aircraft passes horizontal, you again approach vertical, and this time, you'll need right rudder. Remember, use the elevator to control aircraft direction whenever the wings are vertical.

If you stop to think about these movements, you'll see that they are, in fact, a smooth, continuous movement of the sticks, which you will realize is a lot easier said than done. It only comes with practice.

◆ The flat turn is a somewhat simpler, yet interesting-looking maneuver to accomplish while maintaining a level attitude. Its effect is more appreciable with a slower model, such as a Piper Cub, rather than with a pattern-type aircraft, although an Ultimate is also ideal for this maneuver.

As a matter of fact, some aircraft will not slip through the air sideways to a point at which you can even tell that they are flat turning. For example, if you use a Cub to perform a left-hand flat turn, start the maneuver at a higher altitude than you think you'll need. This is crucial because you drastically slow the airplane down during this type of turn, and it could stall and require more altitude than you initially thought to allow you to recover. (Believe me, I'm talking from personal experience; this has happened more than once.)

Start at a level attitude at about ½ throttle, and apply left rudder until you notice the airplane starting to yaw left. Then apply the necessary right aileron to keep the wing horizontal. It will probably take a few tries before you succeed, because to prevent the plane from wanting to snap, you'll need to hold just the right amount of left rudder, elevator and right aileron.

When you're able to hold the plane in the flat turn, you can practice making the circle smaller and smaller as you improve; but remember that the tighter the circle, the slower the airplane is actually flying, and that greatly increases your chance of a stall.

◆ The M-wadd. Now on to something a lot faster and extremely radical! I've never seen this maneuver demonstrated by any-

one else, nor have I seen it diagrammed in a magazine. I call it the "M-wadd." Scott Broughton (another of our club members) and I scratch-built two identical, 72-inch, ⅓-scale BD-8s, with 4.2 engines. We were flying these particular planes when we discovered this maneuver. I've found that only planes designed for aerobatics with a short-coupled fuselage (for aerobatics) will do this maneuver. Planes with a long tail moment will not do it.

Start the maneuver during level flight, at full power and with plenty of altitude. Pull back on the elevator quickly as if to

If this ½-scale Extra were any bigger, I would be able to climb in and fly it myself. This is a great aerobatic platform that gives me hours of flying pleasure.

begin an inside loop, then suddenly throw both sticks to the upper corner of the gimbal. What seems to work best is to go to the full-power, right rudder while pushing full down-elevator and left aileron. When it's done successfully with the proper type of airplane, the airplane goes from straight-and-level forward flight into a tail-forward tumble that comes out in a snap-roll-type stall. As it does so, I let the sticks go back to neutral for just a second, but maintain full throttle, and fly the airplane out of the stall. This is definitely not a maneuver for a beginner.

Don't do this maneuver with an airplane that wasn't designed or modified to withstand the tremendous forces that are being applied to the entire airframe. You're literally threatening to tear the tail off the fuselage when you do this one.

It's also very likely to come out of the stall in one of many possible directions. This maneuver, in particular, can only be mastered through hands-on experience. All airplanes handle differently until you

get accustomed to how the plane handles the controls given to it. I mentioned that the left rudder and right aileron worked best on my plane, but the opposite might work best on yours. Try it!

◆ The whoosh-by. This last maneuver is fairly simple, and I usually do it at the end of my flight because it can be performed without the assistance of an engine (dead-stick). It can be done with just about any type of airplane, but the very last step may vary somewhat, depending on the strength of your wing. This is a somewhat violent maneuver, so only do the whoosh-by while no one else is flying, and be sure that no one will come near your flying pattern.

I begin to set up for this stunt after all other maneuvers have been done and I'm at the end of my flight. First, I climb to an altitude at which the airplane is barely visible, then I kill the engine and continue to soar around until I can tell by testing the throttle stick that the engine is completely dead. I then point the airplane straight down at an imaginary point at least 50 feet in front of me, and I continue to dive toward that point on the ground until the last possible second (about 100 feet of altitude) before I pull back hard and quickly on the elevator, just before the plane would hit the ground. Then I pull the nose up enough to gain adequate altitude to bring the airplane around, and I hope I judge all conditions well enough to land the airplane dead-stick and so that it rolls out right in front of me.

The sound of the air "whooshing by"

Here's one of my favorites—a low inverted pass. My P-47 is a great flying machine and can handle my style of flying with no problems.

the airplane without the engine running will definitely surprise you. It gives you an idea of how much force is actually being exerted against the skin of the aircraft.

When you attempt this maneuver, be sure to have plenty of altitude when you pull out of the dive, and allow enough air speed to make the necessary turn and to glide in dead-stick. Until you know just what to expect from your plane, remember that walking definitely beats rebuilding.

On one occasion, I had changed from one computer radio to another without checking the elevator percentage that the first transmitter was programmed for, and guess what? You probably got it right—

total destruction.

I hope that this chapter will help some of you newer pilots try the more complex aspects of R/C modeling. These maneuvers have provided me with hours of enjoyment over the years, and I hope that they'll do the same for you. ◆

ABOUT THE AUTHOR

Stinger Wallace

Stinger was born at an Air Force base and was a "military brat" until his father retired when Stinger was six. At age 12, he heard an .049 U-control airplane behind his home and became hooked. In 1977, he bought his first 6-channel radio and a Sig Super Sport 3-channel trainer. Stinger loves multi-engine aircraft and, in the Unlimited R/C Air Races, his planes reached 195mph. His main interest is IMAA-size aircraft, particularly the WW II warbirds. He and Walt Bardwell are constructing a 14-foot-span B-29, which will weigh around 48 pounds with four Zenoah G-23s—well within the AMA's 55-pound limit.

CHAPTER 17

Fun-Fly Competition

by Jerry L. Smith

The first time I held a transmitter in my hand, I knew I was hooked. Then the training began. Approaching my 40th birthday, I had found a great challenge. For years, I had participated in competitive go-cart racing, motorcycle trail riding and water sports, but age was becoming a factor in my choice of hobbies. I soon found out that, unlike in past endeavors, in R/C flying, I always walked away unscathed from accidents, mishaps and crashes. Yet the adrenaline rush and competitive spirit were as strong and addictive as in any sport in which I had ever participated.

My first plane was a basic Sig Cadet trainer. With the help of a good friend and a trainer system (which I highly recommend that beginners use to prevent unnecessary crashes and losing equipment), I was on my way to many hours of fun and to opening doors to new friendships in the modeling world.

After my debut flight in 1982, I experimented for a couple of years with different types of aircraft before I became attracted to one highly aerobatic design—the Miss Martha. I discovered this design at a highly competitive fun-fly event in Winston-Salem, NC, where I met its designer, Bob Richards, and his friend Robert Vess. Together, they put on an exhibition of impressive aerobatic maneuvers.

I spent the next three years flying the Miss Martha. These were my formative years as an R/C pilot. Soon I was competing in fun-fly contests in Greenville, SC. Enthusiasm for major fun-fly competition was growing in North Carolina, South Carolina and southern Georgia. I soon realized that I wanted to be a force to be reckoned with among fun-fly pilots.

ONE-WHEEL WONDER

At one competition in Greenville, I saw a new style of plane that was a radical departure from anything I had ever seen. This one-wheel plane had a thicker wing, a longer chord and much larger control surfaces than other fun-fly planes that were popular at the time. It also had a fuselage profile that resembled a control-

line model. This plane (which originated in southern Georgia) was the prototype for the fun-fly designs we use today.

During the evolution of this one-wheel wonder, fun-fly competitions were becoming more commonplace. Gordon Banks, the editor of *R/C Report* magazine in Huntsville, AL, promoted the first highly competitive fun-fly event—the Shootout, which was later referred to simply as "the Nationals." I am pleased to say that, in the eight-year history of this "Super Bowl of fun flying," I have claimed five titles. Last year, I was invited by air-show promoter Frank Noll to participate in an air show in Dayton, OH. I have also been invited to several other such air shows this year. My signature plane designs—the Smith Special and the Smith Super Special—have brought me the most attention in the radical aerobatic design competition fun-fly circle, but my real love is still picking up the transmitter and flying planes. In this chapter, I hope to share my experience and know-how so that you will be able to maximize your skills and fully enjoy our great sport and this drastically different design of plane.

User-friendly logistics and relatively low cost make this plane ideal when you don't have a great deal of time on your hands or money in your pocket. In fun-fly competition, pilots and designers work together to improve both our planes and our sport. My colleagues have been an invaluable help to me, and I hope that my experience will help to improve yours.

THE PLANE'S DESIGN

◆ Airfoil design is the most significant differentiating factor in plane design today. Robert Vess, a professor of experimental aerodynamics at North Carolina State University, is the father of the airfoil on the Smith Super Special (kitted by Air Flair). This airfoil accelerates and decelerates with more stability than any other airfoil I've ever flown. Variations on it (mainly made 10 to 15 percent smaller) satisfy a range of pilot preferences.

◆ Weight is another significant factor to consider when developing a high-

This one-wheel wonder is a Gyro-1. Its thick, symmetrical airfoil and large deflecting surfaces make for some interesting maneuvers. The Gyro-1 has a composite wheel strut that can take the abuse of hard landings.

performance airplane. In my opinion, weight reduction is more important than design improvement. Most competition planes use 4- to 6-pound competition-grade balsa. The ribs of my planes are made out of 1/16-inch-thick balsa and leading- and trailing-edge sheathing. The wing spars are 1/4-inch-square medium balsa, reinforced with 0.05- or 0.07-inch-thick carbon fiber. The tail surfaces are made out of 3/16-inch-thick contest-grade, 4- to 6-pound balsa with carbon fiber to reinforce the trailing edge of the built-up horizontal stab. The most common motor-mount material is 1/4-inch-plywood and Magnalite, which is end-grain balsa laminated with 0.07-inch-thick carbon-fiber sheeting. The tail boom is fiberglass-wound tubing and usually measures about 1/2 inch in diameter. As for glues, high-quality CAs are better than epoxy because they're lighter.

Covering can also make a noticeable difference to weight. Clear coverings are lighter than colored coverings. When the wing has been covered, check it to ensure that it's straight or has a washout of up to 1/4 inch on each tip.

◆ **Washout.** To add washout to the aileron, you must refer to the rib center line at the wingtip. At the fuselage position, the aileron must be at or up to 1/4 inch below

This was taken at a fun-fly that's held every year in Kingston, Ontario, Canada. It has sport-scale, NCFFA and scale contests. There is a wide variety of planes, and the contestants come from all over the northeastern United States and eastern Canada to participate.

the center line. This makes the plane much more stable near a stall attitude.

◆ **Landing gear.** As for landing gear, it seems as if everyone has an opinion. One wheel is far and away the most popular style because it is reliable.

◆ **Radio**. My radios of choice are Futaba and JR. I fly Futaba 9 ZAP and run an SR 6V battery to provide more torque to the servos. A standard, 4-channel radio flies fun-fly planes well, but for maximum performance, a computer radio with high-torque servos is the optimal choice. If your goal is recreational fun flying, the 4-channel radio will be adequate, but a computer radio is better for competition because it provides an air-brake function and an elevator-to-flap coupling that decreases the size of the plane's loops.

◆ **Air brakes.** I recommend that, to start, you set the air brakes to 10 degrees of up-flap movement and to no more than 5 degrees of down-elevator. I find that airplane stability is more predictable with this "progressive" setup. Air-brake setup usually isn't subject to much debate, but I believe that the setup on my designs allows a more gradual movement of the surfaces that gives me a less abrupt, more predictable approach.

To trim the air-brake function, I fly level and watch the pitching motion (nose-up or nose-down) of the aircraft as I apply the air brakes. When trimmed properly, the plane will maintain a level attitude as it lands. Adjust the elevator to correct either nose-up or nose-down deflection.

You must preset your radio before all flight maneuvers, including small loops and air-brake functions. If you preset your radio properly, you'll have much less to think about during flight. (Flipping switches has never been my technique of choice.) There are two ways to reduce

sensitivity levels: dual rates and exponential. Competition pilots generally prefer flying with exponential, because it reduces the sensitivity of the control sticks around the central position. The percentage of expo used is up to the pilot. I recommend starting out at negative-20-percent aileron and elevator.

In a nutshell, up-elevator plus flaps down equals small loops. To decrease your loop size, start with 20 degrees down flaps with full up-elevator deflection (45 to 55 degrees). For optimum loop speed and performance, add deflection until the loop speed decreases and the plane begins to scoot—not fly—through the loop. I prefer larger, faster loops to smaller, slower loops.

◆ **Engine.** When thinking of an engine, weight, not horsepower, is the most important consideration. We fly planes that weigh only 2 to 3 pounds; naturally, the 3-pound planes should be pulled by larger engines such as an HP .40 or an O.S. .40FP. The lighter planes should obviously have smaller engines, such as the Enya .35 heli with the heat-sink head fins removed. On my planes (which usually weigh around 2 1/2 pounds), I use a Webra .32. This offers a good combination of power and weight that helps me achieve maximum performance. These engines weigh approximately 9 ounces without the exhaust system. The O.S. .40FP is an excellent, inexpensive engine for beginners.

I use two types of K&B glow plugs—the 1L and MC-9—because they're dependable. For the exhaust system, I like to use the mousse-can muffler design. I've experimented a great deal with different types of mufflers, and I've always returned to this design because of its instant throttle response and lightness.

◆ **Propeller.** My propeller of choice is 10 inches in diameter with a 4- to 5-inch pitch; this seems to be the most suitable for fun-fly airplanes. An 11-inch-diameter prop would create a gyro effect and prevent the plane from turning as tightly. They turn 14,000 to 17,000rpm according to their setup. I prefer wooden to carbon-fiber props because wood is so much lighter and can be accelerated and decelerated more easily. The heavier props (carbon-fiber and fiberglass) will not accelerate as well.

◆ **Fuel** is basically the pilot's choice, but 15- to 40-percent nitro seems to be the norm. I use 30-percent Blue Thunder, which is sold by Horizon Hobby and made by Cool Power; it has a low synthetic oil content.

TECHNIQUES

The landing area outside of my house on which I practice is 150 feet long by 100 feet wide. When I fly, there are power lines about 100 yards in front of me, and the areas to my right and to my left are very confined. By using a practice field this small, I know that wherever I compete, the field will seem large by comparison. I've set up boundaries that remind me how far I can safely fly. I practice my positioning, maneuvers and landing on this field. If I make practice difficult enough, competition will be easy.

I owe my success to good positioning and consistency, not to speed and "flash." In the unlimited class, competition is so stiff that it's nearly impossible to dominate in all areas. To ensure a chance at victory, you must be able to score well in all of the events, but not necessarily be the best in any one event.

To fly successfully, you must be aware of the wind direction and speed. Thick airfoils are very forgiving and unlike other types, they let you get away with some imperfections and miscalculations. For example, with most types of airplane, you would never make a downwind takeoff, but with fun-fly planes, if you can improve your positioning by doing so, you do it.

If you have trouble understanding turbulence, air pockets and the like, visualize how water would react in the same conditions. Like a boat, an airplane leaves a wake; when you repeatedly enter and re-enter such "churned up" air, it affects your plane.

FUN-FLY MANEUVERS

Let's look at the 1995 NCFFA events: loop, roll-loop-spin, touch-and-go and limbo. With the exception of limbo, all involve three basic maneuvers—loop, roll and spin. To master competitive fun flying, a pilot simply needs to master these three things.

◆ **Loops.** One loop is very simple, but multiple loops are hard to fly consistently. Before attempting the loop, check your transmitter to make sure that your loop coupling (50 degrees up-elevator, 20 degrees down-flap is a good starting point) and air-brake features are active. Familiarize yourself with your plane's optimal loop size and speed.

As I mentioned, larger, faster loops are more controllable than tighter, slower loops. Larger, faster loops are easier to position and to maintain consistently

because you spread your "plane wake" over a larger area. After three or more loops, you'll usually have to make corrections to compensate for "wake" and/or to improve positioning. Always make corrections at the bottom of the loop; neutralize

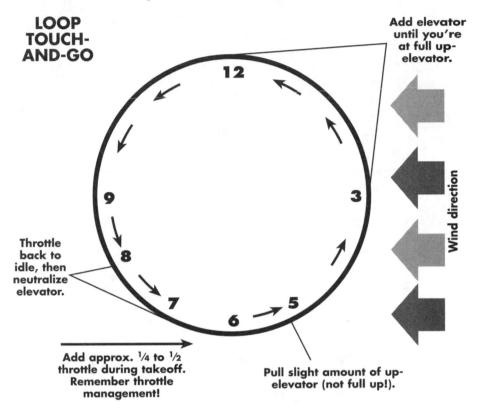

LOOP TOUCH-AND-GO

Add elevator until you're at full up-elevator.

Wind direction

Throttle back to idle, then neutralize elevator.

Add approx. ¼ to ½ throttle during takeoff. Remember throttle management!

Pull slight amount of up-elevator (not full up!).

the elevator and make aileron corrections to the right or left.

To turn in a competitive run when doing a set of 10 loops, a pilot must accurately calculate the best beginning altitude because the plane will gradually descend with each loop completed. Often, what sets champions apart from also-rans is who finishes the loop sequences closest to the ground. In multiples of five, outside loops must be started higher than inside loops because insides are more controllable.

◆ **Rolls.** For success in any rolling maneuver, a pilot must be consistent and comfortable with the direction in which he rolls the plane. I, like most pilots, have always rolled to the right. Most fun-fly competitions allow a maximum of three rolls. I fly the first two rolls at a 45-degree upward angle from takeoff, then I pull the throttle back to nearly idle and stop the third roll with the wings level to position my plane for the next part of the event.

◆ **Spins.** The usual definition of a spin doesn't apply to a fun-fly plane because we don't use rudder. To spin, we combine

up-elevator or down-elevator movement with aileron.

• Of the roll-loop-spin events, roops (a combination of a roll and a loop) are the most popular. To master the roop is to have confidence in your abilities and your

potential for competition success.

The roop is difficult because proper position is hard to maintain. To master successive roops, fly each one thinking ahead to the next one, but don't hurry the combination of the two, because each one feeds from the other. You roll it, then you loop it...you roll it, then you loop it. This seems simple, but you must finish each roll before you loop.

Keep in mind that to achieve a good score, your altitude must be low; the maneuver is so demanding that the event is won or lost in the short span of time it takes each pilot to land after completing all the roops.

• Touch-and-go events require that a pilot momentarily "land" the plane between maneuvers. In this context, landing is simply touching the wheel to the ground. Touch-and-go events require more throttle management than any others.

• When flying a figure-8, the touchdown spot must be consistent. I always try to touch down directly in front of myself, with no more than 25 feet of leeway on either side of center. This keeps me regulated for a good, consistent flight. Don't

Official NCFFA Events

Note: numbers in brackets represent repetitions for which records are maintained. Maneuvers in brackets may be changed by CD but no records will be kept.

LOOP EVENTS

1. **Inside Roops** [10] ....Takeoff, [roll,loop], touchdown.
2. **Outside Loops** [10] ....Takeoff, [outside loop], touchdown.
3. **Outside-Inside** ....5 outside loops, 5 inside loops, touchdown.
4. **Split Outside-Inside** ....5 outside loops, touch-and-go, 5 inside loops, touchdown.

ROLL-LOOP-SPIN EVENTS

5. **Roops** [5] ....Takeoff, [roll,loop], touchdown.
6. **Split Roops** ....3 roops, touch-and-go, 3 roops, touchdown.
7. **Modified Dixie Death**..........[Takeoff, 3 rolls, 3 loops, touchdown.]
8. **Dixie Death** [2] ....Takeoff, 3 rolls, 3 spins, 3 loops, touchdown.
9. **Split Dixie Death** ....Takeoff, 3 rolls, touchdown, 3 spins, touchdown, 3 loops, touchdown.

TOUCH-AND-GO EVENTS

10. **180 Touch-and-Go's** [10] ....[Takeoff and touchdown] with a 180-degree heading change between each takeoff and touch.
11. **360 Touch-and-Go's** [10] ....[Takeoff and touchdown] with a 360-degree heading change between each takeoff and touch.
12. **Roll Touch-and-Go** [5] ....[Takeoff and touchdown] with a roll between each takeoff and touch.
13. **Roop Touch-and-Go** [5] ......[Takeoff and touchdown] with a roop between each takeoff and touch.
14. **Roll Touch Loop Touch** [5] ..[Takeoff, roll, touch-and-go, loop, touch.]
15. **Spot Touch-and-Go** [5] ....Takeoff, [touch in defined area], touch.
16. **Inside Loops** [10] ....Takeoff, [inside loop], touchdown.

LIMBO EVENTS

17. **Limbo** [5] ....Take off away from ribbon, [pass under ribbon], touchdown. Poles are to be 50 feet apart and 5 feet high. Aircraft can not touch the ground until the final touchdown.
18. **Loop Limbo** [5] ....[Same as limbo with an inside loop after each pass under the limbo.]
19. **Roll Limbo** [5] ....[Same as limbo with a roll after each pass under the limbo.]
20. **Inverted Limbo** [5] ....[Same as limbo, but done inverted.]

and ribbons come into play. Practice is the key to successful limbo flying.

FINAL THOUGHTS

Practice sessions, not actual contests, are crucial to becoming a topnotch fun-fly pilot. My methods and tidbits of advice?

◆ Fly the plane close to you. Before a contest, familiarize yourself with the events to be flown, and check that your plane setup can execute these events.

◆ Practice two to five times a week, 30 minutes each time. Fly a few of the more difficult events. Take a close look at the placement, position and wind direction. Once you've done this, you can fly with hand/eye coordination and to an extent, sound. Anticipation is the key; you must always think a step ahead.

◆ Maintain a high concentration level. Blank out everything around you. When I fly, I deal with only two things: me and the plane.

◆ I take three planes to competitions: a pre-competition practice plane, my contest plane and a backup contest plane.

I hope that other pilots will enhance their abilities by using what I've learned through years of practice and competing. The main point that I want you to take away from reading this is to keep things simple in every aspect of the sport. Fun-fly planes provide a great deal of freedom and convenience; this is an affordable and enjoyable sport to a great many people. I believe that the more dedication you put into it, the more enjoyment you will get out of it. ◆

ABOUT THE AUTHOR

Jerry L. Smith
Jerry L. Smith has been involved with R/C model airplanes for 13 years and has devoted 10 of those years to fun-fly competition. He is the author of several construction articles and the designer of the Smith Special and the Smith Super Special—best-selling competition fun-fly planes. Jerry is a five-time national competiton fun-fly winner. He resides in Kentucky where he is a maintenance planner for Lockheed Martin—a gaseous diffusion plant.

consume yourself with worry about how wide your turns are. Obviously, you want them to be as tight as you can comfortably fly, but above all else, maintain a consistent touchdown point in front of you.
• One of the most challenging events for me to watch and appreciate is the loop-touch. It requires throttle management, must always be flown into the wind, and it allows no room for error. Timing is also essential, and practice is a necessity. (Refer to diagram.)
• I've never won a limbo event, probably because I haven't spent a great deal of time practicing. Still, it is a pretty simple aspect of competitive fun flying. In limbo flying, pilots must be comfortable with their vantage point because obstacles such as poles

CHAPTER 18

How to Trim Sailplanes for Aerobatics

by Jef Raskin

I T CAN BE difficult to trim a model sailplane for aerobatics. For example, if a plane never finishes a loop in the direction from which it started, this might be caused by bad aileron trim or rudder trim—assuming that you're flying the plane correctly. The two effects can look the same.

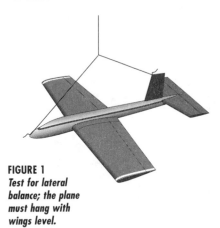

FIGURE 1
Test for lateral balance; the plane must hang with wings level.

This chapter explains how to tell which bugs have got into your plane, how to tell similar effects apart and how to fix them. A lot of these techniques are the same or similar to those used to set up aerobatic power planes; in fact, we have a simpler task, because there's no torque from the spinning propeller and no spiraling slipstream to complicate the way our planes fly.

We want to achieve an ideal aerobatic sailplane. It should have the same

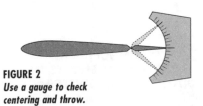

FIGURE 2
Use a gauge to check centering and throw.

response upside-down (inverted) and right-side up and be able to maneuver equally well and with the same control inputs in either orientation. A well-trimmed sailplane should track easily through inside and outside loops without rolling to the right or left, and it should

come out on the same heading as it started on. Applying rudder should yaw the plane sideways without causing it to roll, climb, or dive.

To test your airplane, you'll have to be able to fly upright and inverted and do inside and outside loops. Rudder, elevator and aileron control are assumed, although some of these tests apply to 2-channel planes. The case where there are flaps (usually coupled to the elevator) is also considered.

BENCH TESTING

Trimming starts on the building board. First, check whether one wing is heavier than the other. How you test this will

FIGURE 3
Measure the distance from the wingtips to the center of the aft end of the fuselage. The tips must be equidistant from that point.

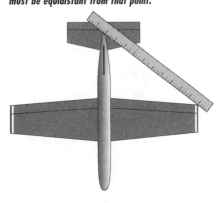

depend on the plane: with some fuselages, you can put a pin in the tip of the nose and another in the end of the tail cone. Tie a thread to each of these pins, and suspend the airplane from the threads (see Figure 1). The heavier wing will, of course, rotate to the bottom. You can correct the condition by putting weights in the tip of the lighter wing.

Flight testing can help you to distinguish incorrect aileron trim from either wing-heaviness or incorrect rudder trim, but it can't help you to diagnose both at once. This is why we must correct any wing-heaviness before we start flight testing (and, unlike the other problems, a too-heavy wing can be detected in the shop).

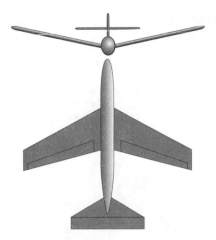

FIGURE 4
Yaw-roll coupling can be caused by too much sweep or too much dihedral.

It's essential that none of the control surfaces has free play. They must center on their neutral position precisely. Don't simply eyeball this, but check it with a ruler or another guide to see that all surfaces return precisely to the center from both sides. If a surface has free play or doesn't return to center, then you won't be able to flight-test for proper trim, because the airplane will be a different beast depending on what you last did to it! You can't fly precision aerobatics unless you have a model built with precision.

The balance point must be as described in the plans or as calculated by the usual formulas. When using a program (such as MaxSoar) that gives you a range of balance-point positions, it's best to choose the rearmost point of the specified range, or even a bit behind it, because most computer programs are designed for non-aerobatic flight.

A fully aerobatic plane shouldn't have differential ailerons because the differential would work against you in inverted flight and outside maneuvers. The ailerons should have no warps and should move the same amounts upward and downward on both wings. Use a ruler or a homemade gauge to check this (see Figure 2). It's also important to seal the gaps between surfaces and controls; unequal gaps can have the same effect as a warped wing. The same goes for all controls. The control motion should never be more than 30 degrees on each side of center.

• **Side view.** If the plane has a symmetrical airfoil, set the ailerons and elevator to neutral, and check that the wing incidence and stabilizer incidence are both zero. I use an incidence gauge or I measure from a flat surface. If your plane doesn't have a symmetrical airfoil, it's difficult to make it behave in the same way when inverted or upright.

• **Top view.** Viewed from above, the wing and stabilizer must be perpendicular to the fuselage center line. In this regard, my planes are square within $1/32$ inch at the wingtips. I make sure the wing is centered and then check the distance from a corner of the wingtips (or some other

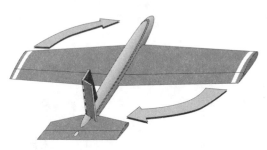

FIGURE 5
Make sure that the plane yaws, but doesn't roll with rudder input.

easy-to-measure-from point) to the center of the fuselage at the rear (see Figure 3). It takes a few tries to equalize these pairs of measurements, but it can be done. The fin should lie directly along the fuselage center line. There's no propeller, so there's no reason for the fin to be angled as it is on some powered planes.

• **Front view.** Viewed from the front or rear, the wing and stabilizer should be parallel and horizontal. If there's any dihedral, it must be equal on both sides; most

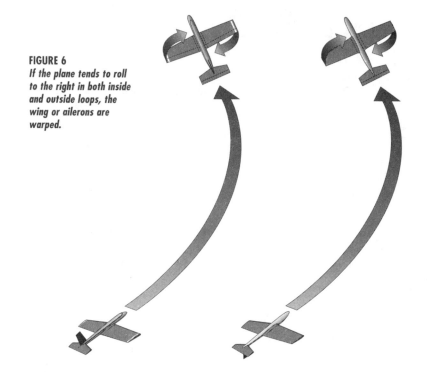

FIGURE 6
If the plane tends to roll to the right in both inside and outside loops, the wing or ailerons are warped.

precision aerobatic sailplanes have no dihedral in the wing or stabilizer. The fin should be vertical and centered.

◆ **Summary.** *If a plane isn't built right and tight, it won't do well in flight. All the rest of these tests will be useless if the plane isn't true and square.*

TEST FLYING

The tests outlined here are given in a certain order. To detect the "culprit" in a

plane that won't fly right, we have to examine our clues one at a time. Only after we've eliminated certain problems can we begin to diagnose others. Unfortunately, pilot error can mask some of the effects we're looking for (for example, you might be unknowingly adding a little aileron whenever you use the elevator), so do each test a number of times and, if you can, with more than one pilot.

HANDS-OFF TEST

To repeat: if, and only if, a plane has been built accurately will flight-testing clearly reveal any further problems. The first test is to put the craft into straight and level flight. In smooth air, a good aerobatic plane is surprisingly stable and can fly for at least 5 seconds hands-off without any noticeable roll, pitch, or yaw. If you can't trim it so that this is the case, then it was poorly designed, built crookedly, has loose controls, or is tail-heavy.

DISTINGUISHING BETWEEN THE EFFECTS OF DIHEDRAL AND SWEEPBACK

Both excessive dihedral and excessive sweep will make the plane roll when you apply rudder (see Figure 4). If your plane has no sweepback (as measured at the quarter-chord line, not at the leading edge), then you only have dihedral to worry about. For example, the model shown in the illustrations has no sweep.

To avoid problems caused by excessive

sweepback, I build my planes with less than 10 degrees of sweep. Here's how you find out whether you have a problem:

Fly upright straight and level. Apply rudder. The plane should yaw without dropping a wing (see Figure 5). If the plane rolls right with right rudder, there's too much dihedral or sweepback; if it rolls left with right rudder, then more dihedral or sweepback is needed. A high wing acts like dihedral.

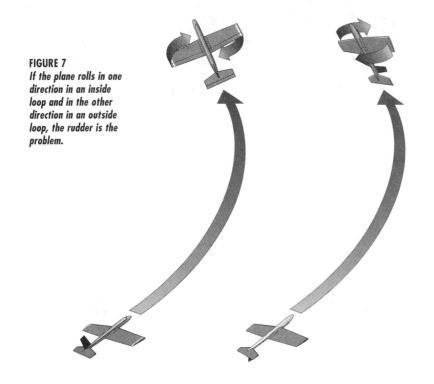

FIGURE 7
If the plane rolls in one direction in an inside loop and in the other direction in an outside loop, the rudder is the problem.

To tell which is which, fly inverted straight and level. Apply right rudder. If the plane rolls right both upright and inverted, the effect is the result of too much dihedral. If it rolls to the right when upright and to the left when inverted, the effect is the result of excessive sweep. In an aerobatic plane, it's better *not* to have sweep (measured at the quarter-chord line).

If the plane pitches upward or downward when rudder is applied, the fin and rudder are probably too large; shorten them. If the plane doesn't yaw, the rudder is probably too small. It's generally better to increase the chord of the rudder/fin assembly than its height, because if the fin and rudder are too tall, you'll get some yaw in your aileron-only rolls. This is the opposite of the advice I'd give for thermal sailplanes where the efficiency of a higher aspect ratio surface is desirable.

◆ **Summary.** *Design with little or no sweep. Then, if right rudder rolls the*

plane to the right in upright flight, you'll know that there's too much dihedral; if right rudder rolls the plane to the left, there's too little dihedral.

SEPARATING RUDDER AND AILERON EFFECTS

Out-of-trim ailerons (or warped wings) and an out-of-trim rudder or fin can cause the plane to roll when you apply the elevator. Here's how to tell them apart. From

a dead-level flight into the wind (perhaps after a dive to pick up speed), do an inside loop upward. Do this a few times. Your plane should loop without requiring aileron or rudder input; note whether it rolls one way or the other.

Say it rolls slightly to the right. This could be because one wing is heavier than the other, or the ailerons are out of trim, or the rudder or fin isn't centered. The wing-heaviness can be fixed on the bench (and it should have been). Technically, even if the wing is static-balanced when you test it in the shop, unevenly distributed weight can still couple pitch to roll. For any reasonably well-built wing, this effect will be too slight to notice.

If the plane rolls while doing an inside loop, try flying it inverted, and do an outside loop upward (just as you did the inside loop upward). If the plane still rolls to the right, the problem is caused by a warped wing or incorrect aileron trim (see Figure 6). This effect can also signal a

warped stabilizer.

If, however, the plane always rolls to the left in an outside loop and rolls to the right in an inside loop, there's some right trim to the rudder (assuming the wings are balanced); see Figure 7.

◆ **Summary.** *If inside and outside loops make a plane roll in opposite directions, the problem is rudder trim; if it rolls in the same direction, the problem is aileron trim.*

DISTINGUISHING WING WARP FROM AILERON TRIM

When flying at a constant speed, you can adjust the ailerons to trim out the effects of wing warp. As your speed changes, however, the amount of aileron you need will also change, and that will make the plane difficult to fly with precision. To test for this, trim the elevator for slow, hands-off flight—as slow as your plane can go without stalling. Then, using only elevator, gradually dive the airplane until it's pointed straight down. (I have a suspicion that it's best to start this test pretty high up.) If it rolls on the way down, you have a warped wing or, what's less likely, a warped stabilizer. Flexibility in a plane can also cause problems; aerobatic models must be stiff! Misalignment of the fin or rudder can also cause a roll when diving, so you'll have to make sure that the fin and rudder pass their tests first.

ARE YOUR WINGTIPS TOO THIN OR TOO NARROW?

Some aerobatic models have a nasty habit of snapping out at the bottom of a downward loop. This can be caused by a stab that's too small, but inadvertent snapping is more often caused by tip-stalling owing

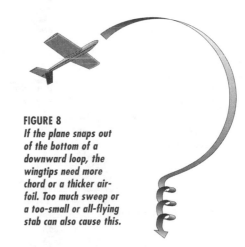

FIGURE 8
If the plane snaps out of the bottom of a downward loop, the wingtips need more chord or a thicker airfoil. Too much sweep or a too-small or all-flying stab can also cause this.

to incorrect wing design, e.g., the wingtips may be too thin. Alternatively, the tips may have too little chord. On an aerobatic model, the tip chord should not be less than half the root chord.

Excessive sweep is another cause of premature tip stalling, but if you have no roll with rudder as mentioned earlier, then sweep probably isn't your problem (see Figure 8). On some models, I've cured tip stalling by limiting elevator travel, but a well-designed plane won't exhibit this problem under any conditions.

A last cause of unwanted snaps is the use of an all-flying stabilizer. A conventional stabilizer with a movable elevator is less prone to stalling. This is because it's a cambered surface and can achieve more force for a given area. It's generally best not to use all-flying surfaces in aerobatic models.

WHERE SHOULD THE PLANE BALANCE?

This is a matter of taste, unlike, say, yaw-to-roll coupling, which is always undesirable for aerobatics. If the plane won't fly hands-off unless you add nose weight, then it's tail-heavy (as I mentioned earlier), but how can you tell whether you've added too much weight? Trim for normal upright flight and then roll inverted. To fly level inverted, the plane should require

only a tiny amount of down—well within the usual trim-control range. If it requires more than this, it's too nose-heavy. My best planes will fly either upright or inverted without trim change; none requires more than one or two clicks of the trim lever.

DECALAGE

If the wing has a greater or smaller angle of attack than the stabilizer, inside and

outside loops won't be of the same diameter, and one will require more control input than the other (Figure 9). But a more precise test is to fly the plane upright and

FIGURE 9
If inside loops and outside loops have different diameters, check the decalage.

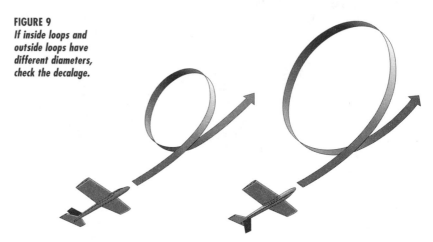

inverted in slow passes in front of you. Observe the elevator deflection; it should be in the same amount but in opposite directions on the two passes. If the angle of attack is too great, there will be more

elevator deflection when flying inverted; if it's too little, there will be more elevator deflection when flying upright. There's too much to think about when flying aerobatics to have to worry about different amounts of elevator input just because you're inverted.

FLAPS

It's becoming more common to couple flaps or flap-ailerons (flaperons) to the

elevator (as with many control-line stunters). The flaps go in a direction that's opposite that of the elevator, although they don't move through nearly as large

an angle. This makes loops tighter, it makes the plane more efficient, and it allows the use of thinner airfoils. If you can uncouple the flaps from the elevator, first make sure that the plane is trimmed correctly without them; then run the same tests with the flaps operational. Any problems introduced will then be caused by the flaps, and you can diagnose them as aileron or decalage errors.

Following this outline will help you to get a sailplane that's capable of precision aerobatics. Flying the maneuvers is now up to you. ◆

FIGURE 10
The Anabat II was designed by Jef Raskin in March '91. It features all symmetrical airfoils and is controlled by ailerons, rudder and elevator coupled into the ailerons used as flaps.

ABOUT THE AUTHOR

Jef Raskin

Jef is well-known in computer circles for creating and overseeing the initial development of the Macintosh computer project at Apple Computer, Inc. An AMA life member and contest director,

he has been flying model planes since the '50s. Thousands of his unique Western Wind R/C sailplanes—among the first computer-designed kits—were sold in the '70s. Jef runs the country's only annual, sanctioned sailplane aerobatics competitions, and his work has been published in technical journals, newspapers and magazines such as Wired and Model Airplane News.

When it comes to scale flying, Terry Nitsch is the "top gun." Winner of two consecutive Top Gun contests, the '95 Scale Masters and numerous other events, Terry knows how to fly in a scale-like manner and how to interact with the judges. For his insight, see "Scale Competition Flying Tips." George Leu, scale competition flier, former Top Gun chief judge and *Model Airplane News* scale columnist, tells you how to drop that ordnance in "Scale Bombing Techniques." There are many different techniques to master, so get a head start by reading these chapters, and make your flying buddies envious of your newfound talents.

CHAPTER 19

Scale Competition Flying Tips

by Terry Nitsch

Who makes the ideal scale pilot? A pattern flier? A full-scale pilot? A hot-dog sport flier? In reality, a combination of their skills can be very helpful in becoming a topnotch scale pilot. Today's scale competitions are so competitive that any little error or miscue can cost you dearly.

The beauty of scale modeling is that all models not only look different, but they also fly differently. Each full-size aircraft has its own speed envelope, wing loading, handling tendencies and mechanical systems. To receive maximum flight scores, you need to duplicate these.

Duplicating full-scale flight is much easier said than done. I always jump at the chance to see a full-scale Sabre Jet fly at an air show or exhibition. Every time I see one, I learn more about how I can fly my model. Not everyone has the opportunity to see the full-scale versions of their models fly, but there are usually similar aircraft that can provide critical flight information. Take note of all aspects: takeoff configurations, speed, turning radii and throttle settings. Watch the landing pattern: how large is it?; when do the flaps and gear come down?; what's the altitude at touchdown? There is so much to be learned to improve flight scores; it's mind-boggling! Videotapes are also available to view the flight characteristics of many types of aircraft.

PRACTICE, PRACTICE, PRACTICE

When weather conditions become adverse, why do certain pilots continue to score well? Because they know their airplane. Ideally, the serious scale competitor has two versions of the same aircraft; one is the competitive machine and the other is to practice with.

Even without the luxury of having two identically prepared aircraft, practice is still the bottom line in knowing your airplane. When the opportunity exists, I prefer to practice in crosswind conditions. Of the last four scale events I competed in, three were crosswind conditions—two of them rather severe! This is where some full-scale experience is valuable. You'll never receive maximum takeoff and land-

ing scores in a strong crosswind without cross-controlling the model. This means using enough aileron to keep the windward side of the aircraft low while applying opposite rudder to maintain the desired heading. This configuration on a landing approach essentially puts the model in a sideslip condition; to take off and land like the big guys and to receive maximum scores, this becomes the requirement.

A rule of thumb for crosswind takeoffs is to lean the aileron stick into the wind and apply the opposite rudder as needed to maintain heading. For landings, apply the necessary rudder input to eliminate most of the crosswind yaw, then use the ailerons to guide the descent onto the runway center line. Either way, rudder input is a must for maximum scores in crosswind situations.

Discipline is the key to any successful practice session. Although scale flying may look rather boring (not a lot of razzle-dazzle), it's quite complex. In competition, you're judged on every phase, including turnarounds. Remember those

Here are a few of the rewards you could add to your collection if everything goes perfectly. Controlled flights and a high static score are essential for taking home the goods.

flight-realism points! To get the most out of practice flights, flip every switch, change every rate, perfect every sequence—even if you aren't flying your contest bird. I wish I had a dollar for every time a contestant has said, "I landed on the wrong rates," or "I forgot to flip the right switch," or "I flew that flight with the flaps partially down." Does that sound familiar?

YOUR COPILOT

Practicing with your regular caller is also very helpful. My wife, Sheila, and I practice together and take notes on all flaws and problems. If the same problems occur several times, these notes are added to our competition call sheet as reminders during competition. It's amazing what you forget when you're in front of the judges. Any hint or reminder your caller gives you can make the difference between winning and losing.

Develop a practice routine that works best for *you*. I like to fly the entire sequence, then re-fly any problem maneuvers before I land; four flights per session are my maximum. Making flights because you want to get in a certain number of flights won't help you to perfect routines.

Quality of practice is more beneficial than *quantity* of practice.

FLIGHT PLANS

Establish a flight sequence that complements your particular aircraft and flying style. There are mandatory and optional maneuvers, but the sequence and direction in which you choose to perform them can add to the overall flow and appearance. I approach a flight sequence the way a figure skater approaches a routine; the show needs to be smooth and interesting to both spectators and judges. Every maneuver should flow into the next and have

The wings are level on this nice loop entrance. Remember to enter all loops on an upwind heading.

a turnaround that's typical of the type of aircraft being flown. Maneuvers that are flown in the same direction and require constant flybys don't score as well as flowing upwind/downwind-type flights. When you're being scored for realism, you'll have too much "dead time" when nothing is happening. A good rule of thumb is to fly all looping maneuvers upwind and all rolling maneuvers downwind.

Use mechanical flight options with some types of flying maneuvers. If the model has flaps or speed brakes, use them along with a descent from altitude or a decelerating pass. Drop your bombs from a

Scale Flight Presentations by Stan Alexander

Most of the judges who go on the circuit—U.S. Scale Masters, Top Gun Invitational, AMA Nationals and FAI F4C—have studied the four rule books thoroughly. When going to a scale competition, they spend at least a week studying that particular rule book. Between some rule books, there are subtle differences in the list of maneuvers allowed (Top Gun and the Scale Masters) and the number of mechanical options you can use; between others, there are major differences. There may even be different wording for the same maneuver, e.g., the split-S in the Top Gun rule book and AMA rule book. These are subtle differences that can affect your scores.

◆ **Rule books.** The most glaring mistake we often see is

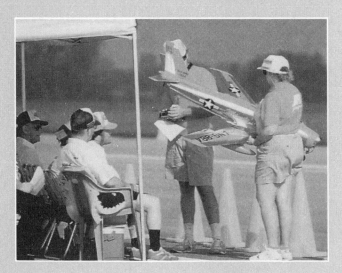

made by contestants who have absolutely no idea what's in the rule book or how to do the maneuvers properly; some have even used the wrong rule book. The rule book (for whichever competition) can help pilots plan their flight presentations. It can also provide ideas about which maneuvers are best suited to your aircraft and your experience level.

What constitutes an "aerobatic or non-aerobatic aircraft"? Every airplane is aerobatic to some degree, and a proper answer depends on what kind of aerobatics a person has in mind. "As far as the FAA is concerned, any maneuver that involves pitch in excess of 30 degrees and bank in excess of 60 degrees is 'aerobatic,' regardless of the aircraft used," states Peter Bowers, designer of the Bowers Fly Baby.

In general, military fighters, military trainers, purpose-built aerobatic aircraft, some biplanes and several homebuilts are considered "aerobatic," while most civic aircraft, transports, seaplanes, floatplanes and bombers would be considered "non-aerobatic." But the term "limited aerobatics" would apply to almost anything that flies.

◆ **Positioning and placement.** Before your flight, briefly explain what you'll do and where you'll place your maneuvers. For example, if the sun is directly in front of you and the judges, you might tell them you'll do the maneuvers to the left or right of center. Only an idiot would risk losing an aircraft

Brief the judges on all maneuvers, and demonstrate mechanical options and functions. This is important to earn a good flight score; the judges like to know what's going to happen.

An F4U Corsair about to make a perfect touchdown on the center line. To achieve a stable approach and landing, everything must be in sync.

steep dive or descending turn with an appropriate realistic pullout; don't pull out too quickly and break the pilot's neck! When dropping tanks, follow with an Immelmann turn or some type of evasive or aggressive maneuver. I guarantee you'll score better in this manner than with a simple flick of a switch.

Keep in mind that, like typical flight maneuvers, mechanical options are scored from 0 to 10. If your wings don't fold or bombs don't drop, you'll get zero—just like a missed maneuver. Always check these options immediately before your flight. It's easy to take mechanical options for granted, only to have them fail when you need them the most. Let's look at the judging criteria for a typical flight maneuver. It's judged on three basic elements: precision, placement and realism. The fol-

lowing descriptions are taken directly from the Top Gun rule book and are typical of most scale competitions.

◆ **Precision.** When the contestant announces a maneuver, the judge will form a mental picture of the model's flight path. The size of the maneuver will depend on the type of aircraft. Judging begins when the contestant announces (usually) "Beginning now," and continues until the contestant calls the maneuver "Complete." Course corrections that aren't part of the maneuver but are obviously needed to correct deviations in the model's path will lower your score because they show your flight lacked precision. If they're executed in a manner that's typical of the prototype aircraft, smooth, unobtrusive corrections to counter wind drift shouldn't result in lowered scores.

For a judge to obtain a reference point

because of poor positioning, and completing a loop around the sun is a very good example of poor positioning. Also know where the (inside) line is on the runway for completing maneuvers such as flybys, landing-gear demonstrations and bomb drops. Performing maneuvers with the aircraft wing 3 feet from the judges' chairs is dramatic, but it won't garner a high score; it's dangerous. Basics such as these, other safety infor-

Always show the judges the mechanical functions that you intend to use in flight. Here, they're checking the landing gear.

mation and exceptions to the rule book are usually covered in pilot meetings at contests before the start.

After you've explained to the judges where you'll do your maneuvers, you must put them where you said you would, and that requires practice. There are exceptions listed in the rule book, but most maneuvers, such as a figure-8 and a loop, should be centered in front of the judges and pilot. Maneuvers that should be done to the left or right of center include a wingover, a procedural turn and a stall turn. If you aren't sure where your maneuvers should be done, ask the judges.

When you go to the local field, practice your flight routine for at least half of your flights. You might try new maneuvers and practice takeoffs and landings the rest of the time. Have a friend act as your caller—as if you were at a contest. This might seem silly to others at your local field, but anyone with contest experience will understand. If you practice calling maneuvers at your

local field, you won't be as tense when you do the same in front of hundreds or thousands of spectators and judges.

◆ **Total flight presentation.** A poor flight presentation is seen all too often when pilots rush through their maneuvers and cut flybys short so they can set up for the next maneuver. They use only half of the recognized field instead of the full circuit. Using the whole field gives you time to think and set up your next maneuver. Use the time you're allotted to properly set up and complete the maneuvers listed on your score sheet (about 15 minutes at most competitions).

◆ **Flight realism.** In most competitions, this is judged from the time your flight begins to after the landing has been completed. Don't use your time to goof around in the sky or play to the spectators. Fly the aircraft as though it were the full-scale bird up there; after all, that's what flight realism is all about. Observe and listen to some of the expert pilots you know; you'll be surprised at what you will learn.

Above all else, be consistent, practice your routine, know your aircraft and the rule book, and have fun at contests!

Stan Alexander has been a judge for the Scale Masters, the AMA Nationals, FAI Scale Competition and Top Gun.

for the maneuvers, most of them should start and finish in level flight. Because models of light aircraft have insufficient power to begin vertical maneuvers (loop, Immelmann) at level flight, a maneuver that allows them to reach entry speed should precede the vertical maneuver. No points are deducted if the contestant announced the intention to build up speed in a dive prior to the start of a maneuver. At the start and finish of all maneuvers, the wings of the model should be level.

◆ **Placement.** To achieve perfection, all flight maneuvers should be presented in a manner that can be easily judged. The optimum location of the maneuver, relative to the judges, will vary according to the type of maneuver. For example, maneuvers with horizontal symmetry (Cuban-8, loop, roll) should have their midpoint immediately in front of the judges. To present a

Before every flight, check all the functions, including the retracts.

clear view of the model, some maneuvers, such as stall turns and wingovers, are best performed to the right or left of the judges. You may receive a zero score for placement if, in the judges' opinions, the maneuver could have been better performed elsewhere. If a maneuver will be

deliberately flown on a heading that isn't parallel to the runway, the judges should be informed before the flight.

◆ **Realism.** Prior to your flight, clear with the chief of judges any maneuver or scale operation that isn't listed in the rule book. You should be prepared to explain any such maneuver or operation and, if necessary, to supply documentation that such a maneuver is actually within the capabilities of the full-scale aircraft.

The size of the aerobatic maneuvers should reflect the capabilities of the aircraft modeled. For example, if both were modeled to the same scale, a loop performed by a J-3 Cub should be smaller in diameter than one performed by a P-51 Mustang. The speed at which maneuvers are performed must also reflect the capabilities of the prototype. Consideration should be given to the forces that would be exerted on the full-scale counterpart. Exceedingly small or tight maneuvers with unnecessarily high rates of roll, pitch, or yaw do not simulate the performances of most full-scale aircraft and should be downgraded accordingly.

Finally, remember that the smoothness or grace of the flight presentation will have a large impact on its realism. The judges should consider themselves passengers in the model and assess the maneuvers according to how they would affect passengers.

As you can see, the pilot has some latitude in tailoring each maneuver to complement his or her particular aircraft. The winning pilots use this to their advantage in every part of their flight sequence. Whether you fly a Piper Cub or an F-16, don't shortchange yourself by not taking advantage of the flexibility in the rules.

In the past, to be in the winners' circle, pilots would aim for the 180 plateau—a static score of 90 points plus an average flight score of 90 points. Unfortunately (or fortunately, depending on how you look at

To eliminate this problem—especially on lightly loaded aircraft—mix rudder and aileron on takeoffs and landings.

it), with the increased caliber of modelers and pilots, to win these days, a plateau of l90 is needed.

Consistently averaging flight scores in the 90s requires not only skill and planning, but also a great deal of hard contest experience. The only way to gain this type of experience is to participate in judged, scale flying events. Competitions are available for novices as well as seasoned veterans, and with the beginners' class, you can even fly an ARF! So get that scale model, go to a local scale contest and just do it. Watch your competitors, listen to what the judges have to say, and don't be afraid to ask questions. Don't become discouraged; use your score sheets as constructive criticism and a base from which to improve. I don't know any judges who wouldn't be happy to discuss your flight or a particular maneuver and recommend ways to improve. The experience is invaluable!

By now, you can see that scale flying at the competitive level requires a total package of maneuvers, options and sequences. Every aircraft has advantages and disadvantages, as does every flight routine. Every pilot has different skill levels. The key is to build your flight package to optimum advantage in all aspects. When this happens, synergy takes place. ◆

ABOUT THE AUTHOR

Terry Nitsch

Terry has been flying R/C since the age of 10. His interests include helicopters, aerobatics, scale and jets, and he has won both Top Gun and the AMA Scale Nationals. He is also a national pattern champion and two-time winner of the U.S. Scale Masters. Terry is currently working with the Jet Pilots Organization and the AMA to develop safety and operational standards for miniature gas turbine engines. He is a senior manufacturing engineer at GM's Delphi Interior and Lighting plant in Columbus, OH, where he lives with his wife, Sheila, and their two daughters, Angi and Jama.

CHAPTER 20

Scale Bombing Techniques

by George Leu

If, at a scale contest, you drop a bomb as a flight option, you should duplicate the techniques used by full-size aircraft. The execution and follow-through for a drop vary greatly. They depend on the aircraft, the era in which it flew and the type of bomb dropped. This chapter provides several examples that could help you to improve your flight scores.

Garland Hamilton's BVM F-80 Shooting Star is equipped to bomb its target for today. Garland placed second in Expert at the 1995 Top Gun Invitational.

Today, there are "smart" bombs that can be released and then safely directed to targets so that the aircraft is less vulnerable to enemy fire. Although electronic devices have made bombing a science, they have not completely replaced free-fall iron bombs.

Many targets are well-defended, so aircraft seldom fly straight and level over them and simply release their bombs. Dropping iron bombs has many variations. A great deal has changed since WW I, when intrepid pilots hand-dropped sharp metal darts and small bombs over the side of the cockpit. Let's see what's involved.

BOMBING TECHNIQUES

◆ **Straight bombing.** In this standard maneuver, the aircraft flies at a given altitude and releases its bombs over the target. This maneuver isn't 100-percent accurate, but when several aircraft are involved, the target is "saturated." Heavy bombers, such as the B-17 and the B-24, used this type of delivery during WW II; during the Vietnam War, the B-52 followed the same procedure, but at an extremely high altitude.

◆ **Dive bombing.** The aircraft climbs to a high altitude and dives directly at its target. At a safe pull-out altitude, the bomb is released and the plane flies away. This is very accurate. If, however, the target can return fire, the aircraft may be in danger on pull-out. The Dauntless SBD-5 employed this technique during WW II,

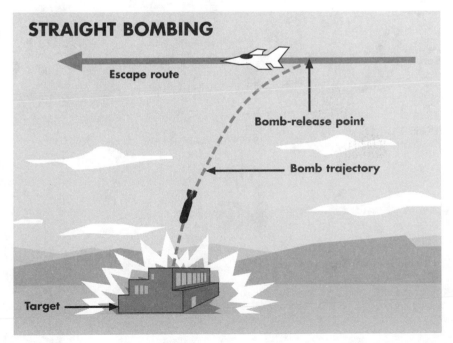

STRAIGHT BOMBING

Escape route

Bomb-release point

Bomb trajectory

Target

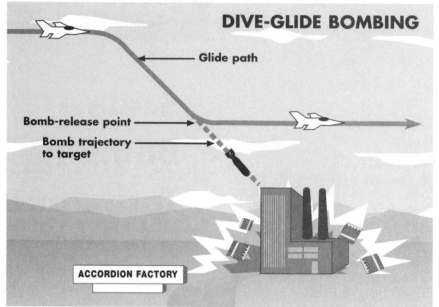

DIVE-GLIDE BOMBING

Glide path

Bomb-release point

Bomb trajectory to target

ACCORDION FACTORY

◆ **Dive-glide bombing.** This technique requires an aircraft to approach its target at a fixed altitude, reduce its speed and, at a slight downward angle, glide toward its target. The bomb is released on the descent, and then the aircraft resumes speed and climbs away. The bomb hits after the aircraft has passed the target. This is a more accurate delivery technique, and it increases the aircraft's safety.

◆ **Catapult-toss bombing.** This new procedure allows an aircraft to escape a heavily defended target. The aircraft starts its bomb run at a very low altitude and high speed. As it approaches the target, it climbs at an angle of between 45 and 90 degrees until it reaches a predetermined altitude for bomb release. After it has been shot out, the bomb continues upward until gravity slows it down and it falls back to earth (preferably right on target). While the bomb does this, the aircraft continues through either an Immelmann maneuver (fighter or light-attack aircraft), or a hard turn (heavy-attack aircraft) and quickly moves away from the target. The A-4 Skyhawk, F-18 and A-6 aircraft use this technique.

and although it was effective, it resulted in a tremendous number of casualties. The German JU-87 Stuka dive bomber also used this technique.

◆ **Direct-delivery bombing.** This is used for close-support bombing. The aircraft dives toward its target at high speed and, when it's close enough to guarantee a hit, it releases its bomb. This method endangers the aircraft and crew, because the escape route begins very close to the target. Marine pilots used this type of bombing during the Vietnam War.

Bombs Away!

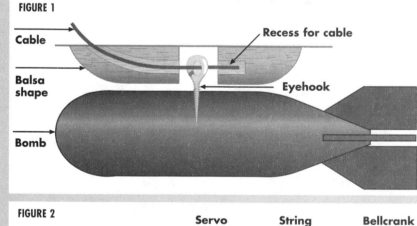

FIGURE 1

Cable

Recess for cable

Balsa shape

Eyehook

Bomb

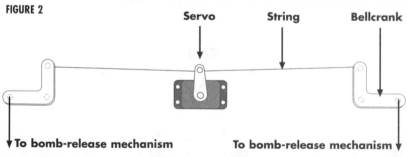

FIGURE 2

Servo   String   Bellcrank

To bomb-release mechanism   To bomb-release mechanism

Use string or a thin metal cable to pull the bellcrank and activate the mechanisms. You can make two bombing passes with only one auxiliary channel.

Models can drop bombs in many ways, but it's best to use a simple, reliable one. For quick, dependable installation, I recommend Vortac bomb-drop mechanisms or one of the units from Hobby Lobby Intl. or Wing Mfg. You can also easily scratch-build a release mechanism out of plywood, a cable and an eyehook (see Figure 1).

If your radio has extra channels, you can hook up several bomb releases; and by using string or thin cable to "pull the pin," you can also have independent bomb drops with only one servo (see Figure 2). The secret to successful bomb-drop setups is to keep everything simple.

The bombs must be light, durable and bear at least some resemblance to real bombs. Solid balsa, fiberglass-covered foam and even small, plastic soda bottles can be used. Fins can be made out of thin plastic or plywood sheets, and these can be reinforced with thin strips of fiberglass cloth. Don't spend a lot of time making perfect, exact miniatures of the bombs; they'll be beaten up when they're used. After all, you're building them to drop them!

The Martin AM-1 Maulers loaded for bear! The "Able Mabel" could carry 10,689 pounds of armament.

Wing Ordnance

A close-up of Garland's bomb installation for this BVM F-80 Shooting Star.

LINING UP

The run toward the target is also a place where differences pop up. During WW II, so that the bombardier could fix the target in his bomb sight, the heavy-bomber pilot flew a straight, constant-altitude course. The Stuka dive bomber often simply nosed over to get the target in its forward gun sight. The British naval bomber pilot flew parallel to and then past his target so that it disappeared under one of the wings; when the target reappeared at the trailing edge, the pilot put his plane into a hard-over turn and dove at it. This method kept the target in sight longer during a bombing run and increased bombing accuracy.

There are more ways to deliver a bomb than I've mentioned here, including:
• **Skip bombing.** To attack ships, B-25s dropped bombs short of their targets to bounce them off the surface of the water.

For all you would-be heavy-bomber and dive-bomber enthusiasts, there's now a source of true-to-scale bombs—Frank Tiano Enterprises (FTE)! These epoxy/glass 500- and 1,000-pounders are suitable for static competition, yet they're strong enough for actual dropping operations. The bombs come in halves that can virtually be snapped together, thanks to a novel indexing lip. When the halves have been securely glued, you fashion your own tail fins with the help of FTE's instructions and the templates that come with every bomb. You must supply or build your own release mechanism.

The bombs are available in 1/8, 1/6 and 1/5 scale and cost from $13 to $24; there's a full money-back guarantee if you aren't completely satisfied.

DIRECT DELIVERY

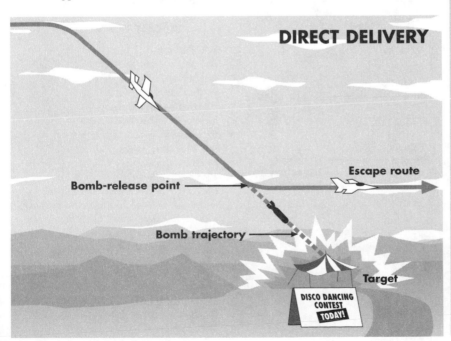

Bomb-release point
Escape route
Bomb trajectory
Target
DISCO DANCING CONTEST TODAY!

Get on target with these beautifully made scale bombs; wing ordnance never looked better!

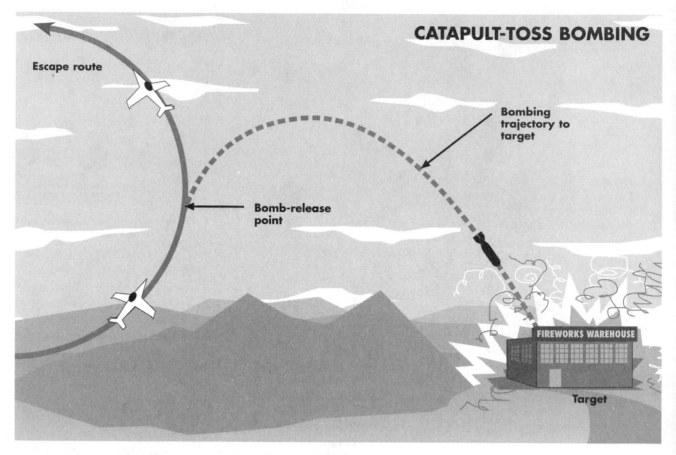

CATAPULT-TOSS BOMBING

Escape route

Bombing trajectory to target

Bomb-release point

FIREWORKS WAREHOUSE

Target

DIVE BOMBING

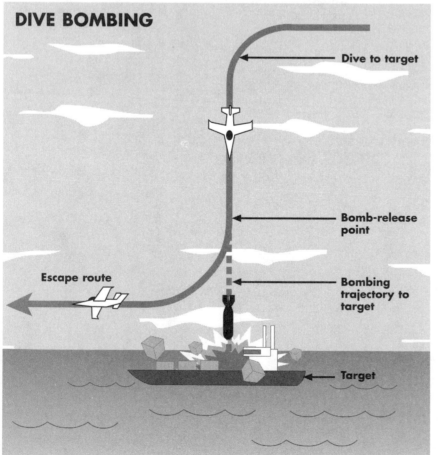

Dive to target

Bomb-release point

Escape route

Bombing trajectory to target

Target

• **Retarded bombing.** To clear areas in the dense Vietnam jungle, A-6 Intruders used small parachutes or pop-up fins to slow their bomb's forward speed.

The next time you attend a scale flying contest, observe the bomb-drop techniques used. The more educated you become on the subject, the better your chances of improving your flight score will be. ◆

ABOUT THE AUTHOR

George Leu

Born into a modeling family, George became interested in R/C flying in the spring of 1968 because he wanted to fly at the Rhinebeck WW I Jamboree, which he did in the fall of 1968. During the '80s, George was active in scale modeling and pattern flying; he wrote for Flying Models, and he was vice president of the NSRCA. He was also involved in changing American pattern flying to FAI (turnaround) style. In 1984, he began to fly jet models; he also continued with scale modeling at the Master's Finals and at many local and regional scale and pattern events. George has been the chief flight judge at Top Gun, and he writes the "Scale Techniques" column for Model Airplane News.

RACING

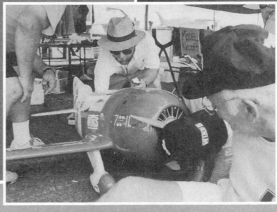

SECTION FIVE
RACING

Many say the thrill of racing is second to none; can any other type of piloting demand as much? In this section, you'll find that winning involves far more than lightning reflexes, finesse and an airplane that's race-ready. In "Go Fast and Turn Left!", Rob Wood, giant-scale racing correspondent for *Model Airplane News* and manager of a successful racing team, provides an overview of techniques and strategies learned from the pros on the giant-scale racing circuit.

In "Enjoy .40-Size Pylon Racing," world-famous, champion pylon racer Dave Shadel offers rare insight into how to win a pylon race. Dennis Crooks, a well-known scale competitor, R/C pilot and successful giant-scale racer, offers his advice on giant-scale AT-6 pylon racing in "So You Want to Try AT-6 Racing?".

Miniature electric pylon racers—long a craze in Europe—have appeared on the scene in the U.S. Tom Hunt tells you how to successfully fly these specialized, inexpensive yet demanding racers in "Speed 400 Pylon Racing." The authors in this section agree that it's not the plane that makes or breaks a race; it's the pilot's technique.

CHAPTER 21

Go Fast and Turn Left!

Secrets of giant-scale racing

by Rob Wood

S o, you've managed to build a giant-scale, Reno-style racer; you've put in several hundred hours of planning, designing, engineering, building, assembling and finishing. You've made your travel arrangements,

A golden-age racer flies down the stretch. Like the Reno and Formula One racers, these make excellent scale subjects.

reserved motel rooms for you and your team, ordered spare parts for every essential element of your aircraft and installed the very best engine and radio money can buy. In short, you're ready for the Big Race—ready, that is, in every way but one: how are you going to fly the course? When I asked veteran racer Bryan Keil (winner of the Formula One Gold at Madera '94) what his advice would be for anyone wishing to win, he said, "Get out front, and stay there!" That's sound advice, but every race has four other pilots who are trying to do just that.

One of the maddening aspects of giant-scale racing is that it's extremely difficult to practice before the races, simply because most of us don't have access to a racecourse with pylons, lights, line judges and—more important—three or four other airplanes to fly against. "They're just model airplanes," you muse. "It's just flying around in circles, isn't it? I can do that—no problem!" In fact, giant-scale racing is unlike any other R/C airplane competition for several reasons.

First, these airplanes are *big* (up to 122 inches in span), and they fly with four other big birds around pylons. That means

that if all five airplanes are evenly matched (as is often the case with AT-6 Texans, for example), the entire pack may very well have to rotate to a knife-edge and pull around the pylon at the same time: more than 40 feet of wings trying to round a 15-foot pylon! Because two objects (or five, for that matter) can't occupy the same space at the same time, the five aircraft have to maneuver around one another as they negotiate the ¾-mile course, and that's part of the exhilaration—and frustration—of giant-scale racing. Though a chapter (or an entire book) can't tell you "everything you always wanted to know" about giant-scale racing, time and time again, the winners have demonstrated some tricks and strategies that I can share with you.

◆ **The course.** The course is a deceptively simple layout: three vertical pylons, approximately 15 feet tall, spaced around a ¾-mile course. The aircraft form up behind a pace plane and wait for the horn that signals the start of the race. (At the Galveston races, they wait around one end of the course in anticipation of a countdown clock.) When the horn sounds, the airplanes dive for the start/finish line, and the six-lap race begins.

This crewman holds the author's Sea Fury and awaits the signal to release it. Your pit crew must concentrate and must know what to do and when to do it.

◆ **The goal.** The goal is simple: fly around (or past) the three pylons six times, and then land.

◆ **The problem.** It's a long, long way between pylons (1,600 feet between pylons one and two, for example), and one's depth perception fails at those distances. When you fly the course, you and your caller will be absolutely convinced that you have flown way past the pylon, when in fact you haven't reached it yet.

Race organizers provide pylon personnel who will switch on a light when your aircraft has crossed the "plane" of the pylon, and you should theoretically wait for the light before turning; if you don't get a light but turn anyway and fail to go around the pylon, you will pay a penalty in time, points, or place, depending on the race (it's known as a "cut"). Thus, the pylons are crucial, and understanding the finer points of negotiating the turns makes the difference between winning and losing.

This Formula One racer has just left the ground after its takeoff roll. These planes have thin, slick airfoils and rely on speed to generate lift.

PYLON STRATEGIES

◆ **Setting up the turn.** If you wait for the light before you start to turn, you'll fly several hundred feet past the pylon before you head back in the opposite direction. The rules say you have to fly past the pylon, but not to the next county! The trick is to "hug" the pylon, and fly the tightest possible course. To do that, you must understand the capabilities of your airplane. Some unlimited airplanes can rival a Quickie 500 in turning ability; for example, just "bank and yank," and fly to the next pylon. Slower (and heavier) unlimiteds, AT-6 Texans and most Formula Ones, on the other hand, must "fly through" the turns using rudder and a wider turning radius. In any race, however, you must begin the turn *before* the pylon light goes on and let the momentum of the airplane's forward motion carry it past the pylon. Thus, your airplane will cross the plane of the pylon halfway through the turn. This is the secret of winning, and it's another argument for getting to know your airplane before attempting to race it.

◆ **Negotiating the turn.** If you start your turn too early, you'll cut the pylon; start too late, and you'll be left behind. Your caller's ability to anticipate the lights is often the element that will make or break your chance of winning, and he or she should coach you through the turns; for example:

"Ready!"—pilot's fingers are poised to move the aileron stick to the left.

"Start your turn!"—slight pressure on the aileron stick.

"Turn!"—full aileron bank, with right rudder.

"Pull!"—up-elevator.

"Straighten out!"—bring the airplane back to straight and level flight.

Because every airplane/pilot combination is different, the caller and pilot must know each other as well as the airplane and course.

◆ **Flying in the pack.** There are two ways to view the aircraft that are vying for the same air space as yours:

—as obstacles you must fly around;

—as accessories to winning.

As obstacles, the other aircraft repre-

A clipped-wing Mustang lands dead-stick—a common practice that helps to avoid breaking those expensive props.

sent hazards and the potential for midair collisions, and many pilots simply fly high or very low to minimize the danger.

On the other hand, some pilots use the competing airplanes to their advantage.

A busy flight line. Pilots need a starter and a couple of holders. These giant planes produce a lot of pull, so make sure you have some strong helpers.

How? For one thing, suppose you're right on the tail of another airplane; if the pylon light-keepers are on the ball, your opponent will get a light before you do, and you can simply turn on *his* light, instead of waiting for yours. Your momentum will carry you past the pylon, and your light will come on after you've already started to head back in the other direction. This is a risky maneuver, but it has worked well for some aggressive pilots.

But let's suppose that you're leading the pack and that the number-two airplane is right on *your* tail. If your opponent and his caller are concentrating on your airplane, you can start your turn early, and then, just before you reach the pylon, bank *right* to avoid cutting it. By the time your opponent has realized what you've done, he has completed his turn *in front* of the pylon, and he has lost points because of the cut!

Here's another risky maneuver used to some effect by pilots: fly high and then dive in front of the leading airplane, thus hitting it with your propwash. This turbulence can cause the other aircraft to veer off the course and lose precious time when correcting for this.

Finally, there's the conservative approach: concentrate on your own airplane, and (more or less) ignore the others. Fly above or below the pack, and complete every race without cutting pylons. Remember the old adage: "If you want to finish first, you must first finish!" Completing every race without cuts will rack up points, and it's the accumulation

of points over the course of the week that determines who flies in the trophy races on Sunday. We've seen some of the slowest airplanes make it into the trophy races simply because the hotshots have self-destructed during the heat races.

STRAIGHTAWAY STRATEGIES

Although negotiating the course between the pylons might seem like a simple case of flying in a straight line, there are also strategies to be considered here. Because aircraft with heavier wing loadings tend to lose ground in the turns, they must make

up for lost time in the straightaways, and there are a few tricks to consider:

◆ **Fly a straight line from turn to turn.** If you veer to the left or right between pylons, you must correct to be in position for the next turn; every correction costs you, because lateral movement bleeds energy off straight-and-level speed. Also, when traveling at high speeds, an airplane that veers slightly can be way off the course in a very short time. Thus, you risk being in the middle of a course correction when you should be setting up for your turn—a prescription for disaster. Your caller's job in the straightaway is to keep you on a straight course ("Bring it in a little bit." "Take it out a little bit." "Good! Hold at that heading."); and your job is to use your rudder to correct your course.

◆ **Dive against the wind, climb with the wind.** If you fly a little too high in the straightaway, you can use gravity to your advantage by increasing ground speed in the dive. To illustrate: suppose your airplane has a top air speed of 100mph, and you're flying into a 100mph headwind; in straight and level flight, your airplane would have an indicated speed of 100mph, but *zero* ground speed.

Because ground speed determines how fast your airplane flies from pylon to pylon, you must use any means at your disposal to increase it. Thus, when you

Silver racers are on the ready line for Friday heats at Reno. Racing conditions can vary greatly depending on location and time of year. Make sure that you are prepared to fly in all weather conditions.

dive into the wind, gravity increases your ground speed. Conversely, wind resistance is decreased in the downwind leg, so climbing expends very little energy; thus, your airplane will be in the proper attitude (and altitude) to take advantage of gravity going into the next straightaway.

◆ **Dive in front of the leader.** If you use gravity to increase ground speed, you can dive in front of an airplane that's flying straight and level; even if your propwash doesn't throw him off course, you might "psych" him out so much that he bleeds off energy in over-correcting. This is another risky maneuver, but it has worked for some pilots.

GENERAL TIPS FOR FLYING THE COURSE

• Conserve fuel while forming up. If you attempt to fly at full throttle during form-up, you'll unnecessarily use too much fuel, thus increasing the amount of fuel you must carry to finish the race. Extra fuel is heavy, and weight is drag. If nothing else, you run the risk of running out of fuel before the race is finished (it has happened to me).
• Anticipate the turns; plan the straight-

Going for the Gold often demands pushing miniature aircraft to the limit. Dick Sizer's immaculate P-63 is pulled through the air by a 17-pound, 12ci twin Husky (a real beauty).

aways. Visualize the entire course as a flight plan, and you'll be in complete control of your race from start to finish.
• Use your rudder! It's amazing to me that so many pilots seem to think that the rud-

der is simply that thing on the back of the airplane that goes along for the ride and moves incidentally only when the tail wheel moves. Use rudder—not

Another popular golden-age racer—the Gee Bee R2—has just passed the finish line and is about to do a victory roll.

ailerons!—to make a course correction in straight and level flight. Ailerons drop the wings and bleed off energy.
• Wear sunglasses with UV blockers, or your eyes will become fatigued, and even giant-scale airplanes look very, very small

1,600 to 2,000 feet away.
• Use rudder—not ailerons!—to make landing-approach corrections. At slow speeds, racers tend to have very little aileron authority.

• Get into the habit of using all the runway you need. Races are always held at airports, where the runway is unlimited. Many pilots land as though they were fly-

ing back at their club field, but it isn't necessary to roll out at your feet. (Racers tend to need a longer runway than sport planes, so try to touch down well downwind of your pilot's box.) If you have the fuel, and you don't like your approach, go around! It's better to suffer a little humiliation than to stay up all night repairing your airplane.

◆ **Go fast and turn left!** These hints aren't all-inclusive, but they do cover the basics. Only experience can provide you with a comprehensive "feel" for racing, but I can sum up all the advice you need in one sentence: get to know your airplane and your caller *before* you get to the races, and practice, practice, practice! ◆

ABOUT THE AUTHOR

Rob Wood

Rob was born in Annapolis, MD, at the U.S. Naval Academy, where his father was an instructor. His first 12 years were spent living on naval bases on the East Coast, so his childhood was filled with the sounds and smells of ships and aircraft. From his first model—a glider with a 4-foot wingspan built from plans that he found in an encyclopedia when he was 10—to his latest giant-scale unlimited racer, Rob has been hooked on airplanes. His team—Classical Racing—has entered every major giant-scale race since 1992 and has won numerous gold and silver trophies.

CHAPTER 22

Enjoy .40-Size Pylon Racing

by Dave Shadel

It hardly seems possible that Jim Shinohara (my caller) and I have been competing in R/C pylon racing for 20 seasons. We have experienced just about every success and failure possible. Fortunately for us, there were many more successes than failures, or we probably would have thrown in the towel years ago! Twenty years in any sport is likely to reward you with some type of success, if you are willing to invest the energy, time and money that it takes to be on top of your chosen game.

Pylon racing is no different from any other sport in that your investments will be rewarded. Obviously, pylon racing has its own idiosyncrasies, and you may gain insight into some of these in the following pages. You might learn some things that will help make your pylon racing road a little less bumpy. My best wishes for safe and successful racing.

PYLON RACING GAMES

◆ **Quickie 500** and its local variations has been around since the early 1970s. Today, Q-500 aircraft that are flown according to AMA rules are faster than the Formula One aircraft that I first raced. Local rules often dictate more sedate Q-500 events in which AMA-legal aircraft powered by sport .40 engines are flown. This is how the events were intended to be; they give beginning racers a place to start. Though you may be the local "hot dog" with an eye on bigger and better things, if you want to get into pylon racing, this is where you need to start: with a Q-500 aircraft and sport .40 engine.

◆ **Quarter Midget .40.** This class was established as the "poor man's" Formula One class. It's nearly equal in performance to a full-blown Formula One setup, but it's much simpler than Formula One, because it requires a variation on the Q-500 engine and low-nitro-content sport fuel. At the national level, aircraft speeds of around 160mph are not uncommon. This event is for those who can easily handle an all-out Q-500 aircraft.

◆ **Formula One** is perhaps the most difficult pylon racing event and the one with the most prestige. Before the competition, the scale-like replicas of full-size Formula One racers are "beauty-judged" to determine their takeoff order; pretty takes off before not-so-pretty. All-out racing engines that burn up to 70-percent nitro are commonly used and, if you miss the engine setting, you can literally melt holes in the piston. High noise levels and speeds above 180mph limit the areas in which these craft can be flown; they're definitely not for newcomers.

◆ **F3D** is a world-class pylon racing event that is usually flown outside the U.S. Though only a handful of U.S. fliers participate in it, the U.S. has owned the World Championship trophy since 1987, and that says an awful lot about our fliers' abilities. These aircraft use custom-built, tuned-exhaust, alcohol-fueled .40 engines with speeds that rival those in Formula One. Again, it isn't a newcomer's game.

YOUR EQUIPMENT

Successful R/C pylon racers seem to cut through the trivial aspects of the events and defeat all obstacles to their goal: to win pylon races. Top competitors in any

Mike Del Ponte's Revolution—one of the available ARF Q-500s.

game are true students of their sport.

I have always maintained that success in pylon racing and other competitive R/C events is determined by 75 percent "you," 20 percent equipment and 5 percent luck.

As you gain experience, the luck factor decreases and the "you" factor becomes more significant. You make a lot of your own luck.

You can buy ready-to-compete packages that are capable of championship-winning performance. Just pay your money, and take your pick. But will you be able to make the plane perform? Not likely. At this point, it's not the equipment's fault that you can't make it work. It's your lack of experience, and that can be increased only over time. That's why it's best to start simply.

For any competitive R/C event, I feel it's important to have the very best equipment, especially when it comes to transmitters and servos. The least expensive versions will work, but they usually lack the precision necessary to fly racing aircraft properly. Servos and transmitters must be extremely accurate to allow the best flight performance. The radio manufacturers have the receiver part of the equation pretty well in hand; nearly all function well.

Support equipment is another factor in your success. To perform maintenance between heats, you should have a neat toolbox filled with things you need. Too

Here's a Nelson .40 Q-500 engine on the nose of Jim Allen's Quick Vee. Note the clean installation.

much junk just makes the right tools hard to find. Your starting equipment should be topnotch, as well. Many zero scores result from failed starting equipment. Remember, if you can't make it run, you can't make it fly (and you can't win the contest!).

BEING CONSISTENT
Early in my racing career, I learned that consistent performance equals winning results.

When I set up my pit area at a contest, my toolbox is always placed to my left, with my aircraft on a holding stand in front of my chair. When I go to the starting line for a heat, my starting equipment is always in the same spot in relation to my airplane. By doing these things consistently, I eliminate errors caused by trivial, thought-cluttering distractions. When I need something quickly, I don't have to frantically search for it.

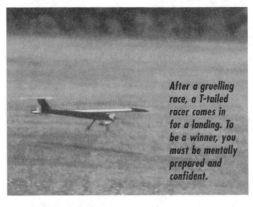

After a gruelling race, a T-tailed racer comes in for a landing. To be a winner, you must be mentally prepared and confident.

The same goes for setting up your aircraft and engine. Through trial and error, I have found that certain things work well in aircraft and engine setup, so I do these things exactly the same way every time; consistency is key.

EYE CONTROL
Your vision is key to your success in pylon racing. To accomplish lap after perfect lap, your sight must be as keen as possible. Many racers need help in this area; they believe that their vision is excellent without having had the benefit of a professional eye exam.

I have worn glasses for most of my life even though I have very good distance vision in one eye. My other eye got the short end of the stick and needs a strong lens to be 80 percent as good as my good eye. If I had never seen an eye specialist, I probably would have figured that my vision was fine. I can fly without wearing glasses, but I fly better with them.

If you wear glasses while flying, try to stick with the type that has little or no frame. In racing, peripheral vision is very important, and thick-framed glasses block too much of it.

Most racers probably choose the colors for their aircraft in an attempt to create a "cool" color combination. Unfortunately, colors that look "cool" on an 18-wheeler or a racecar often don't work on a model aircraft. I have difficulty with white and silver aircraft. They may be pretty on the ground, but they are hard to see in the air. Since the early 1980s, Jim has most frequently painted my Formula One aircraft bright orange, with exactly the same trim schemes and colors. That may sound boring, but it works for me, and no one can argue with success!

YOUR CALLER
A few successful pylon racers have a different caller at every race; but the great racing teams of all time have always been pilot/caller teams who stuck together for years. During my early racing years, I watched guys such as Bob Violett and Cliff Telford (the TV team), Terry and Al Prather, Bob Smith and Jeff Bertken and many other very successful racing teams. I always marvel at the unspoken communication between a pilot and a caller who have worked together for a long time.

It took years for Jim Shinohara and me to become as comfortable with each other as we have. His early calling efforts and my less-than-perfect abilities were well-matched. All I once heard from him was "Ready...turn!" and "We got two cuts." Today, we can talk strategy during the race if we have to, even during laps that take less than 6 seconds!

The only way to establish this intimacy is through lots of practice, so pick someone you really get along with, and start practicing now.

PLANNING A PROGRAM
Many racers, especially beginners with little heat racing or practice experience under their belts, have a lot of variation in their overall performance; in one heat, they enter a stunning performance, and the next heat is "ho-hum."

I still remember those days, and I know what those racers are going through. It is very frustrating and often embarassing, especially if you're a fierce competitor who expects to make a good showing. I also know that the advice you receive from fellow racers is sometimes overwhelming, especially if you're a young person or a beginner.

Well-intentioned fellow racers may offer advice on technical points, psychological tricks, equipment, etc. Most of the advice does more harm than good! It can get so complicated that you may feel you are traveling the path to total discouragement. But these "helpful" hints don't usually address the problems that new racers have.

Beginning racers should expect ups and downs in their performance. When you master the basics of getting the engine to run well and flying the course well every time, then you can experiment with things that other racers claim work for them. Then you find out whom to believe and whom not to believe.

Knowing exactly which moves to make takes years of experience. I know, because it took me many years to realize that, once you've mastered the basics, the "you" part of pylon racing is about 90 percent mental.

◆ **Precision thinking.** Today's high-level competition requires precise thinking and flying. Don't be frustrated by new flying sites, disruptive competitors and other outside forces beyond your control. Adjust your flying style and timing to compensate for varying conditions, but always remember that, if you're mentally prepared, you can handle any situation.

◆ **Interruptions.** Almost everyone has seen the disruptive individual at the club meeting, flying site, or contest. He is the one who wants to argue about everything from the club dues to the color of the sky; then he browbeats the contest officials into giving him "re-fly's" that he thinks he deserves. I have even seen such individuals take their own workers to races to help them cheat for a $5 trophy!

These people need to be shown the door! If you have people like this in your racing group, don't be intimidated by their ravings. Let it be known that their actions will not be tolerated, and if they don't shape up, remove them from your activities. Your racing success shouldn't have to be compromised by these disruptive knuckleheads.

◆ **Negative thinking.** Like any sport, racing has its ups and downs (you know, the dreaded slump). When new racers have a "down" after having struggled slowly upward for quite a while, it's usually because they forgot what they were doing right, or never recognized what they were doing right when they were doing it.

Many factors relate to success in racing: what you eat, how you sleep, whether you party the night before the big race—all affect your attitude and thinking.

Treating this game as an athletic event, with emphasis on the mental side, will help your racing. Don't expect to go to the race with a hangover and do well. It won't happen, and you'll go home disappointed without the trophy in hand. Concentrate on positive thoughts, and always look to the goal of winning.

AIRCRAFT TRIM
This subject is difficult to address uniformly because everyone is comfortable with a slightly different setup.

◆ **Balance point.** If the kit manufacturer didn't give you a starting point, begin at 25 percent of the mean aerodynamic chord. On a constant-chord, no-sweep wing such as a Q-500, it's easy. Just measure the chord (10 inches on a Q-500), and go back 25 percent (2½ inches) from the leading edge. After setting the balance point and control throws, it's time to fly.

◆ **Aircraft feel.** On your first flight, just try to get the feel of the airplane, and don't be too concerned about speed. Set the engine richer than normal, and just get your plane into the air. Check the elevator and aileron controls for correct response. Do they feel right for you? A dual-rate transmitter setup will help this process.

◆ **Balance and throws.** When the elevator and aileron throws have been set to your liking, trim the airplane to fly level (no dive, no climb, no roll). Take the airplane up to 250 or 300 feet, and place it in a 45-degree dive. With the wings level, let go of the controls. If the airplane steepens its dive, it is slightly tail-heavy (add nose weight). If it tries to come out of the dive, it is nose-heavy (add tail weight). Top racers know that, for maximum performance, the balance point should be as far aft as possible. Just remember that an aft balance point can also result in an airplane

allowing the elevator stick to center itself (think about it). I never try to level the wings between the pylons; there just isn't time, and every control-surface movement increases drag and slows the model down.

Once you are comfortable with the above, the airplane can be trimmed to properly negotiate the pylon turns. Take the model up to 100 plus feet in altitude, roll to knife-edge, and pull the elevator hard. The model should make an abrupt 180-degree turn without diving or climbing. If the plane climbs, add weight to the left wingtip in ¼-ounce increments, and try again until the problem disappears. If it dives, put the weight on the right tip, and proceed as above.

These trimming steps are intended only as a guide. Racers develop their own preferred setup over time, but the basics are the same and should get you started.

◆ **Coping with conditions.** If you compete, you will be forced to fly in less-than-ideal weather at some point. Most fliers fear strong wind more than any other condition because it makes contests into "survival of the fittest" matches wherein the losers often go away with damaged equipment.

I usually do a couple of things to be successful on such days. I increase control-surface throws slightly. There are times when the gusting wind will blow

This new entry in the Q-500 wars—the Blackjack by Steve Grattan Enterprises—can be purchased in kit form and in various stages of completion.

that a novice can't handle. So be careful if your skills do not place you in the "expert" category.

When you are satisfied with the control-surface throws and balance point, it's time to trim for the racecourse. I prefer a setup in which the airplane dives slightly if the elevator stick is released during level flight. Because I usually fly the racecourse at between 45 and 90 degrees of bank angle, this setup allows me to move the model out from the pylons by merely

your aircraft down in the corners, and a little extra throw will help prevent it from crashing. Also, for some added safety margin, fly a bit higher than you normally would. Finally, get some practice on these less-than-ideal days. Your contest performance will show it!

◆ **Flying-site conditions.** If you fly contests in new locations, you will undoubtedly encounter flying sites that have less-than-ideal conditions. Trees along both sides of the runway, bad backgrounds for the number-two pylon and a rough runway can make you worry about the safety of your aircraft.

The best approach is to stand out on the course and imagine yourself flying it. Note where the obstacles are, and pick out visible reference points that you can focus on during your flights. Don't forget your landing pattern; plan that, too, because your standard approach may have a big tree in it!

If you do as I've outlined, your fears will be eased, and you'll be able to concentrate on winning the race.

When you are satisfied with the control-surface throws and balance point, it's time to trim for the racecourse. I prefer a setup in which the airplane dives slightly if the elevator stick is released during level flight.

◆ **Nervousness** during competitions is very common. Even top fliers are nervous when competing in an important meet, or when they need an outstanding flight to win. I try to channel nervous anticipation to attain an alert state of mind.

If you focus on how stressed you feel, you can impede your thought processes. You may get so nervous that you forget to fuel the aircraft or change the glow plug before a big heat race. This "stage fright" can lead to serious breaks in concentration.

Incorrect actions result from thinking about your nervousness instead of creating a plan to win the big heat race. Try to convince yourself that you like being "on stage" because it is an opportunity to do your best, not your worst. You can show the other fliers how well you perform under pressure. If you imagine the worst, you almost guarantee a disastrous outcome.

◆ **Have confidence!** If, after all this positive thinking, you're still nervous, you can control it with confidence. Confidence comes from having a strategy to handle any situation that arises. If you have a good plan, you will be confident. When you have confidence in your plan, you can

concentrate on the steps necessary to win the contest.

◆ **Successful attitudes.** Fierce competitors have the desire to excel at their chosen game. My contact with both new and experienced pylon competitors has convinced me that the addage about winners and losers is true: winners expect to win and losers expect to lose. Unless a negative attitude can be reversed, future performances will be determined by past experiences.

A winner's performance is usually the result of past success. His confidence is enhanced by knowing he has the right equipment and a plan and techniques that work. A successful plan usually includes a few personal touches during the "get ready" process. Winners have a plan that works for them, and they practice zero deviation from that plan.

◆ **Fly-offs.** At some point in your racing career, you will probably fly off for a high-placing award in a major competition.

Do not fall into the trap that many competitors do—that of making big changes in your equipment setup. I was guilty of that early in my racing career, and I was not successful in fly-offs because of it. Remember that your basic tried-and-true setup got you to the fly-off and can also take you to the winners' circle.

Examples of changes you should never make prior to fly-offs are fuel, prop and engine changes. Don't set the needle differently; don't try to anticipate your caller. Just keep doing what you have been doing, and your chances for success will be better.

◆ **Hearing protection.** *Pylon racing is hazardous to your hearing.* Read that line again because it's important.

Today, I have permanent hearing loss because of exposure to loud noises during my life. I flew models as a kid in the '50s and '60s when we didn't pay attention to

ear protection. On the flight line in the military I was concerned, but I seldom wore hearing protection because of the need for communication between crew members. I have also used firearms at various times throughout my life.

Most of my hearing loss came about prior to the widespread use of hearing-protection devices and before I was involved in pylon racing; 20 years of that just put the final nails in the coffin of my hearing.

Which type of hearing protection you use is up to you, but I recommend that you use something. If I only knew years ago what I know now.

FINAL THOUGHTS

So, there you have it. Twenty years of various experiences that may help *your* racing. I have, indeed, been fortunate in my racing career. I have had the continuing support of my family and the friendship and assistance of many people, especially Jim Shinohara. It is likely that most people never meet a man like Jim in their entire lifetime. His unconditional generosity is rare in today's world, and I am truly privileged to know him. Thanks again, Jim; we really knocked 'em dead! ◆

ABOUT THE AUTHOR

Dave Shadel

Dave started flying U-control models in the late '50s. By 1962, he was flying combat, stunt and rat-race planes in area contests. While he served with the U.S. Air Force, R/C sailplanes held his interest from 1970 to 1975. In 1975, he began a five-year stint with Kraft Systems (the world leader in R/C at that time), and his ability soared. In 1976, he began Formula One R/C pylon racing and, with the help and guidance of friend and caller Jim Shinohara, he soon became a formidable opponent. The Shadel/Shinohara team has won every major pylon-racing event several times and has represented the USA on five World Championship teams. In '87, '89 and '95, they were named world racing champions. Dave owns Performance Specialties and resides in Nevada with his family.

CHAPTER 23

So You Want to Try AT-6 Racing?

by Dennis Crooks

If you consider the number of entries in giant-scale air racing to be a good guide, the AT-6 class is by far the most popular. At nearly every event, the class is filled and there's a waiting list.

The AT-6 class can be considered an entry-level event, and that undoubtedly

Turning past the number-two pylon and heading toward the third, these AT-6s are in a race for the finish. One little mistake could cause the lead plane to lose its position and allow the one on its tail to win.

adds to its popularity. Because this is a "limited" form of racing, expenses can be kept to a minimum.

AT-6 REQUIREMENTS

◆ **Engine and propeller.** The required Zenoah G-62 engine is very common and very reliable. Engine modifications aren't allowed; you literally take the engine out of the box and bolt it onto the firewall. The only real differences in performance are the result of careful break-in and engine flying time. Bench running is better than nothing, but it isn't nearly as effective as the cycles of heating and cooling (loading and unloading) an engine experiences in flight. It seems that the

more fuel you run through this engine, the better it gets. For the record, race fuel is provided at the event, and it's the *only* fuel you're allowed to use. You'll also be provided with a propeller; currently, the APC 22x10 is the prop used.

◆ **Airplanes.** Choices have increased considerably as a result of racing popularity. Kits are available from: The Aeroplane Works, Bridi Horndog Aircraft, Byron Originals, DW Aircraft, Nick Ziroli Plans, Race Pro Engineering, Saxton Glass, Yellow Aircraft and Zimpro Marketing (see the list of addresses at the end of this book).

The prices and quality of these kits and semi-kits vary considerably. They're all competitive, but some require more effort than others. Before tackling one of the semi-kits, you should make a realistic evaluation of your building skills. Kits typically consist of a fiberglass fuselage and foam wing and tail-cores; construction details are up to you. If you choose this approach, you would be wise to obtain a set of Ziroli AT-6 plans. Before building your chosen kit, request a copy of the AT-6 specification sheet from the

race you plan to enter. I include the most current specs, but changes do occur. As you start to build, you will probably discover that the model exceeds most of these dimensions.

Setting up for the landing takes concentration and good piloting skills. The more proficient you are with landing, the longer you're likely to continue flying the heats.

AT-6 RACER SPECIFICATIONS

WING

	INCHES
Span	100
Root chord	18
Tip chord	9½
Root thickness	2¹¹⁄₁₆
Tip thickness	¹³⁄₁₆
Wing leading-edge radius at dihedral break	⅜
Wing leading-edge radius at tip	³⁄₁₆

STAB

Span	31½
Root chord	11
Tip chord	8
Root thickness	¹⁵⁄₁₆
Tip thickness	½

COWL

Diameter	10¾

FUSELAGE

Length	66½
Width at firewall	10
Width at trailing edge	9
Height from canopy top to fuse bottom	15¾
Rudder top to fuselage bottom	15½

◆ **Wing.** A great deal of attention is given to the AT-6 wing. Most "kit" wings are thicker than the minimum allowed, but making the wing thinner is not the secret to going fast. Keep in mind that the AT-6 racer flies in the 100 to 120mph range—not exactly in the supersonic airfoil category. If there's an "aerodynamic secret" to going fast it is this: parasite drag increases proportionally with speed. To the *AT-6* racer, this means that *all* dimensions should be at the legal minimum, and the airplane should be as aerodynamically "clean" as possible. If possible, avoid having exposed servos, pushrods, control horns, switches, screw heads, etc. They add considerably to parasite drag, and because the AT-6 has a limited amount of horsepower available to overcome drag, it must be reduced.

◆ **Weight.** This must be kept to a minimum also—in this case, 25 pounds dry (no fuel). The straight and level speed of a heavier airplane will be comparable to that of a lighter version, but we don't race

in a straight line. Regardless of your flying style, your racer will slow down in a turn, but a lighter airplane will slow less in a turn and accelerate faster after it.

It is not difficult to build an AT-6 to meet minimum weight requirements. You must pay attention to construction techniques though. Keep in mind that this airplane only has to fly straight and turn left. Admittedly, it turns sharply, but it is not necessarily abusive. You must consider every part of the structure and the stresses it will encounter. As with most models, the tail must be as light as possible. Remember that the loads on the horizontal stab are the opposite of the loads on the wing. An over-stressed wing will fail up; an over-stressed horizontal stab will fail down. I also suggest that the main landing-gear mounts be "over-built," because the AT-6 can be very unruly on landing. It is much easier and quicker to replace bent struts than to reconstruct a damaged airframe.

Now that you have this beast built and balanced, the next obvious step is to fly it. Don't worry about racing yet; just fly. It is very important that you become intimately familiar with your racer. I know it's difficult to sport-fly a purpose-built aircraft, but you must. You'll never be an effective racer if you aren't comfortable with your airplane. On the flight line, there's plenty of nervous tension, and

there's no need to add more with a new airplane. Besides, the AT-6 is an enjoyable airplane to fly.

I should mention that you should not confuse "entry-level" racing with second-class racing. The AT-6 racers are every bit as intense as the unlimited racers. Before a race, most competitors will help a

novice, if asked; during the race, however, a go-fast-or-get-out-of-the-way mentality becomes apparent.

AT THE SITE

◆ **Technical inspection.** Having arrived at the site of the event and completed the required paperwork, you'll go to the technical inspection area. Don't assemble your model; you'll just have to take it apart again. The inspection is very thorough and somewhat time-consuming. The inspectors might find things you have overlooked. Above all, don't argue. They aren't interested in what you have done in the past or at other races. They will also measure and weigh your racer to make sure it meets the minimum specs.

Your engine will also be checked to make sure that it is indeed stock. If it is not, you will be disqualified—no exceptions! When your engine has been determined to be legal, it will be tagged in some way. It's imperative that this tag remain undisturbed; if it's removed or disturbed for any reason, the engine must be re-inspected.

At some point during registration or inspection, you will be given a propeller. You must use *that* propeller—not one just like it. If you break it, you must return the broken blades and buy another. Don't worry about the missing tip, they aren't that picky.

Your pit crew will be a holder and a starter. Have your starter double as your caller; as soon as he has started the engine, he can run back to the pilots' box and immediately start to feed you the information you need.

◆ **Race organization.** When inspections have been completed and the paperwork organized, a race matrix will be posted. This tells you when and against whom you will race. It may also assign a staging position.

◆ **Fuel.** Somewhere between the pits and the staging area will be a fueling station.

Here, they will drain your fuel tank and then refill it with the race provided fuel. Your airplane may also be weighed again at this point.

◆ **On the flight line.** After fueling, you will be directed to the staging area, and when you are staged on the flight line, you will be assigned a color. This color relates to a light on the racecourse pylons. Make sure your caller knows this color.

There are exceptions, but nearly all competitors use electric starters on the flight line. This is not only expedient, but it's also a lot safer. Generally, the race organizers provide starters to those who need one. It's a good idea to practice starting your engine before you get to the race. Depending on the contest director (CD), you will have 2 or 3 minutes to start your engine at the beginning of the race. If you're prepared, this is more time than you'll need.

◆ **Your crew.** You're allowed a three-person crew: pilot, starter and holder. Ideally, your crew will be the same for each race. If that is not possible, you (the pilot) must take charge to make sure every person knows exactly what to do. It works very well if your starter can also be your caller. As soon as the engine starts, the starter should run to your position in the pilot box to become your second set of eyes.

TAKEOFF!

Once the engine is running, the flight-line coordinator will assign you a takeoff sequence. Your holder will probably be directed to position your racer on the runway. You should make sure your holder knows exactly where you want your airplane and that he doesn't release it until you're ready. At this point, it's imperative that you remain cool and disciplined. Do *not* rush the takeoff. There may be people shouting and running around trying to rush you. *Don't get rattled.* If you blow the takeoff, you won't be able to race, and that's why you're there.

Again, depending on the race organizer, there may or may not be a pace plane. If there's a pace plane, find it and stay with it. Some formation-flying experience will help a great deal here. Ideally, you should be able to watch three airplanes at once—yours, the pace plane and one of your more serious competitors. This takes practice and good depth perception. Your comfort level with your own aircraft will show here. You should be able to adjust the position and speed of your racer automatically while watching the pace plane.

Your caller can be a great help. He

should be able to absorb the entire picture, including the person who will start the race. When all the racers are behind the pace plane and the starter is ready, the race will start. Just before pylon 2, the

The AT-6s used in these races have to meet certain specifications, including: 100-inch wingspan, Zenoah 62 engine and a dry weight of 25 pounds.

pace plane will peel away; now you're racing and you must receive a light and go around pylons 2 and 3. But your race time won't start until you cross the official start/finish line, which will be in the vicinity of the pilot stations.

THE RACE

Once the race is under way, your caller's job becomes even tougher. Even though the AT-6 is easy to fly, you will have to concentrate to make sure it stays exactly where you want it. There is no way you can watch the whole race or judge when to turn; your caller must know your flying style, be able to absorb the whole picture and have above average depth perception.

As I mentioned earlier, at the pylons, a light comes on when your airplane has passed a pylon and it is safe to turn. This is where your caller goes to work. In a tight race, you must start to turn before the light comes on. This requires that you judge your speed and position accurately to make sure you do, indeed, go around the pylon.

◆ **Scoring.** This is based on a 12-point scoring system: 10 points for first, 9 for second, etc., and a 2-point bonus for finishing the race.

If you turn and the light does not come on, it is considered to be "a cut." A cut will earn you a penalty of 1 point; two cuts—3 points; and with three cuts, your score will be zero. So, technically even if

you receive a zero for the heat, you'll still receive 2 points for finishing.

Some races have adopted a time penalty for cuts. This is a little more cumbersome but can benefit racers. For instance, if a

cut means a 10-second penalty, but you're 11 seconds in front, you'll still win.

◆ **Strategies.** There are many racing strategies, and you will develop your own. The preferred racing style is so simple that it is difficult. When the race starts, you'll descend to racing altitude, let's say 20 feet. When you reach this altitude try to stay there. Climbing and diving have the effect of lengthening the racecourse.

You must also decide how much risk you're willing to accept. Sooner or later—and probably repeatedly—you'll be challenged for your position—airborne "chicken." Only experience can teach you how to deal with a specific challenger. Regardless of your course of action, any adjustments—assuming you choose to do something—should be made very carefully.

Keeping heading changes to a minimum is not as easy as it sounds. The most common error is to turn too sharply as you round a pylon; this means that you have to weave back out onto the course to avoid slicing the next pylon. Slicing means that you go beyond the pylon and then turn and come back, but you did not go around the pylon. Slicing is not allowed, and it is difficult to see.

Your caller should count the laps; there should be six. This is not crucial information, but it's nice to know. If you're being challenged, knowing the lap number allows you to dive for the finish line for every last bit of speed.

At the end of the race, you'll be told to climb to altitude and hold. You may also be given a landing sequence. Therefore, regardless of your faith in your caller, do not stop racing until told to do so officially. Your first few races will probably seem quite long, but when you climb to altitude, you may start breathing again. Try to relax, but do not take your eyes off your airplane.

At this point, you might try reducing power and adding a few degrees of flap (you do have flaps don't you?—wing center section, at least). They will make your life a lot easier for the most difficult part of AT-6 racing—landing. Within reason, the slower the better. Only practice will teach you how not to bounce, and the AT-6 will bounce with the best of them. Knowing how to land becomes even more important when your other competitors do

A perfectly set up wheel landing. With the AT-6, you must be able to control the plane through the touchdown and rollout.

not know how. It isn't unusual to have the runway littered with airplanes and pieces of airplanes that have to be avoided.

It can be very satisfying to have won the race then to taxi back to your holder. Now go to the pits and tell everyone how easy it was, even though you know, deep inside, that during the race, you were so nervous that you would have given the transmitter to anyone who would take it! ◆

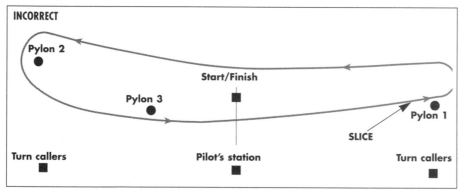

As you can see from the drawing, it is better to fly a straight line between the pylons than to run the risk of cutting it by flying a curved line.

ABOUT THE AUTHOR

Dennis Crooks

Dennis has been involved with aviation all his life. He holds a B.S. in aerospace technology and a commercial pilot's license with multi-engine and instrument ratings. He also held a flight instructor certificate for many years. After retiring from a charter pilot position that he held in Chicago, he began to perfect his modeling skills. He has designed and built many aircraft including a folding-wing TBM, twin-engine ducted-fan SR-71 and an F-14. With his Learjet 35A, he became the U.S. Scale Masters champion in 1993 and won the Toledo static competition in 1995. Looking for a new challenge, he took up giant-scale air racing and became the AT-6 Grand National Champion in his first year. Next, he plans to branch out into the Unlimited class.

CHAPTER 24

Speed 400 Pylon Racing

by Tom Hunt

The Speed 400 pylon racing class revolves around the use of a very inexpensive (less than $12) electric motor to fly small, light models around three pylons at speeds that average 50mph. The electric motor, made by Mabuchi for Graupner of Germany, is called the Speed 400. Pylon racing is just starting to catch on here in the U.S., but many people build the models just to sport fly. In Europe, where this class first emerged, one can find a race somewhere every few weekends. Most model designs are scratch-built, but Graupner and other European manufacturers are beginning to introduce all-wood and ARF versions.

The model designs range in wing area between 130 and 180 square inches and weigh between 13 and 20 ounces. There are conventionally configured models, flying wings, canards and even twins! In Europe, the final rules are still fluid, but the one fast rule is that the motor must be a Speed 400 (any of three different-voltage versions) and have a maximum of seven cells on board.

The power system usually incorporates a BEC-type speed control. A few good controllers have appeared on the market in the last year or so, especially those designed for Speed 400 applications. Two that come to mind are made in Europe. One—the Schulze—is a fully proportional, high-frequency speed control with BEC (battery-eliminator circuitry) that accepts six to eight cells with a maximum current rating of 16 amps. The instructions are written in German only, but those familiar with this type of controller won't find it difficult to set up. It's available through Slegers Intl. of Wharton, NJ.

The other controller is made in England by Gordon Tarling. It is also a fully proportional, high-frequency speed control with BEC, and it's capable of handling six to eight cells, but it has a maximum current rating of 20 amps. Called the Micro-star 20BEC/B, it's only available direct from Gordon.

RULES

In my home club, SEFLI (Silent Electric Flyers of Long Island), we adopted some of the European rules and modified others to suit our environment. The rules and course layout are shown in Figure 1. The battery cell of choice is the SR 500 Max (an "A" cell). In Europe, (because the races are longer), the preferred cell seems to be the red 600 or yellow 650 sub-C. The choice of propeller varies with the choice of motor, but 6x3 to 6x6 are common.

The SEFLI course setup shouldn't be unfamiliar to those who already race models. Each flier requires a timer/caller at the near end and a flagger at the far end of the course. The SEFLI field is atop an old landfill (approximately 50 to 60 feet above surrounding ground level). The number 1 pylon flaggers stand on the crest of the hill. If a model deviates from the course, the flaggers can find shelter on the steep face of the hill. If your field does not provide this natural protection,

Three Speed 400 racers designed by the author. Left: Tom Hunt built this SSP-400 7.2V Speed 400 on seven cells with a Graupner 6x5.5 prop. Foreground: Don Abramson built this 6V Speed 400 on seven cells with a Poli 6x4 prop. Rear: this twin-boom, P-38 look-alike (built by Tom Hunt) uses two fiberglass SSP-400 fuselages and a fiberglass nose pod, foam wing-core, and two 6V Speed 400s on seven cells, each with 6x3 Graupner folders.

The single-motor version—the SSP-400—is available from Modelair-Tech as an all-balsa plan, or a fiberglass and foam semi-kit.

it would be prudent to erect a fence or cage to protect the flaggers. A master timer should also be on hand to verify the winning time.

The SEFLI club limits the number of planes in the air to four. Most races, though, are with three planes or fewer because of manpower constraints or frequency conflicts. With four models in the air, all doing in excess of 50mph on a

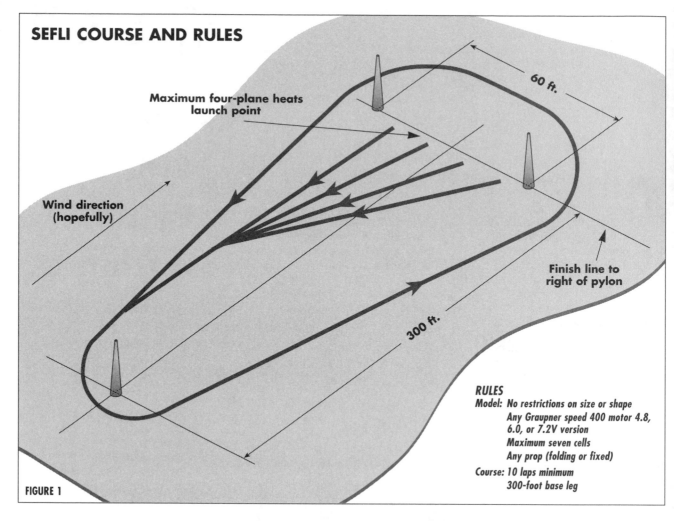

SEFLI COURSE AND RULES

Maximum four-plane heats launch point

60 ft.

Wind direction (hopefully)

Finish line to right of pylon

300 ft.

RULES
Model: *No restrictions on size or shape*
Any Graupner speed 400 motor 4.8, 6.0, or 7.2V version
Maximum seven cells
Any prop (folding or fixed)
Course: *10 laps minimum*
300-foot base leg

FIGURE 1

very short course, the excitement is high, but brief. The race is flown for 10 laps. A cut pylon is a 5-second penalty; the second cut pylon is a disqualification. SEFLI uses these rules because these models only stay in the air for a limited time (owing to battery-pack capacity). Making a flier go another lap because of a cut pylon may cause a DNF (did not finish) if the motor pack runs out. There's hardly ever a delayed start waiting for a pilot to get the motor started; however, DNFs have occurred because of insufficient charge, or a failure in the electrical system. Because the races last only 2 minutes, sport flying in between races is encouraged. There's no need to shut the club field down for an entire day or morning just to race.

FLYING TECHNIQUES
As in most pylon events, the one who doesn't midair or come in contact with the ground usually wins. For the sake of continuing this chapter, let's assume that at

least two people remain in the air for most of the race. Almost every time, smooth, consistent flying technique will win over a

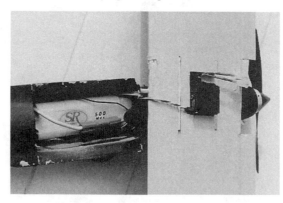

Radio installation is tight in these small models: the speed control and micro receiver are behind the motor; the 7-cell battery pack is under the wing; the elevator servo is behind the trailing edge of the wing; and the aileron servo lies flat on the bottom of the thin wing.

faster airplane flown by a less skillful pilot. The power system limits the model's top speed, and the model's shape isn't very important as long as it can be easily flown. Because the SEFLI course has very

short straightaways, the turns are crucial. The model and pilot must be capable of turning tightly without causing a high-speed stall. Wandering in the straight sections is also a cause of slow times.

The model should have good roll control and stability. Excessive roll rate (aileron) can make the model very difficult to position as it exits the turns, and this means a greater distance traveled and slower race times. Excessive pitch control (elevator) can cause the model to snap-roll in the tight pylon turns and "depart" you from the race. Novices should set up their models with low deflections and increase them as they gain experience. I still prefer models that have a long wingspan (relatively speaking for this class) and long tail moments (with the horizontal tail farther back). This enhances the model's natural pitch and roll damping and allows it to track straighter coming out of the turns. The disadvantage of this type of model is that it weighs slightly more than a smaller, close-coupled model, and it doesn't turn quite as tightly, but it is a smoother airplane to fly at all skill levels. This type of model wins races because it doesn't wander on the course because of pilot over-control.

◆ **The start.** Figure 2 depicts the technique that I use to successfully race in the Speed 400-class pylon races. At the master timer's command, all the pilots launch their models simultaneously toward the far pylon (pylon 1), which is hopefully positioned upwind. The pilot heaves his model—not to gain an advantage, but to ensure that the model will fly safely straight ahead if something fails electrically at launch. A wimpy toss could also make you susceptible to a strong wind gust just when your fingers are *not* on the sticks. If a midair is going to happen, it will occur as you enter the first turn. Assuming that all pilots make this first turn, it's time to settle into a routine.

◆ **The race.** As speed builds (maximum speed will not occur with these models until at least one lap is flown), the pilot should be aware of the turns but should not "anticipate" them, i.e., the pilot should develop a rhythm of leaning into each turn with aileron control and pulling as hard as required with the elevator at the moment the timer/caller yells "Turn." The model should climb ever so slightly during the turn because there is no rudder to prevent the nose from falling.

When the model completes the far, end pylon turn (pylon 1), dive it slightly to remove excess altitude, level the wings smoothly and bolt toward the near, side pylons (numbers 2 and 3). This part of the lap should *not* be two square corners unless the pilot is highly skilled. Lean into the number 2 pylon slightly, and tighten the turn enough to go around pylons 2 and 3 in a constant-radius turn. Also, this turn should be done with a slightly climbing attitude. Assuming the wind is blowing from the number 1 pylon, the model

should be commanded into a slight dive toward that pylon to start the process all over again.

◆ **The finish.** Let's assume the race is close. Out of the number 1 pylon on lap 10, two or more models are within a couple of model lengths of one another. If, after 10 laps, these models are this close, it's safe to assume that they're all traveling at about the same speed. To gain the edge, dive to the finish line with the wings leveled as soon as possible. To transfer as much potential energy (altitude) into speed as possible, the model should cross the finish line at 2 to 3 feet of altitude. Now, pull up quickly and do a victory roll before you mow the grass!

FINAL THOUGHTS
• Speed 400 models should be designed to be reasonably easy to fly (that's why many are flown for sport).
• To fly smooth turns and unwavering straightaways, they should be well-

RACING TECHNIQUE

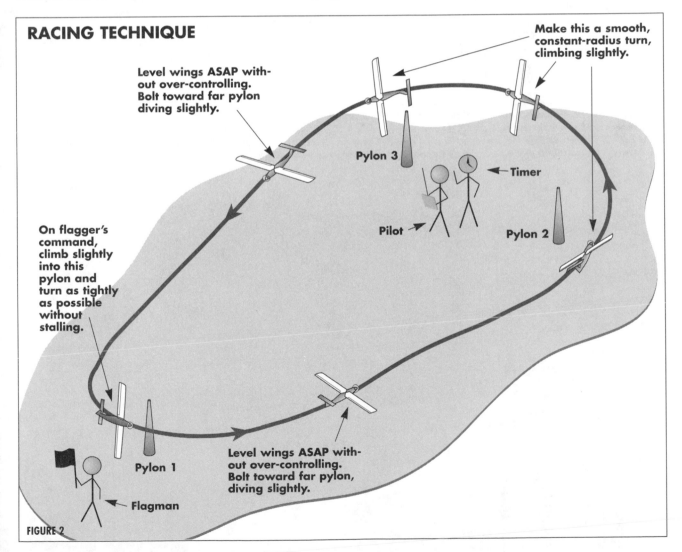

Make this a smooth, constant-radius turn, climbing slightly.

Level wings ASAP without over-controlling. Bolt toward far pylon diving slightly.

Pylon 3

Timer

Pilot

Pylon 2

On flagger's command, climb slightly into this pylon and turn as tightly as possible without stalling.

Pylon 1

Level wings ASAP without over-controlling. Bolt toward far pylon, diving slightly.

Flagman

FIGURE 2

damped in pitch and roll.
• Fly the models with a rhythm. Straight, roll in, pull, roll out; straight.... Repeat as necessary for 10 laps.

• Do not attempt to look around for the nearest plane. Fly as if you're the only one in the race.
• If the race gets close near the end, don't

upset your rhythm; just dive to the finish at a minimal height and prepare for that victory roll.

I hope that these techniques will help to make you a better pylon racer. I'd like to see this event grow as big here in the U.S. as it has grown in Europe. The models are inexpensive, and you can fit two dozen in a small station wagon! Happy racing! ◆

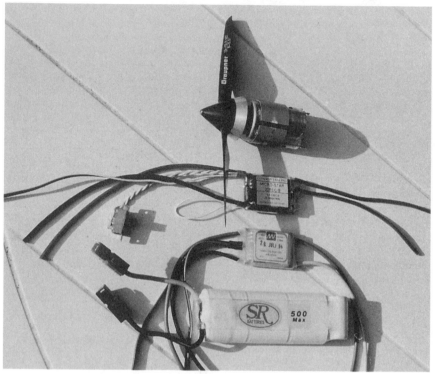

Top: Speed 400 7.2V motor with Graupner 6x5.5 prop. Also, notice the two candidate speed controls: a Gordon Tarling ESC from England rated at from 20 amps for 6- to 8-cell BEC (above); and a Schulze ESC from Germany rated at 16 amps for 6-to 8-cell BEC (below).
  The 7-cell SR 500 Max pack provides the power. Note: the connectors have not yet been installed in the speed controls. The controller is usually hard-wired to the motor, and the connectors go to the battery.

ABOUT THE AUTHOR

Tom Hunt

Tom Hunt has been building and flying model airplanes since the age of 10. In 1979, he earned a B.S. in mechanical engineering and took his first professional job as a wind tunnel test engineer with Grumman Aerospace. Since then, he has pursued a masters degree, worked for Lockheed Missiles and Space as a wind tunnel model designer and, in 1982, returned to Grumman as a senior engineer. He designs and builds ducted-fan, scale and sailplane models, many of which have been published. Recently, Tom has been developing practical VTOL model aircraft and electric model designs and flight systems. He won first place in Class A Sailplane at the 1995 Electric National Championships and is a regular contributor to Model Airplane News.

SECTION 6
SOARING

SECTION SIX
SOARING

The graceful world of soaring and thermalling is more competitive than many sport fliers might imagine. Timed events, finding thermals, aerobatics without an engine, distance runs and the power needed to hand-launch are just a few of the many things that are covered in this section. Mike Lachowski, *Model Airplane News* soaring columnist, sailplane designer and successful competitor, gives you all the answers to finding lift in "How to Soar with the Eagles." Dave Garwood, *Model Aviation* soaring columnist and a long-standing contributor to *Model Airplane News*, offers tips for the newcomer in "Your First Glider Competition" and "Slope Soaring."

Dennis Phelan, a member of the National Soaring Team, covers the competitive sport of F3B thermal soaring, and Brian Agnew, hand-launched glider champion, offers advice on how to get the most out of your glider in "How to Handle Hand-Launched Gliders." Did you know that the fastest R/C plane is a glider? Well, you do now, so keep reading, and check out what these world-class glider pilots have to say about their flying techniques.

CHAPTER 25

How to Soar with the Eagles

Find thermals wherever they lurk!

by Mike Lachowski

On a perfect soaring day, new glider pilots can launch and fly only to find themselves in a landing approach. Why is everyone still soaring? Until you look at what the experts are doing and gain that soaring knowledge, achieving a long flight will be a hit-or-miss affair. The first step is understanding the source of thermals. You also need to know what triggers a thermal and makes it break loose from the ground and head toward the clouds. It seems pretty simple, but it isn't. Weather, terrain and other factors vary, even within a few hours on the same day. After finding lift, it's up to the pilot. How do you fly in lift and sink? What do you need to practice? Let's start with the sources of lift.

SOLAR HEATING

Warm air is lighter air; the molecules move more rapidly and take up more space. Air is a good insulator, but it's poor at conducting heat, that's why winter clothing keeps us warm. Only the air trapped within the clothing is heated. The air heated by the ground retains its heat unless it's mixed with other air.

The heated air in that elusive thermal gets its energy from the ground. Solar energy passes right through the atmosphere without warming the air, but it does warm the ground. Let's look at some factors that affect solar heating.

◆ Shadows from passing clouds will prevent the ground from being heated. Areas that have been in shadow for some time are poor places in which to look for thermals. The shadow cuts off much of the energy that would otherwise be input to the ground. You can watch the clouds move by and predict when areas will be in shadow or sunlight. If you're flying near the edge of a cloud's shadow, you should fly toward an area that's still in sunlight. Another tactic is to preserve altitude until the cloud shadow moves and the ground starts to heat again.

◆ Haze and smog also reduce ground heating. The best thermal soaring weather on the East Coast occurs in the spring and the fall during cool, dry, clear skies of the polar continental air from Canada. Hot, humid days in the summer provide only weak thermals; there isn't usually much you can control here. All you can do is adjust your flying. On hazy days, take advantage of light-lift and low-sink areas ("sink" refers to descending air). On clear days that have stronger lift, be more aggressive in covering ground to get to thermals.

◆ The angle of the sun's rays changes ground heating. The angle changes with latitude, season, time of day and terrain. Hills are great for soaring because of the temperature differences between sunny and shadowed slopes. These differences help to trigger thermals (especially in calm air).

Weaker thermal   Stronger thermal

Hills facing the sun receive more direct heat and are more likely sources of thermals than hills sloping away from the sun. Don't forget the cloud shadows that curtail or shut down thermal generation.

THERMALS, MOISTURE AND HUMIDITY

Air that contains water vapor is lighter than dry air. The combination of water vapor and warm air provides just what we need for a thermal.

Water vapor gets into the air in several

ways, including by evaporation from moist ground. Unfortunately, evaporation requires a great deal of heat, so the actual temperature of the rising air in humid conditions is much lower than the temperature of rising dry air. Moisture in the air conducts heat away from the thermal and spreads it out, reducing the thermal's strength. Also, although air is a poor conductor of heat, water is an excellent conductor. That's why you put a vapor barrier in a house to protect the insulation from moisture.

Can you now see why thermals on humid days are weak and fuzzy when compared with the nice, well-defined "ideal thermals" that you're likely to find on dry days? The dust devils you get on humid days are really big (some folks call them tornadoes!).

Plants are a wonderful source of moisture. Trees put tons of water into the air each day. Trees heat up at different rates, and their rates of transpiration (how much moisture they put into the air) vary. If you must search for thermals in a forest, pick evergreen trees instead of deciduous ones because they put less water into the air, so the air is heated more effectively.

The nicest part about water vapor is that it scatters light and turns a blue sky white. Now you know why some people can just look up and see thermals some days. They're looking at hazy areas of moist air. Most of the time, this air is rising; it might not be rising rapidly, but it's more than enough to keep a plane aloft. If you're

Finding Thermals

So, you want to learn more about thermal soaring, but you don't want any part of the regional or national contest scene. If your club never has enough people to help with its local contests, why not offer to help with the winch?; it's an excellent way to practice observing.

A lot of thermal soaring has to do with carefully observing the air and the objects around the field. As you help with the launch, observe what the pilot is noting. Pick out areas where you think there's lift and where you think the air is really bad for soaring. Then watch the glider to see whether you were right; or did the pilot have different ideas? You won't be able to keep watching because you'll soon have to launch the next glider. After that, try to find the glider you launched previously. This is great practice in finding airborne gliders or birds quickly.

Keep an eye on your watch. Can you pick out lift cycles? With only occasional flights, you may not be able to pick them out, but if you have a nice stream of contestants stepping up to the winch, it's easier to tell what's happening to the air currents. If you find a regular cycle of thermal activity, look for other clues that are related to it. Is there a regular cloud pattern? Do any ground-based indicators like flags or trees show the lift?

Take time out; practice observing when you aren't distracted by flying. There's plenty to learn, and everyone will appreciate the help, too.

used to dry weather, take a trip to the Midwest in late summer. These conditions are quite common there at that time.

THERMALS CAUSED BY MOISTURE DIFFERENCES
The last places you might think to look for a thermal are at a lake or a swamp. Surprise! A difference in humidity can

actually create thermals there, even if the temperature over the area is lower than that of the surrounding area. At the '93 Tangerine, the swamp behind the landing area was often the source of very light lift. The extra moisture was just enough to keep the planes aloft. Sometimes, the lift would break away but, generally, it dissipated downwind. If you fly where it's cold

Evergreen forests produce better thermals than deciduous ones. Less water evaporates from the evergreen trees, so the thermals are better.

and a nearby pond or lake is warm enough, the combination of warmth and moisture is a good source of thermals.

By now, you're starting to make a list of thermal sources. No one source, however, is guaranteed. Thermals depend on specific weather conditions: dry air, moist air, temperature, winds, terrain and time of year. There's no substitute for practice and experience.

WORKING A LIGHT, HUMID LIFT

When flying in light, humid lift, the most frequent mistake is forgetting Dave Thornburg's wonderful analogy of, "the river of air," which implies that the air moves downwind. The effects of this "river of air" can be seen when an inexperienced flier, thrilled that his model is hanging in there so well just upwind of the launch, can't keep his plane in the air long enough to make a "max" because a stream of bad air (no lift) has floated into the plane's space.

To avoid that problem, you need to make a nice, careful circle and drift downwind with the good stream of air. You probably don't need a tight circle; a really good pilot can look as though he's just flying around, not even working the lift. Just keep track of everyone upwind so you know where the lift ends.

SURFACE-HEATING CHARACTERISTICS

The more sun there is, the more energy there is for the ground to absorb. The amount of energy that's absorbed depends on the type of ground surface. Some energy is reflected immediately. (Look outside on a sunny day when the ground is snow-covered.)

The energy that the earth's surface emits forms wavelengths that happen to be in the infrared band, which we can feel as heat but we can't see. This radiation heats the air; it's a source of thermals!

◆ *How is enough air heated to produce a thermal?*
Remember that air—especially dry air—is a poor conductor of heat. So if things are relatively calm, large "parcels" of air are heated. Eventually, they break loose as thermals. Strong winds cause problems; the turbulence mixes the warm surface air with higher air, and that distributes the heat. This greatly reduces the formation of overheated surface air that could otherwise form a strong thermal.

The sun's energy can't all be absorbed by the earth's surface; thermals are the results of the earth's radiating part of this energy (see the Surface Variations chart). We glider

pilots get to take advantage of this. Some of the surface areas that produce more thermals are dark, smooth surfaces such as the tar and cement of our roads and cities, barren brown fields, sand beaches, dry river beds and smooth deserts.

On windy days, we must search for thermals over areas that are protected from the wind. Because the wind is not blowing directly over it, the air near the surface of these areas has more time to heat up. Dense forests and crop fields are good sources to check out.

Also, the leeward side of a slope is a good source, especially if there's an area of

trees just upwind. These trees house thermals that eventually rise, are taken by the wind and deposited over the leeward side of a slope.

A THERMAL BREAKS FREE

OK, we have some hot "light" air on the ground just waiting to become a thermal. It's hot and light but that doesn't mean it will rise. If it rose immediately, you could never have a bubble or column of rising air. In reality, the hot air is more like the drop of water that hangs down until it gets too big or is disturbed and released. Our hot air is a "drop of air" on top of the ground. Something must happen to it for it to leave the ground and rise as a thermal.

A thermal can be triggered in many ways. All that's needed is some surface irregularity to break it free: a temperature contrast, the motion of some object (which will disturb the air), or a small "slope" that causes the air to break free and move upward. Remember, we are looking at triggers; the heat source for the air could be well upwind of the trigger. The air must move along the ground and get to the trigger before it can break free.

A variety of surfaces—the edge of a wood, a river bank, crop fields—reflect and absorb different amounts of energy

thereby causing varied surface temperatures. Who wouldn't prefer to walk barefoot in the grass instead of on the hot tarmac?

◆ *Who says you can't make your own thermals?*
On a calm day, vehicles driving by can provide a disturbance that breaks a thermal loose. Even launching sailplanes or slamming a door has been known to work. Standing in the middle of a field on a calm day, you can feel the bubble of hot air traveling along the ground. It's not a thermal yet. You need to look around and

find the trigger and wait patiently until the thermal breaks free. If you're on the landing approach of a short flight, this is just what you need to pull out that max flight.

When the wind speed increases, small "slopes" become your best friends. When flying, the edges of a wood or a cornfield, or a tree line become primary search areas. Quite often, the local experts know where these areas are and include them in their thermal search. Watch where they first find a thermal, and find out why they like a particular tree line.

Strong winds present additional problems; forget all the low-level bubbles of air. The wind will mix the low air and never allow the warm air to accumulate and start a thermal. You'll still find thermals on these days—quite often, a few hundred feet in the air. All this low-level, mixed-up air is still warmer than air that's higher in the atmosphere, and parts of this layer of air can begin to rise, but you won't find many ground features to use as thermal detectors. Often, the cloud activity is the only guide to lift. All your usual favorite lift spots will fail you, but by watching the cloud activity and the other pilots, you can predict max flights and short flights before the pilots launch.

Thermal Flying Hints for Beginners

- Search for thermals near changes in the terrain, such as tree lines or edges of fields.
- Search where people recently found thermals, i.e., 10 to 15 minutes earlier, not two hours before.
- Turn the plane immediately when you see the tail rising, or a wingtip rises and turns you away from a thermal. Don't wait for the model to start climbing.
- Bank the glider and maintain a

banked turn at low speed. Don't try to slow down too much.
- Keep the speed and the bank angle constant.
- Don't reverse the direction of your turn unless others are flying in the same thermal in the opposite direction.
- Move away from the poor-air part of the circle. Make only a small correction within each circle.
- Don't circle over one spot; move downwind as you circle.

SEARCHING FOR THERMALS

◆ *How should I look for lift?*

Fly as often as possible in all conditions on a particular field; eventually, you'll learn when and where to find thermals (lift).

Whenever I visit a new flying field, I drive around to see what's just beyond it; I look for potential lift sources. There might be a swamp or a river just downwind, and you really don't want to land off the field. I always like to find the east-facing slopes on the field. They're the last search points for first-round flights because they will usually have some lift. After searching other areas, always make sure you have enough altitude to visit the east-facing slopes.

There is one other thing you want to look for. After you've spotted the sources of heat, you must figure out where thermals are "triggered." Where will this hot air break loose from the ground and start rising?

The time of day determines the strategies you need to adopt to find and work lift. How often have you seen inexperienced pilots try to fly all day where they found lift in the morning? They didn't find any lift all afternoon.

◆ **Stability and lapse rate.** During the day, the sun's angle and the stability of the air change. Stability is measured by lapse rate—the rate at which the temperature decreases with altitude. The higher the lapse rate, the more unstable the air and its vertical motion and the more thermals there will be. Also, if temperature increases with altitude, you get an inversion and the air becomes extremely stable with nothing rising through the inversion. Enough with the jargon; how can you get a longer flight?

◆ **Morning thermals.** In the morning, first consider topography. An area that faces the sun is the best place to find lift. If there's one spot in your flying field in which everyone flies in the morning, I bet it's facing the sun. Of course, by noon and later, other areas will be much better thermal sources, and thermal activity over the

Looking at a Field

We arrive at the field and park near the south corner. Looking down the road to the northeast (1), we see a wooded area and some ground just before the trees that is not sod. This requires some investigation. Turning toward the north (2), we see

with some high grass. This depression will allow heat to build up for a thermal. When the wind blows from the direction of the trees, the trees can act as a shield and "degrade" the thermal activity. When the wind blows over the field toward the trees, the trees can trigger thermals. If we took a walk over to the tree line, we would find a

a tree line along the northern and northwestern boundaries. Looks as if there is something beyond the northern tree line. Turning northwest (3), we can't see too much. What's beyond the hill? The field slopes down toward the east. Thermal activity off the field will be better earlier in the day. Finally, turning southwest (4), we see the road and a building along the southwest edge.

Taking a walk to the east corner (5), we find a catch basin

golf course.

With the sand traps, greens and rolling terrain, golf courses provide everything you need to generate thermals.

Driving back to the west corner that we couldn't see (6),

there is another drainage area and a high mound of dirt that shields some historic buildings from the commercial development in the south corner. Of course, who can complain about

morning area will have diminished. Morning air is usually more stable because it's cooler, so it has little chance to rise. In addition, inversions that affect model soaring are more common in the morning. You can see this by how high thermals take sailplanes throughout the day. Often, you can characterize morning flights by light lift, not much sink and not much altitude. You're flying in the thermals that are rising from the ground, but they're being stopped by an inversion. About midday, it's finally warm enough for the thermals to break through the inversion and allow you to reach a much higher altitude.

In terms of flying strategy, keep control movements to a minimum, and don't worry about hitting bad air. You should work the light lift carefully in the morning, and don't expect a rapid climb rate. You're less likely to find bad air early in the day. If you happen to be flying in a contest with open winches, on the first round, wait until you see the thermal activity, then fly the rest of the morning rounds early in the round to take advantage of the more favorable flying conditions with lift and not many areas of sink.

◆ **Noontime thermals.** Around noon, you'll find the proverbial "noon balloon." Often, this is the time at which low-level thermals break through the inversion. If you ride one of these through the inversion, the whole sky seems to go up. This isn't much use in a thermal duration contest, but it's plenty of fun for sport flying, cross-country flying and making your LSF duration flights.

◆ **Afternoon thermals.** The sources of lift have moved, and the air is more unstable. By late afternoon, thermals become more scarce. In addition, there may be larger areas of sink. Flight strategy must be changed to suit these conditions.

If you fly into sink, get out of it quickly, because the next thermal may be farther away than earlier in the day. You can't afford to lose altitude by wallowing in sink. It's also more important to plan flight paths back from a thermal you followed downwind. When thermals are frequent, you can afford to fly straight back through the sink following that thermal. If you do that later in the afternoon, you're asking for an off-field landing. Even though you want to just hang in there to get your max, pick a path to the left or the right of sink, and be aggressive when you fly through it. In the afternoon, you need to be very sure of where lift is before you launch. Start with a flight plan that includes a known thermal, a thermal you think just moved through, or, if all else fails, a flight away from known bad air.

"SEEING" THERMALS

Unless they know what to look for, most pilots start out thinking that "seeing" a thermal is a joke. In reality, there are many ways to see a thermal. Birds or other gliders already flying in a thermal are large, easy-to-see objects. Scanning the sky to locate gliders or birds takes practice. You have to know what the pattern of a bird or a glider in the sky will look like. One good way to practice this is by observing or timing for other pilots. When you see a bird or glider in lift, look away for a while, and then go back and see whether you can pick up the object again.

◆ **Small but good indicators of thermals.**

—Swallows, though very small, are good indicators of thermals. When you see them darting around in the air, they are feeding on bugs that have risen with a thermal.

—Butterflies are also good lift indicators because they're just large enough to be visible from a distance.

—Strong thermals pick up dust and debris, so when you see such things rising, you can be fairly certain that there's a thermal.

having a Home Depot right next to the field? Need some glue? Taking a drive on the road beyond the trees to the west, there is a canal and then more sod.

Overall, it's a good field with close thermal sources on three of the four sides. Just watch going downwind over the buildings or the highway.

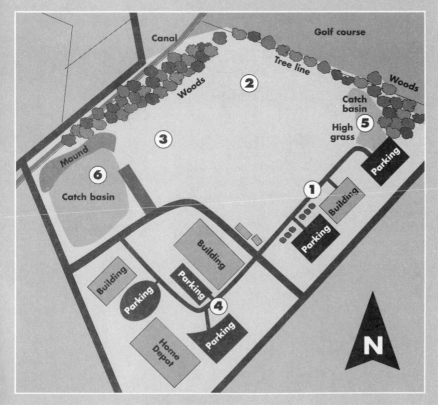

Good eyesight certainly helps you recognize these signs of lift; good hearing can help, too. It's good to be able to recognize the high-pitched sounds of hawks and swallows. Unfortunately, their pitch is too high for many people to hear.

WATCH THE WIND

Changes in wind direction provide another valuable clue to finding thermals. The air in a thermal is moving, and this movement will change the speed and direction of the wind close to it.

When a thermal is directly upwind, the wind speed slows, but if it's downwind, the speed will increase. Thermals to the left or right of you will cause a shift in wind direction. Have you ever wondered why many thermal pilots like to wear shorts? It isn't to show off their legs. They do it so that they can feel changes in wind direction and temperature.

Adding to the wind shifts are temperature changes. Thermals are warmer than the surrounding air. Many people are sensitive to temperature changes as thermals move through the field.

Other objects can help you to see these changes. Strips of thin, light Mylar on tall poles are some of the best thermal indicators around. If you can assemble two or three and position them around a field, you'll learn a great deal about low-level

lift. Confirm your own sense of wind direction changes and temperature changes with the dances of the Mylar in the lift. I always fly with a length of yarn on my transmitter just so I can tell the wind direction at a quick glance (thermal, downwind to the left...).

Tie a small strip of cloth to a fence or a piece of brush in a corner of the field. I bet the local thermal experts notice it's there. Thermal pilots like flags, too. A shift in wind direction caused by a thermal will alter how much of the flag you can see. You may even see the flag billowing off to the opposite side of the pole because of a strong thermal, or it might be totally limp if the thermal is very close to the pole.

Look at the leaves on a tree. You'll notice that the underside of the leaf is a different, lighter, shade of green. Winds and thermals will move the leaves and

Surface Variations

SURFACE	% OF ENERGY REFLECTED
Various cereal crops	3 to 15
Dark soil	8 to 14
Moist sand	10
Bare ground, rocks	10 to 20
Grass	14 to 37
Dry sand	18
Dry, plowed field	20 to 25
Desert	24 to 28
Snow, ice fields	46 to 86

Source: C. E. Wallington, "Meteorology for Glider Pilots," London, 1961.

expose a different percentage of the leaf bottoms. With some trees, you can actually see a pattern in the leaves directing you to the strongest part of the thermal. Another pointer is tall grass. Grass moves with the breeze, and changes in its movement can point you toward a thermal.

Don't forget that lift isn't the only important factor for success. Knowing about sink and bad air is just as important. If you can feel cold sinking air, stay out of the area.

FLYING ON "BAD" DAYS

As a sailplane pilot, you can enjoy flying when power fliers stay home or go home. Strong winds? Add ballast. Cloudy, gloomy weather? That's good for soaring, too. Good flight times are possible even on inauspicious-looking days. I'll discuss:
• how to deal with extremes such as very low ceilings;

Humidity from a swampy area can be a source of lift; just don't land there!

• how to identify the best air for soaring;
• how mist and rain will impact flight performance and how you can deal with these changes.

◆ **Low ceiling.** When the ceiling is very low, the clouds provide a good indication of lift and where to fly. The key indicators are darker clouds and low-level scuds (ragged low clouds moving rapidly beneath another cloud layer). The darker areas are usually the lower clouds where you can take advantage of the air rising into the clouds. You have to be careful or you might see your sailplane disappear into these clouds. Work around this limited visibility by circling at the edge of the clouds, making your model disappear and reappear on one side of the circle. The scuds are good indicators of possible lift and are most useful when the cloud base is higher.

You've lost sight of your model; don't panic. Now is the time to try flaps or spoilers. This will kill some lift and reduce the model's altitude until you can see it again. Always imagine where the model *should be* flying, and this will make it easier to track when it reappears. Don't over-control the model, or you may end up with some violent maneuvers. If you spend more time in the clouds than your competition, you're higher than them and will therefore get a longer flight from the higher altitude.

Launching when there's a low ceiling is another problem, because your model might disappear near the top of the launch. If you're conservative, release below the cloud base and try to launch into the brighter areas of the clouds. A more aggressive approach is to maintain constant altitude and gain more speed on the winch, but don't pull up to zoom on release. Use this speed to cruise off the launch. Look for a launch corridor of bright sky where you know you will reach the clouds. To maximize altitude, launch toward that area. For some excitement with a stronger model, zoom off the winch into a loop, and hold elevator so that you keep doing loops until the model is visible. You can add as much as 30 seconds to your flight time with this energy before you level out to continue your flight.

◆ **Interpreting the air** in which you're flying takes a good eye. You have to know your sailplane's normal attitude and be able to detect the slight difference that will be apparent in very light lift. On overcast days, the lift conditions are similar to those you'll encounter on very humid days. Even though the air looks good, you must have patience with the air. There are no strong

thermals here. Don't forget the lift indicators you use on more pleasant days. There may be thermals, and you'll see small birds feeding and hawks circling, and you'll feel the wind shifting toward the thermals.

Of course, there's rain on these days, too, and it may start during your flight. This can really impact a glider's performance, so you should look to see which side of the field the rain is coming from, and try to avoid the heaviest rain. It's a good idea for your flying buddy to watch

Mylar streamer are very sensitive to wind currents. Flags located upwind are a great aid, too.

for rain and low clouds. You can ride good air downwind, but you might end up downwind with low clouds or rain reducing visibility and impeding your ability to bring back your model.

When flying in mist or rain, flight trim will change. Water builds up on the model, and its most obvious impact is on the CG. When a model starts to stall and doesn't fly smoothly, don't hesitate to throw in a click of down-trim. During longer flights, you may have to do this more than once. After the flight, remember to return the trim to its original position. If you expect rain, why not install a little extra nose weight ahead of time? Whether a model's performance is severely affected by moisture on the wing or not will depend on its airfoil, because the water drops change the airfoil's surface and cause turbulent airflow. The airfoil won't perform as well and might be really badly affected.

I hope these tips will help you when you next fly on a less-than-ideal day. If you're

used to constant beautiful weather, too bad you'll miss out on all this fun.

◆ **Managing sink.** Knowing the quality of the air can be just as valuable as knowing where to find the lift. Nothing teaches you better than a sore arm gained by repeatedly hand-launching for 25-second flights. You won't know where lift is before every launch, but flight groups in a contest may force you into launching anyway.

The most common sign of poor air is cold air. Warm, rising air will be displaced by descending, cool air. Stay out of the cold; fly as far away from it as possible.

STUPID PILOT TRICKS
It's a beautiful day and there's plenty of lift. You enter a strong thermal upwind of the turnaround and are really high by the time you drift back to the winches. You have two choices now: test your eyesight, or increase your understanding of thermals and your ability to find lift and fly through sink. All too often, I see sport pilots just staying with the thermal until their planes are tiny dots in the sky. It's no fun having to help your buddy bring that thing down; worse yet is having to search the sky for a lost sailplane.

My normal approach is to leave the lift, but I sometimes like to practice inverted thermalling. Here are a few things to improve your flying skills:

◆ Practice judging how fast lift is moving downwind. Fly away from the lift for a minute, then point the sailplane toward where you think the lift has drifted. Did you get it right?

◆ Note the down-air conditions you fly through before you find the lift. Remember to fly through these areas faster.

What have you learned? You know what it's like to fly through down air behind a thermal. Having confidence that you know what you'll find is important when you charge through sink to get to the lift you know is just a little farther downwind. You've seen how far lift drifts in a minute. Now, when you step up to the winch, you'll be able to judge whether you want to charge downwind to take advantage of the lift the pilot in the landing pattern used while you were waiting for a winch line.

◆ Search for other areas of lift. There's nothing more satisfying than flying many thermals during a flight. *Don't* fly directly upwind. This has the highest probability

Let's Go Fly

See lift; feel lift; hear lift. The search for thermals is a complex, multifaceted activity; no single technique always works. It takes practice, experience and a knowledge of where to look and how to see the not-so-invisible thermal.

of being the wrong area to fly; you'll be setting up for a landing approach, not flying in a thermal. A zigzag search pattern works well, but the first leg is the important one.

◆ To find a stronger thermal, I fly far away from the initial thermal—often, all the way to the other side of the field. It's amazing how often, just by flying at 45 degrees crosswind, you find another thermal and then watch the pilots who stayed with the first thermal—straight upwind—land before you do.

The crosswind flying concept also works for getting down from high altitudes, when lack of visibility is the biggest problem. While your glider is circling, you can see the planform during part of the circle, but it might "disappear" when it's coming straight toward you. Exit the thermal flying in a direction that allows you to see the wing and side of the fuselage. You'll be less likely to lose sight of your model; if there are clouds, plan your flight path so you'll always have clouds as a back-

ground. Eventually, you'll get your glider down to an altitude at which visibility will no longer be a problem.

Well, that's how I search for thermals and lift in all types of conditions. Beginners who think this is quite a task should practice the theories and watch accomplished pilots. Everyone can learn to find lift and thermals and then go out and soar with the eagles! ◆

ABOUT THE AUTHOR

Michael Lachowski

Michael has been active in modeling for over 20 years. In addition to his Model Airplane News soaring column, he is a member of the Round Valley R/C club and the Millstone Valley Silent Fliers and edits the Eastern Soaring League newsletter. He prefers to design his own sailplanes and is an avid scratch-builder. Mike's interest in modeling led to his chosen field—engineering. He holds degrees in mechanical engineering and computer science and is currently employed by a major petrochemical company where he is responsible for networking at a research site.

CHAPTER 26

Your First Glider Competition

by Dave Garwood

In thermal sailplane flying, as in many sports and hobbies, competition improves an individual's knowledge, skill and ability in ways that are hard to duplicate. It may be that you've been flying sailplanes for two years and have heard or read about sailplane contests, or maybe you've seen a sailplane contest and have thought about entering for the first time.

A leader of club-sponsored contests, the Wintonbury Flying Club has put on spring and fall sailplane contests in Simsbury, CT, every year for the last 20 years.

If you've never competed, you may have some questions. What happens at a contest? How can I find a contest? Which models should I take? How can I prepare for maximum success?

This chapter answers these questions, gives an idea of what to expect at a club sailplane contest and offers tips and techniques for flying well and scoring well at your first thermal competition. This chapter was written for pilots who have learned the basics of R/C sailplane launching, flying and landing, but have not yet entered a competition.

WHY FLY IN A THERMAL CONTEST?

Here are three reasons why sailplane pilots go to contests:

◆ **To see sailplanes, both new and old.** Contests attract dozens of fliers who take along a variety of models, so there's a chance to find out more about a design you may be thinking of building or buying. You can examine the appearance of the finished model, see it fly and talk to the builder about how the kit went together.

◆ **To learn from other pilots** and to see how different strategy decisions affect the outcome of a flight. You'll see good and bad launches, successful and floundering lift-finding strategies and both superb and disastrous landings. You'll get a chance to see how others prepare, trim and fly for maximum duration, how far downwind other pilots will fly in search of lift, how they set up a final approach, and how they hit a spot landing.

◆ **To measure and advance your skill.** Considering the number of fliers and flights at a typical contest, it's pretty hard to compete and not learn something that improves your sport flying. Your launch technique will improve, you'll see how to trim for maximum speed through sink and by using ridge lift from a tree line, you'll learn how to stay in the air when thermal lift fails. You'll find out how good you are, and you'll learn things that will help you improve your flying skills.

Some fliers think that they won't like the excitement and challenge of competition, and this may be true, but the tension

These sailplanes represent a range of cost and sophistication. They wait for a call to the flight line as a contest pilot and spotter fly.

Sailplane Selection and Preparation

The Academy of Model Aeronautics (AMA) recognizes four sailplane contest classes, and they're defined according to wingspan and launching method. The numbers of these classes are from the AMA competition rule book and are used in contest announcements to specify which events are scheduled for that contest.

◆ Class 441 is for gliders of 1.5-meter (60-inch) wingspan or less that are launched by hand. A typical flight task might be to get as many 2-minute flights as possible within a 15-minute window. Examples of sailplanes suitable for hand-launch competition are the C.R. Designs Climmax, Culpepper Models Chuperosa, Dodgson Designs Orbiter, Joe Hahn Monarch, M&M Glider Tech Commoner, Sky Bench Aerotech Sagitta and WACO Mosquito.

The Pierce Aero Paragon on the wing. It flies so well that it can be considered a thermal trainer.

◆ Class 442 is for 2-meter (78-inch) wingspan gliders.
◆ Class 443 is called "standard class" with wingspans limited to 100 inches or less.
◆ Class 444 or "open class" has no limit on wingspan.

Models in these classes are launched by a winch provided by the contest director. Some contests, especially local club contests, are designed to encourage newcomers and will also allow launches from a high start for those who aren't accustomed to a winch.

Beginner 2-meter sailplanes include the Airtronics Olympic 650, Carl Goldberg Models Gentle Lady, Dynaflite Pussycat, Global Kits Easy Answer, Future Flight Thermal Thing and Mimimax Enterprise Minimax 700. Advanced 2-meter sailplanes include the David Layne Designs Saturn 2.0, Dynaflite Katie II, Northeast Sailplane Products 2-meter Alcyone and Slegers International Vulcan 2M.

Standard class sailplanes include the Airtronics Olympic II, Hobie Hawk, Pierce Aero Gemini MTS and Just Plain Fun Models Big Birdy.

Unlimited class sailplanes include the Airtronics Peregrine, Ben Clerx Mako, Dodgson Designs Sabre, Northeast Sailplane Products Alcyone, Slegers International Sky Hawk, the Pierce Aero Paragon, Tekoa Shadow, R&R Genesis and WACO Magic.

The number and type of control surfaces are not limited by AMA rules, so advanced ships tend to have additional fea-tures that give the pilot more control of the sailplane. As a minimum, many contest planes have glide-path controls such as spoilers or flaps. They may have advanced R/C features such as flap and elevator mixing to compensate automatically for changes in pitch caused by deploying spoilers or flaps.

Both aileron and polyhedral designs are represented at contests in all four categories and none seems to have an absolute edge in performance. Beginners are often more comfortable with polyhedral ships, which exhibit greater stability; experienced fliers often prefer ailerons, which tend to offer greater maneuverability. Either design can win.

If your sailplane kit offers the option to build spoilers or flaps, go ahead and include them. The weight of an extra servo is well compensated for by the increase in glide-path control, which gives you more flexibility in hitting the landing spot.

If your sailplane has an option to carry ballast to increase the wing loading—use it. A higher wing loading increases the speed of a sailplane and its ability to penetrate a headwind. On a windy day, having ballast on board may mean the difference between making it back to the landing circle from a downwind excursion or not making it back at all.

Finally, before the contest, experiment by moving ballast to move the center of gravity (CG) fore and aft. A forward CG emphasizes stability, which is good for hands-off flying. A rearward CG emphasizes agility and allows the sailplane to signal the pilot when it has encountered lift.

Consider taking more than one airplane to the contest and entering more than one class. This gives you more

For glide-path control, the Great Planes Spirit 2-meter polyhedral design features a third servo and spoilers in the wing. The Spirit is a little heavier and tougher than planes such as the Gentle Lady and thus flies better when the wind picks up.

experience and keeps you busier during the event.

It's important to fly what you know. You'll be more comfortable with a plane that you've flown in practice than with a 6-channel job you finished the night before the contest—guaranteed.

of competition brings out the best in many pilots and allows them to fly better than usual. Because there are so many sailplanes in the air searching for lift, it's easy to find lift by watching others. Some of your most successful lift–finding days will be contest days.

Whether you win or not, contest flying benefits all its participants.

FINDING A CONTEST

The most immediate source of information on an upcoming contest is a notice in a sailplane publication, a club newsletter, or in a hobby shop. If sailplane contests are not announced in your own club newsletter, you may want to begin reading publications such as *R/C Soaring Digest* and *Eastern Soaring Lines*.

A comprehensive national list of contests can be found in the competition event listings in *Model Aviation*—the Academy of Model Aeronautics' (AMA) magazine. When you find a contest that you want to attend, send a self-addressed stamped envelope to the contest director and ask for an informational flyer and a map, if you need one. Most contest directors will be pleased to receive inquiries from out of town and will be happy to help faraway fliers get to their contest site.

Note that AMA membership is required to enter most contests, because this provides liability insurance.

TIPS, TECHNIQUES AND STRATEGIES FOR SUCCESS

Here are 11 specific tactics and techniques that will improve your sailplane flying and increase your thermal duration contest scores.

◆ **Study the weather.** Begin watching the weather two or three days before the contest and pay attention to the air masses coming your way. A high-pressure system will bring clear skies, bright sun and (hopefully) puffy cumulus clouds, which mark thermal tops.

For sunny days, bring on the lightly loaded, open-bay polyhedral ships—the "simple" sailplanes—because they do well in this weather. Their supposed lack of fine roll control when coring a thermal will be more than compensated for by their low landing speed when shooting for landing points.

A low-pressure system will bring cloudy skies and stormy weather, so faster sailplanes that can carry ballast are more likely to score well. The ability of any sailplane to cope with the wind can be improved by adding extra weight to increase the plane's wing loading and

increase its ability to penetrate the wind.

Watch the weather for one more reason: so you'll wear proper clothing. It's no fun flying while you're shivering because you need one more layer, or when you're dripping sweat because you didn't take shorts for the afternoon sun.

The tailless Peck Polymers Genesis is an example of a 60-inch-wingspan, hand-launch sailplane. Most planes in this class have a traditional wing and tailplane configuration and can have polyhedral or aileron roll control.

◆ **Match your sailplane to your skill.** The casual observer at a sailplane contest may conclude that the more you spend on a sailplane, the more likely you are to end up in the winners' circle. Though it's true that experienced fliers commonly prefer more advanced sailplanes, that is not the reason they win. They win because they fly well. You will perform best with a sailplane that matches your present skill level.

Remember that there is no mighty F3B ship, no glass slipper, no six-servo "wonderplane" that has the low sink rate of a 2-meter Gentle Lady. In the same air, an advanced-design, composite-construction sailplane will come down faster from a given height than will a lightly loaded, balsa-and-spruce, open-bay construction floater-type glider—every time.

It's true that the super ships can do things the floaters can't—like go fast. Fast planes can cover more ground searching for lift, but it takes experience to fly them well; it takes skill to find the stronger lift needed to fly a heavy plane successfully. It takes a finer touch on the sticks to keep aileron wings level than it does for polyhedral wings. Heavy ships land hotter and require skillful use of braking devices such as flaps and spoilers

to score landing points.

To succeed at a contest, choose a sailplane that you fly well and one that is suited to your present skill level.

◆ **Know the rules.** The successful competition pilot knows the contest rules, the local field boundaries and any special rules to meet local conditions. Some flying fields have certain areas, such as neighboring houses, that are out of bounds for fly-overs. Some contest directors are firm about restrictions on over-flying pit areas or spectator areas. Violating these restrictions can result in disqualification.

Make sure that you understand the timing, scoring and record-keeping methods used for the contest. Sometimes, you record raw time and landing-point scores only, and sometimes, you convert these into scores from a round. Know how many rounds will be flown and whether scores from the worst round will be discarded in the final scoring. Know how the radio-transmitter-impound procedure works.

Some contests allow line "pop-offs" to be reflown, while in other contests, there's no such thing as a "pop-off" unless there is a winch-line break. Under these rules, if the model leaves your hand on launch, you fly out the round.

The basic rules are published in the AMA (or other sanctioning body) rule book. The classes to be flown at a specified contest and whether winch-launching assistance is available will be noted in the contest announcements. Local conditions such as field boundaries and daily conditions, e.g., the time of the duration task, will be covered in the pilots' meeting before the contest. That meeting is intended to clear up any uncertainties. Don't leave the pilots' meeting without knowing whether you'll be flying 6-minute or 7-minute rounds.

◆ **Choose a spotter who knows more than you do.** The spotter is the pilot's second pair of eyes and tactical advisor. Because this job requires a fair degree of judgment, it's wise to choose someone with significant contest flying experience. In addition to keeping track of time during

the flight and counting down so the pilot will be able to land on time, the timer also watches for signs of lift and watches the progress of the competition. If a thermal falters and the pilot decides to leave it to search for new lift, having watched other sailplanes and perhaps soaring birds, the spotter will have an idea of where on the course to look. He will be able to confirm whether the sailplane is in lift or not and will watch for traffic that could cause a midair collision. He monitors the competition, especially at landing time, so that he can advise whether the landing zone will become crowded.

In club contests, the spotter also acts as

an official timer. He counts down the remaining time aloud so the pilot knows when to begin his descent and when to set up for landing. In advanced competition, the official timer says nothing except the official time (and then only if asked). In local contests, the spotter advises the pilot throughout the flight, and the spotter's experience may make the difference between a great round and an ordinary round. Do not be afraid to ask an experienced pilot to time for you on a contest day; you'll learn from it.

◆ **Watch the air.** Watching the hawks and vultures, the dandelion puffs and other

What Happens at a Thermal Contest?

A thermal contest consists of a series of precise duration flights followed by precision spot landings. After launch, you fly for exactly, say, 7 minutes, gaining a point for every second flown up to 7 minutes and then losing a point for every second that exceeds 7 minutes. Landing points are added to flight scores for landing on or near a marker. After three or more rounds of flying, final scores are calculated by combining the scores from all of the rounds.

The skills you'll need to succeed are launching, finding lift and landing. Getting a good launch is an advantage as it gives you more time in the air to search for lift. Finding enough lift to stay airborne for the duration task is the cen-

tral concern throughout most of the flight. Bringing the aircraft down under control and on time to score landing points is almost as important as launching and flying.

Deciding precisely when to begin your descent is more important than it seems at first, and careful timing here can really improve your score. Landing points are usually a significant factor, and good landing scores can often make up for marginal flight scores.

The contest begins with registration where the entry fee is paid and proof of insurance (an Academy of Model Aeronautics card) is shown. There may or may not be time or a winch available for practice and trim flights before the contest starts.

At the pilots' meeting, the flight-duration time will be announced. It could be 6, 7, or maybe 10 minutes, depending on the weather and perhaps the number of entries. The field boundaries will be described, (including any areas that are off-limits to fly over). There will be an opportunity to discuss contest rules and any modifications needed to fit the locale or weather conditions. The radio-impound and score-keeping procedures will be explained. At the close of the pilots' meeting, the competition begins.

A pilot is assisted by a spotter who tracks the flight time and advises the pilot as to the location of other sailplanes, finding lift and general strategy. A round consists of a winch or high-start launch, a timed flight and a spot landing. At the conclusion of each round, the scorecard is turned in, and the transmitter is returned to the radio-impound tent.

Throughout a round, when you aren't actually flying, you may be spotting for other pilots. Depending on the level of staffing the contest director has available, you may be helping on a winch or assisting with other contest-management tasks.

At least three rounds will be flown, and scores from all the rounds flown will be combined to determine the winner and the finishing order of the other contestants.

A thermal sailplane begins the climb on a winch tow. The pilot's foot is on the winch pedal, and the man on the left operates the winch-line retriever.

people's sailplanes can tell you a lot about lift on the field: where it's generated and whether it develops in cycles. Between your flights, watch the air to observe the lift and sink. To make your time, see if a tree line can generate lift to extend your flight for two or three minutes.

Don't be intimidated when flying against well-known and experienced

by flying through the same air twice.

If none of these specific strategies seems attractive to you, at least vary your pattern every time and observe what happens. Some parts of the flying field and the surrounding area will produce more lift than others, although the spots may vary throughout the day. Find the productive areas and use them.

confidence, promotes accuracy and quickly improves landing scores.

◆ **Maintain a positive attitude.** If there is any endeavor in human experience that is influenced by a positive attitude, it is thermal competition sailplane flying. Enthusiasm, confidence and positive thinking have an immeasurable effect on your ability to fly well at a contest. How can you improve your score with a positive outlook?

• Quit complaining. Whining about the air, carping about the rules and casting aspersions on the contest management is bad form. Don't do it.

• Take action to improve the situation. Pitching in to help the contest workers with winch problems, working with a less experienced flier to solve radio problems, or helping where you can improve the quality of life for all of us improves your own karma and seems somehow related to doing well in a contest.

• Don't take it too seriously. Few sports capture your interest and imagination like competition R/C sailplane flying, but taking it too seriously can ruin the fun. Keep it light, and never forget that we do this for fun.

An aerial view of the Hudson Valley Soaring Society's thermal contest site taken from a sailplane. Parked cars, the transmitter-impound tent and a few sailplanes are near the tree line (A). The flight line is in the lower portion of the photo; both the winches and the spot-landing areas are in the closely cut grass (B). A graduated tape in the very bottom of the frame is one landing area (C).

pilots, because it's from them that you will learn the most. Pick a good competitor and watch his entire flight.

Watch for changes in the lift-generating pattern as temperature and wind conditions change throughout the day. The more you know about the air you fly in, the better flier you will be.

◆ **Develop a search strategy.** A purposeful search is a more effective way to find lift than is coming off the launch line and striking out in a random direction. Flying toward the area of the field that has been producing lift for the past 2 hours might work, although conditions can change. Following hawks and soaring birds can often be productive. You'll see some fliers leave the line and tear off downwind; they're going to join a thermal that they felt cross the field just before launch, and they're flying to where they know lift is.

A simple but effective strategy is to use your initial launch height to move out fast and far, looking for signs of lift on the way out, and to come back at a more leisurely pace, making sure you don't waste altitude

◆ **Develop a consistent landing pattern.** Coming into the landing area from a different height and different wind direction each time is a pretty good way to guarantee zero landing points time after time. Consistency in approach works small miracles in scoring points on landing.

In one common landing approach pattern (modeled after full-scale aviation), you fly three sides of a rectangle. You enter the pattern on the downwind leg, make a 90-degree turn into the base leg, and then make another right-angle turn into the wind for the final approach to the landing spot. If you always enter the downwind leg at say, 100 feet of altitude with 15 seconds to go in the round, you will be amazed at how accurate your landing times will become. Lengthening or shortening the downwind and crosswind legs can help you adapt to changes in wind speed and leave you in a position where you have sufficient altitude to reach the landing spot.

Whether you use this landing pattern or another, flying the final seconds of the round in the same way each time builds

◆ **Make your own luck.** Luck plays a part in sailplane contests, just as it does in other parts of life. Good luck occurs when preparation meets opportunity. We know "lady luck" visits at irregular intervals, and opportunity only knocks; it doesn't break down the door and pull you out of bed. Those who have inspected and repaired their model the day before the contest, those who have fully charged their batteries the night before, and those who have arrived at the contest site and surrounding area early to study it for possible thermal sources somehow seem to have better luck.

Often, the winch master would like to have his setup checked by a test launch. If you're ready to fly early, grab this opportunity and fly a practice round so that your first flight of the contest won't be your first flight of the day.

◆ **Avoid the exhilaration trap.** Because your concentration is heightened, you're assisted by a spotter, and you're flying in the company of many others who are searching for lift, you're more likely to find lift on a contest day than on a sport-flying day. Beware the siren song of abundant lift, and remember your contest task. Do not get carried away and fly so high that you can no longer see the model, and don't follow a thermal so far downwind that you can't get

A competitor prepares to launch a Dodgson Designs Lovesong at the Wintonbury Spring Sailplane Challenge. The pilot's right foot is on the winch pedal; the man at right is the winch master.

back on the field. These are common ways in which models are lost.

The most insidious form of the exhilaration trap is failing to bring the sailplane down soon enough to make your landing time. In sport flying, we don't practice coming down much; it seems as if we come down soon enough without forcing it. In contest flying, however, a good score depends on nailing your landing time; building up too much speed in a rushed descent can overstress airframes and break models. Keep calm, break off the lift-finding mode, and begin the descent in plenty of time to set up properly for a landing approach.

Contests are exciting, and they tend to get your heart rate up, but stay cool, use your judgment, and maintain control of the plane at all times during the flight.

◆ **Practice, practice, practice.** There is no substitute for practice. To the extent that you follow this rule, you can forget about the others. You can worry less about weather because you've flown in all kinds of weather. You can overcome the untoward effects of exuberance because you've felt the exhilaration many times. You won't misjudge when to begin the descent to landing approach because you've done it over and over. You'll know the signs that your sailplane is in lift because you've flown that plane for hours and hours.

At every contest, there's one competi-

tor who has the world's simplest glider (made from the world's cheapest kit) who does really well. If you strike up a conversation with him, you'll find that he flies 5 or 6 days a week, 10 months a year. He wins because he knows his glider. He has flown it for hours, landed it thousands of times, and he knows his aircraft better than anyone else on the field. Remember that no matter how advanced sailplane designs are, there's no technological substitute for practice with your sailplane.

One way to gain the practice that you need to win is by joining an individual achievement program such as the League of Silent Flight (LSF). The skills you need to progress through the LSF levels are those you need to win at contests.

You thought only superb pilots go to contests? Not true. All levels of experience are represented, and it's almost as hard to finish last as it is to finish first. Don't be afraid to enter a contest because you think you don't have enough experience. All contest winners had a first contest. ◆

ABOUT THE AUTHOR

Dave Garwood

Dave has built and flown more than 45 thermal and slope R/C sailplane designs. He has flown sailplanes in 10 states, in local, regional and national thermal contests and slope races, and he  *presented a seminar on slope soaring at the New England R/C Soaring Convention. He has flown a sailplane every month for the last six years and hopes to do the same in the six years to come. Dave writes a soaring column for Model Aviation, and he contributes extensively to Model Airplane News.*

CHAPTER 27

Slope Soaring

by Dave Garwood

Did you know that the world's fastest model airplanes are slope-soaring sailplanes? Without a prop disk or air intakes to create drag, an Austrian slope-soaring glider called "Dassel" holds a speed record of 248mph. Keep that in mind the next time you hear about a ducted-fan model doing 150 or 200mph.

"R/C soaring simulates the majestic flight of soaring birds." —Ed Slobod

Slope soarers fly some of the simplest models with some of the least expensive radios for relaxing sport flying, demanding aerobatic competition, blistering pylon racing and intense air-to-air combat.

To be successful in slope soaring, you'll need to consider four things: the wind, a hill, a plane and skill. I'll address each of these.

HOW DO THEY STAY UP?

The wind keeps them up. When flying, gliders are *always* descending—relative to the air mass that surrounds the airplane. For gliders to stay up, they must fly in rising air. Thermals provide rising air to support thermal sailplanes, and wind blowing against a hill flows *up* the hillside and provides lift to fly slope sailplanes.

Without wind, there's no slope flying. While the wind blows, a flight can last as long as the radio batteries hold out. It's possible to fly gliders in wind speeds of 5 to 50mph, although the most practical conditions are from about 8 to 30mph. As wind speed increases, slope-soaring pilots bring out smaller, heavier and faster sailplanes.

We can cope with a tremendous variation in wind speed, but we aren't as flexible with wind direction. For our purposes, the wind must blow directly, or nearly directly, into the face of the hill. The more perpendicular the wind is to the ridge line, the greater the lift. Ninety degrees is ideal; 10 degrees either way is nearly as good; and 20 is decent. But more than 30 degrees off "straight-in" is generally "unflyable" or nearly so, because the lift decreases rapidly as the wind direction becomes more parallel to the hill. To test whether the wind is sufficient to fly, hold the model firmly in a launch position out in the wind stream in front of the hill. If the plane tries to lift out of your hand, there's enough lift to fly.

As you think about starting slope soaring, you'll begin to take more and more interest in the wind-speed and wind-direction parts of the weather reports and forecasts. You'll probably find that there are one or two predominant wind directions in your area, and knowledge of the prevailing winds will guide your search for suitable hills. At the slope, an 18-inch

Dennis Phelan and Mike Lachowski, who spend most of their time with thermal sailplanes in F3B practice and competition, enjoy the unlimited lift available on a slope when the wind is blowing. This photo was taken at Cape Cod, MA.

ribbon tied to the tip of your radio antenna will accurately indicate wind direction and relative wind speed; and a hand-held wind gauge from Hobby Lobby will give you accurate wind speed.

CHECK OUT THAT HILL!

If the essence of fuel-powered flying is learning to start and run a miniature engine and the essence of thermal gliding is learning to find and use thermals, then the central task in slope soaring is finding hills.

The perfect slope-soaring hill might be 100 feet high and 500 feet long, rising at a 45-degree angle from the valley floor and covered with grass cut by somebody else. It would be devoid of trees and bushes, run arrow straight, be perpendicular to the prevailing wind and have a paved road to the top that passes a sign that reads, "R/C sailplane fliers welcome."

That hill exists only in our imagina-

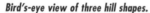

Bird's-eye view of three hill shapes.

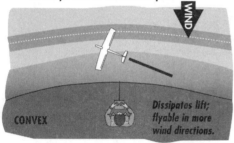

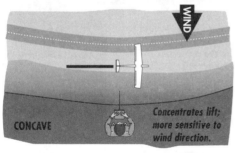

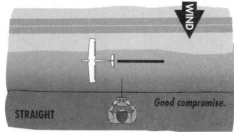

tions, but there are plenty of hills with enough of these characteristics to be quite acceptable. Slopers are searchers; they're always looking out the car window when driving, poring over topographic maps to find hills they can't see from the main roads and asking their sportsman friends where good hills might be.

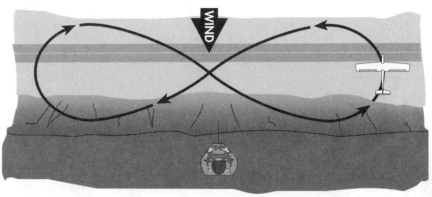

Top view of classic figure-8 slope pattern. It turns into the wind.

Important hill characteristics:

◆ **Height.** The practical minimum height is high enough to generate lift. (It may be as little as a 20-foot-high abandoned highway overpass.) The maximum is limited only by your ability to get to the top. The 100-foot height and 500-foot length are suggested because they're likely to produce enough lift to fly in a variety of wind speeds, and they're long enough to fly straight for a while before having to turn around and come back.

◆ **Steepness.** Generally, the steeper the better, but a true cliff is not necessary. Many hours of productive slope lift can be enjoyed on hills with only a 20- to 30-percent slope. And gentler hills are easier to walk up and down. You have to fly a hill to find whether it's flyable or not.

◆ **Shape.** Few hills are ruler-straight. When you look down on slopes (a bird's-eye view), you'll notice that some are concave and others are convex. A concave slope collects and concentrates the wind, thus increasing the lift, but it's also more sensitive to wind direction. If the wind isn't blowing directly into the "bowl," you'll have a lot of unruly, turbulent air. Convex hills, on the other hand, dissipate wind and reduce lift but are less sensitive to wind direction. Straight hills are desirable for our purposes.

◆ **Ground cover.** Grass is great for walking, landing and finding lost airplanes. Bushes reduce the number of places you can land, and trees interfere with both landing and flying. Cleared land is preferred.

◆ **Upwind turbulence makers.** What's out in front of the hill is as important as the shape and size of the hill itself. If trees, buildings and other hills are upwind of your hill, their "wind shadow" will disturb the wind that produces your lift. Upwind obstructions don't automatically

make a hill unflyable; they just make the air more turbulent. Some of the best-known slope sites are on the coast because they're free of upwind obstructions, but good slope-soaring hills with unobstructed upwind terrain also exist inland.

◆ **Access and owner permission.** You have to get to the top of a hill to launch and be there legally to fly. Sometimes, government-owned land is allocated for recreational purposes, but there may be restrictions. Keep your site accessible; get permission to fly and follow the rules.

If the land is privately owned, you can bet model airplane flying isn't the owner's primary purpose. You can, however, get approval to fly on farmland by talking to the owner in advance. By working around crop schedules and respecting livestock, some soarers are allowed to use the same sites for years. Don't trespass; ask first.

No rolling hills cleared for pasture in your neighborhood? There are many possibilities for soaring sites: landfills, flood-control dams, gravel pits, strip mines, dikes, levees and ramps built for highway overpasses.

Go find a hill or two and, eventually, the wind will come. Meanwhile, choose and build a slope-soaring sailplane.

WHICH AIRPLANE?

It depends. Choice of slope soarer depends mainly on pilot skill and available lift. In light lift, we fly thermal-type sailplanes; as lift increases, smaller and faster models rule. When the wind howls, the lead-sled racers make an appearance.

Most slope soarers fall into these four categories:

◆ **Thermal floaters.** These gliders are most often rudder-and-elevator polyhedral, open-bay wing models with wingspans of 72 to 100 inches. Wing loadings range from 4 to 8 ounces per square foot of wing area. They offer new slope pilots the same advantages they offer thermal pilots: inherent stability (so less control input is needed to guide them) and slow flight (which gives the pilot more time to react). The high wing mounting and upswept tips of these models are less likely to be damaged during landings because the wings are off the ground.

It's hard to imagine more relaxed R/C flying than guiding a polyhedral glider in 8mph winds silently and gracefully, back and forth across the face of a slope, bringing it down when the onboard batteries approach their 2-hour limit. This is *real* lawn-chair flying.

◆ **Purpose-designed slope soarers.** After a season or two of polyhedral flying, most slope pilots migrate to the more precise control of ailerons. A successful slope design requires a rugged airplane with effective control surfaces. These models generally have a semisymmetrical airfoil and a wing loading of 6 to 10 ounces per square foot for speed and penetration in the wind.

Flying purpose-designed slope models requires some experience and skill. Those who are graduating from polyhedral floaters must learn aileron roll control to turn, and those who are "transitioning" from fuel-powered flight must hone pitch-angle control to avoid stalling.

The aileron slope pilot is rewarded with precise control and aerobatic performance. These models are generally capable of inverted flight and maneuvers such as loops, rolls, Cuban-8s and split-S's. Soarers with large fins will perform credible stall turns, even without a rudder, because the wind into the hill provides the necessary yaw force to kick the tail over.

Most of the sailplanes flown on slopes are purpose-designed slope soarers, and they deliver more stick time than any other type. They provide the means for newer R/C pilots to advance their skills and enter the realm of aerobatics and hot-dogging. Which is more thrilling?—your

Lou Garwood makes a close pass with his Sig Ninja, which has a modified fuselage of his own design. The Ninja is aerobatic and is suitable for moderate lift at inland and coastal slope sites.

first loop or your first roll? With a purpose-designed slope soarer, you can learn both in a single season.

◆ **Advanced slope soarers.** Faster, sleeker and smoother than purpose-designed sailplanes, these slope hot-rods meet our needs for more speed and maneuverability. They have faster airfoils and wing loadings of 10 ounces per square foot and higher. Their fuselages are usually made of fiberglass or special plastics, and they may have pitcheron (wings pivot independently to control roll and pitch) or wingeron (wings pivot independently to control only roll) control surfaces to reduce drag. Many

advanced ships still use 2-channel control, while some have a third channel for rudder, dive brakes, or flaps.

Flying these rocket ships is vastly different from what most people think glider flying is like. They're lightning-fast and radically maneuverable, yet silky smooth.

They'll complete 15-foot-diameter loops and perform five axial rolls 20 feet off the deck. "Toto, I don't think we're in Kansas anymore."

◆ **Combat slope soarers.** The competitive spirit being what it is among R/C pilots, sooner or later, you'll find yourself flying wingtip to wingtip with another sloper. One plane will bump another, and then the second will jostle the first. "Ready to go for it?" says one pilot; "OK; you're on," replies the second. Another air combat match begins.

Slope combat scoring sometimes relies on tape streamers or judging, but it's often just a question of "Knock the other guy out of the air" until he can't launch again—not too different from a boxing match in strategy or scoring.

Like no other kind of model flying can, this "fight for your life" element makes a top-gun flier out of an R/C pilot, and slope combat is cheaper than other types. You think you have quick reflexes? This is the place to find out *how* quick.

WIND, HILL, PLANE— NOW WHAT?

You throw it off the hill. The first surprise is that you throw it *downward*. With a hand-launch sailplane, you heave it upward when you launch; with a thermal sailplane, you throw it up; but you launch a slope soarer downward. This is because on launch, speed is far more important than altitude. If you gain flying speed, you'll soon have altitude, but if you stall

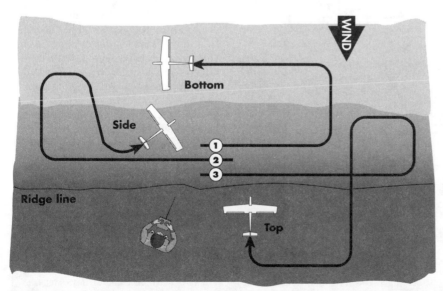

Final approach path and landing location (top view) for: 1—bottom of hill; 2—side of hill; 3—top of hill.

on launch, you'll crash for sure.

Be prepared to have quick reactions on the sticks. Generally, slope flying is far more active than thermal flying, and you have to be flying the model all the time to keep it where you want it, i.e., safely in the lift zone and away from the ground.

A few seconds after release, the sailplane reaches flying speed and follows a path away from the pilot and the hill. Remember that lift decreases as the distance from the hill increases, so you make a turn to keep the model in the lift band that parallels and is also fairly close to the hill. After the first turn, the model is flying parallel to the hill.

Before the model gets too small to see, make a 180-degree turn *away* from the hill and *into* the wind. The model will pass you because it's flying parallel to the hill, and before it gets too far away at the other end, make another 180-degree turn and fly it back toward you. Generally, slope turns are made *away* from the hill and into the wind, and the basic slope-soaring pattern is a figure-8 (viewed from above).

Ha! One complete circuit. This isn't going too badly, is it? For the first few sessions, this may be all you do, or all you *need* to do. It's amazing to see your plane flying out and back, passing close by at eye level, or below and cruising on unseen lift while the loudest sound heard is servo-gear noise.

After getting the feel of the basics, your first "mission" may be to explore the limits of the lift available. By now, you know that the strongest lift is close to the top of the ridge. As you venture out, the lift gradually

behind the hillcrest "the rotor." It isn't a good place to fly; stay out front at all costs.

WHAT ABOUT LANDING?

You have three choices. In increasing order of skill required, they are: at the bottom, on the slope face and on the top.

◆ **To land at the bottom,** you simply fly away from the hill into softer and softer lift. The model loses speed and altitude, and as it descends, lift decreases, too. Finally, you land the model as you would land a thermal glider: by raising the nose to reduce speed and flying it smoothly down to the ground. This is the safest landing procedure; its chief disadvantage is that you have to hike down the hill to get your plane.

◆ **A slope-side landing** begins in the same way, but when the model is well below the hillcrest, bring it back toward the slope and let it regain altitude. As it climbs, it will lose speed; again, land it as you'd land a thermal sailplane, by flying low enough to scrape it along the ground. You'll have a shorter walk to collect it.

◆ **Hilltop landings** are for truly confident slope pilots. Start with a downwind leg (the only time you turn downwind), lose a

Bob Powers (rear left) launches Bill Griggs' Great Planes Spirit into the air at Cape Cod, MA. Tom Atwood (foreground) assembles the Cox Ridge Hawk.

one advantage to this technique: if you don't like the approach, you can go around and just shoot back out into slope lift. Try that with thermal gliders!

FINAL THOUGHTS AND TIPS

R/C slope soaring is interesting, exciting and amazing. The scientist in us will be interested in how slope lift works. Pilots who usually fly with fuel power will be excited about how much aerobatic flying can be done without noise and vibration. Thermal soaring enthusiasts will be amazed that, under good conditions, a single flight can last two hours.

Nearly all R/C pilots will be amazed by how much wind you can actually fly in. Slope soarers have signs in their workshops that say such things as "When it's too windy to fly power, go to the slope."

On the slope, things happen fast. Models get beaten and battered more than in flat-field flying, so always have a repair kit. If you can find an instructor, you'll be able to flatten the learning curve a little. And a buddy-box radio system is highly useful in the first few flying sessions. If these aids aren't available, don't fret; plenty of people have taught themselves slope soaring.

We've covered the basic elements: wind, hill, plane, skill. Now go fly the slope. ◆

To learn about the author of this chapter, see page 140.

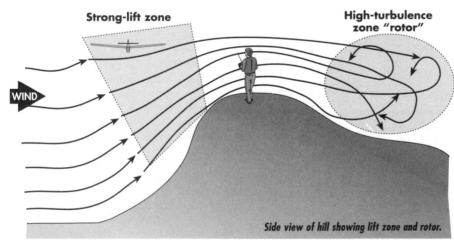

Strong-lift zone

High-turbulence zone "rotor"

WIND

Side view of hill showing lift zone and rotor.

softens. If you get out too far and begin to descend, just fly back close to the face of the hill and work your way back up to the top. Avoid flying behind the top of the hill. As the wind flows over the top of the hill, it becomes turbulent, and lift decreases sharply. Slope pilots call the danger zone

little altitude on the crosswind leg, and turn on final into the wind. The trick is to maintain control while you fly through decreasing lift and increasing turbulence. To maintain control, you *must* keep the air speed high. You'll be landing hot when you land on the top of the hill, but there's

CHAPTER 28

Flying F3B

by Dennis Phelan

World-class thermal duration: that's what this event is all about. It's sniffing out thermals, following thermals, waiting for thermals and flying to, from and through thermals. You do those things already. In this event, you get to look for lift in the duration task, rip off laps in good air for the distance task and, for speed, wait for the best air in which to start your run. It's a thermal-soaring event. Working time, re-launches and normalized scores in flight groups are some of the means by which this fast, fun event is fair to all.

This sport can be very difficult to get started in. This chapter is intended to help those who are interested in learning about the event and to prepare novices for serious practice. It doesn't tell pilots how to fly. Every group of F3B pilots works as a team and practices according to their own wants and needs. I've simply provided some ideas on how to prepare for competition. If, after you have read them, you decide to become involved in the event and have no one to look to for answers, have no fear. Contact the AMA, and ask for the team-selection committee chairman for the F3B event.

TEAMEAST: THE ROAD TO THE NATIONALS

What started as a classified ad in the Eastern Soaring League (ESL) newsletter in early 1991 has brought a new team—Eastern America's Soaring Team (Teameast)—into the F3B arena. Here's the story of how the team was formed and what happened along the way.

I have been flying F3B tasks since 1987. I qualified for and flew in the 1990 Team Selection contest, and I realized that being part of a team was necessary to become competitive in the event. The quality of my practice sessions had been limited because I had been flying alone, and that made it hard to get better at distance and speed.

I decided to advertise for fliers. I called Byron Blakeslee, the editor of F3B/USA. He told me that I had a good idea, but only one person in my area—Steve Syrotiak—subscribed to the newsletter.

Because I already knew him, I turned to the regional pilots in the Eastern Soaring League to find interested people.

I didn't receive a single reply during the flying season, so I sent a form letter to seven talented pilots to see whether they would be interested in flying with me. Mike Lachowski, John Marion and Steve replied to say that they would be there to see what the event was about. Others I sent the letter to replied, but they were too busy or offered to help the team on a non-flying basis. After I had spoken to Mike, I was sure he would form his own team with local people rather than with me. Steve surprised me by pushing to get practice sessions going, and in January and February 1992, we got together with John for some not-so-serious task prac-

tice. We hoped that Jim Tyrie would attend, enjoy himself and join in, but bad weather kept him away.

PRACTICE

Everything started happening the first weekend in April. Three pilots with F3B planes arrived for practice: Steve with

Rich Burnoski loads, unloads and changes the amount of ballast in his plane. The weight at which you fly the plane varies with each flight. Sometimes lead will go in and out several times before the plane has flown once! Usually ballast is made in pieces that will slip over one another, making it easy to make small changes.

Steve Work readies for a "remote" launch. Skip Miller is the official at base A. Steve's helper prepares to toss the loaded plane. With the sky looking pretty dark, lots of tension is put in the line to help get good launch altitude.

his Synergy 91, Mike with his own-design F3B and me with a Comet 89T. I had sent them copies of the rules and, after discussing them, we started practicing Task B—distance. This event involves flying back and forth in a straight line. After a few flights, everyone was doing at least that much. I also had them keeping their noses down and moving faster. I couldn't prevent Mike from circling in lift while on the course. Things got better quickly, and once they had each put up a flight of more than 20 laps, there was a genuine understanding of how the task should be flown. By day two of the weekend, we were flying distance again and paying more attention to the teamwork aspect and calling turns. Mike stayed late to do speed runs, and out of his first six, he came up with some good times.

Because Mike did so well in the first session, I talked him into going out to Chicago for a SOAR qualifying contest for the Team Selection event. Rich Burnoski was our host, and Tom Blood was the CD. The two-day contest provided great practice in what had to be the worst of weather, and Mike and I qualified.

PRACTICING FOR THE CONTEST

Distance practice dominated our next two sessions. We also practiced re-launching, launch techniques and teamwork. Everyone could fly with a wing loading of 20 ounces per foot more, handle the course with any wind and fly both sides of the course. Mike and Steve were ready to dive into speed.

The first weekend in May was windy, and our position on the field had us flying near trees; but we remained undaunted. We were helped by my brother, Roger, another glider pilot named Mike Fritz and a good friend, Bob Hurlburt. They came to the field to help us with chutes and to sight base B for most of our sessions at the Durham field. They were there for the show, and so were the power fliers of my club—the Black Sheep Squadron. We set up the four winches and launched from each doing consecutive practice flights. None of our timed runs broke any world records, and Steve joked that the Portuguese National Team had nothing to worry about!

Two more practices in May and early June were devoted to speed runs, and we worked hard at calling turns, timing and

critiquing flights. We added one more to our crew: Dave Garwood came by to learn the different jobs required of a an F3B pilot at base A during the tasks.

In the two final sessions, we covered the total time it takes to bring a plane down and re-launch it back to altitude. We also covered remote launching for Task C (speed) and, for simulated contest experience, we flew some man-on-man using the working time with re-launches.

Our three-man team had practiced together more than half a dozen times, and considering that two of the pilots had fewer than six months of experience with the tasks, we weren't doing too badly. We were ready to go to the Nats and meet Terry Edmonds—our fourth pilot. A pilot may have four people helping during a flight; we had three pilots for help, and Roger, Dave and Mike were available for duty. We also recruited ESL members Terry Luckenbach and Tony Matyi during the contest. We were ready, and the contest was a week away. Now, let's see what we can do for you.

TEAMWORK IN F3B

Why is teamwork important in F3B? Why did our teams at the last two World Championships do so well? Here are some answers.

◆ During the contest tasks, the pilot who makes the official flight needs to have the cooperation of the team pilots and mechanics.

◆ Good teamwork can really improve a person's abilities and scores. We all use teamwork to our advantage. When you pick an official timer at a thermal duration contest and have him keep track of time, watch the other gliders, get information on the condition of the air, pick a landing circle and straighten the tape, you become a team. There is usually no commitment here, and because these contests do not usually support teams, some timers are better than others.

◆ An F3B team is made up of three or four pilots. A team may have more than four people, but the rules allow only four people to help the pilot at any task. Having extra people means that a pilot who flies in the next flight group has a chance to get ready. The person at the turn-around can be replaced, and it's nice to just watch what's happening or just take a break.

◆ Every pilot will find that he has a preference for who will help at certain jobs;

one person may be best to call the turns and another to launch, etc. By flying and practicing together, the jobs will be assigned so all pilots have the best chance to perform in the air. Each team member may do more than one job during a task and should be capable of performing many, if not all, the jobs.

◆ It is important to practice these tasks as well as learn to fly the plane. In F3B, scores are normalized inside flight groups. When you help your team do well, pilots on the other teams don't get big points against *you*.

◆ Below are the jobs that pilots like to have performed for them while they keep their eyes on the glider and their mind on the task at hand. Some pilots may like more than this done; some will get away with less. Some pilots have been known to complete tasks without help from anyone at all!

At launch

• Man the turnaround to retrieve the line, and return it to the winch for a re-launch.
• Hold and launch the glider; in the distance task, hold the glider up for identification.
• Operate the winch or, if the pilot operates the winch, quickly wind the line down to within 10 meters of the turn-around after the plane has left the line.
• Start the working-time clock, and keep the pilot informed of how much time is left.
• Be ready to retrieve the glider for a re-launch.
• Help pick the air and the tactics for this working time.

Duration

• Clock the flight time from the moment of launch to landing. Supply this information to the pilot in the format of his choice—countdown or time into flight.
• Inform the pilot about working time and his chance of re-launching.
• Inform the pilot about air, the location of other members of the flight group, how well they're doing and their chances of relaunching.
• Inform the pilot of landing-circle position, wind direction, air traffic, trees and other obstacles during the landing.

Distance

• Tell the pilot how much time he has spent on the course, and keep track of lap times.
• Inform the pilot about working time and his chance of re-launching.
• Count the laps.

• Call the base A and B roll-ins and turns.
• Repeat the turn signal given by the officials.
• Watch the flight group members and help to decide whether a re-launch is advisable.
• Advise the pilot at minimum altitude to stay away from the pits, winches and sighting devices, and direct him to a safe landing.

Speed

• Help pick the time the pilot chooses to launch.
• Call the approach to base A as the pilot exits the course.
• Call the base A and B roll-ins; call the turns.
• Repeat the turn signal given by the officials.
• Watch the safety line, and keep the pilot on course.
• Inform the pilot about working time and his chance of re-launching.

GETTING READY FOR PRACTICE SESSIONS

Welcome to your first season of F3B flying. Yes, there's snow on the ground and it's cold, but there's a lot to be done. A few things must be gathered so the actual fly-

can use a rope with a knot every 39 inches. You can also take your hats off and throw them on the ground before you set up for your landing pattern. These should not be used much on practice days—maybe once at the end of the day for man-on-man duration or early in the day before the thermals are rising. Why? Because we have better things to do when there's lift coming through.

To lay out a course for distance and speed tasks, you'll need a, 200-meter-long (656 feet) wire or rope to control the length of the winch line with a mark on it to indicate 150 meters (492 feet). For first practices, measuring the winch line once will suffice; getting close to the length is good enough. Learn to pace off the 200 meters, and it should be easy to determine the 164 feet that base B is short, and pace back to it. For the first sessions, when you are learning to stay on course and make turns, accurate distance is not important.

Sights for base A and base B are needed to finish the course. As you get on with F3B, nice sights will be very important. To get started, a sight could be a reference to a tree on the edge of the field, two tall poles lined up perpendicular to the winch lines, or a piece of aluminum with a hoop on top and mounted on a camera tripod.

Team Selection Finals in 1994. The site is the Toledo Weak Signals flying field. One plane is being launched for a duration task.

ing sessions will be productive and fun.

The most important thing you need is difficult to find, but when you have it, the rest is easy: you need a team. To learn about the tasks quickly, you need three people who want to fly F3B at the field. The team will share the timing, act as officials and become instructors, critics and competition. They will also make it much easier to put together the rest of the items you'll need.

You'll need two, 15-meter-long landing tapes that are marked every meter. You

To signal from base B to base A, you could use something as simple as a flag. Someone must be looking at the flag the moment it is waved, or the signal will be missed. Having a person who is dedicated to this job makes it work better, but an audible signal will work even better. Inexpensive walkie-talkies will work under some conditions, but when man-power is limited at the field, nothing beats a good set of hand-held or voice-operated CB radios.

You should have at least two stop-

Teameast winches set up for a day of practice.

watches for a session. Working time and flight time are important, and you should keep track of both on every flight. A countdown feature is very nice. At an event, the team will probably use more.

Two or more winches—Ford, Bosch, sport; bring what you have. Most winches in use are more powerful than the rules will allow. Worry about legal winches when you want to try for a place on the team. You're going to love launching. On a sad note, there are not many winches out there in the world yet. Do not despair, you can hand-tow and even use a pulley!

Almost last, from the AMA, get a rule book on the FAI events.

Last is ballast. This is what makes your plane go, and you use it for distance and

F3B Rules Summary

The rules for the F3B event are simpler than most fliers think. These rules make competition fair even when the stakes are high, as in international and world championship events. Complete FAI rule books are available from the AMA.

◆ **The event is flown in rounds.** In each round, you fly duration, distance and speed. Your score for a round is the total of normalized points from the three tasks. The highest score in each group is given a 1,000, and the other pilots are given a percentage. In the distance task, your laps are counted. In your flight group, the pilot with the highest number of laps gets a 1,000 for the task. It doesn't matter how many laps he did, he gets the 1,000! If he did 24 laps of the 150-meter course and you completed 12, then your score would be 12 laps ÷ 24 laps = 0.5 x 1,000 = 500, and that would be your score for the task. You will be in a different group each round, maybe for each task. Duration points get normalized also.

◆ **For the raw score,** you get one point for each second in the air up to 7 minutes, and you have one point taken off for each second after. This gets added to the landing bonus. The landing spot is a 2-meter-diameter circle worth 100 points; each meter out is worth 5 points less, out to 30 points. If you're in the air when working time ends, you won't get any landing points, and the flight points stop. The flight group for speed is usually the entire list of contestants.

For the speed task, the fastest person in the group is given the 1,000, and any other score is determined by taking the time of the flight and dividing it into the winner's time for the normalized score. If the fastest speed run of the round was an 18-second flight and you flew a 24-second flight, your score would be 18 seconds ÷ 24 seconds = 0.75 x 1,000 = 750 points. Speed is usually flown in one large group, which gives you a chance to beat your teammates. The scores from all the rounds flown in the contest are added to determine placement.

◆ **The flying field** should be fairly flat, open and free of slope effects. A winch line should be established with the turnarounds upwind, at least at the start of the round. The landing circles, one for each pilot in the flight group, are usually placed on either side of the winches. For distance and speed tasks, a course must be established.

A vertical plane called base A is established at or behind the winches. It extends up higher than you can fly, and for the distance task, it extends to either side as far as you can see.

Parallel to base A, 150 meters in the direction of the turnarounds, is another vertical plane—base B. It also extends out in either direction. One lap is the distance from base A to B or B to A, not out and back. For a lap to count in either task, the nose of the plane must pass through the base plane the glider is flying toward. Distance can be flown on either side of the winches or directly above; you pick the place on the course where you think the air is best and crank out laps.

For safety reasons, all flying in the speed task takes place to one side of the winches. A vertical plane, referred to as the safety line, is set up at one end of the winch line. It runs perpendicular to bases A and B, and flying on the wrong side will get you a score of zero—no arguing allowed. There are safety areas established on the field where a pilot may not land.

Whether a plane crosses the safety line or bases A or B is determined by officials who use simple sighting devices. Pilots may not have anyone signal them from base B, but help is allowed at base A during the flight. Each pilot or team usually sets up a sight and aligns it with the official sight to help turn properly at base A.

◆ **The contest organizers determine the order in which tasks are run.** Each task is assigned preparation time and working time. Prep time is a 5-minute period before the task begins for each flight group. You use it to check your radio and plane and to get your launching equipment set up. Prep time

speed tasks. Make one of them on the heavy side and make one half that weight. A Falcon 880 can easily carry 24 ounces (maybe more). Don't make ballast in small weights; a few ounces do nothing.

FIRST F3B PRACTICE— or how to keep your teammates happy

Ah, spring! The old fingers are getting back their feel for the sticks, and summer is just around the corner. If you had been considering flying the tasks of F3B, you may have gathered a few or all of the items necessary to be serious. That means you should have a *team* to practice with, or at the least someone who will be coming to the field to help you at base B and with other things.

I'm going to talk here of your first work with the tasks, not the first practice you'll have with the team. What you want to learn flying as a team is what you can't learn yourself. Respect must be given to the others at the field; you should not be there wasting their time. You must try things on your own before you ask for help, and have some good advice for them when they ask.

To put yourself in this position, do it alone. Start by going to the field and setting the winch, the course and the practice schedule, and try to set up repetitive maneuvers and individual practices to teach yourself something about handling your plane; learning to roll is very good.

Set up the airplane. Learn to fly it.

When your team needs you on a team day, they don't want to hear that you have to take time out to dial in your CG or re-set the elevator trim. They need you *now* or the day is going to be wasted. You don't want to hear that "Nothing is being learned" or "This F3B stuff is for the birds." You will know trouble is brewing if someone on the team wants to put up a flight while things are being straightened out.

Get the plane flying right. Much of the flying in practices is done at high speed and in straight lines. Make sure the plane flies in straight lines without input from you. Just as the plane should not turn in the horizontal plane, it should fly hands-off in the vertical, as well. If you drop the

---

ends with the start of working time. All official flights take place in working time. You may launch any time within the working time. Your last flight is the official flight.

• **The task for duration** is 7 minutes, working time is 9 minutes. Flight points count from the time the plane leaves the launch line to when it comes to rest on the ground. The end of working time is the last chance for flight points. There are no landing points given if the plane comes to rest after working time has ended.

• **Distance** has a 7-minute working time. The pilot has 4 minutes from the time the plane enters the course to do as many laps as possible. After launching, the pilot flies the plane behind base A then turns to fly to base B. Only whole laps of the last flight are counted.

• **The speed task** has a working time of 4 minutes. The plane must enter the course within 1 minute of leaving the launch line or be re-launched for another attempt. This rule prevents thermalling to extreme heights for an entry onto the course. Unlike the other tasks, only one attempt for an official flight may be made. The plane may be launched as many times as the pilot demands. Once the plane passes through base A and goes to base B for the first of four laps, the flight is official! A shout of "Abort" tells the officials of a failed attempt and imminent re-launch! Flight time starts when the plane enters the course and ends after it has completed the four laps. A zero is given if the four laps have not been completed.

◆ **"Re-flights."** Much of the fairness in the rules comes from the inclusion of "re-flights" for those pilots who have been hindered during their attempts to make an official flight. The idea is to give everyone the same opportunity to find air and fly in it. The normalized scoring for each flight group rates performance on a man-to-man basis.

Common reasons for re-flights include being unable to launch because someone has fouled your line, not being scored properly, midair collisions or other unforeseeable events. The decision to continue a flight for the best or take a re-flight of the task adds

an element not found in other forms of competition flying.

◆ **You may enter three planes in a contest.** The FAI limits for plane size and weight are the same for AMA and F3B competitions. No landing aids or skegs may be used. The rules actually dictate the planes' characteristics. Limited winch power and the 7-minute duration task do as much to shape the plane as the need for pure speed and the weighty distance task. The plane that starts a round must be used for all three tasks. If an airplane is lost owing to an incident, you would be offered re-flight, and you may use another plane to finish the round.

◆ **To get the best score possible, you may have four helpers.** A team is not necessary, but it's very helpful. At international events, a team is made up of three pilots. At a proper contest, only the team manager is allowed to discuss event business with the officials.

◆ **Launches** can be made in one of several ways. The most preferred way is the winch launch. Winch motors are limited in power by a specification for the internal resistance, which must be greater than 15 milliohms; battery power is also limited to 460 Cold Cranking Amps. A typical Ford long-shaft motor has a resistance of 9 milliohms, and a hot one can be rated at 6 to 8. Older, more powerful F3B winches were rated at 4 milliohms!

Motors must be standard production items. You may modify them only to support the shaft on the ball bearings. Drums must be at least 2.95 inches long and of a fixed diameter. The line is 400 meters long, and the turnaround is 200 meters from the winch. The used line doesn't foul anyone's launch; it must be run down to the turnaround. The winch must be equipped with a device to prevent the line from being let out while under tow. Launching must take place within 3 meters of the winch. Turnarounds can be no higher than 0.5 meter above the ground.

Hand-towing is also allowed. The length of the towline is 175

F3B FLYING FIELD LAYOUT
(left-hand layout shown)

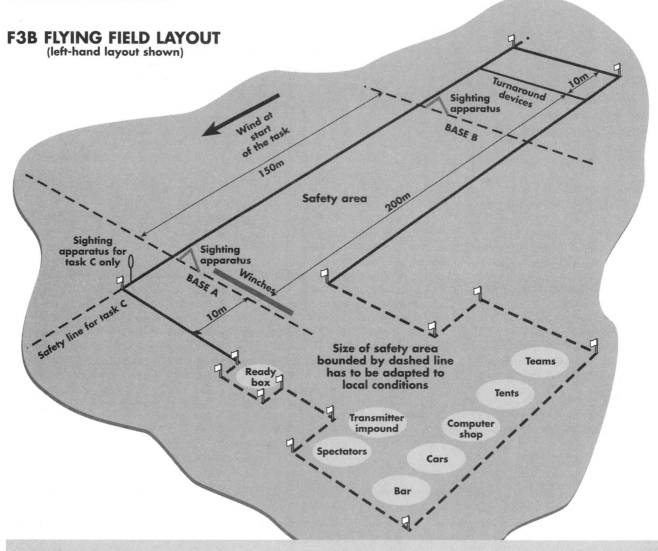

Wind at start of the task

150m

Safety area

200m

Turnaround devices

10m

Sighting apparatus

BASE B

Sighting apparatus for task C only

Sighting apparatus

BASE A

Winches

10m

Safety line for task C

Ready box

Size of safety area bounded by dashed line has to be adapted to local conditions

Teams

Tents

Transmitter impound

Computer shop

Spectators

Cars

Bar

F3B Rules Summary continued

meters. Pulleys can be used to gain some advantage. This method of launching is employed most when the wind has changed and the winches have been positioned to face downwind. The plane is towed into the wind to a better position and hopefully a high launch!

HINTS

Working time is precious time; don't give any away! "You can win the event in the speed task; you can lose it faster in the distance task!"—a quote from at least 100 F3B fliers.

◆ **Advanced teamwork.** Calling air: before sending anyone to better air, be at least 85 percent sure it is better air. Realize the altitude loss during transit. Don't look at someone up high and believe there is still good air underneath. Don't believe an airplane going up is in good air or that one going down is in sink. Conditions change, air moves; help your pilot stay in good air.

◆ **Duration.** F3B is tough, so don't go running to good air and let everyone know where it is. It's you versus them for 1,000 points. How close do you want them to get? Pick at the

air; use it as necessary to stay up. Decide early to re-launch or stick with the flight. If you're on your second flight, be sure to get down before working time runs out. We're talking about what could be 20 to 40 percent of your points. Land safely; land close.

◆ **Distance.** Pilots won't take their eyes off their plane in this task. You must be their eyes and, at times, their minds. Pilots can't look at the clock, so give them time checks more often than you think is necessary. Pilots, if you feel the information from your mates is confusing, ask if you should re-launch. Help maximize the number of laps for the pilot. His flying here helps or hurts you. Get the information out on time; give it out so he can make a decision, not just waste time listening. Land safely; land close on re-launches.

◆ **Speed.** Be ready to start working time right after the pilot in front of you. Be ready to launch at the start of working time. You have a team; don't enter the course on a bad launch or in bad air. Be ready to go back for the missed turn. Relax, go back, make an assessment and finish the course. Land safely and close on the re-launches; time is very precious in this task.

nose to pick up speed, the plane should go faster; it should not start to climb and slow down, and you shouldn't have to hold the nose down or up with the stick. Get the trims set, and get to know the plane. If you've been flying your old trusty thermal ship only to thermals, this new stuff will create some problems. Fly in front of yourself, from right to left and then from left to right, and use *both* right and left turns. On the next flight, fly to and from your position and some point on the horizon, back and forth to the same spot, using right and left turns.

How far should you go before turning? How far is 150 meters? How many seconds does it take to go 150 meters? How small is the plane one lap out, at altitude and low to the ground? An excellent way to get a feel for these is to set the plane down near the winch so you can see the full span, then walk the course to base B and look at the plane where it is without any altitude. To see what it looks like at altitude, walk across the course. Every foot you walk across the field is adding a foot of altitude; got it? Take a hike; you may be doing laps at 600 to 800 feet. This is the kind of thing that you should do alone. If everyone on the team goes out on his own, the team sessions will be excellent.

Put ballast in on these solo days, and get used to it. Distance and speed will be done with the plane loaded. Master slow- and moderate-speed flight, shallow-bank and steep-bank turns, both right and left. Fair warning: don't make low-altitude, downwind turns with the plane set up this way until you have some experience. Stop doing laps with enough air to easily get in position for a landing.

Here's a novel idea: try practicing launches. Typically, you go up the line, zoom and steer your plane toward where you think the lift is, and then you usually drift and try not to lose altitude. Instead, do something else that's a must for speed and distance: before you launch, decide which side of the sky you will do the laps in. Run up the line and, just before the zoom, turn the plane slightly in the direction you want to go; zoom, and do it nearly vertically. The plane should be going up to one side; I hope it's the one you picked. Pull just enough up-elevator so the plane is pointed back toward base A before it runs out of steam; roll it out to level flight; set the speed, and get ready to exit the course. Now the plane is ready to roll over for the entry of a speed run or turn in or out on the course for the first lap of distance.

Before you get tired or your batteries become run down, try speed. Just do four laps. Burn off altitude to keep the speed up, but save altitude so you can do all four laps. Do not go so fast that the plane goes out of control. If you want to see *fast*, keep flying out of control. Crashes happen *real* fast when you're learning. Before you begin the run, try to figure out in which directions you'll be turning so you don't get confused on the course. Don't hold aileron and elevator simultaneously when executing 90- to 110-degree banked turns! Turning into the wind is good, cutting the safety line is bad—zero points for that maneuver. These are some things you should get used to from the beginning.

After this session, I'm sure you'll feel you've done something really different. With the knowledge that you gained, the first team practice will go a lot better and so will all those that follow. The harder each pilot works at his flying, the more will be learned by all. Keeping a group together is easy if everyone is happy. I hope you have a small group to fly with.

words shouted by a pilot, his launcher and the pilot again, before the switch on the winch gets jammed down. They're very common words at our field—heard 60 to 80 times during a six-hour practice. "Ready!" "Turn!" It takes a minimum of three people to make those calls happen during a flight. We hear them often. "I'll get the plane!" is commonly heard at base A when the person flying has more flights left in his turn at the course. It's a friendly gesture that lets pilots stay in tune with the flying, and it provides good practice for re-launching. "What do we do now? More distance or speed?" Uncrossing the used winch lines, beeping the turns and retrieving the lines at the end of a series of launches give you a chance to think about the flying of the day—yours and theirs.

Those will probably be the thoughts you remember at the end of a team practice session. But what will you be doing? The first thing to do is to lay out the course. Set up base A at the winch line,

Teamwork during a remote launch for the speed task; Jim McCarthy launches, Tom Kallevang operates the winch, Dennis Phelan pilots from the safety line with officials behind him, and Rich Burnoski stands with the pilot to provide time and course information. Another team member is 200 meters away manning the turnaround.

TEAM PRACTICE—
or are we having fun yet?

Checklist time. Do you know what the wind direction at the field will be? Does everyone know what time to be at the field? Is your transmitter charged? Are you ready? It's time to get together, have some real fun and do some serious learning. A team practice will improve more than the flying skills of the pilots.

"Ready!" "Set!" "Go!" Those are the

point it down the course, measure the 150 meters to base B and set up the second sighting device. Make it nice and square! Make sure everyone has only 200 meters of line to the turnaround. Now you're ready to put planes together.

You have to assign some tasks now. You need a person to be the base A official, and a person to launch the plane, operate the winch and wind down the line and another to call the turns for the pilot.

I just described the tasks for two people. One is the official, a second person does all the rest. We'll need one person at base B to call turns, so if there's someone left with nothing to do, he can help that one

Seth Dawson's winch. The handle, wheels and winch parts fit into the box for transportation.

guy who's really busy! The last person we need is the pilot with a plane. (Now we'll see who has been doing their homework.)

There are three good ways to hold practices. When people are learning the tasks, the best way is to have one pilot at a time launch, fly the task, then launch on the next winch. Fly the task again, and so on down the line until there are no more lines to hook up. Then rotate the people helping so they all get a chance to do each job. The next pilot comes out of the rotation and does the same thing. How did this pilot get winch lines, you ask? The person

at base B brought them back with him during the rotation. Hint, if you're short on winches, rotate tasks every time you run out of lines, but keep the same pilot. It really pays for the pilot to fly enough times to learn something. Round and round we go, through the rotation. Time to change tasks. After you've gotten warmed up on distance, move on to speed! Speed is simple. Just keep doing the same rotation, but with each launch, the pilot will fly only four laps around the course.

When you know how to handle the plane on the course and everyone feels they know the tasks, it's time to add pressure. Now add working time and flight time. When a pilot steps up to the winch line, his job will be the same as in a contest, only he won't fly against anyone. Give him a short preparation time, and then start the working time clock. He has all the winches and all the help he needs to pick the air, put the plane in it and fly the course. He has all the working time to do it—just like a contest. He does one working time and then everyone rotates. The next pilot up does the same thing with no competition, but when you've just moved up from learning the tasks, this is tough.

If you worked hard to put a practice together, you may have enough people to have an excellent practice session man on man, with officials. The officials are anyone who's not flying or launching. These are the sessions you work for. When all the pilots in the group can handle the pressure and the planes don't need to be trimmed or repaired at the field, this is what you do. Make sure all your friends who wanted to see you fly come out, along with the pilots you know who didn't want to try F3B and any relatives who happened to drop by. Manpower is what you need now. To run distance man on man for two requires: two pilots, two

launchers/helpers, two base A turn-callers, two more at base B and someone to do the timing and lap counting. Go back to the last sentence and add up all those "two's"; it's an easy 10. Of course, the helpers can count laps, keep track of working flight time, try to locate the best air for the pilot and inform him of the whereabouts of his opponent! Isn't F3B *great*?

If this session and other team sessions work well for you, then you must be out there practicing on your own. That's good to do all the time. You may find that you want to do some re-trimming after the first team session. Do this on your own time before the next team session.

It's tough to have man-on-man practices. You can save four official positions by having the launcher/helpers act as the officials at base A. Coordinated teamwork is essential. Have fun, and be careful with those winch lines! ◆

ABOUT THE AUTHOR

Dennis Phelan

Dennis was born in 1945 and, around the age of 10, he added wooden airplanes to his plastic model collection. In 1960, he was introduced to some fine pilots who formed the Southern Connecticut Aeromodeling Association (SCAMA) and introduced him to competitive flying. Chasing free-flight models took up a lot of his time from then on. A tour with the U.S. Air Force found him as a member of that team at the 1965 AMA Nationals. He raced motorcycles for a few years, but in 1980, R/C soaring gained a firm hold on him. In 1987, he began to fly F3B and was soon hooked. He has been flying the event competitively since 1990.

CHAPTER 29

How to Handle Hand-Launched Gliders

by Brian F. Agnew

Introduced 10 years ago as a spinoff of R/C sailplanes, hand-launched gliders have developed into one of the most popular and challenging types of soaring. The reasons for this ongoing and increasing interest in them are many. Most pilots do it simply for the thrill that only "sky-ing out" from a hand-launch can provide. I've never met anyone who has experienced this and didn't immediately become an enthusiast.

Pilots who fly hand-launched gliders (HLGs) are the "purists" of the sport of soaring. Just as soaring pilots frown on those who put power pods on their gliders, HLG enthusiasts frown on the idea of using winches and high-starts.

R/C HLGs span 60 inches or less and typically weigh between 12 and 14 ounces. They generally have a wing area of 350 to 400 square inches, which gives them a wing loading of about 5 ounces per square foot. While larger sailplanes can also be hand-launched into lift, the 60-inch models have become the "official" size for competitions and have been officially recognized by the Academy of Model Aeronautics.

HLG designs have gone through quite a few trends since their inception. At first, they were "built-up" models covered with iron-on films. These tended to be fragile and required more time to build than today's obechi-over-foam models. Today, most competitive models have fiberglass fuselages, which make them stronger, lighter and faster to build. In the last few years, the most successful designs have been polyhedral models with V-tails. The V-tail can be built lighter and makes the glider do flat, efficient thermal turns low to the ground. Lately, pilots have been experimenting with thinner airfoils (6 to 8 percent thick) and have been playing with flaperons. The airframes can now be built light enough to allow the addition of two extra servos in the wings. With flaperons, pilots can use traditionally faster airfoils, and they can use camber to enhance the thermalling abilities of the faster sections. It remains to be seen whether this is just a fad or whether it's the shape of future winning designs.

HLGs appeal to a wide variety of fliers. They are a cost-effective and simple way to get airborne, without the hassles and costs that come with the more complex multi-channel competition machines. Most HLGs are 2-channel models that can be flown with 4-channel radios. A radio with V-tail mixing and a micro airborne pack will allow you to fly competitively. Competition HLG kits cost anywhere from $60 to $150 depending on the degree of prefabrication. Many do-it-yourselfers enjoy scratch-building their own models and trying different ideas until they find a winning combination. HLGs are perfect for scratch-builders because of minimal costs and short building times. Compared with other soaring events, hand-launch contests typically have more scratch-built models.

Given today's ongoing struggle to find and keep flying sites, HLGs are perfect, because every open lot is a potential flying site. Any football- or baseball-size field is more than adequate. The gliders

The author follows through on an HLG toss. Remember, it's not the strength of the throw that's important, it's the accuracy.

are small and light enough to minimize the hazards that accompany flying R/C in a congested area. The abundance of potential flying sites and the compactness of these planes are why few enthusiasts would be caught without one in the back of their car.

Another compelling reason for the popularity of HLGs is the physical nature of the sport. It is good exercise, it never gets boring, and it works most of the major muscle groups. Unfortunately, the physical challenge is also one of the major reasons many people don't try it. But you don't have to have the arm of a gorilla to hand-launch a 60-inch, 13-ounce sailplane! If you can throw a football 10 yards, there is no reason why you can't throw an HLG hard enough to get two or three thermal turns. With HLGs, the accuracy of a throw is far more important than the strength; but strength certainly doesn't hurt. Besides, what better reason is there to get in shape than to be able to fly longer! All the same, those who feel that their arms just aren't up to the task have found that a small upstart (25 feet of surgical tubing and 75 feet of line) gives them all the fun of a hand-launch without the sore muscles.

Most top soaring competition pilots are also avid HLG pilots. They find that an HLG helps them to sharpen their flying skills and, more important, teaches the art of "reading" the energy in the surrounding air mass. The ability to read the air for lift and sink is something that all soaring pilots strive for. The most significant byproduct of flying HLGs is this sixth

In this launching sequence, you can see the author move up the field to look for some signs of lift. He's sure of where he wants to launch and search for lift when he starts the throwing motion. You don't have to be big to throw well in HLG. To get good launches, you need to extend your throwing motion and to practice. Throwing a model the same way you throw on a winch launch just isn't good enough.

sense that develops from countless hours of hand-launching and studying the air. Most of today's top competition pilots credit their love of HLGs as the most significant contributing factor to their status and success.

HLGs improve flying skills by providing pilots with immediate visual feedback to control inputs. Standing in close proximity to the flying sailplanes, pilots can plainly see their mistakes and make adjustments. HLGs accelerate the learning process; they fly low to the ground, and mistakes often require immediate repairs—a strong incentive to avoid them. Beginners would do well to always have their next HLG on the building board so that precious flying time is not lost during building. Once bitten by the bug, you will want at least two planes anyway.

MEETING THE COMPETITION

Once a pilot has become proficient at flying his HLG, he will undoubtedly want to see how he "measures up" against others. Hand-launch competitions present some of the ultimate challenges in R/C soaring.

The typical HLG contest will pit six to eight pilots against one another in 10-minute rounds that include various tasks that are scored man-on-man and "normalized" to 1,000 points. Typical tasks include longest flight of the round, two 5-minute maxes, three 3-minute maxes, most consecutive flights in increasing duration (starting with 15 seconds) and first-one-up, last-one-down. The most difficult task is the five 2-minute maxes in 10 minutes; I've seen this done several times with the pilot getting all five maxes on all his throws and only being 8 seconds off 10 minutes; that allows a little more than 1 second to re-launch between flights!

If you've never seen an HLG contest, it really is entertaining to watch pilots picking their air, running around in search of lift and following it downwind. Pilots will try different strategies—some piggy-backing on others, some going off on their own. Contests resemble three-dimensional

HLGs are much smaller than thermal and soaring gliders. They generally have a wingspan of 60 inches or less and weigh between 12 and 14 ounces.

chess matches; they are as entertaining to watch as they are to fly.

The possibilities for HLG competitions are endless. Within the last couple of years, "hand-launch golf" has become popular. Pilots throw their planes, then

Assuming your glider was built as straight and light as possible, take it to the nearest schoolyard on a calm day. Balance the glider according to the manufacturer's suggestions (usually on the nose-heavy side), and be sure that whatever weight is

want to drop its nose in the turn? Does it climb sharply when thrown? If the answer is "Yes" to either question, then nose weight should be removed and down-trim applied. If your model has a fixed stabilizer, the trailing edge of the wing will need to

jump into a golf cart and literally chase their sailplanes down the course. The "hole" is a hula hoop placed in the middle of the green, and the object is to land your plane in the hula hoop. The lowest score after 18 holes wins.

HAND-LAUNCH STRATEGIES AND TECHNIQUES

◆ **Trimming.** Trimming your HLG is the first and most crucial step toward success.

added can be easily removed a little at a time. (I tape lead to the front of the battery pack.)

Gently toss the plane into the wind. Don't worry about turning; just make whatever adjustments are needed to get the model flying straight and level. Throw the model harder with each subsequent flight, and get a feel for the rudder response; if there is a headwind, gently fly S-turns into the wind. Does the model

be shimmed up $\frac{1}{32}$ inch at a time until the model flies level without down-trim in the elevator.

Setting up an HLG for optimum performance can be a long, tedious process. In dead air, you will also want to time your flights to determine whether the adjustments you make really increase flight times. Keep moving the CG back until you are no longer comfortable flying the plane and your times start to suffer; then move the CG slightly forward. On some models, you may even need to go to a smaller battery if you have removed all your nose weight.

After scouting the field for signs of thermal activity, you should launch your glider into the direction of the thermals. Here, the author is just about to release an HLG into a thermal.

◆ **Launching.** This is a learned motion that, when done properly, closely resembles a javelin throwing motion. Throws should be made on the run and with very little bend in the elbow. A common mistake made by first-timers is failing to keep the wrist straight on the follow-through; unlike when throwing a football, the wrist must not rotate, otherwise, the release will be sideways and the model will "wiggle" to altitude. The throw should be made out (not up!) and should always be made into the wind—regardless of which direction the lift is in. A properly trimmed HLG will have a gradual climb-out without any control input. As your launches get harder and the climbs get higher and steeper, you will find that the model will need plenty of down-travel to top off the launches, or the model may stall; typically, you will need twice as much down-travel as up-travel.

◆ **Finding thermals.** When your model has been trimmed, you can get down to the business of finding thermals. There is plenty of literature available to help you understand the dynamics of finding thermals, so I won't go into detail here. Once your lift has been spotted, throw into the wind for maximum launch altitude! If the lift is downwind, throw into the wind, but do a climbing turn so that at the apex of the launch, the model is headed straight for the lift.

◆ **Common mistakes.** The most common mistakes in HLG flying are poor energy management (flying too fast in lift and too slow in sink) and flying too timidly. Flying at low altitudes requires a steady but firm hand and fast decision-making. A moment's hesitation can make the difference between coring a thermal and walking to pick up your plane. At low altitudes, the thermals are often weak, so don't hesitate to put the plane up on a tip and fly tight circles. Thermals often want to spit your glider out, so it takes a firm hand to keep the plane cored. As altitude is gained and the thermal broadens, flatten the turns. If you've secured a max, leave that thermal and find another; you'll never learn anything by flying in one thermal.

Whatever your background in R/C soaring is, your experience in the sport can only be enhanced by the addition of an HLG. Everything learned from flying HLGs will carry over to other aspects of soaring. It is no accident that the best fliers in soaring are also avid HLG pilots. If your experience with HLGs is anything like most others', you will undoubtedly find that, if you could only have one sailplane, it would be a hand-launch. ◆

ABOUT THE AUTHOR

Brian Agnew

Brian has been flying R/C sailplanes for almost 20 years. From 1991 through 1994, he designed and kitted the Vertigo HLG and Banshee 2-meter competition sailplanes under Agnew Model Products. Both designs won national championships. In 1994, he left model manufacturing to do social work for Catholic Social Services. He currently does kitting and research and development for Slegers International in New Jersey and will soon begin a 13-month commitment to Covenant House in New York City—a shelter for teenage runaways. He holds a B.A. in religion.

SPECIAL INTEREST

There are many fun, specialty areas of R/C flying. The contributions from top R/C pilots in this section will help you become proficient in several of them and help to improve your "fun quotient." Have you experienced the unique excitement of combat flying? It's a must in your R/C flying career. Greg Rose, *Model Aviation* combat columnist and long-time expert, gives you an edge on the competition in "Flying R/C Combat." F5B world champion Jerry Bridgeman discusses how to win when flying battery-powered "rocket ships" in "Tips from an F5B World Champ!".

Want to do better at the next fun fly? See Dan Luchaco's "Sport Fun Fly" for pointers that will help you take home the honors. Perhaps you'd like to compete in an arena that's a little more laid-back but still demanding of skill and careful engineering, such as limited-duration electric competition; national champion Tom Hunt gives you the lowdown in "Flying Class A and

B Electric Sailplane Events." If you enjoy the slow-flying elegance of old-timer aircraft and would like to compete in OT'er events, then Bob Aberle's "Flying Old-Timer Model Aircraft" is for you. If you like the sound of high-revving engines and have the need for high-tech speed, then "Basics of Flying Ducted Fans" by nationally renowned ducted-fan modeler and pilot Bob Fiorenze will answer your questions.

The experts say that to be the best R/C pilot you can be, you need to fly many types of model aircraft. Take advantage of the years of experience distilled in these chapters, and happy landings at the flying field!

CHAPTER 30

Flying R/C Combat

by Greg Rose

It has been around almost as long as R/C modeling itself, and R/C combat is undergoing a fresh surge in popularity. This newfound popularity is due, in part, to one of the hottest new AMA events to come along in years—Event 704, "Scale WW II R/C Combat." Whether they're scale or non-scale, R/C combat events are popular because they offer affordable fun to average modelers.

The competition is fast and exciting and will really get your adrenaline pumping, yet the events focus on affordability and broad appeal to intermediate fliers. Whether you choose scale 704 or a non-scale R/C combat event, both offer a great way to have fun that won't require a second mortgage on your home. As a matter of fact, the cost for an R/C flier to "get into" R/C combat is quite reasonable. You can count on spending just enough to buy a 3-channel sport radio (if you don't already have one), a .15- to .25-size sport engine (again, if you don't already have one) and the typical $30 to $60 price tag for a kit. As you get a little more serious, you can add the cost of a second or third model.

HOW TO WIN

Because sanctioned R/C combat events are relatively new and because new converts are joining all the time, many fliers interested in R/C combat want to know one thing: "How do I win?" Three things determine the outcome of any R/C event, regardless of whether it's pattern, scale, or R/C combat: preparation, flying skill and luck. Let's look at those items one at a time, with some expert advice from full-scale combat pilots.

◆ *"In order to ensure the success of a patrol, it is necessary to do a lot of work on the ground."*
—"Bring Down Your Hun"; British manual published in 1918.

Preparation for winning always starts long before the event. Even before your knife touches balsa, you may have already limited your chances for success. The very first step you must take if you are interested in R/C combat is to spend the time

needed to carefully read the rules of the event in which you plan to participate. Skipping this important step will lead to nothing but frustration. If scale combat is what interests you, read the current AMA rule book for Event 704 rules (see "AMA Event 704 Rules"), paying particular attention to the size, weight and engine restrictions that apply to your model. You can't win if the contest director (CD) won't let you fly your model because its features don't follow the rules. In non-scale events (not an AMA event at the time this was written), ask the CD for a copy of the rules that will be used, so you don't end up building a design the local club won't allow.

◆ *"The smallest amount of vanity is fatal in aeroplane fighting."*
—Captain "Eddie" Rickenbacker; U.S. Air Service; 26 victories in WW I.

Next, come up with a realistic plan for flying and competing in the event. Just like R/C pilots who are new to many other events, first-time combat pilots sometimes come up with unrealistic plans that are often based on an overestimation of their flying skills. You won't win any R/C combat event with a plane you can't

Pilot and pit crew work as a team in R/C combat.

fly. Match your *current* level of flying skill with the model and the event to which you are best suited. If your flying skills aren't quite as good as you would like, choose a model that's easier to fly and has a lower wing loading (see

Even 704 models are occasionally confused with posthole diggers!

"Typical 704 Model Wing Loading and Thrust/Weight Ratios" and "Non-Scale R/C Combat Kit Statistics").

Don't be concerned that you may not be competitive with a lower-powered or lighter wing-loaded model; history offers a long list of superb fighters who had lower wing loadings than their less successful opponents. Simply having a model that you can launch and fly reliably will automatically keep you ahead of a portion of the pack. If your wing area is fixed, as it is in non-scale "one-design" events, make every effort to keep your model's weight down to decrease its wing loading. The most important thing to remember about model selection for either a scale or a non-scale event is to build models that you can fly without slamming them into the ground.

◆ *"Too many men with little time behind the controls of fighter planes never lived to fly into combat. Their familiarization flights killed them."*
—Ensign Saburo Sakai; Imperial Japanese Navy; 64 victories in WW II.

Because most combat events are multi-round affairs, any serious pilot should have a backup model, or even better, two backups. Unlike our control-line combat comrades, you won't need half a dozen models for these events because midairs just aren't that common. The temptation here is to have several types of plane; but if you want to improve your chances of taking home that prize, you'll want to campaign a single design, with several planes set up identically with interchangeable equipment.

◆ *"I regret that I only have one life to give for my country. I'd feel safer if I had two or three."*
—Anonymous USN pilot; WW II.

Now, before you go racking your brain for the best possible R/C combat design, let me give you a hint: such a design just doesn't exist. Just like designs of full-size fighters, every R/C design is a compromise; you pay for every advantage with a disadvantage somewhere else. The best you can hope for is a model in which the design's advantages match your flying style. To do this, you must determine which type of combat flier you are or want to be.

From WW I to the present, two divergent theories of what makes a good fighter have existed: some argue that fast monoplanes are better, while others believe that maneuverable biplanes are. In a nutshell, with both full-scale and model aircraft, the planes that fly the fastest do not turn well, and those that turn well do not fly as fast. Decide which of these two schools of thought (or at what point of compromise between them) you believe in (at least for now), and you'll at last be able to start building your fighters.

◆ *"In aerial warfare, the factor of quality is relatively more decisive than the factor of quantity."*
—Major Alexander de Seversky; USAAF; 13 victories (with Imperial Russian Naval Air Service) in WW I.

When building any model, the key to success is keeping it as light as possible. The strategies for producing such a model are as varied as the building skills of individual modelers, so I won't discuss how to build them light. I will provide, however, a few simple building pointers that are sometimes overlooked, yet offer some of the most effective weight savings.

First, smaller models weigh less than larger models. If you use the same construction techniques to build two $\frac{1}{12}$-scale models, you can build the smaller Me-109 lighter than you could build the larger P-47. Second, never carry extra non-structural weight. In other words, don't use a full-size servo where a smaller one will do, and don't carry one large battery for a full day of flying when you can put in a fresh, smaller pack before each round and avoid that useless weight.

FLIGHT-BOX FUNDAMENTALS

◆ *"Months of preparation, one of those few opportunities and the judgment of a split second are what make some pilots aces...."*
—Colonel Gregory Boyington; USMC; 28 victories in WW II.

The next step may be surprising to some, but it is possibly the single most effective thing you can do to improve your chances of winning in R/C combat. Overlooked

The flight line at a combat meet.

because it never leaves the ground and is rarely a pretty sight, a properly prepared flight box can make the difference between winning and losing.

Many factors can make R/C combat rough on models: relatively high wing loadings (and their corresponding fast glide speeds); hand and catapult launches; bellying-in dead-stick after each round; and the ever-present possibility of a midair. Your flight box must be equipped well enough to keep your model in the air. Piece by piece, check over every model you'll fly to make sure you have all the replacements you need. Don't just carry a couple of extra props; make sure you have a pre-drilled replacement motor mount, a couple of spare needle valves, a spare carburetor and an extra fuel tank. Many fliers carry a complete spare engine that's ready to be popped into place between rounds, if necessary.

Check your radio supplies next. Have a spare of each servo in the sizes used in your model, in addition to spare servo arms and screws. Have at least one extra fully charged battery pack of the same weight. Airframe repairs are common in combat, so a repair box filled with adhesives and reinforced tape is essential. Be sure to carry the right adhesive to repair any part of your model; a fast CA and kicker are useless if your foam wing needs to be repaired. Most R/C combat rules have the option of inter-round safety inspections, so don't just fix it well enough to "get by"; repair it correctly, or hold off flying until you can fly it safely.

◆ *"He must be able to loop, turn his machine over on its back and do various other flying stunts; not that these are necessary during combat, but from the fact that he has done these things several times, he gets absolute confidence, and when the fight comes along, he is not worrying about how the machine will act. He can devote all his time to fighting the other fellow, the flying part of it coming instinctively."*
—Lieutenant Colonel William Bishop; RAF; 72 victories in WW I.

There is one final thing to prepare before you fly combat. Many R/C pilots, even those with years of experience, are not used to flying small, high-powered models that are hand-launched. Because, with new pilots, most combat models are lost during the launch and not in combat, it is important that you practice and perfect your takeoff procedure (see "Hand-Launching Combat Models"). Too many

Hand-Launching Combat Models

Because they're relatively small (compared with many other R/C models), most R/C combat models must be hand-launched. Most scale combat models are of a low-wing configuration, which is difficult to hold because it doesn't allow you to grasp the fuselage at the center of balance. To avoid this problem, try these suggestions:

◆ To get a grip at the center of gravity (CG), indent a handhold into the bottom of the wing. This technique requires some

Fly them in any weather! Merlin Gorowsky tosses a Corsair at 20 degrees—Fahrenheit!

Lee Tait demonstrates a perfect underhand launch.

forethought during building, but it can reward you with a handhold that is practically invisible from the ground when the plane is airborne.

◆ At the CG, make a "drop tank" or "bomb" that serves as a handhold for launching and hides a single wheel for landing. The drop tank and bomb look very scale-like because in full-scale they

would be placed on the CG to avoid having to make trim changes after the bombs have been released.

◆ Learn how to launch a 704 model with an underhand toss, which allows you to hold the fuselage at a point that's directly over the CG for better balance. A few words of caution though: larger fuselages, such as those found on a Zero, can be difficult to grip securely.

In non-scale events, models such as the Wild Thing and the Combat 20 are easy to launch. Often, near "flying wing" designs, such as the Sport Bat II and the TailGator, are best launched by gripping the trailing edge and allowing the model to fly out of your hand.

In any case, a patch of coarse sandpaper glued to the model wherever you hold it can help you to maintain control of it. Avoid throwing the model like a javelin (a common launching mistake), because that often causes the engine to

Bruce Tharpe shows how the high-wing Wonder can easily be launched overhand.

sag at the worst possible time. Launch in a smooth, but firm, motion, and let the model fly out of your grip.

R/C pilots ruin their chances of success by not practicing enough with their combat models. Fly your model regularly, not just during meets, and practice in all sorts of weather, not just on those perfect, sunny days. Combat models are small, so there is no excuse not to toss yours into the trunk and get some stick time with it.

◆ *"A good fighter pilot, like a good boxer, should have a knockout punch. You will find one attack you prefer to all others. Work on it until you can do it to perfection...then use it whenever possible."*
—Captain Reade Tilley; USAAF; seven victories in WW II.

◆ *"You fight like you train."*
—U.S. Navy Fighter Weapons School (Top Gun) motto.

Your model is ready, your flight box has been prepared, your launching technique and flying have been practiced; you are finally ready to fly R/C combat. But which types of flying skills—beyond the basic level of skill almost all R/C pilots have—do you need to be successful in combat? Combat pilots from WW I to the present have found that a list of tips (some basic do's and don'ts of combat flying) is often the best way to get this information out to the newcomer. I've made a list of 10 "commandments" for R/C combat fliers. The first few may be the most important, but ignoring any of them could cost you the prize.

1. Be aggressive; seize every opportunity to take the offensive.
The very first thing is to show aggression. All the preparation in the world won't do you any good unless you are willing to pursue an aggressive flight pattern. Aggressive does not mean reckless; aggressive means always looking for the kill and taking every opportunity to go for the opponent's streamer. The willingness to always seek the offensive will form the cornerstone of your R/C combat ability.

◆ *"The aggressive spirit, the offensive, is the chief thing everywhere in war, and the air is no exception"*
—Baron Manfred von Richthofen; 80 victories in WW I.

◆ *"No guts, no glory. If you are going to shoot him down, you have to get in there and mix it up with him."*
—Major Frederick Blesse; USAF; 10 victories in Korea.

2. Make quick decisions.
The time for dreaming up a clever flight plan is back in your workshop, not when your thumbs are on the radio. Fliers tend to over-complicate the situation by reading something into the actions of the other

Flying and Winning

"Lag pursuit" describes a form of combat in which the attacking aircraft lags behind the target to stay on its tail and be in a good position to make a kill. With full-scale aircraft, lag pursuit is commonly used in heat-seeking-missile combat where the missile's guidance system must lock onto the hot tailpipe of the target before the missile can be fired. For lag pursuit in R/C combat, your propeller must be where the target's streamer is, and that's how cuts are made!

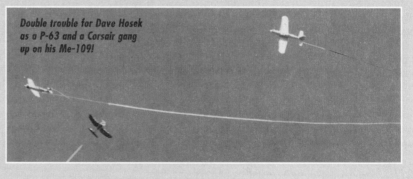

Double trouble for Dave Hosek as a P-63 and a Corsair gang up on his Me-109!

The problem is, if you're fast enough to catch your target, how will you slow down enough to stay on its tail? In addition to properly using the throttle, there are a number of delaying maneuvers you can use to remain on the target's tail.

An Me-109 tries for another piece of a Kingcobra's shortened streamer!

◆ **Snap roll.** The first maneuver, which can be used either to retain a tailing position or to reverse positions with an opponent who's tailing you, is the snap roll. It's now a common airshow maneuver, but it was born in combat—developed by the Soviet ace, Aleksandr Pokryshkin. As an offensive lag maneuver, the snap roll slows the attacking plane's total forward movement, and that forces the target to remain in front of the pursuer. As a defensive maneuver, it's a startling apparent change in direction that can easily catch your pursuer off guard.

◆ **Lag-pursuit roll.** The second maneuver is the "lag-pursuit roll," or "barrel-roll attack." During a turn, this maneuver allows you to remain behind a slower target that turns more tightly; you do this by performing a barrel roll in the opposite direction of your target's turn. Although you'll momentarily lose your tailing position, when the turns have been completed, you'll still be behind your target. True to the idea behind lag pursuit, your faster model goes the long way around to complete its turn.

◆ **High yo-yo.** In a turn, this is also used to out-maneuver a slower, more tightly turning opponent. You respond to your target's turn by going vertical through your turn to increase its radius. Because you're no longer on the same "plane" as your target, your longer turn will put you behind it when you return to the same plane.

fliers. They are just as confused as you are; just find a streamer and go for it!

◆ *"See, decide, attack, reverse."*
—Major Erich Hartmann; Luftwaffe; 352 victories in WW II.

◆ *"Make your decisions promptly. It is better to act quickly, even if your tactics may not be the best."*
—Wing Commander A.G. Malan; RAF; 32 victories in WW II.

3. Always keep your nose toward your opponent.
I have yet to see anyone's tail cut a ribbon. The only "weapon" an R/C model has in combat is its propeller. Always turn into the attack; always keep your propeller pointed at your opponent. This also keeps your prop between the opponent's propeller and your streamer.

◆ *"Always turn and face the attack."*
—Wing Commander A.G. Malan; RAF; 32 victories in WW II.

◆ *"The only proper defense is offense."*
—Air Vice-Marshal J.E. Johnson; RAF; 38 victories in WW II.

4. Always keep one eye on your plane.
Ignore this rule, and you're in for a nasty surprise. It starts out simple enough: you control your plane in a series of maneuvers until, suddenly, you give a command that your plane ignores. At first, you think your radio has been hit, but then you notice that the Mustang you've been watching has a red tail; but you never put a red tail on your Mustang so how could that be…your…? Usually, there's a delay of a few seconds (the "disbelief delay") before panic hits you, and you finally admit to yourself that you've been watching someone else's model and have no idea which one up there is yours.

Here are some tips that may help you to avoid this problem. In scale combat, if you fly a popular plane (P-51, Me-109, FW-190, etc.), find a unique scale paint scheme that no one else will have (bare metal Mustangs are tough to tell apart). In non-scale, one-design events, show up with a unique covering job and, just to be sure, carry a few rolls of wide, brightly covered tape for last-minute changes. In either event, If you do become confused, fly out of the melee (even if it means you'll lose points) to reorient yourself before you re-enter the combat box. If you realize that you have lost your plane, *cut the throttle immediately.* If you're lucky and your plane is still in the air,

AMA Event 704 Rules

The 704 event was designed to recreate the "excitement of World War II fighter combat in a fun, safe, scale competition." The event uses $^1/_{12}$-sport-scale replicas of combat aircraft that were produced or were in service between 1935 and 1955. An important part of the 704 rules requires that, for safety reasons, a maximum weight of 2.2 pounds is allowed for a single-engine model. A provision allows twin-engine-powered models to have a maximum weigh of 2.5 pounds.

Models of full-size planes powered by water-cooled engines (P-51, P-40, etc.) are allowed a .15-size engine. To counter the effects of the drag from larger radial cowls, models of full-size planes powered by air-cooled engines (P-47, FW-190A, etc.) are allowed .21-size engines. Twin-engine models, regardless of the original aircraft powerplant type, are allowed a combined displacement

with three channels that control elevator, aileron and throttle.

The event is flown within a 420-foot-wide, open-ended "combat box," and there's a safety zone that keeps the spectators well behind the flight line. Every pilot is allowed to fly only one model in each round, but inter-round changes are allowed. There is no builder-of-the-model rule for this event.

The contest pits up to six modelers against one another in three non-elimination rounds that last 7 minutes each. This is followed by a final 7-minute round that's flown by the six contestants who have the highest scores and are still capable of competing.

For scoring, actions that involve remaining airborne within the combat box and cutting opponents' streamers earn positive points, while those that involve avoiding combat and having your steamer cut earn negative points.

Safety first! The flight director at a 704 meet clears pilots for launch, one at a time.

of .21ci. Any type of engine is allowed, but tuned pipes are forbidden. During combat, every model pulls a 30-foot streamer that's attached by 5 feet of string. The typical 704 model is set up

Safety violations are penalized by large point deductions or disqualification from a round. Consult the most current edition of the "AMA Competition Rules Guide" for full details of the 704 rules.

odds are that the rapidly decelerating model is yours.

◆ *"One of our prime weapons in all-out war is recognition; it is a weapon we cannot afford to misuse."*
—"U.S. Army-Navy Journal of Recognition," January 1944.

◆ *"Not until the white stars against the blue wings became clear did I realize my error."*
—Ensign Saburo Sakai; Imperial Japanese Navy; 64 victories in WW II (describing

his joining a formation of 15 Hellcats, which he mistook for friendly Zeros).

5a. Keep your speed up, but…

We've all learned maneuvers such as stall turns and spins that really look great in the air. As neat as these maneuvers look, you should save the hot-dogging for before or after the meet and rarely use it in R/C combat. This is because the control of any fixed-wing model depends on maintaining forward speed and, without control, gravity takes over. You know exactly where gravity will take your plane a few seconds after you have begun a stall/spin maneuver (and so does everyone else) because you lack the control to make it do anything but fall. Avoid maneuvers that kill so much speed that your next move is predictable. This rule comes with a built-in proviso (see 5b).

◆ *"Speed is life."*
—Israeli combat tactics manual.

◆ *"Don't let the enemy trick you into pulling up or turning until you lose your speed."*
—Major "Tommy" McGuire; USAAF; 38 victories in WW II.

5b. Keep your speed up, but…*use your throttle!*

Most newcomers to R/C combat are not familiar with using their throttle as a weapon. New fliers tend to launch at full throttle and stay there. Because it lacks the guns and missiles of the full-size counterpart, R/C combat is based on "lag pursuit." Lag pursuit requires that the pursuing craft

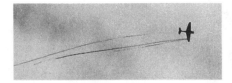

A victory trophy! A fighter flies off with an opponent's streamer caught on its wing.

ply throttling back suddenly, causing the pursuer to become the pursued. Flaps linked with your throttle at low settings will slow you down even more quickly. If you try to stay behind a slower model or one that turns more tightly, use delaying maneuvers to hold on to your position of advantage (see "Flying and Winning").

◆ *"Speed is the cushion of sloppiness."*
—Commander William Driscoll; USNR; five victories (as intercept officer) in Vietnam.

◆ *"Acceleration is of key importance and often overlooked."*
—Lieutenant General Adolph Galland; Luftwaffe; 104 victories in WW II.

6. Gain altitude whenever the opportunity presents itself.

Don't go crazy on this one and climb out of sight. You have to stay within striking distance to be effective; but anytime you can gain an altitude advantage over your opponent, do it. You can always trade off altitude for speed later. When appropriate, use altitude-gaining maneuvers such as the Immelmann turn. Avoid the use of stalls or spins, because they both lose altitude and speed. Use the split-S infrequently, because it eats altitude quickly and it demands a precise determination of whether you have enough altitude to begin with.

◆ *"Altitude confers tactical advantage."*
—"Bring Down Your Hun"; British manual published in 1918.

◆ *"The advantage of height is half the battle."*
—"Forget-Me-Nots for Fighters"; RAF manual published in 1940.

7. Know what your plane (and your opposition) does well.

Typical 704 Model Wing Loadings and Thrust/Weight Ratios

Here's a quick look at some 704 designs rated for their wing loadings and thrust-to-weight (TW) ratios. Designs with low wing loadings tend to be easier to fly and are typically considered to be more maneuverable fighters. Models with high TW ratios are considered fast fighters. Weights and wing areas given in the table are typical of these designs. The engine brake horsepower (b.hp) figures given here are for the O.S. Max FP series—the most popular engine used in 704 combat.

Design	Typical weight (ounces)	Wing loading (oz./sq. ft.)
Corsair	35	17.02
P-63	35	20.32
P-51	33	20.39
A6M Zero	35	20.91
LA-5	29	22.21
FW-190A	32	23.51
MC-202	31	24.80
Me-109	30	24.82
He-100D	28	25.84

Design	Engine size (b.hp/pound)	T/W ratio
LA-5	20ci (.5)	0.2581/lb.
FW-190A	20ci (.5)	0.2500/lb.
He-100D	15ci (.41)	0.2342/lb.
Corsair	20ci (.5)	0.2285/lb.
A6M Zero	20ci (.5)	0.2285/lb.
Me-109	15ci (.41)	0.2186/lb.
MC-202	15ci (.41)	0.2116/lb.
P-51	15ci (.41)	0.1987/lb.
P-63	15ci (.41)	0.1874/lb.

The Prop Busters sure are sold on R/C combat!

stay behind the intended target—in its "kill zone." From the kill zone, a full-size fighter is ideally positioned to fire its missiles or guns, and the R/C fighter is ideally positioned to cut the target's streamer. When your model is being tailed, it is sometimes easiest to get someone off your tail by sim-

If your plane rolls like a log but climbs like a cast-iron stove, don't plan to climb out of trouble. Know what your plane does well and use that to your advantage. Also, keep an eye on what the planes you are fighting do well. Force them into a fight that doesn't let them capitalize on their best features.

◆ *"Know and use all the capabilities in your airplane. If you don't, sooner or later, some guy who does use them all will kick your ass."*
—Lieutenant Dave Pace; USN; Top Gun Instructor.

◆ *"Don't fight the way your opponent fights best."*
—Major Robert Johnson; USAAF; 27 victories in WW II.

8. Think in three dimensions.
Sometimes, turning left or right isn't the best way to turn around. Banking and turning are easily anticipated because the whole plane banks and signals your intentions. Maneuvers based on elevator movements are much harder to anticipate. Use

Launch! The catapult's dolly falls behind as the fighter climbs away.

vertical moves—up or down. Remember that, although full-scale pilots avoid outside maneuvers, R/C pilots don't have to.

◆ *"I decided the thing was to fight more boldly in the vertical plane."*
—Lieutenant Aleksandr Pokryshkin; Soviet Air Force; 59 victories in WW II.

◆ *"He's intelligent but not experienced; his pattern indicates two-dimensional thinking"*
—Spock to Captain Kirk during battle with Kahn.

9. Always keep your (other) eye on your target.
Carefully watch and listen to your opponent. If you're allowed a pit crew/safety helper (as you are in 704), have that per-

son watch your opponent, too. Keep an eye out for signs of intent, such as the beginnings of a bank or the sudden loss of the smoke from a muffler when the

throttle is pulled back. Also, keep your eyes peeled for the stopped prop of a dead engine, because they won't yell "Dead stick" for you (OK, maybe some rookies will!).

◆ *"Always keep your eye on your opponent, and never let yourself be deceived by ruses."*
—Captain Oswald Boelcke; German Air Service; 40 victories in WW I.

◆ *"Never stop looking around."*
—"Forget-Me-Nots for Fighters"; RAF manual published in 1940.

10. Be adaptable.
Ah, finally we get to the only *true* rule out of the bunch: stay flexible. Flexibility is the key to remaining successful.

Non-scale R/C Combat Kit Statistics

MANUFACTURER	DESIGN	ENGINE	WEIGHT (oz.)	WING LOADING (oz./sq. ft.)
J.C.	Sport Bat	.10 - .15	20	7.78
Capstone	Pattern Bat	.10 - .12	26	9.98
Generix	TailGator	.15 - .25	32	12.12
1st Step	FS .20	.19 - .25	40	12.30
Quality	Wild Thing	.10 - .15	32	12.72
Sig	Wonder	.09 - .19	32	13.63
Lynch's	Combat 20	.15 - .25	36	14.40
RA Cores	Gremlin	.25 - .40	56	14.66

Remember that each time you cut a streamer with your favorite move, you've also taught your opponent how to be a little better next time. If you stay with the same moves, those who fell for them earlier may teach you a new lesson at your expense. Change things, keep it fresh, and try to develop new tactics. Watch and learn from others. You'll need new ideas to remain competitive.

◆ *"Nothing is true in tactics."*
—Commander Randy Cunningham; USN; five victories in Vietnam.

◆ *"In this game, there is a great demand for the individual who can 'play by ear'."*
—Major Frederick "Boots" Blesse; USAF; 10 victories in Korea.

Now, the final factor—luck. Even if you explicitly follow every hint in this chapter, and even if you're the best flier around, nothing can stop your winning ways as

A 704 fighter is set up for a catapult launch.

Enough Wild Things for a wild time!

even if you're not having your best day.

◆ *"A MiG at your six is better than no MiG at all."*
—Anonymous USAF fighter pilot. Every day, more and more R/C fliers decide to try the excitement and fun of R/C combat. The events are affordable, fair and fun to fly; and nothing I know compares with the adrenaline rush that a combat round gives. The sight and sound of half a dozen R/C fighters jockeying for position is fun to watch, but is even more fun when you join in. So get started today, and give R/C combat a try. ◆

ABOUT THE AUTHOR

Greg Rose

Greg started his R/C modeling career at the age of three with a milk carton glider. Since then, he has become an avid aero-modeler and enjoys R/C, control-line and free flight, especially in scale events. In 1990, he combined his war-gaming and R/C interests to develop a set of scale R/C combat rules that was later accepted by the AMA to govern event 704. He currently writes an R/C combat column for Model Aviation, and a newsletter for the 704 event, and he's working on a set of R/C combat rules for non-scale models. Greg also flies an R/C blimp at a sports stadium in the Detroit area. He considers his best modeling hours those spent flying with his children.

quickly and as completely as a good dose of bad luck.

◆ *"Any soldier knows that during a war it is not always the ponderables that count, but that a great deal depends on luck."*
—Lieutenant General Adolph Galland; Luftwaffe; 104 victories in WW II.

◆ *"I'd rather be lucky than good any day."*
—Anonymous USAAF fighter pilot.

Many people confuse bad luck with bad planning; so, every time you feel you were dealt a bad hand, stop and ask your-self this question: "Could I have done anything that would have made things come out differently?" If the answer is "No," you had bad luck; if it's "Yes," you could have planned better. Learn from your mistakes, and you will be better pre-pared next time. But nothing can de done about plain old bad luck (except, perhaps, to remember that even a bad day of R/C combat can still be a lot of fun).

The issue of luck should also serve to remind us that, as competitive as R/C com-bat gets, you shouldn't forget to have fun. Although it's not a commandment, it's still good advice. Enjoy what you're doing,

CHAPTER 31

Tips from an F5B World Champ!

by Jerry Bridgeman

On the second day of the World Championships in Wangaratta, Australia, we're called to the flight line at 2:30 p.m. The conditions are ideal—light wind and good thermal lift. My callers, Steve Neu (timer and flight coordinator) and Bob Sliff (course caller) help carry out my two airplanes. As the pilot in front of me finishes the course, I

1994 USA F5B Team. Left to right: Bob Sliff, Jerry Bridgeman, Keith Finkenbiner and Steve Neu.

make sure that my number-one airplane is ready. As the pilot completes the limbo, the officials announce I have 2 minutes to launch. Now, the adrenaline is really pumping. Bob asks if everyone is ready, then he takes five quick steps and yells "On" as he launches the airplane! The motor ramps up to 14,000rpm, and the plane yanks itself out of his hand. I immediately pull up to climb steeply away from the course.

My airplane accelerates and really starts to climb. At 4 seconds, my plane has climbed past 450 feet. I pull up the elevator and aim toward the course. My plane is on its back accelerating. I roll it upright and turn off the motor when Bob yells "Off!" The plane enters the course at 120mph, heading for the far turn.

In 3 seconds, I roll and start to pull the turn. When I hear the signal (beep) that I have finished the lap, I complete my turn and fly back to the near gate. Approaching the near gate, I roll and get ready to turn. At the beep, I'm heading toward the far gate again. I turn on the signal at the far turn and fly back to the near gate, crossing 5 feet off the ground. I hear the beep, turn on my motor and climb for more laps. At that instant, Steve calls out the crossing time.

After climbing five more times, I have

completed 24 laps, and there are 32 seconds to go. I now need to climb higher than before, because I have just enough time to complete five laps. I climb for 6 seconds and enter the course. I have only 32 seconds, so I decide to fly a shorter course in hopes of getting five laps. It works! I get five more! With no seconds to spare, I have 29 big laps—my best round at the World Champs.

Now I have just a minute to do an exciting maneuver called the limbo, during which bad things can happen. The airplane could disintegrate because of the high "G" forces, or loss of control can cause it to slam into the ground. Trying not to think about these things, I climb straight up 400 feet, do a split-S and dive toward the limbo gate. Going in excess of 140mph, I scream past the limbo at 5 feet off the ground. Using the momentum from my dive, I climb to 300 feet with the motor off.

At base A, Jerry Bridgeman flies while Bob Sliff looks through the sighting device, calling for climb to, motor off and turns. Larry Tuohin runs the 3-minute countdown watch.

Now that I have passed the limbo gate, my 5-minute flight duration has started. My team manager/helper, Keith, motions where the pilot before found lift. I head in that direction and the plane lifts. I turn left

What is F5B?

by Keith Finkenbiner

Formerly called "F3E," F5B is an electric sailplane aircraft classification of the Federation Aeronautique Internationale (FAI). It's a specialized event in which pilots seek optimal performance from the airplanes, power sources and motor/prop combinations. The event consists of two tasks—distance flying and thermal duration—followed by a spot landing.

◆ **Distance flying.** The event starts with this task, which is flown between two parallel planes, or stations, that are 150 meters apart (see diagram). The stations' respective bases are referred to as base A and base B.

While the pilot stands at base A, the plane climbs under power behind base A and then enters the course, motor off. Within a 3-minute window, the pilot must try to fly as many laps between the two bases as possible. A pilot earns 10 points for every lap completed—typically, 26 to 28 laps. The motor can't be run while the plane is flying on the course.

As the pilot flies, sighting and signal devices are used to determine the completion of every lap. In most cases, the pilot would run the motor and climb out three or four times during the 3 minutes to maximize the number of laps.

◆ **Thermal duration.** This must be completed immediately after the distance event. The pilot climbs out, turns off the motor and then dives down and zooms under a 20-meter-wide, 3-meter-high "limbo" gate. The pilot has 1 minute to do this; then he climbs out—with or without power—to start the 5-minute thermalling portion. Each second of flight time counts for 1 point, but for each second of motor time, 1 point is deducted. A typical thermal flight will use 10 seconds of motor run during this segment.

◆ **Spot landing.** This is completed directly after the duration task. Extra points are awarded if the model comes to rest in a 15-meter circle (for an additional 30 points) or a 30-meter circle (15 additional points). Many world-class pilots will dive through the limbo gate and not use any motor time to accomplish the 5-minute thermal task, then they'll land in one of the circles for additional points. Note that completing more laps in the distance portion will outweigh the few seconds of motor run required to complete the duration task.

In world-championship competitions, top pilots sometimes fly 29 laps (for 290 points) and will use only 5 seconds of motor run to finish the 5-minute thermal duration task (for an additional 295 points). They then may land in the 15-meter bonus zone for a total of 290 + 295 + 30 = 615 points. World championships are usually decided by fewer than 15 points after the pilots have flown eight rounds and "thrown out" their lowest score (best of seven).

Which skills make a good F5B pilot? Most—but not all—of the best pilots learned racing skills by flying slope racing. The hand/eye coordination needed to slope race is similar to that needed to fly distance laps on an F5B course. But thermalling skills are also needed for the duration portion.

◆ **10-cell competition.** Bonus points are given when smaller power systems are used: for 8 to 10 cells, 15 additional points per lap in the distance leg; 10 to 14 cells: 1 point is deducted for every 2 seconds of motor run.

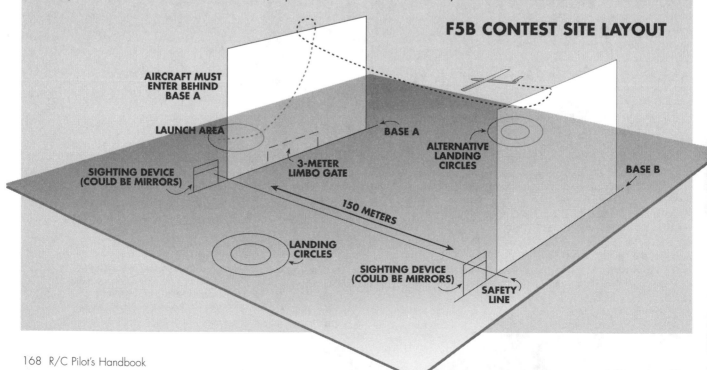

F5B CONTEST SITE LAYOUT

AIRCRAFT MUST ENTER BEHIND BASE A

LAUNCH AREA

BASE A

ALTERNATIVE LANDING CIRCLES

BASE B

SIGHTING DEVICE (COULD BE MIRRORS)

3-METER LIMBO GATE

150 METERS

LANDING CIRCLES

SIGHTING DEVICE (COULD BE MIRRORS)

SAFETY LINE

Constructing a Competitive F5B Model

by Jerry Bridgeman and Bob Sliff

An F5B model must be very light and the wing must be very strong because, in competition, the plane reaches very high speeds. These basic requirements have to be balanced carefully. A lighter model will climb faster, but if the wing is not strong enough, the model will lose speed on turns owing to wing twist. On the other hand, a heavy airplane will not climb as quickly, and in F5B competition, the fastest climb often means a win.

Motor choices (left to right): Astro Flight 60 (light), Plettenberg Evolution and Aveox 1817 with a throttle controller. The Aveox was the choice of the 1995 USA F5B Team.

◆ **Materials.** To produce a light model with the strongest wing, you must use high-quality, high-tech materials. In other words, the model should be made of epoxy/carbon/Kevlar and foam. To do this effectively, you will need some knowledge of epoxy lay-up. We'll assume that you have experience in this or that you know someone with experience who will help you.

◆ **Fuselage.** To produce a fuselage that will be light enough to be competitive, you must use high-quality composite materials and lay it up carefully in a good mold. The halves must be vacuum-bagged to remove excess epoxy. When it's finished, your fuselage (with elevator servo) should weigh less than 110 grams. For the fuselage lay-up, use two layers of 1.8-ounce Kevlar cloth. Place pieces of 1mm-thick Rohacel foam between layers in the tail boom and rudder to ensure that they'll resist bending loads. Use several strands of 12K carbon running full length for extra stiffness and strength. Finally, before joining the fuselage halves, fit the servo inside the rudder. Then glue the servo into place when the halves are joined.

◆ **Stabilizer.** This is next. It is made out of a foam-core with a 2-ounce fiberglass skin. We recommend 1/64-inch-thick plywood shear webs (vertical grain). Use vertical-grain balsa where the stabilizer will be bolted to the rudder. Wet out the fiberglass on 14-mil Mylar, and vacuum-bag it to the foam-cores.

◆ **Wing.** This is the most critical structural part. It must be very strong, very stiff and very light. Our models for the World Championships used hollow wings made in a two-part mold. This is the best way to produce them, because you get a lighter, stronger and more accurate wing, but it's a long and involved process.

Because molded-wing making is complicated and very time-consuming, we recommend that you build wings using foam-cores. It's also a fast and economical way to test various airfoils and wing shapes.

To make a foam wing, start by cutting an accurate foam-core out of 2-pound-density blue foam. Next, make a spar out of carbon and foam to fit into a slot you will cut into the core. Then install the wires for the servos and put in the hard points on which you'll mount the wing on the fuselage. With the spar inserted into the slot, complete the wing by laying up the surfaces. The wing skins are cut out of 2-ounce glass cloth—one for each surface (cloth must be cut on a 45-degree bias; this is very important). Cut 14-mil Mylar to the full size of the wing. Then wet out the cloth on the Mylar surface using good-quality epoxy. Add other reinforcements by placing them on the glass/Mylar surface, and wet them out thoroughly. Next, align the two surface lay-ups on both sides of the core, which is then vacuum-bagged. After this, a conventional clean-up and finishing is required. Next come servo installation, control-surface completion, final assembly and preparation for flying.

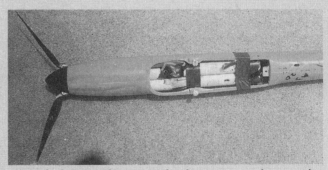

The F5B fuselage: everything goes in; then the wing is mounted on top with aluminum bolts. Notice that the throttle control nestles inside the battery.

◆ **Propellers.** These are the second most important part of performance because, though you can buy hubs and spinners, you must make blades, and it's really very easy. Begin with a prop you like; then make a mold and produce as many as you want. It takes about two nights of work to make a mold and one day to make each blade. After that, you won't have to worry about breaking your favorite prop, because you'll own the mold. The details of making blades go beyond the scope of this chapter, but if you get seriously involved with F5B, you'll soon learn the techniques that other active U.S. competitors use.

History of F5B

by Bob Sliff

F5B (originally F3E) was brought to the United States by Mike Charles in the early 1980s. Soon afterward, Calvin Ettel emerged as a strong supporter of the event, and he tendered the first offer for the USA to host the F5B World Championships. It was eventually held in Lommel, Belgium, in 1986, but the second was held in Cal's hometown of St. Louis, MO, in 1988.

F5B competitors at Wangaratta, Australia.

From that point on, the prospective USA team members began to prepare for the coming Team Selection, which was to be held in Costa Mesa, CA, in the spring of 1988. At that point, Jerry Bridgeman entered the competitive arena. Held on a weekend with good California thermal activity, Jerry's best lap count during the Finals was 20, though he averaged 18 for the seven rounds.

For those of you who are new here, F5B competition involves performance in distance (called "doing laps"), and the drive for "more laps" has been apparent since the beginning. In fact, this one aspect seems to make the most difference to the results of a competition.

◆ 1988 World Championships—St. Louis, MO.

This was held in very hot and humid Midwest August weather. Furthermore, it was here that an "immediate" change in the rules came about as a result of the actions of some European judges and managers. Up to this point, the "laps" had been flown after a single climb; but with this change, fliers were required to climb more than once to altitude; this emphasized motor-power management more than model glide and good eyesight.

In the end, Rudolph Freudenthaller again became world champion doing an average of 21 laps (best was 23). Our USA team placed 11th (Jerry), 13th (Steve) and 20th (Felix). At Jerry's first World Championships, he averaged 19 laps with his best being 21.

Having learned much by observing the European fliers, Jerry and Steve immediately began to generate ideas that could improve their performance the next time. On returning home,

they began by designing new models that were smaller, lighter and faster. They experimented with new propellers, and they sought improvements to their Astro motors. Their flying was analyzed to find ways to improve their skills and techniques.

In preparation for the next World Championships in August, 1990, the USA Team Selection Finals were held on June 1 and 2 of that year in Costa Mesa, CA. After eight rounds, it was Jerry Bridgeman and Steve Neu from the previous team and newcomer Jason Perrin. Bob Sliff was elected the team manager. (Jerry averaged 24 laps—a significant step up from St. Louis.)

◆ 1990 World Championships— Freistadt, Austria.

(Rudolph Freudenthaller's hometown), second week of August. The flying conditions were excellent—warm and dry. Rudolph Freudenthaller was again the champion, but to the surprise of all the fliers and the European press, Jason finished a strong second. Jerry and Steve placed eighth and ninth, respectively, which was enough to give the USA team a strong second in the team competition, behind only the Austrian home team. Regarding the lap counts, the best was 26, which both Rudi and Jason did once. Though the knowledge and experience gained was less this time, our team immediately began to prepare for the 1992 Championships, which were to be held in the Netherlands. By the time of the next Team Selection Finals, new planes had been built, and Jerry, Jason and Steve had practiced and were ready.

Held again in Costa Mesa, the 1991 Finals had low, overcast conditions that made it impossible to climb very high when doing laps. In fact, it was possible to do only four lap sets instead of our usual six. At any rate, after seven rounds, the selected team again comprised Jerry Bridgeman, Steve Neu and Jason Perrin with Bob Sliff as team manager. This time, the lap scores were similar to those in Austria; Jerry averaged 25 laps (with a best of 26).

The team now had a full year to prepare, and activity began immediately with new wings to test airfoils. Several foam wings later, and after consultation with Joe Wurts, it was decided to go with Dr. Michael Selig's SD 7003 airfoil. In addition, planning was begun to make fully molded models. With this decided, Jerry started on the wing plug while Steve began the fuselage plug. Shortly afterward, the first airplane came out of the molds.

As had been the case from the beginning, the radio of choice was the Airtronics Vision because it gave all the mixes we needed. The motor of choice was the locally made Astro 60L ("L" for lightened). Battery cells, as always, were Sanyo 900 SCRs (later called 1000 SCRs). Propellers were homebuilt.

◆ 1992 World Championships—Arnhem, Netherlands.
(The movie "A Bridge Too Far" was about the battle that took place there in WW II.) Weather was variable—from rain and fog to sunny. Rudolph Freudenthaller was again world champion, but this time, he was followed very closely by Jerry, only 4 points behind. Jason and Steve were third and seventh, respectively. This gave Team USA the team championships by a 200-point margin. So, even more than in Austria, the USA served notice that it had really arrived. During the competition, primarily because of medium to poor weather, the best lap count for both Rudy and Jerry was 27.

Back home in Southern California, the team's preparation for the next Team Selection again got under way. For the next 12 months, many ideas were exchanged, but little design and testing activity took place. The only significant actions were that Bob Sliff built a couple of models in the mold to use at the next Team Selection, and Jason Perrin decided to retire. A few advances came during that year: Steve Neu developed a motor dyno that interfaced with his personal computer. From this came some better comparisons among motors. After testing all our motors, both Steve and Jerry switched to Plettenberg motors for the next Team Selection.

The Team Selection Finals for the 1994 Championships took place in Poway, CA, in August 1993. This time, Jerry, Steve and Bob Sliff were selected to go to Wangaratta, Australia. Keith Finkenbiner, who directed the team selection, became team manager.

Poway had excellent thermal conditions, and Jerry and Steve's lap average was up to 27. The following 12 months involved some of the usual experimentation with wing airfoils. When Steve returned after meeting Dr. Michael Selig at the Western Soaring Championships in Washington state, we tried

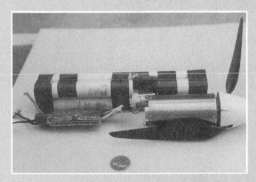

Team USA's power system: 27-cell Sanyo 1000 SCR pack; a new Aveox motor controller; Aveox 1817 motor.

the new S7012 airfoil and decided to go with it. We kept the fuselage we had used before and adapted the wing to it.

Beyond this, the real push was for better motor performance. In the end, after much dyno-testing by Steve, we started to work with David Palombo of Aveox on a new brushless motor.

The existing Aveox motors had shown superior performance, especially with regard to efficiency. But they weren't made in the size we needed for F5B; we needed one to be made specially for the power requirements we were seeking. After much design work by David and testing by Steve (and a motor con-

Austrian team member H. Aigelsreiter made this beautiful Trio F5B model.

troller redesign by Steve), the motor was significantly better than any currently used in F5B. The very best Plettenberg motor tested out at about 84 percent efficient at 60 amps, but the final Aveox tested out at more than 90 percent efficient at nearly 70 amps. Not only that, but the motor turned another 1,000rpm, and it did not heat up and lose speed (sag) during critical phases of the flight.

◆ 1994 World Championships—Wangaratta, Australia.
With Aveox motors in our hands just weeks before our departure for Wangaretta, we began to practice with them. Practice was needed! With the greater power, climbing and course entry were faster, and this necessitated a significant change in our timing and rhythm while we were flying the course. On arrival in Australia some seven days before the Championships, we started to practice full time, and by the start of the competition, we were pretty much accustomed to our models' increased performance.

From the first flights, our power advantage was obvious, even though a new geared system from Robbe of Germany looked very good. Of course, Rudy, with his traditional Plettenberg and his superior flying, was right up at the top.

In the end, it came down to the last flight of the competition for first place. Flying earlier in the day, Jerry did his usual (28 laps); Rudy, on the other hand, having to fly later and in more wind, tried too hard and cut turns a couple of times—25 laps. (He needed 28 to keep up and possibly beat Jerry.)

Jerry became the new F5B world champion—not only the first from the USA, but also the first to beat Rudolph Freudenthaller. Jerry's finish was not only an exciting achievement, but it was also the culmination of a long, challenging and interesting experiment. It was something that Jerry and the rest of us from the good ole USA can be truly proud of.

Results—F5B 1994 World Championships

POS./PILOT	COUNTRY	AVG. LAPS PER ROUND	TOT. LAPS	AVG. SCORE PER ROUND	TOTAL
1. Bridgeman, J.	USA	28.17	169	605.17	3,631
2. Freudenthaller, R.	Austria	27.83	167	603.33	3,620
3. Schaffer, W.	Germany	28	168	602.83	3,617
4. Hainzl, K.	Austria	27.17	163	595.17	3,571
5. Leodalter, U.	Switzerland	27	162	592.83	3,557
6. Neu, S.	USA	27.17	163	592.67	3,556
7. Fraisse, J.	France	26.5	159	585.00	3,510
8. Nizri, T.	France	26.67	160	583.17	3,499
9. Aigelsreiter, H.	Austria	26.17	157	583.00	3,498
10. Wolter, J.	Germany	26.67	160	580.33	3,482
11. Vauth, W.	Germany	26	156	578.67	3,472
12. Schilling, E.	Switzerland	26.17	157	578.00	3,468
13. Strebel, R.	Switzerland	25.5	153	577.67	3,466
14. Sliff, R.	USA	26	156	577.00	3,462
15. Aghem, G.	Italy	25.34	152	575.00	3,450

With seven rounds flown, scores reflect the best six (the lowest score is dropped). The highest number of laps in a round was 29. Bridgeman, Freudenthaller and Schaffer each flew 29 once; no other contestant achieved as many.

and circle in the strongest lift area. As I continue to circle in the thermal, the plane gradually drifts toward the course. I soon find myself flying in the middle of the course while the next flier is running his laps. Realizing that this is a hazardous spot, I know that I must stay with the thermal or lose points because if I have to run my motor, I lose points. Usually, the duration is the most boring part for spectators. Now I have to dodge an airplane going at more than 100mph. Luckily for me, we don't make contact. After several near misses, the thermal drifts clear of the course. It seems like an eternity, but only 4 minutes have passed. Now, with a minute to go, it's time to prepare for landing.

I leave the thermal, fly toward the landing circle and get there with 40 seconds to go. I am going too slowly and losing altitude. I have to blip my motor for a small burst of power to give me just enough lift to ensure a safe landing. During the final 30-second countdown, I set up my approach to the landing circle and make my final turn with 8 seconds to go. I touch down at the far edge of the inner circle and barely slide to a stop inside the 30-point circle.

What was my score for this round? I received 30 points for the landing in the inner circle, 295 points (out of 300) for duration (I was 5 seconds early and I had no points left for motor run) and 290 points for the laps. That gave me a final total of 615 points—the best round flown at the World Championships.

I was very excited and happy with the flight I just described. It was one of the true high points of my life; but I could not have done it alone. My two helpers, Bob Sliff and Steve Neu, and our team manager, Keith Finkenbiner, were absolutely essential. Without their help, I would not now be the world champion of F5B. This competition is a team sport! ◆

ABOUT THE AUTHOR

Jerry Bridgeman
Jerry holds an A.A. in commercial aviation and a B.S. in business administration. He started flying R/C gliders 14 years ago, after he had obtained a private pilot's license. For a while, he flew a Cessna 150, and then he discovered that model airplanes were a lot more fun. Since then, he has flown slope, electric pylon racers and thermal gliders and has attended four electric glider F5B World Championships. He is a self-taught aeronautical engineer who designs and builds his own models. He designed and built all his planes, including his World Championship plane. When he isn't flying his models, he designs and manufactures video poker machines, for which he holds two patents.

He lives in Huntington Beach, CA, close to the flying field, so when the wind comes up....

CHAPTER 32

Sport Fun Fly

by Dan Luchaco

Flying R/C planes presents many challenges. After you have learned to successfully control your plane during takeoffs, basic maneuvers and landings, fun-fly contests provide a way to compare your skills with those of other fliers. Because the first word in the name of this contest is "fun," the pressure on pilots during events is minimal. At a fun fly, you may not be a winner, but there is no reason to feel like a loser. By the end of the contest, you will have learned something that you can apply to your everyday flying. In reverse, you can "practice" for a fun-fly event every time you fly at your local field. The equipment you use, your flying skills, strategy and tips on certain events all influence your performance at fun-fly contests.

EQUIPMENT

To not "beat yourself," you need reliable equipment. Your aircraft should be trimmed for straight and level flight at all engine power ranges. The engine and fuel system should be tuned for steady performance in all attitudes of flight. The radio, servos and batteries should be up to the manufacturer's specs and fully charged.

The first step to improving your score is to get a score; the first step to getting a score is to complete the event. The radio can be set up for maximum performance by using high and low rates (or exponential) and setting the control surfaces for maximum throw. If you do not have a radio with dual rates or expo, set the surface throw for the rate of control with which you feel comfortable. Some events require fast loops or rolls, and other events require smooth flying; set up the radio and plane to cover both. Another option is to change the throw of a control surface at the control horn to maximize your plane's performance for a specific event. Increase or decrease the setting and, after the event, be sure to readjust it for normal flight.

◆ **Engine.** Your engine does not have to be the most powerful, high-rpm unit available. It just has to perform steadily for a complete flight. If, during the flight, you hear it lean out or sag, reduce throttle to keep it running. If you are climbing, reduce the angle of climb and continue the flight.

Before each flight, hold the plane up at a 45-degree angle and check the engine on high speed. Any change in rpm indicates a problem that needs to be solved. Adjust the needle, change the glow plug, or try different fuel. Also, check the fuel tank for a hole in a line or a pick-up clunk at the wrong end of the tank (possibly the result of a hard landing). The tuned-pipe exhaust or pump system (if you use one) must also be working perfectly to maximize your performance. (But these extras mean that more can go wrong, and they're not *necessary*.)

◆ **Aircraft.** Many aircraft have been designed specifically for fun-fly contests. These aircraft usually have a speed envelope of 10 to 100mph and perform well in all attitudes; they glide well, roll and loop quickly and exhibit great ground-handling characteristics.

But guess what? The plane that you have been flying for the past 50 flights is better for you to use at a contest. You are

In the spot-landing contest, this is what you strive for—dead center on the X. Sometimes clubs use flour or powder to make landing circles, and they place a bull's-eye in the center.

familiar with the flight envelope of this aircraft. You can fly it where you want, when you want and how you want. Most fun-fly events are set up for standard aircraft. A 3-channel trainer and a 4-channel sport plane can perform all contest events. If your plane is not competitive in the high-speed roll/loop event, it will probably be great in the climb-and-glide or limbo event.

fly in both windy and calm conditions. At the end of each flight, try to land in the center of the target. If your engine stops during a flight, try to land as near to the target as possible. To practice, climb to altitude, stop the engine, glide for as long as possible, and then land on the target. You can practice this instead of just boring holes in the sky. You will be amazed at how much you can learn about your plane.

plane for maximum performance in each of these maneuvers. Experiment with different controls for spins; try to obtain a flat spin that is easy to enter and exit. Determine how much altitude you need to recover from a spin. As you improve your flying, you will learn the limits of both your plane and your skills.

AT THE CONTEST
So, you're at a fun-fly contest and want to maximize your scores. A few simple rules will help you do well.

◆ **Have a positive attitude about your chances.** If you are not the first flier in the event, observe all those who fly before you to determine the best format to use. The mistakes that other fliers make are what you should avoid during your flight. If you are the first flier in an event, you must do your best to complete the flight and post a score that will be a challenge to the rest of the entrants. If the fun fly is set up with multiple rounds of the same events, you can use the first flight of the day to get rid of the jitters and just post a score that can be improved in later flights. Beware that adverse weather conditions can eliminate later flights, or make events more difficult.

◆ **Complete a flight and obtain a score.** Because not all entrants will score during every flight, you can usually "beat" half the pilots just by getting a score. If you do not complete the flight, you have just defeated yourself. Don't be afraid to ask other entrants for suggestions on an event. (Remember the word "fun" in the contest name.)

Here is a good approach and an off-the-mark approach. To manage your altitude, keep your wings level, and use your throttle. Use the rudder for directional control.

After you have entered or attended a few contests, you may see a design that has more capabilities than your plane. This model can be your next project. Be sure to plan about 50 flights with this new aircraft so you will be comfortable flying it. The best contest aircraft are light, durable, aileron- and flaperon-controlled, semisymmetrical designs. Most have conventional landing gear with a steerable tail wheel or skid. Iron-on covering is easy to patch, an exposed fuel tank allows quick inspection and adjustments, and oversize control surfaces provide tight maneuvers.

When trying to decide which plane to build for a contest, remember the words of Baron Manfred von Richtofen, "The crate? The quality of the crate matters little. Success depends upon the man who sits in it."

FLYING SKILLS
To improve your scores, practice your basic flying skills. Mark a target in the center of the runway, and use it to practice straight ground handling and takeoff control. Also use this target to sharpen your touch-and-go's and landings, and be sure to practice them in both right-to-left and left-to-right directions to imitate different runway layouts.

As your flying improves, challenge yourself to fly a tighter course while you perform the same maneuvers. Be sure to

Experiment with rudder versus aileron control, elevator trim, low and high rates, thermalling for duration, side-slipping in crosswind conditions and any other skills that help you to land on the spot. A longitudinal line in the center of the runway is a good reference point when taking off and landing. Flying the length of the runway with this reference line in view will improve your ability to fly in a straight line, to line up a balloon burst, limbo, bomb drop and execute other precision maneuvers.

Another skill that you should perfect is inverted flying. Be sure to start high and work your way down. If inverted flight doesn't feel comfortable, you are flying too low! Always use the multiple-conditions scenario: left to right, right to left, calm and windy. Fun-fly events usually include these basic maneuvers: takeoff, landing, inside loop, horizontal roll, spin, glide and touch-and-go. Try to perform these maneuvers during your normal flying routine. When possible, do the maneuvers at an altitude "one-mistake high," and try to do sets of three to get used to the required controls. Your goal is to perform the maneuver as quickly as possible, or to do the most loops, rolls, spins and touch-and-go's within a set time (usually 30 seconds).

When you feel comfortable at altitude, go back and combine a routine of takeoff, flying at altitude and landing. Trim the

In every round that you fly, try to maximize your score in at least one event, and then concentrate on the other events. The events at the contest can be "plane" events (loops, rolls, spins) or they can be "pilot" events (spot landings, touch-and-go's, limbo). If you do a "plane" event a couple of times and your score doesn't improve, you have probably reached your max and should put your efforts into the other events. Until you ace the score on a pilot event, your score should improve with each attempt. At fun-flys, the final round is usually when many fliers earn their best score in pilot events.

EVENT HINTS
◆ **Timed events.** There are three types of timed events. The first requires that you perform set maneuvers in the shortest time from takeoff to touchdown. An example of this is "Ten inside loops"—takeoff, 10 inside loops and landing. The time starts as soon as the plane moves,

and it stops when the plane touches down on the runway.

As you perform this flight, distance and altitude are your enemies. Perform the loops immediately after liftoff and close to the ground, and land as soon as you have finished the last loop, and you will have a good time. Such timed events are usually called "Death," "Drill," or "Suicide," because if you make a mistake, you may be in line for the "Crash Award" of the weekend!

Another timed event requires that you perform maneuvers within a prescribed time. An example of this would be "Inside loops for 30 seconds." This flight would be timed from takeoff for 30 seconds. The number of inside loops completed after 30 seconds would be your score. Again, altitude and distance would reduce the number of loops completed in the set time. Your main goal in this type of timed event is to set parameters in your flight "window" and try to stay inside the box during the flight. If you have a helper during the flight, have him coach you for correct placement. A mountain ridge, runway markers and even clouds can be used as "window" markers.

If the event consists of maneuvers followed by touch-and-go's and then more maneuvers followed by a landing on the field, you must try to perform the maneuvers in a pattern that allows you to end the last maneuver over the runway for a touch-and-go. Do not fly all the maneuvers in a straight line away from the runway and then waste a lot of time flying back to the runway for the touch-and-go or landing.

The third type of timed event is usually set up as: climb for altitude for a set time; then perform some maneuver or glide for duration. The altitude climb is maximized by flying into the wind at all times and maintaining the most vertical angle the plane and engine can take that also provides a good speed. Hanging the plane on the prop is no good if the plane is not moving. As you climb for altitude, plan your placement at the end of the climb for optimal visual and wind-velocity conditions. Do not climb into the sun, or the sky (or a cloud) if it matches your plane's color.

If the event is "spins," plan the end of your spins over the lowest part of the flying area. If the event is dead-stick duration, plan the glide to end over the runway or target area (if applicable). Most fun-fly events require that the plane land on the runway in "flyable" condition if the score is to count. Always keep this in mind during a duration or altitude-type event.

To achieve maximum altitude, build up as much speed as possible on the runway before liftoff, because timing doesn't begin until the plane leaves the runway. If the event is spins, a flat spin will usually lose less altitude per spin.

Here's how most planes can be put into a flat spin; try this three mistakes or more high:
- Climb to altitude and cut the engine to about ¼ throttle, hold full up-elevator, full left rudder and full left aileron.
- After the plane has started a nose-down spin, move the elevator stick to full down while still holding full left rudder and aileron. The plane should begin to level out as you move past neutral elevator into the full-down position.
- When you reach full down, slowly change the aileron from full left to full right. The plane is now in a flat spin. If possible, use the throttle to speed up the rotation.
- If the plane reverses direction when you change the elevator or aileron control, stop the input just before its direction reverses. The surest way to exit a flat spin is to move the sticks back the way you came, to the full left rudder, left aileron and full up-elevator position, and then go to neutral and recover. If this does not work, try full down-elevator and high motor.
- A plane without ailerons will also do a type of flat spin; just go to down-elevator after getting into a normal spin. Do not use any flap/elevator mixing in the spin maneuver. Experiment with your plane to see what it takes to enter and exit with enough altitude to complete the flight.

◆ **Target events** include bomb-drop, balloon-bust, carrier, spot-landing and limbo maneuvers. They usually aren't timed, and the goal is precision flying, not speed. Use low rate or exponential controls. Smooth and level approaches to the target at minimum speed are the most accurate.

If the event is bomb drop with a cup or stick holding the bomb, the smooth and

With flaperons, a slow, high-angle-of-attack approach can land the plane right on the spot. With this technique, there is very little forward rollout.

level flight must be from liftoff to drop. To drop the bomb, try to pull vertical just before the target, and push down to fly out from under the bomb. If the vertical or down is not violent enough, the bomb will not come off. Excess speed will cause the bomb to fall forward from the point of drop.

An optional (but more risky) method of dropping the bomb is to roll inverted over the target and push down to climb vertical. *Do not* watch the bomb after the drop; fly the plane, and let the judge score the event. Wind velocity and direction can cause the bomb to drift if it's dropped from a high altitude. For best accuracy, try to drop at the minimum altitude allowed. During the approach to the target, try to line up on something on the runway before the drop area, and try to maintain a steady altitude and heading. Your main concern is to release the bomb at the correct spot near the target.

Balloon bust, carrier and spot landing require the same type of skills. Smooth and straight approaches to the balloon at a steady altitude are important. You can change only two of the variables when you get to the balloon; climb and dive, or steer in and out.

As you control the altitude, have your helper guide you in or out. If the sun is overhead during the flight, use the shadow on the ground to indicate your position. If you have to adjust altitude at the balloon, remember that a little up is usually enough, and any down is always too much! Carrier landing and spot landing require that you fly just above the runway until you reach the target, then land immediately. Slow, controlled flight is an advantage in these events. If allowed, flap or air-brake controls can help with the landing accuracy.

If the plane must stop on the target for the score to count, be ready to use rudder to steer or position the plane as soon as the wheels are on the target. If you wiggle the rudder from side to side, you can slow or stop the rollout after landing.

Limbo is another type of target event, with the ribbon and poles being the target to fly under, or in some cases, between. If the event is to fly under the ribbon, use the straight, slow, low approach. Do not try to fly just under the ribbon; fly just above the ground between the poles. The ground and the poles do not move, the ribbon moves with the wind. If the event has two ribbons and you must fly between them, fly just above the lower ribbon, it

learn your plane's ground-handling limits. When it is too windy to fly, remove the wing and practice your taxiing skills.

LUCK EVENTS

Some fun-fly events are "luck" events that give all contestants a chance to win, regardless of flying skill or equipment. If the

As the announcer would say, "High and away, ball one." The plane has landed to the right of the line and too far past the X to achieve a high score.

usually doesn't move because it is closer to the ground and at the more solid part of the poles. If you are allowed to stand at the inner pole, fly close to yourself to eliminate the risk of hitting the far pole, which is at the limit of your depth perception. If the event is timed for most passes in a set time, or for three passes that are as quick as possible, remember that distance equals time, and speed usually doesn't improve accuracy. The main goal in limbo is to complete the event and get a score. Don't break a plane trying to sacrifice accuracy for speed.

◆ **Ground events.** Taxi or racecourse events on the ground test your ability to control the plane at maximum speed without hitting markers or crossing lines marked on the runway. If the event involves a target, such as a balloon, it is sometimes best to close one eye and aim for the target. If you miss, continue past the target, and then aim for it on the return pass. A long, straight approach is more accurate than a circular or zigzag attempt.

Most two-wheel planes can be made more stable on the ground by adding tail weight. Low rate or exponential control on the rudder channel can provide more precise steering on ground-type events. Spend some time driving around on the ground to

event is "hidden spot landing" or "be in the air when the bell rings," luck is the only way to win. If the event is a two-minute timed flight, you can improve your time counting by tapping your foot while you fly.

If you keep the throttle at a steady speed and fly a simple rectangular pattern, you should be able to count to within 15 seconds and then land on the runway. If the event requires a touch-and-go or another maneuver during the time, concentrate on counting while you fly the maneuver, or estimate the time it will require to perform the maneuver, and count for the balance of the flight.

If you can fly passes up and down the runway, just count for one circuit and then fly as many laps as are required to cover the time, with time allowed for landing. Multiple rounds of flying this event will allow you to adjust the number of laps to improve your score. Watch and time other fliers to see how long it takes for their takeoff, maneuvers and landing, and use this information in your flight.

Another luck event is trying to hit a ribbon that has been dropped at altitude. In this event, try to fly through the ribbon while you fly the plane straight away from yourself, or while you fly straight at yourself. Close one eye to narrow your field of vision while you aim at the ribbon. Do not

waste time trying parallel passes at the ribbon. Other luck events require that you perform some type of non-flying game, such as throw dice until you get doubles, or draw cards until you get a pair, run across the field with a prop, etc., then start your plane and complete some type of flying event.

The flying part of the event usually requires that you start the engine and complete a circuit of the field. The way to improve your luck in this event is to have your equipment ready and tuned for a quick start and flight. Be sure your radio trims are correct before you start the event. In most cases, the winner of this luck event will be the pilot who had his engine start quickest, and who flew the most direct course around the field. Most of the luck came from good preparation, not from the ability to draw the right card or to run fast across the field.

You have entered a few fun-fly contests and want to enter the winners' circle at the next event. Check your equipment, set up your aircraft, practice your flying skills, and try to learn tips about specific events. The chances are good that you will reach your goal. Your success will depend on the effort you invest. Have fun; and good luck at your next fun-fly contest! ◆

ABOUT THE AUTHOR

Dan Luchaco

Dan's interest in model aviation was sparked in 1955 when he was five years old and his father, George, started flying R/C planes. Over the years, his father's cast-off equipment, including single-channel to digital proportional radios and .049s to the latest Schnuerle engines, helped Dan hone his skills. His first fun-fly contest was in 1971 and, with his club—Valley R/C—he has become involved with competition flying and contest format development. Dan is currently president of the National Competition Fun Fly Association (NCFFA) and regularly attends events in the United States and Canada. He lives in Sayre, PA, with his wife, Lou Ann, and their daughters, Amy and Melynda. His son, Steven, is a third generation R/C'er and his toughest competition at contests.

CHAPTER 33

Flying Class A and B Electric Sailplane Events

by Tom Hunt

This chapter discusses the flying techniques I developed to be competitive in the AMA Class A and Class B Limited Motor Run (LMR) electric sailplane events (AMA event numbers: Class A—610; Class B—612). Before I discuss the techniques, I'll discuss the rules of the two events and the types of model that do well in them.

MODELS AND RULES

AMA events 610 and 612 are precision-duration sailplane competitions. You are given 8 minutes to climb to altitude, shut the motor down and glide to a soft contact (we hope) with earth (time includes motor run); *and* you must land in a circle that's generally no more than 60 feet in diameter. In event Class A, you have 45 seconds to reach maximum altitude. In event Class B, you are allowed only 30 seconds. There is a rule governing the amount of "energy" you can put into your model. In Class A, the number of cells in the battery pack that drives the motor is limited to seven; in Class B, up to 30 cells are allowed! The only rule governing the size of the model is that the wing loading must not exceed 24.75 ounces per square foot (probably a moot point, because anything over 12 or 13 ounces per square foot is rarely competitive).

Although the scoring procedure can be modified by the contest director (CD), it is usually done as follows: the point totals from all three rounds of flying are combined to determine the winner. One point is assigned to each second of flight up to 8 minutes (so, if you flew the entire 8 minutes and no more, your score would be 8x60 or 480 points). One point is subtracted for every second the model remains in the air after 8 minutes (hence the term "precision duration"). A "spot" landing in the circle generally earns you 30 to 50 extra points, depending on the mood of the CD that day. I've placed second in many contests because I missed *one* spot landing out of the three.

With these few rules, many of today's models can be competitive *if you practice!* Models such as the Electra, Spectra, Gentle Lady and many other 2-meter/6-foot elec-

tric sailplanes or converted pure sailplanes—weighing no more than about 42 ounces—are very competitive in Class A on seven cells. A high-power cobalt or ferrite 05 motor up front, drawing in excess of 40 amps and swinging 12- or 13-inch folding props, routinely gets to about 1,000 feet in 45 seconds. This altitude does not guarantee an 8-minute flight without a thermal, but it will get you close.

These models can make good Class-B ships, with the cell count reaching nine or 10 and with a smaller prop installed on the 05 motor to keep the current in the low 40s. The models generally weigh about 2 or 3 ounces more because of the added cells. This will hurt the glide slightly, but only a very experienced flier would be able to tell the difference. Separate Class B models can be built to accommodate even more cells (remember, you can use up to 30!), but to be competitive, the wing loading should be kept to 10 ounces per square foot.

TECHNIQUES

Now that you have a feel for the rules and the type of model that's flown, I'll show you how to fly it to the winners' circle! As in an Olympic 100-meter dash, the start is everything. The model should be launched at an angle that's equal to or slightly less

The author holds two of his favorite electric gliders: in his right hand, an all-wood version of his own-design sailplane—the Defiant; in his left hand, a fiberglass fuselage version with a slightly different wing planform.

EFFECT OF WIND ON CLIMB ANGLE

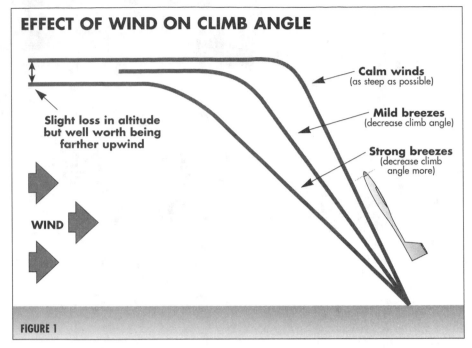

Slight loss in altitude but well worth being farther upwind

WIND

Calm winds
(as steep as possible)

Mild breezes
(decrease climb angle)

Strong breezes
(decrease climb angle more)

FIGURE 1

straight flight. During a climb that's too steep, the model goes too slowly to be controllable. A wandering model is a sure sign that the climb angle is too steep. Burn up a few packs in the same weather conditions to find the best climb angle, then practice, practice, practice. As soon as the model starts to "wander," reduce the climb angle slightly. When the breeze picks up, don't let the gusts confuse you when they make the model have too steep or slow a climb. Let the model fly through the gusts. As more altitude is reached, the air will generally become less turbulent.

Figure 2 depicts how the last 5 seconds of the motor run should be flown. Like that 100-meter dash, the finish is also important. At about 40 seconds (Class A) or 25 seconds (Class B), begin a slow "pushover" to get the model level at exactly the cutoff point. This ensures that the model does not pitch up and stall at motor cutoff. Believe me, that extra 50 feet you may gain by continuing a steep climb right to the end will be lost in the porpoising and stalling that occurs while you try to recover after motor cutoff. In fact, a net loss (as much as 100 feet) in altitude can be expected.

◆ **Thermals.** Thermal flying techniques are the same with electric sailplanes as they are with the motor-less sailplane

than its best climb angle. Don't be afraid to throw the model hard. If something fails electrically moments after launch, a good throw will allow you to fly the model forward to a safe landing. A wimpy launch may stall the wing, and you'll be picking up pieces and watching the rest of the contest from the viewing stand.

◆ **Climb angle.** The best climb angle for the model depends on many factors. Battery and motor health, model weight and, probably the most important, the wind. Figure 1 shows the effect of wind on the best climb angle. Notice I did not say "best rate of climb"! A high rate of climb in a stiff breeze may not be as important as sacrificing a little altitude to get a little farther upwind after motor shutdown. If you took the route of maximum altitude in a stiff breeze, your model might head very far downwind (looking for thermals) and never make it back to the field, even if you did achieve an 8-minute flight. Trading a little altitude for remaining farther upwind is prudent. It gives you more time to look for thermals before having to return to

the field. Remember, if thermals are present, they're blowing downwind, too!

Let's assume the wind is nil or light for some practice flights. The best climb angle for your model is very easy to assess. Launch the model with the nose raised only slightly. Increase the climb angle until it's difficult to maintain

OPTIMUM CLIMB PROFILE CLASS A AND CLASS B ELECTRIC SAILPLANE AMA EVENTS 610 AND 612

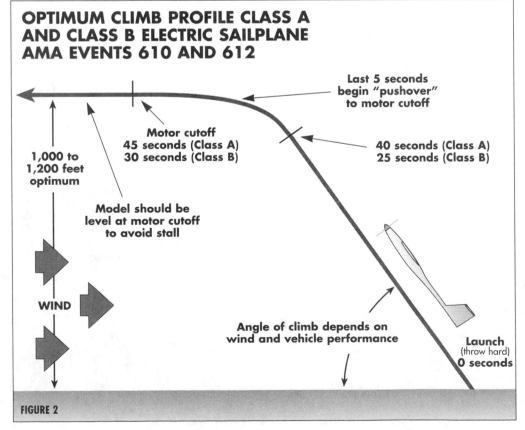

Last 5 seconds begin "pushover" to motor cutoff

Motor cutoff
45 seconds (Class A)
30 seconds (Class B)

40 seconds (Class A)
25 seconds (Class B)

1,000 to 1,200 feet optimum

Model should be level at motor cutoff to avoid stall

WIND

Angle of climb depends on wind and vehicle performance

Launch
(throw hard)
0 seconds

FIGURE 2

types. Many good articles have been written on this subject by much better thermal soarers than I. Therefore, the only thing I'll mention on this subject is about the time it takes to bail out of a good thermal to make it back to earth in exactly 8 minutes. Let's assume that at about the 5-minute mark, you are still as high as you were when the motor was shut down. Thermal hunting or bailing out of the current thermal should be initiated. Until about the 7-minute mark, if the wind is light, circle the boundaries of the field or, if the wind is strong, execute "S" turns upwind of the spot-landing area. At this point, decide whether the spot is obtainable. If the answer is "Yes," Figures 3 and 4 show the way to hit it consistently. If the answer is "No," just concentrate on putting the model down *safely* anywhere on the field, as close to 8 minutes as possible.

HITTING THE SPOT

◆ **Light winds.** Figure 3 shows the method I use to "hit the spot" on light-wind days. At about the 7-minute mark, plan to be at no more than 200 feet of altitude. Circle directly over the spot at a diameter with which you and the model are comfortable (observe local field rules of not flying over the pits or the spectators). At about 7:30 minutes, come out of

the circle and head downwind slightly. With about 10 seconds to go (7:50), make a tighter turn onto final approach. At this point, it's helpful to ask the timer to count off the last 10 seconds or so. Put the

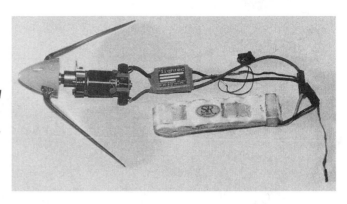

Components of a typical electric glider setup. The folding propeller is connected to a gear-reduction unit that is attached to the front of the electric motor. The motor is connected to a speed control (which is wired into the battery pack), a fuse, servo lead and an arming switch.

model into a shallow dive, so that it will touch the ground just before the spot.

The energy that's left in the model should allow it to slide right up to the center of the spot. Remember, although the goal is to touch the ground at exactly 8 minutes, being long or short by even as many as 5 to 10 seconds but coming to rest within the spot is far more point-rewarding than being out of the spot at exactly 8 minutes. Above all, do not ever attempt a second try at the spot if you are

too high, regardless of the time left. I have never, *ever* seen anyone (including me) get a second chance at making the spot. More often, models are tumbled into an unrecognizable pile of MonoKote and balsa.

◆ **Windy days.** On a windy day, the technique is a bit different. At about 7:30 minutes, begin a downwind leg from the "S" turns you've been doing upwind of the spot. The wind speed will determine how far downwind you should travel before you make a turn onto final approach. A stiff breeze will require that you turn onto final very close to the spot, keeping the nose down to penetrate. With 10 seconds to go, the approach looks a lot like the calm-day

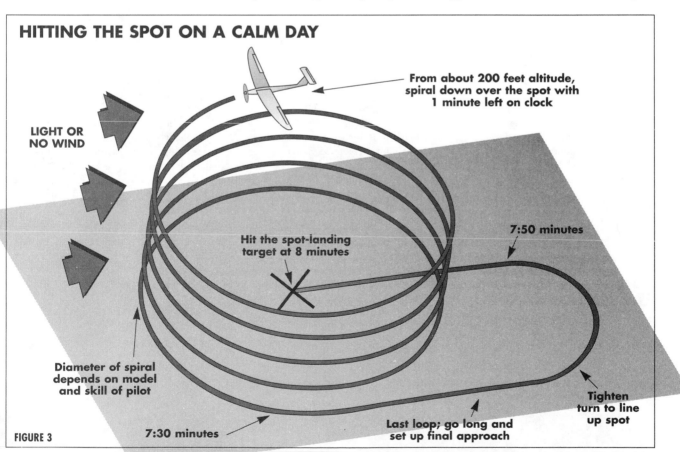

HITTING THE SPOT ON A CALM DAY

From about 200 feet altitude, spiral down over the spot with 1 minute left on clock

LIGHT OR NO WIND

7:50 minutes

Hit the spot-landing target at 8 minutes

Diameter of spiral depends on model and skill of pilot

Tighten turn to line up spot

FIGURE 3

7:30 minutes

Last loop; go long and set up final approach

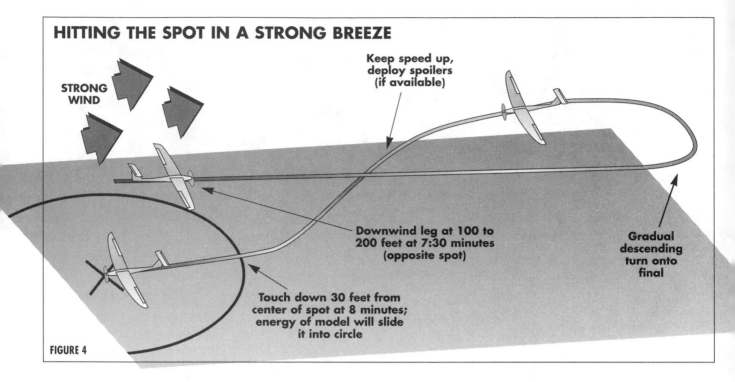

HITTING THE SPOT IN A STRONG BREEZE

STRONG WIND

Keep speed up, deploy spoilers (if available)

Downwind leg at 100 to 200 feet at 7:30 minutes (opposite spot)

Touch down 30 feet from center of spot at 8 minutes; energy of model will slide it into circle

Gradual descending turn onto final

FIGURE 4

approach, but speed should be greater, and that means you'll have to start from a higher altitude.

If you have them, deploy spoilers/crow or flaps *only if the model is flying straight and level toward the spot.* I can't count the number of times I've seen fliers try to dump some altitude near the spot with the model banked or the nose too high. Most often, they miss the spot, and the ensuing crunching noise usually means the competition has just been reduced! With the extra speed necessary for good control in windy conditions, you should actually target the ground just at the edge of or slightly outside the landing spot, and let the energy of the model skid you into the center of it. If your entry speed is too high and there's a chance of exiting the other side of the spot, apply full down-elevator and full rudder (either direction)

to "ground loop" the model; this will bleed off any remaining energy.

KEEP PRACTICING

Practicing these techniques is difficult to stomach with a competition sailplane because of the inherent danger to the airframe; but practice you must. Building a second model (which should look, weigh and fly exactly the same) to practice with is time-consuming for the casual competitor. Many modelers also like to jump on the bandwagon and fly exactly what the winner flies; but all it really takes is learning to fly *your* chosen model well.

I started flying (and winning) these events with a 47-ounce, 8-year-old, modified Gentle Lady. The model is now 12 years old, it's a little lighter, and it sports a new wing and a rebuilt fuselage. (The only things that are original are the servos

and horizontal and vertical tails.) I attribute my success with this airplane to three things: it's light, it's strong, and I didn't give up on it when someone beat me with "something better." I have recently retired the model—primarily because of fatigue; I'm tired of looking at it, and it's tired of flying in competition. The stress on it is just too much at that age. My new model (my own design—the Defiant), though it uses everything I have learned from the Gentle Lady, will be flown again and again in *and* out of competition until it and I are one!

You do the same with your model, and I promise you that if we meet at the field, we'll both go away winners, regardless of the final standings! ◆

To learn about the author of this chapter, see page 124.

CHAPTER 34

Flying Old-Timer Model Aircraft

by Bob Aberle

Old-timer flying encompasses several categories defined by the Society of Antique Modelers (SAM). Categories are:

◆ **Antique**—model aircraft that were designed, kitted, or had plans published prior to December 31, 1938.

◆ **Old-timer**—models that were designed, kitted, or had plans published prior to December 31, 1942.

◆ **Nostalgia**—models that were designed from January 1, 1943, through December 31, 1956.

The type of powerplant used is another sub-group. Antique and old-timer models can be flown with fuel-powered engines (spark ignition, glow and diesel), rubber power, electric power, by towline (for gliders) and even by hand-launching (also for gliders). Old-timer kits are available from The Aeroplane Works, Balsa Products Engineering, Custom Kits, Klarich Custom Kits and Spirit of Yesteryear Model Aircraft Co. For this article, I won't get into the nostalgia class, which also has a wonderful story behind it.

John Tatone's 1941 Atomizer, as flown to first place by the author in the ½A Texaco event (January 1994, three-day, SAM 77 Winter Fly contest, near Tampa, FL). Bob had the only two 15-minute max flights of the day; 300 square inches; 16 ounces total weight.

For an annual membership fee of $15, you can join SAM and receive a complete rule book and a subscription to the newsletter "SAM Speaks."

The SAM rule book is essential because of the many events that can be flown using a variety of powerplants. Basically, there are several popular subgroups in the antique and old-timer categories, i.e., R/C-assist (where a radio-control system does the in-flight "steering") and free-flight (as it was back in the '30s, where the model is pre-trimmed on the ground and is on its own in flight).

The front end of Bob Aberle's electric Lanzo Bomber showing the Astro Flight geared FAI 05 motor that's powered by seven SR SAM 800 cells. This model earned more than a dozen firsts during a three-year period.

SAM RULES!

In compliance with SAM rules, some events have limited engine runs. These limited run times are specified for types of engines (spark ignition—original or replica), converted ignition (glow engines converted to ignition), cross-scavenged glow and Schnuerle glow. Engine run times are also determined in some events by the model's weight rounded to the nearest pound. In addition, there are fuel-allotment events in which fuel is limited according to a model's total weight, e.g., so many cubic centimeters of fuel per pound of model weight. Back in the '30s, these fuel-allotment events were sponsored by Texaco Oil, and they're still referred to as the "Texaco events." There is also a Texaco event for electric power; the battery is allowed to be fully depleted of its charge during a flight.

Antique and old-timer models can be flown just for the fun of it or for competition. If you want to simply sport-fly an old-timer model using an equally old ignition engine, there's nothing wrong with that. These models basically fly like powered gliders because they are lightly loaded. The engine (or rubber motor or tow-line) takes the plane up to an altitude where it can glide around, sometimes with the extra help of thermals. If you like, you can install a modern-day glow engine with an R/C carburetor and cruise around using low-throttle settings to conserve fuel. Electric power can also be fun because the motor can actually be turned on and off by the R/C system while the model is in flight. The results are long, pleasurable flights that are generally very undemanding.

Larry Davidson's Lanzo Bomber off on another max flight at the SAM 75 chapter contest held at Calverton, Long Island, NY.

OLD-TIMER TOURNAMENTS

It's safe to say that, eventually, every old-timer enthusiast will want to try some form of competition. If you're interested

What a priceless photo! Carl Schmaedig (left), Mike Granieri (center) and Dr. Walt Good at the January 1992 SAM 77 Winter Fly contest near Tampa, FL. Both models are versions of Carl Schmaedig's Flying Stick design of 1937. Carl holds the very first Stick he ever built, some 50 years later, using Bob Aberle's reduced-size plans. Back in 1937, Carl only published the plans; he never actually built the model. Walt Good holds Bob Aberle's full-size Schmaedig Flying Stick; Granieri is saying, "My MG-II is better!"

in competing, you could start by visiting a local SAM flying field or, better still, attend a SAM contest. The organization has a brochure and a directory that it will gladly send to you. From your own observations and by reading through the SAM rule book, you'll be able to pick the events that you want to participate in. All kinds of detail come into play in old-timer competition flying.

◆ **Choosing a design.** Selecting a model design is one of the most important jobs. By attending SAM contests, you'll quickly learn what the better contestants fly and win with. Old-timer models take time to build, so try to make the correct choices the first time around. As an example, some of the most popular designs now being flown are the Lanzo Bomber, the Playboy Sr. and the Kerswap. By changing an engine size, you can enter a different event. For example, I successfully flew a 350-square-inch Lanzo Bomber in Class A LMR glow, Class A LMR ignition and Class A Texaco simply by using three different engines. That was a great advantage because I had to transport my models in a small vehicle.

◆ **Engine displacement.** This is important because there are classes of events determined by engine size. The model's weight is important for determining engine run time and fuel allotment. Most important, to win, you need a plane that is at the minimum weight (at or close to the specified minimum wing loading).

For information on old-time engines, you would be wise to join the Model Engine Collectors Association (MECA), which circulates a bimonthly "Swap Sheet" in which members list the engines they need or want to sell. This is one of the best ways to obtain original old-time ignition engines, or some of the fine replica engines manufactured today. MECA also sponsors and advertises "Collectos," at which people gather to buy and sell old-time engines.

◆ **Building from plans.** Most modelers who build old-timer aircraft generally build from plans, although several fine companies produce excellent kits. A great source of plans is John Pond's Old Time Plan Service. John offers several catalogues that provide extensive listings of antique and old-timer model designs,

many of which are offered in different sizes. Plans are also available from Modelair-Tech, Bill Northrop's Plans Service, Dan Lutz and Ken Sykora.

O/T Organizations

Academy of Model Aeronautics (AMA), 5151 East Memorial Dr., Muncie, IN 47302.

Model Engine Collectors Association (MECA), Secretary/Treasurer, Bob McClelland, 3007 Travis St., West Lake, LA 70669.

Society of Antique Modelers (SAM), Secretary/Treasurer, Larry Clark, P. O. Box 528, Lucerne Valley, CA 92356 (also SAM Library of Plans).

If you become a serious competitor, you'll probably build a considerable number of models so that you'll be able to fly in a variety of events. At most major contests, there is a high-point award that goes to the person who wins the most places (earning points for each

Don't laugh! Many a beautiful old-timer model has been damaged by flying-field wind gusts. Here, Larry Davidson uses homemade sandbags to weight his model down. This full-size Lanzo Bomber is flown in the Texaco fuel allotment event.

place). At the annual SAM championships (held every year in a different part of the country), the Grand Championship award is the most coveted, both for the R/C-assist and the free-flight categories.

◆ **Preparation.** I fly the R/C-assist events and almost always attend contests at which I end up flying spark-ignition,

glow, diesel and electric power. Having a van is most helpful. However, I've traveled from Canada to Florida and out to Ohio in my little Honda with as many as eight models and all the support equipment. Before you consider the flying aspects of old-timer contest flying, consider such things as tools, props, fuel and field-type battery chargers.

While preparing and packing for every contest, I refer to my supply checklist. Ignition engines run on a gasoline/oil mixture. Glow fuel can get complicated because the little Cox ½A Texaco engine may only need 10-percent-nitro fuel, while a big, powerful, K&B, 6.5cc, Schnuerle-ported engine may need at least 40-percent-nitro fuel. For my diesel engines, I need one type of ether-based fuel for the Class A Texaco event and another formula for my Elfin 2.49cc diesel for the Class A LMR event. I also need an SR Batteries Smart

Charger/Cycler to charge my electric-motor battery packs and some of my R/C system batteries while I'm at the field.

TOURNAMENT TIPS

Keep in mind that people do a considerable amount of flying at an R/C-assist old-timer contest; you may see 15 or more models in the air at any one time. To get the longest official flying time, the contest director generally prohibits practice flights and engine run-ups (both of which require an R/C system).

◆ **Be ready to fly your official flights** *without practice*. For electric-powered events, have an extra motor with a prop installed on it attached to a test board. Use that motor to run the charge down on all of your flight battery packs; then recharge them for your official flights. A battery that has been cycled once at the start of flying will always have a greater capacity. Keep that trick in mind!

◆ **Have your eyes checked regularly.** The SAM ½A Texaco event is particularly trying on a flier's vision. You may get a 6- to 7-minute engine run (on the 8cc fuel allotment), pursuant to a 15-minute max flight. These models usually have wings of only about 300 square inches. Many models have been lost simply because their pilot lost sight of them. For that reason, try to cover your models with the most visible colors, e.g., red and black. The use of special reflective tapes is also encouraged.

◆ **Attend the pilots' meeting.** At the start of any contest, the CD will usually hold a meeting to explain the events and any special rules that apply to the particular flying field. Out-of-bounds areas are usually specified, and if you fly outside the accepted boundaries, you forfeit your flight (and probably the event). Some CDs add other requirements, such as precision flight time and/or precision landing. If they stipulate a 7-minute max flight, you lose 1 point for

every 1 second you exceed that time. They also mark a circle of 30 to 50 feet in diameter in the landing area. If you land within that circle, you receive bonus points. These extra rules can be a lot of fun. They also help eliminate many of the tied scores that require time-consuming fly-off rounds at the end of the contest. To prepare for such

The ½A Texaco scale event is a wonderful new departure as a provisional SAM R/C-assist contest. This is Bob Aberle's Aeronca L-3 Defender; Cox .049 Texaco engine; weighs 18 ounces; 300 square inches.

eventualities, I usually mark a spot at my flying field when I'm practice-flying or testing new aircraft. I try to hit that spot on every single landing. Everything I do is related to what might help me at a contest. In other words, I'm not casual about anything!

◆ **Check the weather forecast**—at the start of every contest day; make your own

observations, too. I prefer not to be the first to fly. Patience can be a virtue to the contest flier. Of course, from a practical standpoint, you can't just stand around watching one another with no one flying. Assuming that the wind almost always picks up during the course of the day, I try to fly my smallest and lightest models first. If I have an electric-powered event scheduled that day, then that model will be the first in the air. On a 75-second limited motor run (cobalt motor rule), I can usually obtain a 7-minute max flight in dead air without the aid of a thermal. If the wind is calm or near calm, I try to climb vertically as high as I can—almost on the verge of a stall. If there's a good breeze (even early on), I tend to hold the

More popular old-time engines: the Shilen replica Torp .29 (left) and the John Targos replica Elfin 2.49cc (.15) diesel, which is SAM-legal for the Class A ignition events, even though it's a diesel.

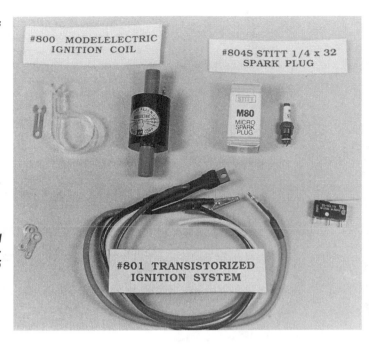

The components that go into a spark-ignition system for old-timer models. The Schmidt transistorized ignition system is now very popular; ModelElectric coils are as they were back in the '30s and '40s. Replica spark plugs are now showing up from several sources (cost— from $9 to $15 each).

#800 MODELELECTRIC IGNITION COIL

#804S STITT 1/4 x 32 SPARK PLUG

#801 TRANSISTORIZED IGNITION SYSTEM

model to about a 45-degree trajectory and attempt to get as far upwind as possible, even though some altitude will be sacrificed. Avoid using down-elevator to get the model to fly back upwind. When you're forced to do that to stay inside the field boundaries, you may lose too much altitude and fail to get a max flight.

Next up, and usually later in the morning, are the tiny, 1/2A Texaco fuel-allotment models. Both the 1/2A Texaco and SAM electric events have minimum wing-loading requirements of 8 ounces per square foot. That works out, in the average case, to a 35-ounce electric old-timer and about a 16-ounce 1/2A Texaco. Again, with the little Texaco, if it's windy, go for the upwind penetration rather than the altitude. Later in the day, I usually fly two more events (four being the most I can handle in a day). In the stronger winds, the Class C LMR and the glow-engine events are the better choices.

◆ **Be patient.** In almost all SAM events, you're allowed so many attempts to make a prescribed number of official flights. The decision point for voluntarily declaring an "unofficial" flight or attempt is usually during the engine-run period for that event. Up to 4 minutes is permitted for the 1/2A Texaco event. Be patient in that regard, because this is a very important strategic point at any contest. If you have an engine run that's too rich or lean and you aren't reaching your normal altitude, tell your timer you want to attempt another official flight. Kill the engine, get the plane down in a hurry, and make the necessary adjustments. Contests have been

won with that kind of patience.

Treat every flight as if you needed every last possible second of flight time; contests have been won by only a few seconds. If you're up reasonably high, but you don't seem to be catching any thermals, have a friend spot several other nearby planes and see whether they're

doing any better. When you catch a thermal (the model begins to climb rapidly), turn back into it. Don't just keep flying straight, or you will quickly lose it.

◆ **Don't let the model get away from you.** Common sense will tell you the approximate altitude you'll need for a max flight. Save your flying nerves for the fly-off round, and get your model back down safely. Safely does not mean a 75-degree down-angle terminal dive. Doing that could easily rip the wings off your plane, so when you have to descend, do it gradually and carefully. If you break up your model after the first or second flight, you have surely lost!

◆ **Fly-off tips.** If you're lucky enough to get to a fly-off round with other contestants, prepare yourself. If you use a lightweight receiver battery pack, fast-charge it for that last flight (it may be down after those first few flights), top off the fuel tank, take the wing off, and store the model so that it doesn't get damaged; or at least put a white cloth over the radio compartment area so that the equipment doesn't "cook" in the sun. Above all, put a rag or a cloth over the entire engine so that dust and dirt don't work their way into the venturi, and check the prop for possible cracks.

The author's Stealth Bomber is really a 630-square-inch, 35-ounce Lanzo Bomber that has been flown in both the SAM and AMA Old-Timer electric events. Bob says its name comes from its entire bottom being covered with clear Mylar to save weight. When you turn the plane over, it almost disappears!

The best of the best—three-time (consecutively) SAM R/C-Assist Grand Champion, Larry Davidson (East Northport, NY) who has been flying model aircraft with the author since 1951 (44 years!). Here, he holds one of his Lanzo Bombers—75-inch span; hot Orwick .64 ignition original; flies in the Antique class; completely covered with dyed silk with a dope finish—as the original was!

Winning is easier when you're careful!

At many old-timer contests, the contest director will halve the motor run for a fly-off round. This is done to save time when most people are tired. Keeping that in mind, you'd be wise to practice flying (in advance of a contest) at reduced engine runs. Because you will probably not get much altitude, thermal flying will be difficult. If it's a windy day, stay into the wind as long as possible. One 360-degree turn in the glide could easily knock you right out of contention, so do everything you can to stay up as long as possible. Most important, if you are all flying (in the fly-off) at the same time, don't take your eyes off your model to look at your competitors.

FINAL THOUGHTS

Old-timer competition flying can be very rewarding. The degree of flying skill necessary need not be that great, because there are so many events to choose from. Although I concentrated on the R/C-assist events, which are my favorites, the free-flight events are also challenging and a lot of fun.

In addition to the SAM organization, the Academy of Model Aeronautics runs old-timer events according to their own rules. Models intended for one set of rules can usually be flown under other rules. Space didn't permit a separate commentary on these events, but they are described in the AMA rule book.

Whatever the rules, these models of yesteryear provide wonderful opportunities for sport and competition flying for all ages. ◆

ABOUT THE AUTHOR

Bob Aberle

Bob, a retired aerospace engineering manager, has devoted 45 years to model aviation. Over the past 20 years, he has been a part-time contributing editor and later, technical editor of Flying Models magazine. He has published more than 30 R/C designs and is a prolific writer. In the early '80s, Bob chaired the prestigious AMA R/C Frequency Committee that petitioned the FCC for the 80 R/C channels in use today. For that effort, he was appointed AMA fellow in 1983 and received the AMA's Distinguished Service Award that same year. In 1982, he won the Howard McEntee Memorial Award and, in 1993, he was inducted into the Vintage R/C Society Hall of Fame. At the 1995 AMA/NEAC Electric National Championships, Bob won third place in both the Class A and Class B old-timer category.

CHAPTER 35

Basics of Flying Ducted Fans

by Bob Fiorenze

It's no wonder that the number of ducted-fan (DF) modelers is growing. Ducted-fan airplanes are exciting to fly and impressive in the air, and many are scale beauties that vie for top honors at major scale meets. There's nothing quite like the metallic roar of a ducted-fan aircraft in a high-speed flyby (the fastest top 200mph).

Ducted-fan aircraft vary in complexity, but most use high-performance engines with rpm of over 20,000. Maintenance and monitoring of the power system require a little more attention than your typical sport model. To get the best flight performance out of your ducted-fan ship, bear its unique features in mind.

In this chapter, I'll cover the basics of DF flying technique, and I'll summarize the maintenance checks I recommend to ensure your plane's flightworthiness. Also included is an excerpt from *Model Airplane News* that describes how I fly my scale model of the F-117 Stealth bomber; it adds some insight into the complexity of advanced, scale ducted-fan aircraft.

RUDDER NOTE

To prevent tail-heaviness and to reduce expense and potential complications, 50 percent of the DF models out there do not have a functional rudder. This helps to avoid tail heaviness and reduces expense and the potential for complications. In my opinion, it's better to use a rudder, but having one is not essential (bottom line: it's your call).

Ducted fans do not allow you the same margin of linkage "play" as you may enjoy with a sport plane. If you do install a rudder, use a mechanical linkage that can be made rock solid, with no play. At high speeds, there is no room for slop, because it will probably cause flutter and endanger your aircraft.

IN THE AIR

When you first fly a ducted fan, don't go for any "wild and crazy" exhibition flights—even if you consider yourself something of a crackerjack pilot.

A ducted fan does not have propwash blowing directly over the control surfaces

of its tail feathers. The only aerodynamic forces acting on the tail surfaces are generated by the relative wind the aircraft "sees" as a result of its forward flight. Accordingly, the forces acting on the rudder and elevator will be greater when the aircraft is flying faster. This means that the responsiveness of the plane, compared with a sport aircraft, is likely to feel muted at lower speeds. Although these differences are subtle, be mindful of them during takeoff and landing.

Because there is no rudder, use normal nose-wheel steering during takeoff. Similarly, don't expect to do a snap roll on takeoff, because there is no propwash over the control surfaces.

Your control inputs and the ducted fan's response in the air are generally more linear and gradual than those of a typical sport plane. For example, assume you are flying a sport plane at cruising speed. When you transition from half throttle to full power, the sport aircraft will jump forward, i.e., it will show a much more dramatic control response than a ducted fan. Jets do not react as

abruptly, but instead tend to perform smoother transitions. There is an aesthetically pleasing side to this, which some describe as "scale realism."

These handling characteristics should be kept in mind when you first fly a ducted fan. On the first flight, get a feel for the

The author with his Jet Model Products F-4 Phantom at the '84 Kansas City Scale Masters Championships. Good maintenance ensures success.

way the aircraft handles and how it responds to your control inputs. Pay particular attention to how the airplane behaves in slow flight and in high, banking turns. If you are accustomed to flying sport aircraft, you may feel a certain complacency when you transition to ducted fans, because they will not respond as crisply. Don't assume anything; stay keenly attuned to your aircraft's attitude, heading and handling at all times.

These tips will help make your first flights successful.

◆ **First landing.** Practice setting up for a landing while you're at 500 feet altitude and imagine the runway is at 450 feet. Then yank and bank, and see how it feels to abort the landing and come around again. In about 5 minutes, you will have to do this for the first time on the actual runway. Preparation comes first; be proud later.

If you are coming in at a fairly hot speed and want to flare the airplane, think it through in advance. With a sport plane, a little blip of power will help flare the airplane without delay because of the advantage of the propwash. With a jet, there will be a slightly delayed response because there is no propwash. Again, think ahead.

Engine/fan vibrations can loosen hardware. These 4-40 landing-gear bolts, which are close to the engine, are checked for tightness. Don't forget to check those axles for lubrication.

◆ **Dead-stick landings.** If you go dead-stick, you ought to be able to land, because in terms of wing loading, glide ratios and turning ability, e.g., steep angle of bank, ducted fans are like scale airplanes. Scale airplanes tend to be a little heavier and less well-suited to gliding in dead-stick. Although there are notable exceptions, the typical ducted fan poses the same challenges. You want to minimize the angle of bank, because it cuts down on the proportion of lift that keeps the aircraft aloft (the other percentage helps to turn the plane).

◆ **Use a timer.** It is critical to use a timer on a jet. Suppose, in initial flights at high altitude, you have determined (by flying till you dead-stick) that you have 9 minutes of fuel. If that's the case, you'll want to set your timer to 7 minutes on future flights.

Header/tuned-pipe damage can be expensive to fix. Avoid completely blowing away the silicone O-ring, which results in header/pipe metal contact.

◆ **Aerobatics.** Jets tend to excel at large, sweeping, high-speed maneuvers. With many models, knife-edge is doable, but I would start off with simple rolls and loops and gradually work toward more involved aerobatics. When you have developed a feel for the way your jet flies, the maneuvers you can perform should be fairly evident.

◆ **Radio setup.** To the extent that it's feasible, try to minimize the length of servo extension cables. This is true for any R/C aircraft and particularly important for ducted fans. If you do need to use long extension cables, I recommend a PCM radio.

◆ **Fuel choice.** Typically, you want to run the lowest-nitro fuel you can; 5- to 7-percent nitro is appropriate. But in colder temperatures, you may need up to 10-percent nitro to achieve good idling characteristics.

POST-FLIGHT MAINTENANCE

What do you do with your ducted-fan model after a typical day of flying at the club field? Do you just put your jet away? Of course not. You should inspect it and prepare it for storage so that it's ready to go the next time you head for the field. Here are some of the things that I check before I put my plane away.

◆ **Oil.** With most tuned-piped systems, oil stays in the muffler. If you store your airplane nose down (assuming you have a tractor-configuration ducted fan), oil tends to seep into the engine's front bearing, possibly into the fan rotor area and into the fan intake. Residual oil from all sides of the exhaust tailpipe can leak into the frontal area. I usually hang up my plane, tail down, as if it were on a meat hook. I let it hang there for an hour or two to get

the residual oil out so that it doesn't make a mess later.

Next, I turn the plane upside-down. If it's a rainy or humid day, the oil on the axles will probably wash away. Spin the tires to make sure the axles aren't dry. You might have to pull the wheel collars off and re-oil your axles.

◆ **Linkages and hinges.** When your jet is upside-down, the horns and clevises are usually exposed and easily accessible. Now you can test your pushrods, i.e., the rods that are connected to the ailerons, flaps, elevator, rudder and motor control. Make sure that the screws that hold the horns in are secure, as well as the hinges. Pull on your servo to make sure that it's tight. Even though you don't inspect the actual servo tray, you can just pull and tug on everything. Sometimes, the landing-gear bolts can vibrate loose, so I check them, too.

Next, I flip the model right-side up to inspect the inside. I check all the bulkheads, the wiring and the air lines for wear. There's a bulkhead here with a wire going to one of the aileron servos. The wire looks as if it's making contact with a section of the plywood bulkhead. Make sure that the wires aren't frayed, because this is an area where there could be problems.

◆ **Exhaust-system fittings.** The engine is a critical area that requires careful inspec-

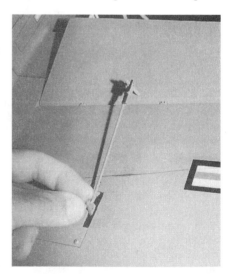

To check the integrity of the servo tray and clevises, pull and tug on the servo horns, hinges, linkages and control horns. You're looking for excessive play and potential for failure.

tion after a few flights. Take, for example, a typical O.S. 91 Dynamax-type setup. If the muffler-pressure fitting on the tuned pipe becomes loose, the pressure will be intermittent. (Fittings are usually attached

Flying the F-117

Editor's note: in this interview, Bob sheds further light on the challenges of flying scale, ducted-fan models (first published in May '95 Model Airplane News).

The awesome ability of the F-117 Stealth Fighter to deliver laser-guided bombs with pinpoint precision, and without being detected by radar, has captured the popular imagination since the Gulf War. But how does the R/C model of this unusual-looking aircraft fly? I asked Bob Fiorenze, who served as a test pilot in the R&D program for Yellow Aircraft's scale F-117.

• **Setup.** The 25-pound, 9-channel model is powered by twin O.S. 91s driving Dynamax fans, and it uses 7-percent-nitro smoking ducted-fan fuel. Two channels allocated to elevator and aileron actuate elevons. When you give an elevator command, the canted rudders (which act as partial elevators) and the elevons move. When Bob first set it up, a rudder command actuated both the rudders and the nose-wheel steering. Later, realizing that rudder was not essential in flight, Bob split the rudder channel into brakes and parachute using a single, three-position switch. Two channels control left and right engine mixture in flight. Three redundant pneumatic systems drive landing gear, gear doors and brakes.

The front view of the F-117 shows its angular shape which helps in avoiding enemy radar. When landing the model F-117, parachute deployment acts as an air brake. As the roll out slows down, the brakes are applied.

• **Flight.** The F-117 is designed to provide a stealthy, stable platform for delivering warheads. The model, with a relatively forward CG, turns out to be a docile, stable aircraft that does not need gyros (the full-scale plane, with an aft CG, requires constant computer flight corrections). Because there is no propwash directly over the control surfaces, the

model is relatively smooth in its response to power and control inputs, and that contributes to a sense of scale realism.

• **Takeoff.** Prior to takeoff, brakes are applied, and engines are spooled up to approximately 60-percent power. Then brakes are released, and engines powered up to 100 percent for the approximately 250-foot takeoff roll. Bob notes, "When takeoff velocity has been achieved, you input

Bob's scale F-117 flies quite well without any need for gyros.

about half to three quarters elevator to rotate the plane, and it naturally lifts off. The rate of ascent is about 1,000 feet per minute, so I usually bring it back to about 200 feet per minute, so that it looks more scale-like."

• **Flying.** Overall, the plane "flies like it's on rails." The effective dihedral—from the tremendous sweep—makes it quite stable when flying upright. Bob does caution that because of its unique profile, its heading can be a little ambiguous, so you always want to keep in mind where it has just been. Lift-robbing, steep-bank angles are to be avoided, particularly at low altitude.

The F-117, which has a relatively flat bottom, is not designed for aerobatics. Inverted, with full down-elevator, it will hold sustained flight. It will also do a nice military arcing roll. Bob notes that he tries not to fly at full throttle all the time. The carbs tend to go rich in the mid-range, so it's good practice to throttle back to 65 or 70 percent in cruising flight to reduce rpm and engine heat. Bob has circled the field on one engine.

• **Landing.** Bob sets up for landing with a long downwind leg. "Ease your throttle down by a few detents as you start adding up-elevator. At all times, you want to watch the nose-high attitude of the plane so that you won't get behind the power curve. As with any larger, scale airplane, you don't want to take a chance of wallowing into the ground."

He observes that, after touchdown, 50 percent of the parachute deployment is for actual braking, and 50 percent is for "wow." A 20-inch-diameter chute without holes lets the plane track like an arrow. After it has slowed a bit, brakes are applied.

—*Tom Atwood*

with JB Weld or silicone.)

Adjusting your engine at the flying field can make you pull your hair out. No single adjustment will work. The O-ring that holds up the tuned pipe can snap, and this puts undue stress on the header, which can then break the header bolts. If this happens,

◆ **Glow plug.** Pull your glow plug after three or four flights, and check the coil. If it's pushed off to one side, chances are that the plug should be thrown out. Another candidate for the garbage is a glow plug that looks crystallized. This is the most dangerous time to reuse the plug.

check your tank for cracks and leaks, and make sure that nothing rubs against it.

◆ **Battery.** Now is a good time to check your battery capacity. Let's say you're getting 200 minutes on a full charge and cycle, and your jet has made three flights.

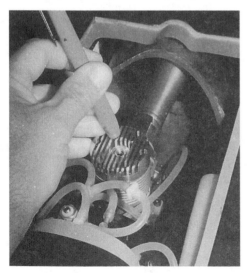

The area behind the cylinder head is prone to vibration. Check the tightness and integrity of the throttle linkage, the carburetor bolts and the header bolts.

Vibration and direct wire/bulkhead contact make it mandatory to check these contact points for servo-wire wear. Also note masking-tape "safety" (see arrow). The servo-horn screw can never "back out" because of vibration. Additional redundant safety precautions include a jam nut, fuel tubing and a metal safety clip on the clevis (Sullivan no. 256 shown). All this adds up to less concern about your equipment and more concentration on flying.

you have to remove the engine and re-tap the bolts (another hassle to avoid).

Check the heat-seal O-ring—the one that's between the header and the tuned pipe. It should be replaced every three or four flights. I know they're expensive, but if they fail and you're on a pipe-pressure

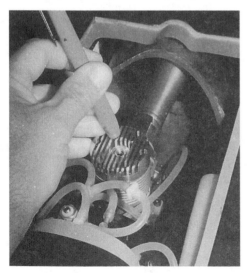

Using a flashlight, check the color of the piston's top. If it's a caramel color, it indicates that the engine is being broken in properly.

system, you'll lose pressure and probably fry the engine (go super-lean instantaneously). If you're on the Pitot system, you won't go lean but, in either case, you could still damage the front of the tuned pipe, and it would have to be sent back to the factory for header-pipe repairs.

It glows when you put a Ni-Starter to it and appears fine when, in fact, it's on the critical list. Flash a light on the top of the piston while the plug is out. When a new engine has been broken in properly, the top of the piston will turn a caramel color during five to 15 flights. This color is a good indication that you're breaking in your engine with plenty of oil, i.e., the engine is running rich, and it stays cool.

◆ **Rotor blades.** On certain aircraft, the inlet design allows you to reach in and pull on the rotor. Shake the rotor to see if anything feels loose. Excessive play means worn bearings and reduced plug life; bearing replacement is a must. Check the blades; maybe you picked up a stone. If a blade is chipped, it will fail; it will also make the other blades fail, cause vibrations and possibly kick the rotors off the crankshaft. I've seen rotors cut aileron and elevator wires and chew up the inlet. I've also had the carburetor fall off the back of my engine because the carburetor bolts have loosened.

◆ **Engine and fuel system.** If you're careful not to run the O.S. 91 too lean or too hot and you throttle back during certain maneuvers, loose head bolts won't usually be a problem. Don't forget to check the throttle arm. It can develop cracks that can eventually cause throttle failure (runaway throttles are no fun). If you use a ball link, make sure there isn't too much play in the plastic link, the bolt, or the nut. Also,

If you discharge the batteries as soon as you get home, and there are 100 minutes left, then you actually used half of your battery capacity. You probably could have safely made at least two more flights.

This inspection procedure should take all of 20 minutes—a small price to pay for a trouble-free day of flying. As with all modeling activities, remember to "make haste slowly."

I hope this information contributes to the success of your ducted-fan endeavors. Safe flying! ◆

ABOUT THE AUTHOR

Bob Fiorenze

Bob Fiorenze was born in Queens, NY. He graduated from the Academy of Aeronautics College in 1969 with an A.A.S. degree and then signed on with Islandic Airlines. He started a business building racecars and transmissions and later sold the business to open a diagnostic repair center. In 1974, he received his pilot's license and, in 1988, he moved to Florida and opened Fiorenze Hobby Center. Some of Bob's achievements in R/C include first place at the AMA Nationals, U.S. Scale Masters and Top Gun. When not flying, he enjoys writing magazine articles. He was retained by the AMA to do the evaluation on turbine engines. Bob has a wife and three daughters.

USEFUL ADDRESSES

1st Step, 503 Esparada, Georgetown, TX 78628.

Academy of Model Aeronautics (AMA), 5151 E. Memorial Dr., Muncie, IN 47302-9252.

Air Flair, P.O. Box 11702, Kansas City, MO 64318-0202; (816) 353-7854.

Airtronics, 11 Autry, Irvine, CA 92718; (714) 830-8769.

All American Kit Cutters, 365 Dutchneck Rd., Hightstown, NJ 08520; (609) 443-3175.

Anabatic Aircraft, 8 Gypsy Hill Rd., Pacifica, CA 94044.

APC Props; distributed by Landing Products, P.O. Box 938, Knights Landing, CA 95645; (916) 661-6515.

Astro Flight Inc., 13311 Beach Ave., Marina Del Rey, CA 90292; (310) 821-6242; fax (310) 822-6637.

Aveox, P.O. Box 1287, Agoura Hills, CA 91376; (818) 597-8915; fax (818) 597-0617.

Balsa Products Engineering, 122 Jansen Ave., Iselin, NJ 08830-2601.

Bill Northrop's Plans Service, 2019 Doral Ct., Henderson, NV 89014.

Bob Fiorenze, P.O. Box 953042, Lake Mary, FL 32795-3042; (407) 327-6353.

Bridi Aircraft Design Inc., 23625 Pine Forest Ln., Harbor City, CA 90710; (310) 549-8264; fax (310) 549-8268.

Byron Originals, P.O. Box 279, Ida Grove, IA 51445; (712) 364-3165; fax (712) 364-3901.

Capstone R/C Suppliers, 562 W. Schrock Rd., Westerville, OH 43081; (614) 899-6313; fax (614) 899-6070.

Carl Goldberg Models Inc., 4734 W. Chicago Ave., Chicago IL 60651; (312) 626-9550; fax (312) 626-9566.

Cheetah Models, 14725 Bessemer St., Van Nuys, CA 91411.

Cirrus Ventures, 115 Hunter Ave., Fanwood, NJ 07023-1030.

Cox Hobbies, 350 W. Rincon St., Corona, CA 91720; (909) 278-1282; fax (909) 278-2981.

CR Aircraft Models, 205 Camille Way, Vista, CA 92083; (619) 630-8775.

Culpepper Models Inc., 2526 Washington, Dubuque, IA 52001.

Custom Kits, 127A Fox Hollow Rd., Glen Gardner, NJ 08826; (908) 638-6902.

D&W Aircraft, 409 Mid Pines Way, Modesto, CA 95354.

Dan Lutz Plans, 455 South Stage Coach, Fallbrook, CA 92028.

DCU, 1564 S. Anaheim Blvd. Unit B, Anaheim, CA 92805.

Dodgson Designs, 21230 Damson Rd., Bothell, WA 98021; (206) 776-8067.

Don Smith R/C Aircraft Plans, 219 Goolsby Blvd., Deerfield Beach, FL 33442; (305) 570-7551.

Douglas Aircraft Model Aviation, P.O. Box 92742, Long Beach, CA 90809.

Du-Bro Products, 480 Bonner Rd., P.O. Box 815, Wauconda, IL 60084; (708) 526-2136; fax (708) 526-1604.

Dynaflite, P.O. Box 1011, San Marcos, CA 92069; (619) 744-9605; fax (619) 744-7923.

Eastern Soaring Lines (newsletter), 253 Bloomsbury-Pittstown Rd., Milford, NJ 08848.

Florio Flyer Corp., P.O. Box 88, Dagus Mines, PA 15831.

Frank Tiano Enterprises, 15300 Estancia Ln., W. Palm Beach, FL 33414; (407) 795-6600; fax (407) 795-6677.

Futaba Corp., P.O. Box 19767, Irvine, CA 92713-9767; (714) 455-9888; fax (714) 455-9899.

Future Flight, 1256 Prescott Ave., Sunnyvale, CA 94089; (408) 735-8260; fax (408) 735-8260.

Graupner, Henriottonstr., Postfach 1242, D-73220 Kirchheim/Teck, Germany.

Great Planes Model Distributors, P.O. Box 9021, Champaign, IL 61826-9021; (217) 398-3630; fax (217) 398-0008.

Hobby Horn, Midway Hobbies, 15173 Moran St. B, Westminster, CA 92684.

Hobby Lobby Intl., 5614 Franklin Pike Cir., Brentwood, TN 37027.

Hobby Shack, 18480 Bandilier Cir., Fountain Valley, CA 92728-8610; (714) 964-0827; fax (714) 962-6452.

Horizon Hobby Distributors, 4105 Fieldstone Rd., Champaign, IL 61821; (217) 355-9511; fax (217) 355-8734.

House of Balsa Inc., 10101 Yucca Rd., Adelanto, CA 92301; (619) 246-6462.

Irvine Engines; distributed by Altech Marketing, P.O. Box 391, Edison, NJ 08818-0391; (908) 248-8738.

JB Weld, P.O. Box 483, Sulphur Springs, TX 75482.

J'Tec, 164 School St., Daly City, CA 94014; (415) 756-3400.

John Pond Old-Time Plans Service, P.O. Box 90310, 253 N. 4th St., San Jose, CA 95109-3310.

Jomar/EMS, 22483 Mission Hills Ln., Yorba Linda, CA 92687; (800) 845-8978.

JR Hobbies, RR #7, P.O. Box 249A, Springfield, IL 62707.

JR Remote Control; distributed by Horizon Hobby Distributors (see address above).

K&B Mfg., 2100 College Dr., Lake Havasu City, AZ 86403; (602) 453-3579.

Ken Sykora's Old-Timer Model Supply, P.O. Box 7334, Van Nuys, CA 91409.

Klarich Custom Kits, 2301 Sonata Dr., Rancho Cordova, CA 95670.

Larry Jolly Model Products, 15781 Empire Ln., Westminster, CA 92683.

League of Silent Flight, 10173 St. Joe Rd., Fort Wayne, IN 46835.

Lynch's Hangar, 2525 Center St., Caro, MI 48723.

Madden Model Products, 255A Horicon Ave., Brant Lake, NY 12815.

Minimax Enterprise, P.O. Box 2374, Chelan, WA 98816 (509) 683-1288.

Model Engine Collectors Association (MECA), Rt. 1, P.O. Box 766, Milano, TX 76556.

Modelair-Tech, P.O. Box 12033, Hauppage, NY 11788-0818.

MonoKote; distributed by Great Planes Model Distributors (see address above).

Nick Ziroli Plans, 29 Edgar Dr., Smithtown, NY 11787; (516) 467-4765; fax (516) 467-1752.

Northeast Sailplane Products, 16 Kirby Ln., Williston, VT 05495; (802) 658-9482.

O.S. Engines; distributed by Great Planes Model Distributors (see address above).

Peck Polymers, P.O. Box 710399, Santee, CA 92072; (619) 448-1818; (619) 448-1833.

Plettenberg Motors; distributed by Hobby Lobby Intl. (see address above).

R/C Soaring Digest, P.O. Box 2108, Wylie, TX 75098-2108.

RA Cores, P.O. Box 863, Southbridge, MA 01550 (508) 765-9998.

Race Pro Engineering, P.O. Box 445, Sutter Creek, CA 95685; fax (209) 267-0923.

Robbe, 2655 N.E. 188 St., Miami, FL 33180; (305) 932-1575; fax (305) 937-2322.

Sanyo, 2001 Sanyo Ave., San Diego, CA 92173; (619) 661-6620; fax (619) 661-6743.

Saxton Glass, 3709 Longbridge Dr., Modesto, CA 95356; (209) 575-5067.

Scale Aviation USA, 115 Hunter Ave., Fanwood, NJ 07023.

Sig Mfg. Co. Inc., 401-7 S. Front St., Montezuma, IA 50171; (515) 623-5154; fax (515) 623-3922.

Slegers Intl., Rt. 15, Wharton, NJ 07885; (201) 366-2525; fax (201) 366-0549.

Society of Antique Modelers (SAM), P.O. Box 528, Lucerne Valley, CA 92356.

Spirit of Yesteryear Model Aircraft Co., 40 Holgate St., Barrie, Ontario, Canada L4N 2T7; (705) 737-0532; fax (705) 737-0532.

SR Batteries, P.O. Box 287, Bellport, NY 11713; (516) 286-0079; fax (516) 286-0901.

Sullivan Products, P.O. Box 5166, Baltimore, MD 21224; (410) 732-3500; fax (410) 327-7443.

Sun Fair Aircraft Design, 415 Stony Point Way, Unit 106, Oceanside, CA 92056.

SuperTigre; distributed by Great Planes Model Distributors (see address above).

The Aeroplane Works, 2134 Gillbridge Rd., Martinsville, NJ 08836; (908) 356-8557.

The Birdworks, P.O. Box 1320, Port Orford, OR 97465.

Top Flite; distributed by Great Planes Model Distributors (see address above).

Vortac Mfg. Co., P.O. Box 469, Oak Lawn, IL 60453.

VS Sailplanes, 2317 N. 63, Seattle, WA 98103.

Webra; distributed by Horizon Hobby Distributors (see address above).

Wing Mfg., 306 E. Simmons St., Galesburg, IL 61401; (309) 342-3009.

Yellow Aircraft, 203 Massachusetts Ave., Lexington, MA 02173; (617) 674-2222; fax (617) 674-2188.

Zenoah; distributed by Indy R/C, 10620 N. College Ave., Indianapolis, IN 46280; (317) 846-0766; fax (317) 848-1015.

Zimpro Marketing, P.O. Box 5776, Oak Ridge, TN 37831; (615) 482-6188.

Zinger; distributed by J&Z Products, 25029 Vermont Ave., Harbor City, CA 90710.